Kingdom on Mount Cameroon

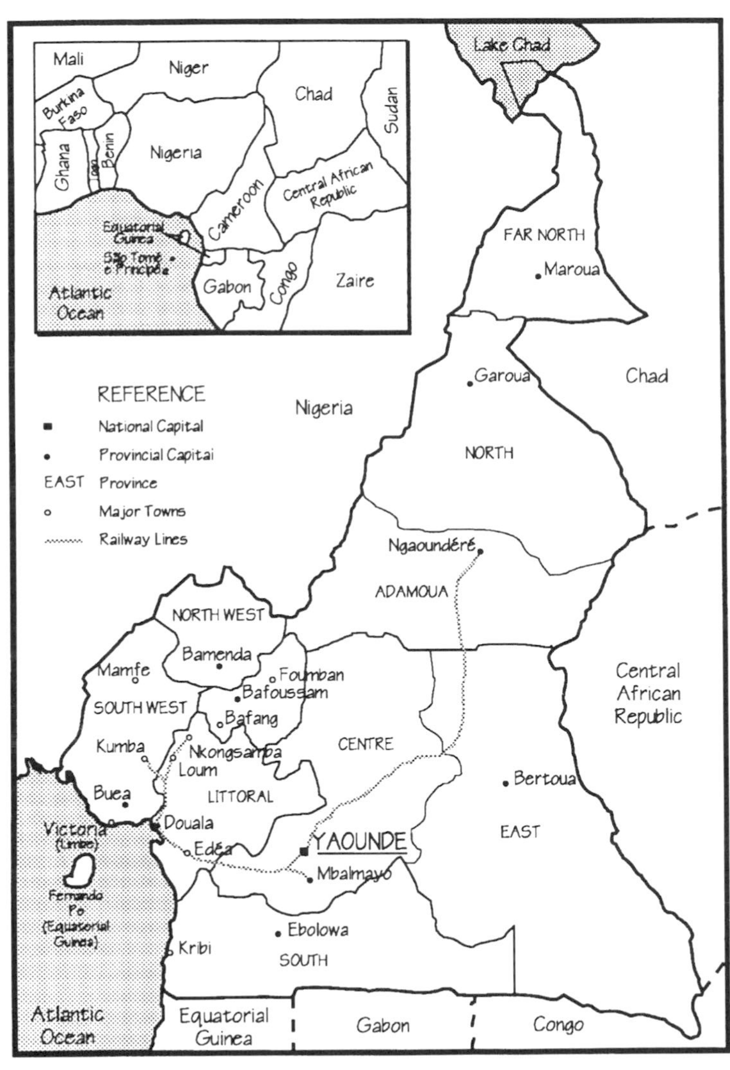

The Republic of Cameroon

Kingdom on Mount Cameroon

Studies in the History of the Cameroon Coast 1500–1970

Edwin Ardener

Edited and with an Introduction by
Shirley Ardener

First published in 1996 by

Berghahn Books

Editorial offices:
165 Taber Avenue, Providence, RI 02906 USA
Bush House, Merewood Avenue, Oxford, OX3 8EF UK

British Library Cataloguing in Publication Data

A catalogue record for this book
is available from the British Library.

Printed in the United States on acid-free paper.

ISBN 1-57181-929-0

Contents

Appendices

Illustrations

Maps

Figure

Editor's Introduction

The Bakweri people who occupy the slopes of the immense, volcanic, Cameroon Mountain, a few degrees north of the equator on the West Coast of Africa, have unrivalled views across the plains, creeks and shores which skirt their highland. For centuries the waters around the shores and up nearby rivers have attracted traders and fishermen from Cameroon and from Nigeria, as well as men in merchant vessels and warships from Portugal, Holland, Spain, Great Britain and Germany. Some have merely completed their business and left; others have stayed to wage war, establish colonial administrations, to found missions or to settle and engage in work as farmers or take up a variety of other occupations. This book by Edwin Ardener tells of some of the episodes in the history of the peoples of the mountain and their encounters with strangers.

The Bakweri refer to themselves as *Vakpe*. Their own name has long been modified by others, both Cameroonian and stranger, by the use of the more common prefix of local Bantu languages, *Ba* (for people), while the implosive *kp* in Vakpe has been rendered as, for some, the more pronounceable *kw*, hence Bakweri.[1] The heights of the Cameroon Mountain are referred to by Vakpe as *fako,* but as with the name of the people who use this term, in this volume the more widely known terminology for both has been followed. The translation of African terms into English provides many problems. The term 'kingdom' itself may seem inappropriate, not only to some people who are used to it being applied to much greater territories and populations, but also because the term, and its associations, might not be chosen by some Bakweri-speakers. As times change the nuances of words evolve and their meanings, and ideas concerning their fields of relevance, are interpreted according to the socio-political environment and the personalities of the day, in a continuing process. When my husband used the term for the text which forms the second contribution below, which was written in Cameroon primarily for local readers, it did not seem to be especially problematic when applied to the history of Buea.

As Edwin Ardener explains in his first contribution here, three centuries ago the term *Ambos* was used by some for people living on islands between Fernando Po and the Coast, probably on those in what is still called Ambas Bay. The Dutch who followed the Portugese took up the term but, as is shown, its exact applications and its variants are difficult to determine, and one cannot simply assume that the Bakweri were ever intended by it. Nevertheless the appellation still echoes in Cameroon today, where the term Ambozania has been coined by someone, whether in jest or prophetically I know not, for an imagined new anglophone polity. Edwin wrote a brief account of the distinctive Wovea people when most of them were living on one of the islands in Ambas Bay. Their recent forebears, who may once have had connections with the people of Fernando Po, were courageous whale hunters, and his brief study in *Nigeria* was illustrated by many photographs of their fishing equipment; the text and some illustrations can be found below.

In the nineteenth century the Germans called the people on the mountain Bakwiri, but today we hear of 'the Bakweri', 'Bakweris' (thus anglicized for the plural) and of 'a Bakweri' (for an individual—in place of their own singular term Mokpe). When Edwin Ardener lived on the mountain in the 1950s and 1960s the total Bakweri population was thought to be about 16,000 (see below). Though a small group, Bakweri have held a pivotal position in the area, both strategic, economic, military and political, which is striking even today. Their impact on the history of Cameroon—both in its early days in relations with European traders, those with military power, with administrators and with English, Jamaican, Swiss and American missionaries, and throughout and currently in relation to other Cameroonians—derives from their unique geographical position and the advantages they have grasped as a consequence. This volume contains eye-witness descriptions of Bakweri dating back to before the middle of the nineteenth century (see for example, that of Missionary Merrick and later of von Puttkamer below), but here we may cite a contemporary account by the German Max Esser, published in 1898, who said he was

> astonished by their unusually handsome figures. They are clever at any task and intellectually well-endowed. Moreover they are outstanding for their bravery and mettle, and these qualities are seen in their raids. They stood up to the Germans as fierce enemies in the battles on the Kamerun Mountain.[2]

The Battles of Buea are vividly described in the second contribution here, in a long account originally written in 1969, but published here for the first time. Spectacular success for the Bakweri people led by the King of Buea, (described by Zintgraff, after visting the three Bakweri villages of Upper, Lower and Middle Buea at the end of January 1887, as 'wearing his beard in three plaited tresses,'[3] was eventually followed by dramatic defeat. As a result the population of Buea, according to Esser, dropped from 2,000 (a rather high estimate) to 800; this was probably mainly due to relocation. The Germans, including the admiring Esser, immediately took advantage of Bakweri weakness by acquiring land for plantations from the people on the mountain and around its base. The plantation system which has experienced a series of metamorphoses in various hands, private and public, since these early days, still plays a crucial economic and social role in Cameroon today. The story of the establishment of the plantations and the overwhelming social consequences to the Bakweri are dealt with in Edwin Ardener's studies below.

Edwin himself made lengthy visits to West Africa over twenty years from 1949 onwards, which for the last seventeen were to Cameroon. For seven years he was based in Cameroon, taking leave in the United Kingdom from time to time to write up his material. He was financed by a series of research grants, which for much of the time he received as a member of the West African, later Nigerian, Institute of Social and Economic Research (NISER) based at Ibadan University, Nigeria. It was to undertake a three-pronged study, which arose out of local concerns, that Edwin first came to Cameroon. This involved consideration of the welfare of the workers living in the plantation camps, a report of the effects of the plantation system and its demographic consequences as seen by the Bakweri, and finally the people of the grasslands area in Cameroon from which the labour largely came were considered. This research took him up-country to the chiefdom of Esu, where he lived for the best part of a year.[4]

Text from that part of his contribution which deals with the Bakweri and other peoples local to the plantations in the resulting *Plantation and Village in the Cameroon* (1960) has been included below, as this book has long been out of print. This section takes forward the story of the establishment of the plantations up until the 1960s, and the resulting 'land question' for the Bakweri. It describes Bakweri agricultural practices and marriage arrangements and other cultural features, the fundamental changes in immigration patterns,[5] and the overwhelming impact these had on Bakweri village life. By this time many Bakweri were afraid they were dying out. The majority of men and many women associated this with the breakdown in traditional marriage practices. Casual, or long-standing relations with men where no marriage payments had been made, which were often regarded as a form of prostitution (the appellation 'harlot' was in constant use), were widely blamed. The 'one-parent family', or 'woman-headed household', was not then a generally accepted or advocated alternative to traditional unions, least of all by the majority of Bakweri. Nevertheless some women were voting with their feet. In *Plantation and Village*, as well as touching on these social matters Edwin also examined and contradicted the widespread outsider view (of non-Bakweri) that Bakweri were 'apathetic' and not active in the economy.

Because of this anxiety among the Bakweri regarding their supposed decline in population, the research lead to a follow-up study of the effects on Bakweri family life of the presence of plantations workers, who greatly outnumbered the Bakweri, and of whom many were without wives. In innumerable conversations in various villages, the women's views were especially sought; moreover one thousand or so women in five villages were separately interviewed and their marital and fertility histories systematically collected. A conference paper by Edwin summarizing the results, of which only a few copies have been available in cyclostyled form, has been printed here for the first time. The full study, which was again sponsored by NISER, appeared as *Divorce and Fertility, an African Study* (1962). His conclusion was considerably more optimistic than that of the Bakweri themselves at that time.

All the rapid and drastic changes which took place in the wake of the political and economic innovations introduced by the Germans had an unsettling effect on other Bakweri beliefs and practices. As economic booms and recessions alternated, new patterns of old ways emerged. In the 1960s an old cult appeared to spread through Bakweri villages, which required the introduction from up-country of new witch-finding and neutralizing institutions. Descriptions of these events by friends who participated in them were documented and analyzed by Edwin in a paper entitled 'Witchcraft, Economics and the Continuity of Belief' published in 1970. This study, included below, shows in vivid detail how economic changes in the world economy can enmesh and be dealt with through traditional beliefs concerning the supernatural. Edwin reported the supposed eradication of *nyɔngo* witches. In 1996 I found such witches flourishing due, it was said, to their having 'captured' the witchfinding institutions which controlled them; the coincidence with the present economic crisis might be noted.[6]

In his writings Edwin shows that, far from conforming to the then long-standing view of non-Bakweri outsiders that the Bakweri were 'apathetic', they had retained far more of their culture than was usually then perceived by others. Within the fences around their villages, many of their traditions were preserved, although like traditions everywhere, they were adjusted to the circumstances of the day. Among the high points of the year for some villages were wrestling contests and the *Malé* dance, the public display put on by members of the secret elephant society. To end on a positive note, included here is a short account of one public display in Wokpaongo village, just a mile from the centre of Buea, which was printed in *Nigeria*, and which was illustrated by a professional photographer from and still living in Wokpaongo, Mr Mbwaye; some of his excellent photographs are included here. It is good to be able to note that this dance, is still being held, and wrestling continues.

Soon after Nigeria became independent in 1960 and split off from the then Southern Cameroons, Edwin was offered a post at Oxford University which he accepted provided he could first return to Cameroon for another nine months. A request to the University from the then Prime Minister Foncha to permit him to extend that stay was turned down in Oxford. However, Edwin continued to revisit Cameroon regularly during his university vacations as a guest of the Southern, later West, Cameroon Government to continue his research into the history and culture of its citizens. Given the honorary title Adviser on Archives and Antiquities, during this period he helped to establish the Buea Archives office, by collecting material from ant-ridden cupboards and hot and dusty lofts throughout the then Southern Cameroons, by choosing a site and sketching a design for the new building which the government had the foresight to finance.[7] He then trained staff, the first of whom was Mr Kima who shared many of the orginal discomforts, and Edwin set in motion a system for the general care of public, private and other records. The building was officially opened in 1969 by S. T. Muna, by then Prime Minister of West Cameroon. Despite many problems deriving from the recent financial difficulties facing Cameroon currently, the Buea Archives office is still in active use by students, local and overseas scholars, and members of the public.[8]

Edwin was always determined that our work should be read in Cameroon by the general public. When *Coastal Bantu of the Cameroons* was first published he had to guarantee the first order put in by a sceptical Basel Mission Bookshop (predecessor to the existing Presbook shop) in Victoria. In fact this book was always in demand and stocked locally thereafter, and is still sought in Buea, though now long out of print. *Divorce and Fertility* was also circulated in Buea.[9] Later, aware of the shortage in Cameroon of historical material on the area, especially of primary sources, Edwin Ardener issued a series of booklets from the

Archives Office which were printed for him by the then government printer in Buea.[10] These included *Traditional Bamenda; the Pre-colonial History and Ethnography of the Bamenda Grassfields* (1967) by E. M. Chilver and P. M. Kaberry, *Historical Notes on the Scheduled Monuments of West Cameroon* (1965) written by himself, which was also issued in a German translation for the first organized tourists to come to Buea, *The Prime Minister's Lodge* (1969) by Margaret Field (formerly published as *The Commissioner's Lodge*)[11] which describes what is now a Presidential residence, an abridged translation from the German text of *Zintgraff's Explorations in Bamenda, Adamawa and the Benue Lands, 1889–1892* (1966) by E. M. Chilver, and *Eye-witnesses to the Annexation of Cameroon, 1883–1887* (1968) by myself. The latter contained excerpts from long out-of-print contemporary accounts in English and translations from similar texts in German.

On his last visit to Buea Edwin Ardener prepared the text, which is published for the first time as the second section of this volume, which deals with the history of the settlement of Buea, the war with the Germans, and its aftermath. For this study he drew partly on German materials then in the Buea Archives, some of which were, years later, moved to Yaounde, and partly on the research notes he had made during his discussions with the Chief of Buea, Gervasius Endeley, and other local experts. Regrettably, though intended for local distribution through the Buea archives series, this text has lain unpublished until now.

When political independence was achieved in 1960 by Nigeria and francophone Cameroon (the latter until then being a United Nations Trust Territory, and known in anglophone Cameroon as French Cameroon) the anglophone Cameroons, both Northern and Southern, continued for some time to be administered by the United Kingdom as U.N. Trusts. Buea, the residence of Chief Gervasius Endeley, successor to the famous King Kuva, became the focus of much political activity because Buea held the official seat of the Prime Minister of Southern Cameroons, John Ngu Foncha, as well as various Ministries, and housed the meetings of a House of Assembly and a House of Chiefs. Chief Endeley's nephew (and brother to the present encumbent), Dr E. M. L. Endeley, who had long played a prominent role, being the first Premier of the Southern Cameroons, was at this time leader of the main opposition party.[12] Now the United Nations demanded that the people of the Cameroons, both Northern and Southern, should determine their own political future and accordingly a plebsicite was held giving a choice between integration with Nigeria and reunification with French Cameroon. In addition to the strong lobbies for each of these choices, there were also views in the Southern Cameroons in favour of a period of continued Trusteeship under United Kingdom administration, at least for a short time, or for a separate independent political future which would not unite the Southern Cameroons to either neighbour. In 1959 (2 January) the Secretary of the United Nations, Dag Hammarskjöld, stopped in Buea to meet separately members of the government (Dr Foncha, S. T. Muna and A. N. Jua) and of the two main opposition parties (Dr E. M. L. Endeley, P. Mbile and P. Motumbe-Woleta) to ascertain their intentions. As the recording machines were not working properly, I was asked to take notes at the meeting.

To cut a long story short, at the plebiscite the people of the Northern Cameroons decided to amalgamate with Nigeria. The Southern Cameroons people voted overwhelmingly to integrate with the French-speaking Cameroonians on their eastern border. Reunification had occurred, but not within an exact replication of any pre-existing sets of borders, as Edwin pointed out at the time. No other choice was permitted by the United Nations, because of the pressure of the anti-colonial lobby there, and the belief that the Southern Cameroons would not be economically 'viable' as an independent state.

During this period of uncertainty and in the years following reunification Edwin Ardener knew most of the politicians in both the main lobbies and of many persuasions, from all parts of the Southern Cameroons. He talked to the British administrators and became familiar with those brought in to run the plebiscite. He, like most of the Europeans on the spot, maintained a neutral position, feeling that this was no time for outsiders to intervene: Cameroonians had to work this one out for themselves. He wrote a number of accounts of these events in *West Africa*, as they occurred, and made lengthier contributions to *The World Today*, and to Hazlewood's *African Integration and Disintegration*. The latter has been republished here, preceded by a brief note on the boundaries of German administered Kamerun. Edwin points out in these publications that the Southern Cameroons had long been relatively isolated from the centres of political power and commerce in Nigeria. He stated that during the first five years after reunification 'the isolation was maintained...The physical isolation of the representatives from Yaounde [who came to what was by then called West Cameroon] was increased by the sense of psychological distantiation.' It should be remembered that there was then no bridge over the Mungo River at Douala, and the land route from Yaounde to the forest areas was circuitous and badly maintained. He was prophetic when he wrote, following an administrative reorganization, 'Possibly the creation of the six adminstrative regions, of which West Cameroon is taxonomically one, may foreshadow a future, more centralized, republic, in which the position of West Cameroon will be reduced in constitutional importance. But the basic realities will have to be accommodated in any succeeding structure', (see the seventh chapter in this voloume).

Edwin concluded his study of the federated State in the work published here, by noting that in 1966 the politicians in power had decided to operate under a one-party system; this continued until recently. With the demise of the federal structure the ministries in Buea were closed down, the old 'Schloss' built by Puttkamer became a rarely visited, and out-of-bounds to the public, Presidential residence, as it is still. Although some individuals gained from centralization, the dissolution of the West Cameroon state certainly had a diminishing effect on Buea, as decision-making and staff moved to Yaounde. This decline was later exacerbated by the drastic economic cut-backs of so-called 'structural adjustment' policies and the even more recent devaluation of the French franc, to which the local franc is tied. Those 'basic realities' to which Edwin referred indeed came to the fore as anxieties grew among some of the people of the anglophone areas that their economic opportunites were diminishing in relation to those elsewhere, They linked this decline to their 'anglophone identity', forged in their particular history, which some saw as being overwhelmed by that shaped by another set of experiences. A pressure for decentralization built up, which has taken various forms—from a request for a more balanced development policy for the republic as a whole, through various forms of local autonomy even to outright seccession and the formation of a new independent state. In response to agitation in various parts of Cameroon, multi-party democracy became the official policy, though, as in many countries, its implementation still presents problems.

Recently, however, the aspirations of anglophone Cameroon have been met to some extent by the foundation of the University of Buea (which has brought new employment and population to Buea) and other developments in the North-West and South-West Provinces of anglophone Cameroon. They also probably stimulated the admission of the Republic—for anglophone Cameroon, readmission—to the Common-wealth. On the day in October 1995 that Cameroon became a member of the Commonwealth joyous parades of women marched the streets of Buea, as elsewhere. After many vicissitudes, the publicly-owned Cameroon Development Corporation, the largest plantation system in Cameroon, is currently being administered again by the Commonwealth Development Corporation. It remains to be seen how these and other developments will affect the Bakweri people as a whole, still vastly outnumbered by, but generally on friendly terms with, neighbours of other language groups. In the 1950s and 1960s the outlines of tidy Bakweri villages could be identified by the 'living fences' which, though by then hard to maintain, marked them off from the straggly 'stranger quarters' on Bakweri land beyond the village fence. Today in many places the fences are mere skeletons of their old structures, and to the casual eye there appears a blurring of the boundaries as infilling by Bakweri and non-Bakweri has linked the old settlements. But Bakweri in the various villages still control some important stretches of land, and their permission must be sought for its use by the tens of thousands now living on the mountain slopes near Buea, including those on Soppo and Bokwaongo land. How future political and economic changes will in the long run affect the people in these and other villages lying on the slopes of the Cameroon Mountain remains to be seen. The history of the area, as described by Edwin Ardener in this volume, will certainly affect the shape of that future.

Two years after Edwin's untimely death in 1987, Malcolm Chapman brought out a collection of some of Edwin's theoretical papers, most written in Oxford after his last visit to Cameroon. To this Chapman contributed a general biographical introduction and a full bibliography of Edwin's published work.[13] He omitted from this collection Edwin's papers on Africa both for lack of space and because we foresaw that a separate publication or series of publications would be useful. A selection of the papers that focus on the Mount Cameroon area, are now belatedly presented here.[14] Not included are his studies dealing with Nigeria, nor the papers he published in various issues of *West Africa*, and in *The World Today*, as listed below.

It must be emphasized here that all writings are very much products of their times. The material available to the writer, the contemporary concerns of the public and of scholars, moreover the language in which they are expressed, all shape every written text. Edwin would be the first to acknowledge that his writings have to be seen in their historical contexts. Since he wrote there has been a great deal of new scholarship of high quality, much of it home-grown in Cameroon, especially recently with its expanded academic facilities. Among the new collections which can be recommended is the second volume in this series entitled *African Crossroads: Intersections between History and Anthropology in Cameroon* (edited by Fowler and Zeitlyn) which has been inspired by the work of E. M. Chilver. Moreover, we now have the advantage of the published works of trained Bakweri scholars, among whom one of the most prolific is Dan Lyonga Matute, who has followed up the work of earlier writers, such as Edwin, and added the results of his own enquiries among his people; see for example, his *Facing Mount Fako: An Ethnographic Study of the Bakweri of Cameroon* (1990). In works such as these—for others see Appendix D—new data has come forth with fresh insights and I am sure that, were he here today, Edwin would take pleasure in the advances on and amendments to his data and propositions. He always said that scholars should regard their work as provisonal, and he would applaud the Bakweri proverb (cited by Dan Matute) 'one hand cannot tie a bundle'. It is certaion that he would be delighted that so many books cite the Buea Archives office as the source of much of their information.

There is no doubt Edwin would write on different topics and generate further ideas had be not died. He intended to write new introductary and final chapters for this volume. It would be wrong to write on his behalf or to up-date his finished texts.[15] A decision has therefore been taken to retain them basically unamended, conserving the political and other terminology of the day; I refer you here to note 1. Thus you will read of West Cameroon and of the Southern Cameroons, when these terms have no current administrative recognition—though surprisingly they can still sometimes be heard and have meaning in some contemporary political discourses.

Having been published separately for different readers, within and beyond Cameroon, who could not be presumed to be familiar with his previous publications, some repetition will inevitably be found in the texts below. They have been put, not in exact order of composition, but in a sequence which does not offend too much the chronology of events. The content of the studies together, as the title suggests, span a period of four-hundred years. To put the local material into a general West African framework, a reprint of some 'Preliminary Chronological Notes for the South' of the Republic of Cameroon, taken from a collection published under the editorship of Claude Tardits in 1981, has been included as an appendix.

When Edwin gathered his ethnographic data on Mount Cameroon he brought up to date the genealogies he first presented in his book *Coastal Bantu of the Cameroons* (1956). After his death in 1982 Chief Gervasius Endeley was succeeded in 1991 by his nephew, the former Chief Justice, now referred to as HRH Nakuve S. M. L Endeley, Paramount Chief of the Bakweris (or Bakweries).[16]

On a visit to Buea in October 1995 I was distressed to see the burnt-out remains of the late Chief Endeley's dwelling. Gone, I was told, were all the records he had inherited from his brother, the chief before him, and the genealogies and other records he had himself painstakingly compiled. This tragedy, together with the loss of the paper-packed house of another local historian, Esasso Woleta of Soppo, are two disasters which have robbed the Bakweri and scholars generally of irreplaceable information.

Edwin's material, relatively scanty though it is in comparison to that which has been lost, has therefore particular value. It is likely that some of those living today may have cherished alternative versions of their history, deriving from other family traditions. One can only say that Edwin was as scrupulous an ethnographer as he could be, where possible checking the accounts he was given against the alternative sources then proferred, as he describes below. If there are other versions current today, they must be defended by those who assert them. Similarly there will be politicians and others who lived through the 1950s and 1960s who may have seen the events described differently. Past events are made up of many experiences, not all known to everyone. History is indeed multi-stranded, and alternative scenarios may be expected. Others who have steeped themselves in Cameroon history, and who have contributed their own writings on the themes raised, may especially feel that Edwin's work lacks the novelty of recent published work, including their own, and that I should have given this more detailed reference. It is beyond the scope of this undertaking to do more than make the occasional acknowledgment of recent work.[17] This book is a record of some of the work done by one man in the 'fifties and 'sixties, and has the virtues and weaknesses of a time when Cameroon Studies were in their relative infancy. Friend to many—chiefs, farmers, students and politicians alike—Edwin wrote as he saw and heard things then. On a recent visit to Cameroon I was touched by the warm regard in which he is still held in all walks of life. My name immediately evoked the query 'Edwin Ardener - anthropologist?' from Bakweri farmers who knew him twenty-five years ago and from teachers in Mamfe he had never met. I have been encouraged by many of those friends in Cameroon and elsewhere, and those who know of him only through his scattered publications, to bring together these studies, which include some yet unpublished accounts of the kingdom, and make them more accessible.

Shirley Ardener,
Oxford, 1996

Notes

1. Following the practice of linguists of the time, and in conformity to the style of the Ethnographic Survey of the International African Institute to which it belonged, in *Coastal Bantu of the Cameroons*, which includes descriptions of the beliefs and cultural practices of the Bakweri, Edwin dropped the prefix altogether and rendered Bakweri as *-Kpe*. This was the only time he used this confusing practice—confusing because there are no people called Kpe! In *Coastal Bantu* (p.9, note 4) he notes that the 'V' in Vakpe is bilabial. 'The stem *Kpeli* also exists, parallel to the Duala *Mukwedi*, pl. *Bakwedi*, but is rare. Its appearance in *Mokpeli'a Nembongo* (*Bambongo*), the name of the Kpe ancestor, suggests, however, that the form may be ancient. *Kpe* country is also known as *Wojua* by the Mboko and Isuwu of the coast.' See also pp. 3–4 of Matute (1990).
   As for the name of the State itself after it obtained independence in 1961, Edwin wrote 'The use of *Cameroun* in English is now inappropriate, and hybrid forms such as *West Cameroun* especially so. A rule of thumb for English-speaking usage is: Period of Mandate/Trusteeship: *The Cameroons* (division: British [Northern, Southern]/French); The independent French-speaking Republic of 1 January1960–1 October 1961: *Cameroun Republic*; the independent reunified Federal Republic of 1 Oct. 1961: *Cameroon*; (divisions: West/East), French-speaking usage has been consistent through all periods: *Cameroun*.' (See below.) Currently, now the State has ceased to be a federation, it is officially designated as the Republic of Cameroon. In common parlance it has recently become the fashion to refer to anglophone Cameroon—for that part which was formerly called Southern, later West Cameroon—and francophone Cameroon—for the rest of the territory. These have political as well as descriptive meanings for some. T Southern/West Cameroon no longer pertains; the area referred to being divided into North West Province and South West Province. The map of Cameroon (see frontispiece) is a modified version by R. McIntyre of one in Delancy and Mokeba, 1979.
2. Translation by E. M. Chilver from Max Esser's *An der Westküste Afrikas*, Berlin-Köln-Leipzig, Ahn, 1898. Chilver notes that Esser 'was responsible for obtaining the first of the W.A.P.V. lands (Ngeme), later greatly enlarged in 1896. The largest contemporary plantation companies in the "Victoria district" were the K.L.P.G. with headquarters in Bimbia and the Jantzen and Thormählen properties with a centre at Bimbia and lands in Debundscha, Isonge Udje and Mokundange. Knutson had a small property at Bonge, chosen to be near the sea, but found it to be on "poor soil"' (personal note). For further details see Ardener's third contribution below.
3. Zintgraff noted in his *Nord-Kamerun* (1895) that he stayed a few days in the area, noting the rich volcanic soil, that there was plenty of water and that this healthy area was 'made for plantations'. He also observed Bakweri

wrestling and their 'erotic dances' (p. 33). I am indebted to E. M. Chilver for drawing my attention to this material in her translated epitome of pages 1–168 of Zintgraff's book.

4. The Ba'atum of Esu and his elders kindly allocated a site for a mud and thatch dwelling. Some of the fieldnotes taken during his stay in Esu are being edited and will soon be made accessible to researchers, together with that section of *Plantation and Village in the Cameroons* dealing with Esu.
5. The fuller text was accompanied by more tables, detailed by notes, than are included below.
6. Further details describing the resurgence of *nyɔngo* can be found in Geschiere and Konings, 1983. Edwin Ardener described the Bakweri institution of *liengu*, along with some other material, in a paper of general theoretical interest entitled 'Belief and the Problem of Women' first published in 1968, but reprinted together with a follow-up called 'The Problem Revisited' in *Perceiving Women* (ed. S. G. Ardener, 1975). Edwin (with Macrow) also published an illustrated paper on the eruption of the Cameroon Mountain.
7. His duties included the refurbishment of the Bamenda Museum, the clearing and restoration of the German graveyard in Buea, the restoration of the Bismarck Fountain, the repair of the clock on what was then called the Secretariat in Buea, the drafting of legislation concerning the protection of antiquities needed following the split with Nigeria, and giving of advice to customs officers on how to identify antiquities.
8. Over recent years the physical condition of the deposits had deteriorated due to lack of finance for maintenance of dehumidifying equipment, and shortage of staff. At the moment a process of rehabilitation and up-grading is in hand under the guidance of the current Director of Patrimony, Dr Verkijika Fanso, which it is hoped will be maintained both by government funding and from grants and donations from well-wishers. That the deposits are still available for the eager readers who wait upon the office is due largely to the devotion, over the years, of its dwindling archive staff. For tributes to Edwin's work at the archives office see Dr S. Epale (1985), and the obituaries by Prof. M. Njeuma 'Pioneer in African Studies—Edwin Ardener' in *West Africa*, 5 Oct. 1987, and in the *Cameroon Times*.
9. The late Paul Kale liked to tell how some Europeans had quizzed him as to whether or not the material in this book was true. (It was common for Europeans to say to us that social anthropologists would only be told, and believe, lies!) Paul told us that he replied: 'If not 100% true, then it is 99·9% true'—a statement that, even if over-generous, was gratefully received!
10. Some of these texts were written in the morning and set half an hour later in hot metal by, among others Mr Mbah and Mr Eseke, whose skills must be acknowledged. They said it was a change from setting goverment forms!
11. A limited reprint by the Friends of the Buea Archives Office in Oxford in 1996 has been renamed *The Old Lodge*. Limited runs of other booklets have also been made available. The Lodge is currently kept ready for use

by the President. There is talk of it becoming a national museum.

12. For photographs of Chief Gervasius Endeley, E. M. L. Endeley, O.B.E., as Premier, and of Chief Manga Williams, O.B.E., '"father" of the House of Assembly', see p.95. For the House of Assembly in session, see *Introducing the Southern Cameroons*, compiled by the Government of Southern Cameroons, Lagos, 1958. The photographs are by the Gov-ernmentt. Information Service. For the House of Chiefs, see B. Chem-Langhee, 'The Origins of the Southern Cameroons House of Chiefs', *Int. Journal of African Historical Studies*, Vol. 16, no. 4, 1983.
13. Malcolm Chapman has kindly permitted us to draw upon his full bibliography of Edwin's publications in *The Voice of Prophesy* in order to compile a list of Edwin's publications on African topics; see Appendix C.
14. Deciding what to leave out has not been easy, and E. M. Chilver has, as always, been unstinting with her advice on this and other matters. Her sharp eye reduced my errors considerably. In addition to compiling the index, Ian Fowler, whose work on iron-smelting in the Grassfields will soon be published (see Berg Publishers, and other forthcoming studies), has also given much time and made many valuable suggestions. The editor's work in preparing camera-ready copy for the publisher has also been greatly facilitated by the computer skills of Bob McIntyre, a former resident of Buea where he was an education adviser in the early 1990s, who has also taken a personal interest in this book.
15. I cannot be sure that proof-errors, even in crucial matters such as names, have not crept in, as his original handwritten MS is no longer available. Some of the terms and names have been given in the English spelling, rather than in an orthography which would better reflect Bakweri pronunciation. Edwin's card index of *Mokpe* words has been put on disk; it is currently being edited by Bruce Connell and will soon be published.
16. See the University of Buea Newsletter. Vol 2, no.2, 1995.On the death of Chief Gervasius Mbele Endeley protracted discussions took place before his nephew was installed. Peter Geschiere, who was present in Buea then, has given his account of local opinion at that time as he saw it, and of the history of the chieftaincy as revealed in colonial documents. His two subtitles—'The British and the "Invention" of the Endeley Chieftaincy in Buea' and 'The Bakweri of South-West Cameroon: The implantation of a New Chieftaincy'—indicate his approach to this topic, as does the title of his paper, 'Chiefs and Colonial Rule in Cameroon: Inventing Chieftaincy, French and British Style' (*Africa*, 63 (2), 1993). Edwin Ardener (1956) and Dan Matute (1990) discuss the position of leaders among the Bakweri, and the use of the term *Sang'a mboa* ('Father of the village'). The term *kinge* (clearly a term derived from the English term king) was an alternative for *sang'a mboa* used when Edwin was in Buea. Edwin Ardener had used the title 'Kingdom on Mount Cameroon' when he wrote the second text published here while the late chief was still on seat.
17. A short list of selected texts is given as Appendix D below, in order to provide a starting point for any reader unfamiliar with recent work. The list is very far from comprehensive.

1

Documentary and Linguistic Evidence for the Rise of the Trading Polities between Rio del Rey and Cameroons, 1500–1650*

The early historical material for the area between the Cross River and the Cameroons estuary is full of ambiguities. Dapper (1668) and Barbot (1732) between them imposed upon the seventeenth century a canonical scheme. Peoples such as Ambozi and Calbongos dominate the scene, and many of us have been tempted to try to interpret at its face value, a system of toponymy which derives in part from a corrupt manuscript 'tradition', and in part from the compilation of a few independent sources into layer upon layer of variants. This paper attempts to unravel some of the tangle, and by the addition of as yet unconsidered sources to advance the matter a little further from the point reached in the original scholarly study by Bouchaud (1952), the standard work in this field.

I shall be primarily considering the early contact of European trade with the stretch of the West African coast from Rio del Rey to the Cameroons River, places now in the Federal Republic of Cameroon. Some indirect light is also thrown on the situation in Old Calabar. This is not a political study but a clearing of the decks for such a study: of the growth of the trading hegemonies of Duala and Bimbia, which led to the establishment by the end of the eighteenth century of mercantile spheres bounding that of the Efik. I have tried to establish more precisely the period in which this political dawn occurred. This attempt has been aided by new evidence for the presence on the coast of speakers of Bantu languages, specifically of Duala type—indeed we may now virtually say speakers of the Duala language—before 1665. Certain personages may now be said to be 'historical', one of whom stands near the head of the genealogy of the trading dynasties of the Duala people: the later Kings of the Cameroons River (Ardener, 1965, pp. 17-21).[1]

---

* *From* History and Social Anthropology, *ed. I. Lewis, London:Tavistock, 1968*

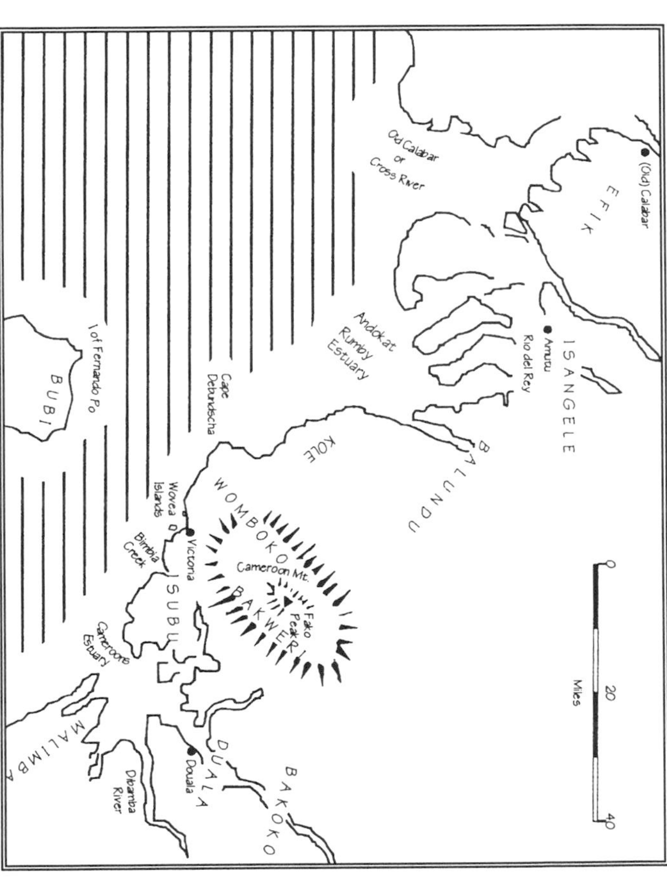

The Cameroon Coast in 1600

Literary Sources of the Onomastic Problems[2]

The Portuguese discovery of the Cameroon coast is usually linked with that of the neighbouring island of Fernando Po, on various good grounds. The island and the coast present the appearance of two mountain peaks only some 25 miles apart at their bases. The date of the sighting of the island itself is, however, never clearly stated in Barros (1552), who merely says that 'at that time' the island of Fermosa was discovered by one Fernam do Pó and that it now bore in Barros' day the name of its discoverer instead of this earlier name. The time referred to appears to mean 'in the contract of Gomes' (beginning in 1469) and not to the period of 1474 which has also been referred to as *'neste tempo'* just before. Bouchaud has clearly demonstrated by the weight of evidence that early in 1472 is the most likely date for the discovery of Fermosa by Fernam do Pó, and by implication of the opposing coast.[3]

There is no direct contemporary evidence concerning the area until the years about 1500, when the veil of secrecy concerning the Portuguese discoveries begins to lift. The *Esmeraldo de Situ Orbis* of Pacheco Pereira is here, as elsewhere, of great value and interest, but the standard English translation (Kimble, 1937) is misleading at precisely this point. The *Esmeraldo* was written at some time about or after 1505 (Basto, 1892, p. ix; Dias, 1905, p. 4; Kimble, 1937, pp. xvi-xvii).[4] The information for our area may relate to 1503-1505, the time of Pacheco's second visit to India. Since he was governor at S. Jorge da Mina in 1520-1522 and since one terminus for publication is 1521 (the end of D. Manoel's reign), a date for the acquisition of hearsay information as late as this cannot be excluded (Dias, p. 4), improbable as it is.

After an account of Rio Real (the joint estuary of the New Calabar and Bonny Rivers), and after mentioning minor rivers to the east in the Niger Delta area, Pacheco's Chapter 10 is entitled '. . . *da serra de Fernam do Poo'* (S. Dias, p. 124). Some confusion in the interpretation of this chapter comes from the fact that the Cameroon Mountain was at this time called 'the mountain range of Fernam do Poo' a name it did not lose for about a century.[5] This chapter therefore is concerned with both the *serra* (on the mainland) and the *ilha* (the island), and it is not therefore accurate to state as Kimble does (1937, note to p. 131), followed by others, that Pacheco says nothing concerning 100 miles of coast between the Rio de S. Domingos (in the present Eastern Nigeria) and the Cameroons River. Pacheco refers to *esta serra e ilha* (S. Dias, p. 125)—'this mountain range and island'—as having been discovered by Fernam do Poo. Kimble, apparently unaware of this local peculiarity of nomenclature, was reduced to the translation: 'This island with its mountain range', taking the latter (as his note confirms) to be the peak of the island of Fernando Po itself. In what follows Pacheco refers sometimes to the *ilha* and sometimes to the *serra.* It is the *serra* (13,350 ft) to which he refers as being visible in clear weather from 25 and 30 leagues, not the lower eminence of the *ilha.* 'And the island at the mouth of this bay', he continues immediately (*this* referring still to the mainland in the Bay of Biafra), 'is very populous and there is in it much sugar cane and the mainland (*terra firme*) is five leagues distant; and a ship coming to the said land (*dita terra*) for anchorage will be in 15 fathoms a half-league from the shore. Slaves may be bartered there (*aly*). . . .'

Stopping here, we may note that *aly* refers to *dita terra* and the latter refers to the *terra firme* which is five leagues distant from the populous island with the sugar cane. We may rest assured therefore that what follows refers to the mainland and not the island. To continue:

> Slaves may be bartered there at eight to ten bracelets (*manilhas*) of copper apiece. In this country (*nesta terra*) there are many and large elephants, whose teeth, which we call ivory, we buy, and for one bracelet of copper one gets a big elephant's tusk [the mention of elephants confirm that we are on the mainland and not on the island]; and in addition there is in this country (*nesta terra*) a fair abundance of malagueta of fine and good quality. There are many things in this Ethiopia which yield a good profit when brought to this kingdom.

We have then clearly set the scene as the mainland at the *Serra de Fernam do Poo:* Mount Cameroon. This falls to the sea by way of a range of foothills and the spur of the Small Cameroon (5,570 ft), at a point comparable with the 5 leagues (the Portuguese league was 4 miles) from the *Ilha* of Fernam do Poo of Pacheco. There are elephants, and good-quality *afromomum*—as at the present day. There are inhabitants, and they sell tusks and slaves for a handful of manillas. The end of this sentence is of great interest:

> . . . e ha jente d'esta terra ilha chamam em sua lingoajem 'Caaboo' e dentro no sertaão sincoenta leguoas da costa dó mar está hua [corrupt text] linguoa que há nome 'Bota'.[6]

The meaning of this sentence, so crucial, is in doubt: 'The people of this country are called "Caaboo" in their language' (this is clear) 'and in the bush 50 leagues from the sea-coast is a [break] *linguoa* which has the name "Bota"'.

Kimble's translation of *linguoa* is 'language', and he suggests an original something like: 'another people, called in their language "Bota"' (Kimble, p. 134). Basto (p. 111) suggests *'lingua de terra, ou baixo'*, that is: 'tongue of land, or reef'. Whatever this Bota was it is clearly stated to be 50 leagues from the sea-coast at the *serra de Fernom do Poo.* In later centuries a Bota was located *on* the sea-coast, and it is so called today, although not in the vernacular of the inhabitants. Were it not for this modern circumstance it would probably have been generally assumed that the Bota in question was the *Serra Bota* which Pacheco actually mentioned later at a distance (by his own reckoning) of 48 leagues from the *Serra de Fernam do Poo,* southward along the African coast, north of Rio Muni. This range appears in the Strasbourg Ptolemy map of Africa of 1513 (Santarem, 1899) as well as regularly in later sources. The name means in Portuguese: 'the blunt range'. We are then presented at the outset with at least the possibility that the Cameroon *Bota* is a ghost name which acquired reality through a long life in the travel literature. The same question arises indeed for the *Caaboo.* These matters will be discussed below. There it is enough to make clear that Pacheco's test concerning the *people* so called intends to locate them at the mainland coast of the *serra,* not the *ilha* de Fernam do Poo. This is further confirmed by the evident continuity of the coast assumed in the next sentence:[7]

> Item. All the sea-coast from this *Serra de Fernam do Poo* to *Cabo de Lopo Gonçalvez,* which is eighty leagues, is densely populated and thickly wooded.

After general remarks, including one on the presence of whales, he continues:

> Item. Two leagues from this *serra de Fernam do Poo* to the north-east is a river which is called *dos Camarões* (Cameroons Estuary), where there is good fishing; we have not yet had any trade with the natives; great tornadoes accompanied by very violent storms are experienced on this coast, and as a safeguard you should furl sail while they last.

The statement that the distance from the Serra de Fernam do Poo was two leagues suggests that a promontory near Bimbia Creek was the point on the mainland from which the measurement was made. Also it is to be noted that the Cameroons River was not yet the place to which local trade came. It has been necessary to consider carefully this authoritative Portuguese source for the condition of the Cameroon coast about 1500, because, although the interpretation given here was clearly made by Bouchaud, the English translation has helped to confuse the position for English-speakers.

Approximately contemporary with Pacheco's account is one by João de Lisboa, published in 1514 in his *Tratado de Agulha de Marear* ('Treatise on the Compass'). I have been unable to consult the Portuguese edition (Brito Rebello, 1903), and here rely on Bouchaud's French translation (1952, pp. 51-53). This source fills the geographical gap left by Pacheco. After the *Rio de sam domingo* (the Andoni river of the Niger Delta: Jones, 1964, p. 34), he names the *Rio da cruz* (the Cross River), and the 'anse de la pêcherie' or 'Fishery gulf': the *Angra Pescaria* of contemporary and later maps, at the entrance to the Rio del Rey. From Rio Real (the Bonny-New Calabar estuary) to the *Pescaria* the whole coast was wooded.

> Know [he says] that from this *pescaria to* the bar of the Rio *das Camaroys* [sic] there is a distance of 15 leagues. In this coast there is a mountain range which is called *serra de fernam do poo,* and if you wish to go to the *Rio dos Camaroys,* passing between the island and the mainland, you must navigate with the lead, because there are shoals.[8]

Pacheco and Joao seem to be independent sources here, but, despite this early mention of the Cross River and of the *Pescaria,* we need not question the conclusion, based upon Pacheco, that these areas at this early date did not attract a great deal of trade (Jones, 1964, p. 34). The *Pescaria* probably received its name because of the dotting of the sea by fishing traps on its bed, like those which are still a prominent feature today.

We next have to deal with a group of sources, in various languages, clustered round the name of Martin Enciso, who in 1518 appears simply to have translated into Castillian a manual written early in the same year by a Portuguese, Andreas Pires, whose own manuscript is in the Bibliothèque Nationale (Taylor, 1932). The latter was a pilot who had transferred his services to Spain. Enciso refers to the distance between Rio Real and a 'Cape of Fernando Po' (*cabo de Fernãdo polo*) as 30 leagues. To the west of this cape, he says, was the *rio de los santos* ('river of saints'), and to the east the *golfo d' l galo* (Enciso, 1518). The Cape would appear to refer to that point on the sea-shore at the Cameroon Mountain already referred to by Pacheco. This may be Cape Debundscha or, more probably, one of the points near Victoria. The *golfo d' l galo* probably contains a misreading of *delgado* (Port. 'slender') a term consistently used at the period of the Suellaba point at the entrance of the

Cameroons River. The 'river of saints' may be the Rio del Rey or the Cross River.[9]

Enciso continues:

> These three rivers are large and have good entrances and the land is very hot. And it is a land of much gold. Here there is a fruit from palms which is called Cocos: and it is big and yellow. They make wine of it and it is also good to eat. In this country they make cloth of wool [=fibre] of palms in such a way that it is good to wear. And in all those lands they use that cloth. They have iron and steel.

The three rivers include the Rio Real, and so a long stretch of Eastern Nigerian coast is evidently included in the description. The land of coconuts (possibly confused also with palm-wine), and of raffia cloth, is possibly intended to be closer to Rio del Rey than to the Cameroons River. Very small amounts of gold have been panned in the Ndian affluent of the Rio del Rey estuary, but Enciso here may be fanciful. The statement of the possession of iron may be noted.

Ambos

The Enciso relation was itself pirated and translated into English (with almost no addition) by Roger Barlow, in an MS. dated to 1541, and published by Taylor (1932). A French version was made by Jean Fonteneau (alias Jean Alfonse) and Raulin Sécalart, pilots of La Rochelle in 1545. This uses French forms (translations and quasi-phonetic renderings) of the Portuguese names: we read of the *cap de Frenandupau, rivière de Tous les Sainctz,* and *l'ance de Jau* (='The gulf of the cock'='golpho de' l galo'). They try to adjust the cape of Fernando Po to the island, which they state to be full of cannibals. This bungled text becomes of interest because they also interpolate into Enciso in this passage certain remarks concerning a people they refer to under the name *Ambous* and like forms. They write:

> And turning to the coast, I say that the rivers are big rivers and along them grey pepper and malaguetta can be obtained. And the people of the country are called *Ambous.* And they are people *qui ont les plus grandz natures que gens du monde et sont puissantes et maulvaises gens* (Fonteneau, 1545, ed. Musset, 1904, pp. 337-38).

Then comes one of those confusions that bedevil all inquiries in this field. Of Cape *Lope Gonsalvez* (Cape Lopez in the modern Gabon), the authors make the further statement:

> And at the said cape. . . the nation of the *Ambons* [sic] finishes, the *Manicongres* people begin, who are continually at war with the *Ambos* [sic]. The *Ambos* eat them when they catch them being cannibals. The *Manicongres* for the most part are Christians. These Ambos have several kinds of wild beasts. The land is very hot (p. 339).

These latter *Ambos* were a people of the Congo area, who are mentioned by Pigafetta (1591): they are placed by Ravenstein between the coast of Congo and Anzica, and he identifies them with the Balumbu (Ravenstein, 1901, p. 191). The *Amboas* who appear on Pigafetta's map (1591, end) thus should be seen in relation to the Anzicos of the Congo basin near which they are placed, and not as in the hinterland of Cameroon near which the distortions of the map also place them. We are not, however, concerned here with the identity of the Congo basin *Ambo* (Doke, 1961, p. 6. identifies them with the Ovambo). Our difficulty is in deciding whether the Cameroon Ambo really existed. This is important, because, from the seventeenth century, their name is permanently with us.[10]

It must be stressed that ghost names of all kinds became attached to the West African coast, partly during the Portuguese period, but more especially during the seventeenth century. Numerous cartographical and route-book recensions of the names occurred in the early period, but the Dutch produced a kind of definitive series of terms which remained unamended virtually until the nineteenth century. Bouchaud has shown the probable purely graphic development of the shadow region of Biafra from the Mesche Mons of Ptolemy.[11] In any investigation of the toponymy the null hypothesis must be to assume a ghost name, and here the possibility of a deformation of the form *Caaboo,* given by Pacheco, cannot be excluded. We find a possibly intermediate form (*isolas canboas*) in Martines' map of 1567 (Santarem, 1899). Confusion with the Ambo of the Congo may have made the fixing of the form *Ambos* all too plausible. It must be said that the argument that *Caaboo* was a corruption in the reverse sense carries as great conviction. None the less, until recently there was no unequivocal evidence available that the term *Ambos* was ever actually applied to Cameroon in any early non-cartographic Portuguese source.

Luckily we now have the following reference, which at least removes doubt on this score. It is in a letter from Duarte Rodrigues (Roiz) to the

King of Portugal, dated 10 May 1529 (MMA, IV, 1954, p. 144). The writer had been sent to the Congo, and was delayed there for six months. The letter advises the King about irregularities observed in the trade of São Tomé, Axim, and Mina. In one passage he says:

> Your highness has a country in the *Ambos* which is between the island of *Fernã do Po* and the mainland, from which there comes much malagueta, and it seems to me that 30 or 40 moyos [1 moyo=822 litres] may be taken out, and, if the country became accustomed to it [the trade] there would be much more; this malagueta is denied to you because no factor of yours in the Island of *Santomé* has ever declared it to you;I have informed you of it; and because my desire is great to serve you I rejoice in looking out for everything, and for this reason give an account to your highness, for it seems to me that in this I do you sufficient service. . . Today the 10th May, 1529.
>
> Duarte Roʋjz.
>
> Address: For the King our Lord.
> This letter is highly secret; let it be opened in front of his highness.
>
> Vay de Colỹ[12]

The name *Ambos* thus existed in 1529, and was applied to a spot somewhere between the island of Fernando Po and the mainland—clearly an island or islands, and thus probably either the islands in Victoria Bay or the island near Bimbia known as Nicoll Island. We have confirmation of the existence of the malagueta mentioned by Pacheco, and further evidence that the area was neglected by Portuguese trade at that time. This solitary contemporary reference to the Ambos in the Portuguese period, outside the shifting onomasiology of the maps and route-lists, enables certain hypotheses to be suggested. First, out of many corrupt forms, *Ambos* (plural) can now be established as not a ghost name. Second, the later references that relate the *Ambos* to islands off the coast can be given special weight, and the question whether the use of the name for the mainland by the Dutch was secondary may be raised.

A source which now comes into a certain focus is the *Hydrographia* of Figueiredo, which was licensed for Publication in Lisbon in 1614. It says (folio 44, reverse) that from the island of *Fernam do Pâo* [sic] to the mainland was five leagues and that 'looking to the north you will see a very high mountain range, which is called *serra de Motão,* and which is above *os Zambus* which is a little island to the south of it.' He says that care should be taken not to go too much on the mainland without someone who knows the country, even if short of water,

> for all the people here are warlike, and there are no people acquainted with the Portuguese, except those of the *ilheo dos Zambus* which is half a league, and seeing people in this island do not go ashore, as they too are warlike people, but go two leagues distant from the island that the peak is to the east of you. . .

This account is circumstantial, and if the common name of the island was *os Ambos* or *'the* Ambos', the spellings *os Zambus, dos Zambus* can be explained as an artifact of word juncture. Figueiredo's account is now greatly strengthened. Of course, it may be countered that the error in word division is not Figueiredo's but that of Duarte Roiz, who was after all writing from the Congo. There is also hovering in the background the difficult shadow of Pacheco's *Caaboo,* which with its peculiar doubled vowels has the look of a scribe's corruption for a word of about the length of *Zambus.* If indeed *Caaboo* did not apparently re-emerge in the later seventeenth century in a Dutch form, discussed below, we should already be well advised to reject it altogether.

Before considering this question further, Figueiredo has a further significance—the last of the major Portuguese sources, he is also used as the basis of an early major Dutch source: Dierick Ruiters whose *Toortse der Zee-Vaert* was published in 1623. When he reached the points in Figueiredo cited above, he used the following forms:

> 1. . . . *eenen hooghen Bergh sien, noorden van u, ende werdt ghenoemt Monton, ofte Maton: 't is eenen Bergh gheleghen op Amboes*
> 2. . . . *'t eylant Amboes 't welck oock Zambus ghenaemt werdt.*'[13]

In the first passage, *Amboes* has been substituted for the *Zambus* of Figueiredo. In the second, it has been offered as an alternative. Considering the corrupt forms of Figueiredo's *Motão* in passage (1), Ruiters' emendations on their own have little status. With the establishment of an independent Portuguese form *Ambos*, however, it now seems more likely that Ruiters is here emending from other, possibly oral sources (*oe* to represent the *u*-like Portuguese *o*). The Dutch and Flemish definite articles would not introduce the same ambiguity of word division (at this point in its history Ambos soon ceases to be perceived as in itself plural). Naber (1913b) suggests, improbably, that Zambus has a Portuguese etymology from the citrus *Djambua,* but on balance I think that the current Portuguese name was *os Ambos* and not *os*

Zambus.[14] Further, the *Ambos* seem to have been people continuously associated with an island or islands off the mainland—islands, from Figueiredo's description, identifiable as one of those with which their name has always been associated in Ambas Bay off Victoria. There is no mention of any people called *Ambos* as living on the mainland in any early source. This situation was blurred by the writers of the succeeding period, as will be shown. If Figueiredo is anything to go by, the later Portuguese were already in doubt as to the form of the name.

Elements in the Dutch tradition

The Dutch *bouleversement* of the Portuguese position in the Gulf after the attack on São Thomé at the end of the sixteenth century, culminating in the capture of S. Jorge de Mina in 1637, used a mixture of Portuguese maps and textual sources of different ages, and to some extent rationalised them. The Portuguese had already been under competition from the Spanish and part of the nomenclature which the Dutch popularized was derived from Spanish forms.[15]

In another part of Figueiredo's work, and not connected with the account already cited, which is an independent source, he gives for good measure a copy of Pacheco, slightly paraphrased, in which the doubtful portion in which Pacheco refers to the 'Caaboo' and 'Bota' is rendered as follows:

> . . . esta terra chamão o *Chaquim*, do cabo pera dentro no sertao cinco legoas està hum lugar a que chamão Bòta' (this is called *Chaquim*, and from the cape into the bush five leagues is a place which is called *Bòta*).[16]

This attempts to tidy up the lacuna in Pacheco, and puts the mysterious Bota only 5 leagues away and definitely inland. This version of Pacheco is of interest in the present context because of the blunder: *Chaquim*; by which the name of a well-known place in Dahomey is substituted for Pacheco's even then incomprehensible Caaboo. This was then copied by Ruiters in his *Toortse*, which says that the inhabitants called the coast *Chaquin* [sic]. He rephrases the whole passage but refers to the malagueta and elephant's teeth of Pacheco, and says, still paraphrasing, that trade takes place four [Dutch] miles inside the cape at a place named *Botas*, and that the natives like nothing but good arm- and leg-rings.[17] It is important to stress that Ruiters is not an independent source here. The line is direct: Pacheco, with Figueiredo's emendations, paraphrased by Ruiters. This point has to be established, because from Ruiters the two placenames *Chaquin* and *Bota* enter the Dutch arm-chair sources. By the time of Dapper and Barbot, the former has, I believe, become the *Cesge* which is coupled with Bota in these classical and misleading texts to give alternative names of an inhabited place near the Cameroon Mountain.

In view of the separate life of the nomenclature of the coast, it is a certain relief when an actual visitor appears—Samuel Brun (or Braun or Bruno), a Swiss surgeon on a Dutch ship whose account (published in 1624) was very influential.[17] In 1614 he reached Benin and then he says '. . . we went to the *Land von Ambosy* and *Camarona, Rio de Anckare* and *Rio de Ree'*. He has something to say on the economic life of the area and he is a valuable independent source.[19]

For our present purposes, we may note the form *Ambosy,* now with a suffix added to the original Portuguese plural form. The proximate source is said by Brun to be Spanish. We may, however, bear in mind the possibility of a 'feedback' of the very word *Ambos* in a form shaped by West Coast African traders or interpreters who, we may think, would by now be cognizant of the Portuguese usage. Brun it is, however, who first likens the Cameroon Mountain to the Peak of Teneriffe, and derives its name from the Spanish *Alta tierra de Ambosy*. All of which was lifted whole later by Dapper, broadcast by Barbot, and was being cited from Barbot by Burton as late as 1863.[20] Nothing illustrates more sadly the lack of corroborative value of so much of the literature on this zone. From now on, forms such as *Ambosy* and the like become firmly attached to the Cameroon Mountain itself, as well as remaining attached to the island or islands off the coast. The mountain ceases to be known as the Serra de Fernam do Poo before the end of the sixteenth century.

Bota and the Cameroon Mountain

Once again Figueiredo occupies a critical place. Where Pacheco talks of a people, called *Caaboo,* and a 'something', called *Bota,* fifty leagues away from the coast in the *sertão,* Figueiredo speaks of *os Zambus,* and, to the north of them, a high mountain called *serra de Motão*. If the *Caaboo* are possibly *Ambos* or *Zambus,* we may wonder if the *serra de Motão* is not the peculiar Bota. It is indeed nearer five leagues inland to the peak than fifty. Once again there are no certainties. The considerable misstatement of numerals is not uncommon in the courses: thus Enciso gives the latitude of *Cap Fernam do Poo as* 'xl [40] and a half degrees' instead of 'iv [4] and a half'—the error may stem basically from a confusion between V and L in the MSS. of the period. Figueiredo himself corrects Pacheco's fifty leagues to five as we have seen above. I am of the opinion that Pacheco's inland feature was the Cameroon Peak and that this was what was called Bota. Whether it should have been *Motão*, while his own form was influenced by the *Serra Bota* of lower down the coast, may be left an open question. What may now be explained is why a name located by Pacheco far inland could also have been given to a point on the coast. The mountain and parts of the coast have often exchanged names.

We may now ask from what language, or languages, *Motão* or *Bota* were derived. The most conservative conclusion is to offer Portuguese etymologies. *Motão* may be a colloquial augmentative of *Mota* 'mound', 'motte'. *Bota,* 'blunt', was already used elsewhere of mountains, as we have seen. It may be argued that Pacheco at least is sometimes reliable on local West African forms (*Jos:* Ijaw, *Ogani:* the Oni of Ife), but he does not clearly say that this is a local form. An alternative hypothesis; much less firmly based, is that these are Portuguese folk-etymologies, even possibly for the same word, from some local language. It will be worthwhile pursuing this hypothesis in order to demonstrate the ambiguities that hedge it round. *Bota* has frequently been taken to be of Duala, or other Coastal Bantu origin, and thought to mean something like 'hatching of fish'.[21] The name seems not to be indigenous to the area. *Bata,* meaning 'a kind of net', seems more possible—since the other *Serra Bota* down the coast gives us *Bata* in Rio Muni. However, etymons from the language of the Bubi of Fernando Po are also possible, if *motão* and *bota* are to be linked.

In Fernandian dialects *b* and *m* are interchangeable, especially in the angular prefixes, as forms for this people's name (=*mome-* in certain dialects) themselves exemplify. *Môte* means 'big' in Bubi (Tessmann, 1923, p. 153). The inhabitants of the present inhabited island in Victoria Bay claim to be of Bubi descent, and were already called *Boobees* in 1855. They now call themselves by a version of the name *Bobe* (Ardener, 1956 pp. 30-31). The Island and its neighbours have a continuous history of occupation after Dapper's account, and one of these is probably also the *ilheo dos Ambos*, as we have seen. It is, of course, plausible that the Portuguese should have taken Fernandians when visiting the mainland opposite. It may well be that the Bubi settlement of the island dates from this time, whatever the origin of the Bota/Motão nomenclature.

There are a few more speculative comments that might be made. The present indigenous population of the mountain (the Bakweri) refer to their 13,500-ft peak as *Fako* 'cleared land', in reference to the grass which covers its upper ranges. This is burnt spectacularly in the dry season at a time which Tessmann gives in the calendar of the Bubi as *asamôte,* which he renders as *asa* 'dry, burnt' and *môte* 'big'. The deity of the Cameroon Mountain among the Bakweri is *Êfásamòtè* a name which is translated in folk-tales as 'half-man' (Ittmann, 1953, p. 19; Ardener, 1956, p.107). We may be dealing with a pre-existing topographical name and with an onomastic tale to explain it. We should not then assume that Bubi ever occupied the mainland mountain—only that the Bakweri were in contact with Bubi speakers, possibly at the coast, during the time of their settlement of the lower slopes of the mountain. With great landmarks like Mount Cameroon, of course, the range at which independent names may be given extends very far.[22]

Calbongos

We now turn to the other important name of this time. Pacheco's *Caaboo* seem to be suddenly resurrected in 1668 as *Calbongos.* No form of this sort occurs in any intermediate source. We have in fact merely to contend with Dapper (1668) on this point, for the great vogue of the Calbongos in maps and compilations of the eighteenth century is due entirely to his work. This applies equally to Barbot's account, which adds nothing independently on this subject.

In a well-known passage concerning Rio del Rey, Dapper, after referring to the trading settlement of a certain Samson (of whom more later) adverts to the nature of the land round the river, and then says:

> The people who live higher up the river, by them called *Kalbongos,* are bold men, but villainous rogues (De volken, die hooger de reviere op wonen by hen genaemt Kalbongos zijn kloeke mannen, maer snode guiten).[23]

Dapper is not referring to Samson's people but to a people 'higher up'. It is not perfectly clear by whom they are called Kalbongos—it seems to be by themselves. They are fishermen with filed teeth, wearing penis-sheaths and smeared with camwood. They swear an oath by sucking the blood from a cut in the swearer's own arm, a custom which (also) the people 'on the high land of *Amboises*, in *Amboises* and *Boetery* observe; whose inhabitants continually wage war against the blacks on the *Rio del Rey*'. We recognise here derivatives of the *Ambos* and *Bota* of our other sources. An account of the *Landschap van Ambosine* then follows, which we may pass over and come to the account of the Cameroons River. Dapper says:

> On the north bank of the river Kamarones live very many people, called *Kalbanges,* who wage war against those above (*tegen tie van bovenen*), there the trade takes place. These *Kalbangen* are subject to a head (*Opperhooft*) named *Monneba.*[24]

As we shall see, Monneba's village is certainly the modern Douala, and, taking into account other evidence to be given below, we can state with virtual certainty that speakers of a Bantu language of Duala type were established there by 1665. The *Kalbangen* of Dapper would certainly then have to refer to the latter.

Barbot (in Churchill, 1732) merely repeats Dapper on Rio del Rey and Cameroons. He tidies up ambiguities in his source. 'The nation of the Calbonges' are firmly described as 'inhabiting about the upper end of Rio del Rey.[25] After passing by *Ambozes,* Barbot says:

> The lands opposite to the latter places, on the north of Rio Camarones, are inhabited by the Calbonges, and as I have said before, extend to the upper part of the Rio del Rey, and are a strong lusty people very knavish and treacherous dealers, and miserably poor, continually at war with the Camarones Blacks, living higher on that river, governed by a chief of their own tribe, called by them Moneba. . . [26]

Barbot here collates Dapper's *Kalbongos/Kalbanges* into one, and interprets them as different from the Cameroons inhabitants with whom they are at war. Later maps and globes collate both Dapper and Barbot, stating that the Calbongos are at war with each other.[27] It cannot be too strongly emphasised that we have one source here—that is: Dapper. Barbot merely appears to doubt that there are *Kalbanges* as well as *Kalbongos* (as well he might) and that Moneba's people were either.

First we must ask: what is the status of Pacheco's form? Unfortunately, Dapper and Pacheco tend to be used to give each other mutual support without either being firmly founded. As we saw, Pacheco's doubled vowels are suspicious.[28] They may be corruptions for other letters, as we have seen. *Caaboo* never turns up again in the Portuguese period. The Italian form *Isolas canboa* merges with readings of *Ambos*, and I incline to see the *c* as merely misread: for *d'anboa* or the like. The status of Pacheco's form is then in doubt, and it is best to leave it out of consideration and to discuss Dapper on his own merits. Calbongo might be a ghost form for *Calborch*, an early (perhaps the earliest) Dutch name for Old Calabar, a form of which Dapper gives as an alternative to (Oudt) Kalbarien. How Old Calabar got its name is a well-known mystery in its own right (see Forde, 1956; Jones, 1963). The Calbongos are possibly part of the same mystery.

There are, however, the following points: we are by 1660 at the head of several genealogies of the Cameroon Coast. As we shall see, Moneba is probably the Mulobe of Duala, who is genealogically placed as the son of the eponymous Ewal'a Mbedi of the Duala.[29] Behind the eponym himself stands, however, the unexplained *Mbongo,* a form which lies at the heads of the genealogies of many local peoples, for example: the Bakweri, in the forms *Mbongo, Nambongo,* and *Nembongo* (for others see Ittmann, 1953; Ardener, 1956, p. 22). The full honorific form for a 'person of the Bakweri tribe' is *mokpel'anembongo.*

Indeed there is no dearth of local forms at these genealogical levels to play the jingling changes on the Calbongo theme. The Kole (Bakolle), a people of the Cameroon coast close to the Efik, traditionally descend from a separate offshoot of the Duala migration under a brother of Ewale of Duala. With Kol'a Mbongo and Ewal'a Mbongo, we can almost keep Dapper's Kalbongos and Kalbanges.[30] It is clear that a halt must be called: too many here is too much. Suffice it to say that, with the form Mbongo at the back of so many tribal histories, Dapper's sources could have heard a number of forms like *Calbongo.* It may be that such a form lies behind the name of Old Calabar (*Calborch*), with which New Calabar from Kalabari would then be quite unconnected.[31] Finally, the inland peoples of the Rio del Rey may have looked, and behaved, as described by Dapper. This is a separate question from whether the name *Calbongos* was 'real'.

The weakness of the onomastic evidence

I have ventured thus far into the onomastic morass, in order to set out how treacherous is the field to those approaching it either from the literary remains or from local knowledge, unless armed with the profoundest scepticism. The excessive range of coincidence alone must at once deter and amaze. There is no place for simple equations. It can easily be seen how, by the erroneous procedure of taking the sources at their face value, and then of taking each subsequent quotation of a key source as independent confirmation, a picture such as the following was built up, and it lies implicitly behind many statements on this area: The Calbongos are non-Bantu. As Caaboo they still occupy the Cameroon Mountain c. 1500 (Pacheco), but by Dapper's time, c. 1660, they are being pressed back by the Ambos who are Bantu. The Calbongos by this view are vaguely felt to be Efik- or Ekoi-speaking because of the similarity to the name for Old Calabar. A romantic variant of this view was Massmann's (1910) who saw the Calbongos and Kalbanges as *Zwergvolk*—Pygmies. The indefatigable Avelot, in his treatment of the population of Gaboon, imposed from afar an order on this scene.[32] He identified both Cameroon and Congo *Ambos*, linking under this name (*Ambou*) the Bakota and other peoples, whom he took to have preceded the Bakongo founders of the Congo kingdom, together with the Duala of Cameroon, in 'a period before the twelfth century'(!) (see Poutrin, 1930).

Upon the most charitable view, the literary sources are just not precise enough for this kind of thing. Onomastic evidence should, in any event, never be confused with evidence from other sources, even when the latter is relatively soundly based. The compulsion to provide nomenclature from an 'historical' source for patterns derived from other data, has bedevilled equivalent fields in European studies for many years ('Celts', 'Scythians', 'Belgae', and the like). The connexions of the north-western Bantu among themselves form a separate and complex study, which is not helped by attempts to attach shadowy labels to already shadowy hypotheses.

From the survey of this first set of evidence, I wish to bring out the following points: for the period from the Portuguese discovery until the seventeenth century we can rescue *Ambos,* and probably *Bota,* as current terms. The former was primarily associated with the islands in Ambas Bay; the latter was probably a name of the inland peak of Mount Cameroon, the main ridge of which formed the *Serra de Fernam do Poo.* Doubtless this could be confirmed or denied by careful search in Lisbon. The peak was in any event also called by the name of *Motão*. We cannot even say of what people the Ambos Islanders were. Bubi of Fernando Po were there in historical times. I have merely added speculative remarks that would keep as an open question whether the Bubi settlement dated from a period as early as the Portuguese discovery. Pacheco's Caaboo remain unconfirmed. Calbongos are part of some confusion of Dapper's. Later, in the seventeenth century, the term *Ambos* was certainly applied to the area next to Rio del Rey, but the application is purely secondary at that time. The most we may be permitted to ask is: whether the early sixteenth-century name for the home of the islanders was given to the Portuguese from any local source. Only the peoples of Fernando Po or of the Rio Real (Ijaw) are likely to have been in a position to propagate such a name so early. Although there is evidence that the inner gulf was widely known by names of which *Moko, Womboko, Mumoko,* and the like appear to have been variants, applied to overlapping places, it would be premature to connect these with the name *Ambos,* let alone with some single people.[33]

Early Evidence for the Duala and Efik Polities

In Dapper (1668) occurs a famous statement concerning the river of *Kamarones* (the Cameroons River):

> In deze reviere worden by d' onzen ook slaven gehandelt, voor een en de zelve waren, gelijk in Rio del Rey. Zy gebruiken met die van de *Kamarones* een selve getal: *Mo*, is by hen een; *Ba*, twee; *Mellela,* drie; *Meley,* vier; *Matan,* vijf. (In this river our people also trade in slaves for the same goods as in Rio del Rey. They use the same numbers as the people of the *Kamarones: Mo* is among them: one; *Ba*, two; *Mellela,* three; *Meley,* four; *Matan,* five).[34]

This is repeated by Ogilby (1670, p. 483), who mistranslates (or possibly amends) it to read that the speech at Rio del Rey is different, instead of the same, but gives the same numerals with slight copying errors. Barbot (p. 385) follows Dapper accurately. The numerals are of Coastal Bantu type (shown in Ardener, 1956, p. 17n.). It is to these that Johnston refers when he says (1919, p. 27): 'the numerals of the Bakwiri or Barundo at Ambas Bay (Cameroons) written down by some French or Dutch trader at the close of the seventeenth century are almost identical with the modern form'. The numerals are not really of these specific types, but more important: there is nothing at all in these sources to show that they were written down at Ambas Bay. Elsewhere Johnston (1922, p. 144-145) refers specifically to the 1732 volume in which Barbot was published. Doke (1961, p. 20) follows Johnston.

This evidence for Coastal Bantu numerals at the Cameroons River by c. 1668 has always been very useful. Dapper's further statement that the language was the same as at Rio del Rey could have been taken fairly seriously as evidence perhaps of the activity of the Bakolle offshoot of the Duala whose traditions start at the same period. It was not to be expected that any further light could be thrown upon this situation, but this can now be done. In an edition of Leo Africanus issued at Rotterdam by Arnout Leers, bookseller, in 1665, there begins at p. 289 a description of the coast of Africa to supplement Africanus' account of the interior. This description is without doubt a chief source for Dapper in this area, or one which drew upon a common source with him—possibly that account by Samuel Blommaert referred to in Dapper's own introduction.

Leers' publication in any event clarifies much in Dapper. In particular it gives a vocabulary containing thirty-seven words and all the numerals from one to ten. Since this material has not previously been extracted I have included it in an Annexe to this paper.[35]

This section is headed (translated): 'Words, in the *Cameronis, Rio d' Elrey,* and the high land of *Ambosus'*. That description is pretty well what it is: the list contains a mixture of Bantu words, many now visibly of Duala type, and some Efik-type non-Bantu words, together with their meanings in Dutch (or possibly Flemish). The two languages are clearly separated in the gloss for 'water', for which two words are given: *amom* (=Efik *mmɔŋ*), and *mareba* (=Duala *madiba,* in which *d/r* are allophones). The numerals are of completely Duala type, with the exception of 'nine' which is an interpolation. The detailed linguistic interest of this list cannot be gone into here, but it establishes that, by 10 March 1665 (the date of Arnout Leers' preamble), Efik- and Duala-type languages were spoken in an area bounded by Rio del Rey, where Efik is now spoken, and the Cameroons Estuary, where Duala is now spoken. The likeliest conclusion is that Efik and Duala were spoken then as now at Rio del Rey and Cameroons respectively. Dapper's statement that Rio del Rey and Cameroons spoke the same language can now be seen to derive from the somewhat ambiguous heading of this word list.

Since this is a mixed list, it is quite possible that some of the forms were collected between these extreme points—that is: from the highland of *Ambosus*. But the Leers vocabulary is not a jargon, that is: not a trade language of mixed origin. Nevertheless, it goes back to the period in which the Duala language, as we know it, was laid down. As Ittmann early noted (1939, p. 32), Duala contains many Efik loan-words, and two of them actually appear in this list, one in basically Efik form (*macrale*≡Ef. *makara,* borrowed as Du. *mokala,* 'European'), and one probably already in borrowed form (*tocke tocke*≡*Du. tɔkitɔki,* borrowed from Ef. *etuk etuk,* 'small, a little'). The preservation of *k* in *kinde*, 'go', is less typical of Duala than of the neighbouring Isubu—a people between the Duala proper and the Cameroon Mountain, who formed by 1800 the rival trading kingdom of Bimbia. Yet the Bantu vocabulary as a whole shows none of the clear Isubu stigmata (see Ardener, 1956, pp. 33-36). Possibly the loss of *k* was less advanced in Duala at the time. Two Coastal Bantu entries appear in Barbot's Old Calabar list which, unlike that of Leers, is largely a jargon and dates from the last quarter of the century: *kinde nongue-nongue* (Barbot: 'go sleep') which would be *kɛndɛ nanga o nɔngɔ,* or the like; and *meraba* ('water'), cf. Leers' *mareba* from *madiba.* In the corrupt context of Barbot's list these words are not evidence on their own for the presence of settled Bantu-speaking people at Old Calabar (even though some of such people were probably there): the rest of the list contains reduplicated forms of possibly Efik-Ibibio origin, as well as entries like *'Negro—A black'* and *'Basin—Basons'*, and many hypochoristic or baby-talk forms. This is merely evidence that forms of Coastal Bantu were among the scraps picked up by Barbot's rather unsophisticated informant in the Old Calabar area.

On the whole, the linguistic evidence, old and new, confirms the present distribution rather than any other, and suggests that the Efik and Duala trading clusters were already separately established, meeting in the Rio del Rey and Old Calabar zone, by the 1660s. It is of interest that further west, for the Bonny-New Calabar area, Dapper gives the numerals 'one' to 'five' (*barre, ma, terre, ni, sonny*) which are appropriately in an Ijaw form (*gbere, mme, tere, ini, sono*—cf. Thomas, 1914, p. 21). They are clearly from that same reliable source that must lie behind Leers for the Efik and Duala words, suggesting the presence of a fairly accurate linguistic observer along the coast at the time.

Samson and Moneba

Given the refreshing solidity of Leers' source, we may turn to his trading remarks with interest. They are separately appended in a section called: 'On the Customs in *Rio Calbary* or *Rio Reaal'*. After a few words of advice on the payments to be made at New Calabar, he moves straight to the Cameroons River, and afterwards adds a few words on Rio del Rey:

> There is little [to pay] at *Rio Cameronis* so the following should be noted, otherwise the Negros will make demands as unreasonable as they usually do. When you are in the river off the village, which is four [Dutch] miles up, in order to trade, the chief (*oppersten*) *Monneba* comes on board. You give him one iron bar and two copper bars. He is satisfied with this—if you want to give more you can.
>
> At *Rio d'Elry,* there is also little, so the following should be noted, as aforesaid. The chief (*oppersten*) there is called *Samson*. When he comes on board, if he is given a half measure (*mas*) of beads (*koralen*), with two copper bars, he should be satisfied: he will pester you for more in trade, but give as little as you can, or he won't think highly of you (Leers, p. 313).

Clearly Samson of Rio del Rey counted for more than Monneba of Cameroon, but neither for very much: the next entry is for the Gaboon (*Riviere de Jambon*) where the king and four notables had to be given many more goods. The historical existence of Samson and Monneba is probably firmly based. The author names another chief (*Abram*) at Cape Lopez, the names of the Portuguese owning sugar mills at São Thomé, and the names of fifty-four mills themselves. Once again, this was a meticulous reporter.

Old Calabar River, as we shall see, was not visited. The Rio del Rey was the trading-spot of the time, and Samson's people, it appears, spoke an Ibibio dialect. The present Isangele of Oron-Amutu seem to be their successors (see below). The trade of Duala must have been in its very early stages. Given this firm ethnic fix in the middle of the seventeenth century, we may now attempt to relate it to the trading situation some years before.

The nature of the European contact

Samuel Brun, in his account of his voyage of 1614, described the trade of an area, as we saw, somewhat imprecisely bounded, but mainly covering the zone from Rio del Rey to the Cameroons River. The trade was both in *accory*—a stone of indeterminate nature (Fage, 1962) which was bought by exchange against cowries—and in slaves captured by the local people, and sold at a low price: three or four measures of Spanish wine, or two or three handfuls of cowries (Brun, ed. Naber, pp. 32-33). Brun noted that they would be sold at 100 ducats apiece 1,000 leagues away. The picture here and elsewhere in Brun would suit the mountain area: fruitful soil, no palm-wine (both oil- and raffia-palms have been relatively scarce), and leaf-mat houses (very characteristic—for the volcanic soil does not compact to make mud walls). The impression is of the same kind of trade as that described by Pacheco a century earlier. By 1614 the trade was still unsophisticated, and almost laughably inexpensive. There are hints, however, that some regularity in the trade may have been beginning. Brun's ship bought four boys in the area for nine measures of wine. They were offered by the 'towns' (*Staden*), a usage reminiscent of the later trader's terminology for the Cameroons River, and there is striking evidence to suggest that the people of this estuary were now known.

When Brun visited Cape Mount on the (Liberian) Grain Coast (Bouchaud (p. 84)—grossly misled by the Latin version, and followed by Mveng (1963, pp. 161-162)—places it in the Congo),[35] where he found a king, Thaba Flamore:

> This king or Thaba Flamore spoke French, but his wife (called Maria by us Dutch) spoke good Netherlandish, black of body though she was. For

> another supercargo [*comes* ≡ Dutch *kommies*] had brought her from *Camaronas,* desiring to keep her near him, and she learned the language from him. She afterwards became the wife of the Thaba, however, in this way: the Thaba was involved in a war six years since, and he asked this *comes* to take part in the fight with him, and in return he would give him eight *centner* [c. 8 cwt] of ivory. The *comes* did this with pleasure, as he was well acquainted with the Thaba. They went together into battle but the *comes* and a cabin-boy perished, and so the Thaba took the wife of the *comes* to himself.'[37]

This '*curieux petit roman colonial*', to use Bouchaud's felicitous Gallic phrase, occurred, from Brun's dates, in the year 1608. The French had already a big establishment near Sestos by 1602 (Naber, p. 39 note), which would account for the Thaba's proficiency in French.

One senses that the contacts with the Cameroon coast still had some of that amiability (soon to be lost) that marked the contacts of the Fernandian Bubi and the English in the early nineteenth century. Brun's voyage probably occurred when the Dutch had barely begun to exploit this part of the coast. In the description of Guinea, bound in with the voyage of Linschoten, published in 1596 at Amsterdam, the author recommended sailing straight from the Gold Coast to Cape Lopez or to São Thomé.[38] The inner portion of the Bight of Biafra was probably not easily navigable until the seventeenth century. Pieter de Mareez, referring to about 1600, advises that it is necessary to leave Benin straight for Cape Lopez:

> and to pass by all the rivers which are inside the bend (*destour*) because there is nothing profitable to do there, and if one happens to fall behind the island of Fernando Po, one is in danger of staying there all one's life without escaping (Mareez, 1605, p. 93).

Sometimes, he adds, the wind would not even serve to reach Cape Lopez direct, and one ended up at the Rio d'Angra and Corisco Island at its mouth.

Indirect confirmation of this navigational problem, in the Portuguese period, comes from a report of João Lobato to King John III (dated 13 April 1529), dealing with the economic and social state of São Thomé, under which, at the time, the Bight of Biafra nominally fell.[39] He is asking for gear to rig out ships for Elmina. Of one of them he says:

> The ship Toyro Santo, which is still in the shipyard, as I have written to Your Highness, and which I have made so that it can be rowed in order to

> go to the Island of Fernã do Poo (*fiz pera se poder remar pera hir á ilha de Fernã do Poo*) . . . is not yet finished.

There was a shortage of cables and anchors. It seems very likely that the Portuguese visits to the coast opposite Fernando Po also required the use of oars. This would explain the salience of the Cameroon Mountain coast nearest to Fernando Po in the early material, rather than the later emporia of Rio del Rey and the Cameroons River.[40]

After 1600 the technical difficulties were apparently less important. In about 1618, not long after the time of Brun's visit to the area in a Dutch ship, Gaspar da Rosa, the Portuguese factor at Elmina, wrote that the Dutch had been under-cutting the Portuguese for years along the Guinea coast with up to thirty ships, and that:

> the evil has gone so far that the Dutch in addition go with their ships to the trading ports of *Sam Thomé, Benim, Jabu, rio Forcado,* and *rio do Camarão,* where they obtain much cloth, cotton, fowls, accory and other precious stones for the coast of Mina, and ivory and pepper which there is in Benim, and no more trade remains for Sam Thomé than that in slaves, because these Dutchmen purchase the other goods. . . [41]

The reference to Cameroon and the accory for Mina are Portuguese confirmation of Brun's story, besides specifying the Cameroons River as a trading-place.

By the time of Leers' source, trade, as we have seen, has become regularised, with recognised middlemen and dues to pay at Rio del Rey and Cameroons River. There are now detailed sailing directions for passing up the Rio del Rey estuary. The writer makes a reference to the Old Calabar river under the form *Oude Calborch,* with the surprising statement that a great reef lies before its entrance which blocks the whole river so that it cannot be navigated.[42] Nothing could be more indicative of the critical date of this source. From Rio del Rey, the route down the Cameroon Mountain coast is given with detail on soundings. The mountain is called the *High Land of Bota.* On its coast is a trading place near a cape, from which the coast runs south east to the Islands of *Amboises.* These are described as 'two small islands' between which it was possible to sail. They are now said to be merely a good spot for provisions but of little value for trade, and little visited. From here the sailing directions take us past the 'small' or 'old' *Cameronois* (the Bimbia River) and to the Cameroons Estuary itself with minute directions to reach the trading-place of Moneba. Ivory in small quantities is obtainable in the estuary. There is no longer need to speculate upon the source of these directions, for maps of the type to which the Leers' source referred are in the Dutch Archives at The Hague. On a large-scale chart of the Cameroons Estuary, *Monna Baes dorp* [sic] is marked on the present site of Duala, and specifically on the later site of Bell Town. The creek at which ivory was picked up led westwards towards the present Mungo river, and thus to the mountain hinterland. On a collated map which includes material from this chart also, the Rio del Rey area is shown. Villages near the Rumby estuary, as well as the *dorp* which was probably Samson's on the Andokat arm, are marked. The charts will be the subject of a separate paper.[43]

This cluster of sources with its cartographical, linguistic, and trading documentation clearly lay behind much later knowledge of the area. It confirms strikingly, once again, that the term *Ambos* and the like referred specifically to the islands, and not to the mainland, and gives further support to the hypothesis that Pacheco's *Bota* was the Cameroon Mountain.

When did this dawn of the new trading situation on the coast between the Cross and Cameroons rivers occur? For the position had developed spectacularly when Dapper received his charter to publish in 1668. His text follows the Leers source closely, but passes by Old Calabar without mentioning its unnavigability, and comes to the Rio del Rey, to the trading-place of Samson. But something is changed; Dapper amends his source (Ogilby's translation of 1670 is here adequate):

> At the Northerly shore thereof lieth a Township, over which (some years since) one Samson had the command; but driven out by those of Ambo, he hath ever since maintained himself by Robbing; for his village was so wasted by fire, that very few houses remained, and those all made of Palm canes [Dapper: *Palmitasbladen:* 'palm-leaves'] from the top to the bottom as well the Sides as the Roof.[44]

If Samson had declined in the world, Moneba appears to have risen in fortune. His people are dubbed *Kalbanges,* as we saw earlier, a matter we may now ignore. They are, says Dapper:

> under a headman (*Opper-hooft*) called Monneba, who is taken to be the strongest of the princes round about. The village where this headman has his residence, lies upon a height, which has a very tidy cover of natural vegetation, and it is taken to be the pleasantest spot in the whole bight. There is an abundance of provisions such as yams, bananas, palm-wine and bordon-wine [raffia-palm wine]. This bordon-wine is like palm-wine,

> but is not so good because it grows in swampy country. The houses are built in a rectangular shape.[45]

Dapper adds little on trade, but he notes the ivory that was collected there. Other items he mentions seem to come in some obscure way from the Leers' word-list (see Annexe).

For the zone between Rio del Rey and the Cameroons River, we are offered a collation. Samuel Brun's terminology on the 'Highland of Ambosy' is substituted for the 'High Land of Bota' of the Leers' source, and, together with Brun's remarks on the Spanish and the Canaries Peak, it becomes, with Dapper and Barbot, canonical. The trading-place of the Leers' source on the mountain coast becomes: 'various villages, among others one called Bodi or Bodiwa, otherwise Cesge'. *Cesge,* at least, I have suggested to be a ghost-name ultimately from Ruiters, (see above). *Bodi* or *Bodiwa* is quite possibly a ghost from *Bota.* Although only *one* village has these three names in Dapper, Barbot turns it into three and, in later maps based on him, three are accordingly marked. From Brun are lifted directly references to the lack of palm-wine and to a certain *Gayombo* drink, now ghosting its way through the literature as *Gajanlas.*[46] 'In the village Bodi', Dapper adds, possibly as if to mark a change since Brun's day, 'there is trade in slaves but little accory.'

Lastly Dapper contributes, from an unidentified source, an independent section on the Islands of Amboises, which is classic and need not be repeated in detail here. The inhabitants lived, it may be noted, on the middlemost island of three, that is: the one named on Admiralty charts to this day as *Ambos* (although known as *Ndame* to the coastal peoples). The islanders spoke Portuguese at the time, thus surely confirming that these were the *Ambos* of the days of Portuguese supremacy. The tradition from now on runs unbroken, through Barbot and the English period of the eighteenth and nineteenth centuries, down to the present day. After Dapper, the islanders take second place to their neighbours of the Cameroons River in future contacts with European trade.[47] The Isubu trading chieftaincy of Bimbia began on another island in a creek on the edge of the Cameroons Estuary—the 'small Cameroons' of Leers—for traders now preferred middlemen with organized contact with the hinterland, which the islanders could never have had. Some of their trade in ivory had been coming through the creeks from the Cameroons River (Dapper, p. 138), probably via the future Bimbia. Moneba's Duala-speaking trading-spot was to become firmly established. I believe the identification with Mulobe of Duala to be sound, and others of his dynasty can be identified in the second half of the eighteenth century when independent English sources begin for the area. But the standard geographies and the great maps of the time showed no advance. Indeed, nearly a century and a quarter after the Leers' Publication, Moneba was still said to be ruling on the 'River Kamarones', in an English volume commemorating Captain Cook's voyages (Bankes *et al.*, 1787, p. 365).

Historical Conclusions

Samson's decline at Rio del Rey was certainly succeeded chronologically by the development of Old Calabar. When Samson flourished, Leers' meticulous source thought the Cross River entrance was unnavigable. Barbot says that, on his first voyage in 1678, he met an English ship which had spent ten months in Old Calabar, and had obtained 300 slaves. In another well-known passage he records that, in April 1698, the *Dragon* collected 212 slaves and indulged in a valuable trade there, in which a long list of notables was involved.[48] The advantages of Old Calabar, as a trading-point, far outweigh those of Rio del Rey. For one thing, the Cross River Estuary leads to a real river, and an important one. Rio del Rey was in effect an anchorage in the eastern delta of the Cross, into which only minor streams ran. We do not have to visualise Rio del Rey rendered uninhabitable by attacks from the Cameroon Mountain followed by a retreat to Old Calabar, for slaving took place in Rio del Rey through the next century. Dapper's remark that Samson's village at Rio del Rey was burnt by people 'of Ambo' is however of interest. By *Ambo* is now meant, as we have seen, the geographical area towards the Cameroon Mountain. Some degree of conflict on this coast is referred to by several writers of the seventeenth century. Samson's attackers may have been Bakolle congeners of the Duala movement. This is the parsimonious conclusion. Nevertheless it is probable that movement towards the estuary by the inland Bantu-speakers now known as Balundu and the like had begun by this time.

The Ibibio group known as *Effiat* (Forde & Jones, 1951, p. 89), who occupy fishing villages in the estuary of Rio del Rey, seem to have lost their foothold on the mainland, and especially on the Rumby Estuary, to these peoples, whom they call *Efut* and *Ekita*, and who called them in turn *Ifiari* or *Fiari* (Langhans, 1902). Efut mingled with Efik in the group known as Isangele to the north of Rio del Rey, and some became part of the population of Old Calabar (Forde & Jones, p. 90; Forde, 1956, pp. 4, 121, 123).

The Ibibio speaking Isangele population of Oron and Amutu villages were the traders of the later Rio del Rey, at the head of the estuarine system. Their traditions, as assembled by Anderson (1933), speak of movement to Rio del Rey from Enyong and the establishment of trade with the Portuguese, upon hearing of the success of Bonny; of contacts with the Balundu (the Efut who joined them); of fights with Ifiang cannibals to the north; and of the departure of trade because of an invitation by the chief of Obutong (Old Town, Calabar) to the Europeans. Samson's people seem to belong somewhere in this story, as may Dapper's wild up-river people. Later a group straight from Old Calabar (Archibong: Asibong) dominated this already mixed group.

In addition, Old Calabar acquired an 'extended family of Creek Town' (Simmons, in Forde, 1966, p. 71) called *Ambo,* and various personalities in Old Calabar had, in Antera Duke's time (c. 1785), names such as: Sam Ambo, King Ambo, and the like (see also Jones, p. 160, and elsewhere). The association of the Ambo family with the Cameroons seems to have survived into the nineteenth century. The name is said to be regarded by them as a foreign name of Portuguese origin (Jones, p. 160) although their etymology is fanciful.[49] The name would rather have belonged to the pidgin used with the foreign frequenters of Old Calabar, to denote an origin from the general Cameroon area. Their own name *Mbarakom* is of interest and confirms this, as it appears to derive from the milieu of the Upper Cross River Bantoid-speaking peoples, and not from that of the coastal Bantu. Several inland movements seem to have been set off by the growth of Old Calabar as a trading centre, which affected the whole Cross River Basin, and by the nineteenth century had touched the inland grassland plateau.[50]

Samson and Moneba are the earliest named coastal Cameroonians recorded, after Maria, the queen of Cape Mount. The period they inaugurate is broadly, in ethnic and linguistic respects, that of today. The widest limits for this appearance lie between 1614 (Brun) and 1665 (Leers). If Leers' source was really Samuel Blommaert (referred to by Dapper in his introduction as his own source), then the terminus 1665 may be pushed back. Blommaert was born in 1583, and made his first voyage to the Indies in 1603. His prime was from 1622 until about 1646, during which period he was influential in the Westindische Compagnie of Amsterdam.[51] The Leers' linguistic material is first-hand. If Blommaert was personally involved in its collection (which is not, of course, necessarily so) we may have to look back at least to the 1630s. The 1630s are also suggested by the possible date of the large-scale map of the Cameroons Estuary already mentioned.

If Moneba was Mulobe, with a floruit at A.D. 1650±15, his father Ewale, the supposed founder of Duala, and his grand-father Mbedi, would belong to a milieu datable to c. 1600. That would be about the time of the early informal contacts: the opening of the Rio dos Camaroes to trade, and the Maria and Samuel Brun period. Jones (1956) has provided a useful insight into the interpretation of genealogies in the trading states. The lack of any tradition between the shadowy Mbongo (Ardener, 1956, pp. 22-23) and Ewale, son of Mbedi, would suggest, by the principle Jones uses for Kalabari, that the Mbongo tradition validates the origin of the Duala and their congeners, while the stories of Ewale, and of the other Mbedine lines, validate the dynasties that grew out of the trading contacts. Mbongo belongs to the 'proto-tradition'. The Mbedine events themselves (Dugast, 1949, pp. 10-21; Ardener, 1956, pp. 17-18, 20-21) can hardly have occurred later than some time in the sixteenth century (for their time-span will have been compressed) although we need not imagine that they had any great conspicuity. There is, traditionally, a movement from a place called *Pitti* above the Cameroons Estuary on the Dibamba affluent: the creek later known, indeed, as Moneba's Channel.

Other small ethnic groups attach their ancestors to the same movement, including the Kole who moved within sight of Rio del Rey and the Malimba who settled on the south of the Cameroons Estuary. These lengthy although exiguous movements (even the Duala numbered less than 20,000, three centuries later, while the Kole were numbered in hundreds) are surely to be accounted for by the response to the growing demands of that early trade mentioned by Pacheco at about 1500. This, mediated by the Ambos islanders at first, directly involved the Cameroons Estuary only Jater.[52]

The foundation of the Duala dynasties may then be securely pushed back to at least a century before Asmis' unsupported date of 1706 (Asmis, 1907, p. 85)—to which Brutsch (1956, p. 56), followed by Mveng (p. 140), gives a surprising weight—with its roots probably in the sixteenth century. Less securely, I would guess that the presence at Rio del Rey of an Ibibio-speaking element was no younger. The early mention of the *Pescaria,* in João de Lisboa, 1514, and the unbroken reference to it thereafter, suggests that the estuary presented much the same appearance as today. Today the fishing traps belong to Efik-Ibibio and to Kole. One or other people was probably old-established by c. 1500; the former are perhaps, in view of the preceding, more likely to have been first.

Final Remarks

Of late, historians of Africa have rightly become very conscious of the problems of the use of oral tradition (Vansina, 1965). It may well be, however, that social anthropologists for their part still tend to underestimate the intricacies of the 'documentary tradition'. That completely uncritical use of documentary sources remarked upon by Professor Evans-Pritchard (1961) is becoming a thing of the past, but the course of the maize controversy reveals that it is not yet dead (Teixeira da Mota & Carreira, 1966, p. 79 note). The nature of the documentary tradition must of course be worked out, as far as possible, independently of hypotheses from other bodies of evidence, for in the field of African history cross-tainting takes place almost insensibly. Nowhere is this more likely than in the onomasiology. Thus the Basa have been sought in the Cameroons sources, because oral tradition suggested that they should be sought, although the onomastic variants upon which conclusions were based belonged to corrupt sources. For a sufficient and critical examination there can be no substitute for recourse to the original texts: even the best editions (and all translations) may let us down.

On the other side yawns a different pit-fall. Local knowledge, the social anthropologist's forte, may be dangerous (although far less so than lack of it). Etymologies do not necessarily become any more trustworthy because they are derived from local languages: their deficiencies may become merely harder to detect. I have offered some, because it is the duty of those placed to do so to offer a certain amount of controlled speculation. But the difference between this kind of etymology and that scientific kind which rests upon even fair linguistic evidence is, I hope, revealed by the valuable Leers' vocabulary given in the Annexe. It is a pity that those students who work, for example, among the linguistic fragments remaining in the toponymy of early Europe, do not, before applying etymologies to them, turn to us for evidence of the welter of conflicting possibilities that exists before the process of oblivion reduces the problem to more manageable proportions.

For political history this paper adds, I think, to the evidence for the great value of the genealogies of the trading dynasties of West Africa. They tend to open and shut like concertinas according to the chronologies offered, but I believe that Jones's attempt to separate the validating tradition of the dynasty from that part validating the origins of the ethnic group at large does throw real light upon the foreshortening found so frequently in them.

Notes

1. In this paper I have usually been compelled to make my own translations of European sources. Fortunately the language, often that of seafaring men, is usually very simple and where it is not I have taken advice. I am especially indebited to Mr R. Cinatti, on specific points but must also mention the suggestions of Mr R. Feltham, Mr. G. Stuval and Mr Cutileiro, on specific points. None of these is responsible for any errors that remain. Save for the rather elementary commentary on Pacheco, there is no point at which any interpretation of idiom could be, I hope, crucial.

   Geographical forms and proper names when cited in a source in translation are in the form of that source. When not citing sources in quotation marks, standard spellings are used. Specifically the four basic forms: *Rio del Rey, Fernando Po, Cameroons River*, and *Cape Lopez* will be used. The name *Moneba* in certain sources has two *n*s, and so although I take the former as standard I also use the latter in those contexts I have tended to use the term 'Efik' for the Ibibio dialects of the Bight of Biafra. It may be that this is a misuse. I use the term to distinguish not Efik from other Ibibio dialects, but Ibibio-speakers in the present Efik area from speakers of Bantu languages.
2. The status of onomastic studies in many fields is to be seen in, for example, the symposium edited by Blok (1966).
3. This part of Barros' text is reprinted in MMA, I, pp. 438–439. See also Bouchaud (1952, Chapters 3–4). The Portuguese *Camarões*, 'prawns', refers to the migrations of a particular species (Monod, 1928, p. 177; Ittmann, 1939, p. 5; Ardener, 1956, p. 42). But *Camarão* (singular) was a name also given to island in the Red Sea (Ramos-Coelho, 1892). See also Note 15.
4. The edition of Silva Dias is used here. Bouchaud discusses Pacheco in his Chapter 6.
5. This is quite clear from all sources.
6. S. Dias, p. 125.
7. After the words *Aquy mapa*: 'here is a map'—an irony: for this important map, like all his others, is missing.
8. South of the Cameroon estuary was the *Cabo do Ilheo* ('Cape of the Islet'), which Bouchaud identifies with the western extremity of the islands which form the delta of the Sanaga River, south of Douala on the present Cameroon coast (Bouchaud, 1952, p. 53).
9. Enciso (1518)—there is no pagination. Bouchaud (pp. 56–57) uses Barlow's English translation (mentioned below) which gives *de galo,* and so obscures the source of this folk-etymology (as if 'gulf of the cock'). On the *Rio de los santos* I am not absolutely happy, but it is clearly a river between the Rio Real (New Calabar-Bonny) and the Cape of Fernando Po.
10. Also on Jean Fonteneau, see Bouchaud (Chapter V, and notes). The

accessible edition is Musset (1904). Pigafetta (1591), who was published at Rome, translated the work of Duarte Lopes, a Portuguese, into Italian. Pigafetta says that *le nationi chiamate Anziquese* are bounded on the seaward side by *populi d'Ambus* (p. 14). I take Pory's (1600) description of the position of the Ambus to be a verbal description of Pigafetta's map, rather than an independent statement. Pigafetta is the source of the spelling *Ambus* on the Italian map in Brown's Edition of Pory, which otherwise owes a great deal to Ortelius' *Theatrum Orbis Terrarum* dated 1570. Of the Cameroon coast, Pigafetta says that the inhabitants of São Thomé had commerce with those of the mainland who gathered (*si riducono*) at the mouths of rivers one of which was called after '*Fernando di Poo, cioè di Polue*' (Po was taken commonly to mean 'dust'—thus he is frequently called *Fernando Poudre* in French sources) who discovered it. There was an island opposite its mouth 36 miles away. The 'Fernando Po river' was probably the Cameroons river, but one doubts whether this name was actually used. It looks like an attempt to explain Pigafetta's own map in which the corrupt name *Serra de Bisenscias do poo,* referring to the mountain, is placed along the Cameroons river.

11. Bouchaud (pp. 170–171). He traces forms in the maps from *Biafra* and *Biafar* back through: *Biascar, Giafar, Maffra, Masra, Mascha, Mescha, Mesche*. Bouchaud gives reasons for the rejection of other etymologies. The name became 'kingdom' and later a city was erected on the maps. Of late, some in Cameroon have wished to find the name *Basa* (an important people of Sanaga-Maritime) in the word.
12. MMA, IV, 1954, pp. 144–146. The document is now also listed in Ryder's recent guide (1965) as item 41, p. 12. (On the amount of a *moyo* see Mota and Carreira, 1966, p. 81n.) Mr Cinatti suggests to me that Roiz is complaining that the malagueta was denied to the king, not by peculation of the *feitor*, but by the failure of the latter to open up the market. This letter, and one to be cited later by Lobato of the same year, suggest an active period of interest in Fernando Po and the coast. There is a well-known document of 26 March 1500 by which the inhabitants of São Thomé were accorded rights in perpetuity to trade on the mainland 'from the Rio Real [New Calabar-Bonny estuary] and the island of Fernam de Poo, as far as the country of Manicomguo, excepting that they cannot trade in the country where there is gold. . .' (Text in MMA, I, 1952, p. 183; also Ramos-Coelho, 1892, p. 107; Blake, 1937, Vol. I, pp. 89–92). The bishopric of S.Thomé was established on 3 Nov. 1534, and comprised the coast of West Africa and South-West Africa. The area from Cape Lopes to the Cunene was excised as the Diocese of Congo and Angola, at S. Salvador, by the Bull of 20 May 1596.
13. Ruiters (1623). The Edition of Naber (1913a) gives only part of the text. Further portions are cited in the notes to Naber (1913b).
14. A derivation from Portuguese *zambos,* 'half-castes', would be better than

Naber's: in that it is not excluded that the islands had a population of this type, although from Figueiredo's words this does not sound very likely. At most this significance may account for the faulty word-division.

15. The union of the Portuguese and Spanish crowns lasted from 1580 to 1640. The Dutch were, of course, in close contact with the Spanish Netherlands. The English name Cameroon(s) comes via Sp. *Camarones.* The name *Jamoer* appears in Dutch sources as an alternative for *Camarones* or the like. I take this to be a reading from Italian maps in which *gamaro* or deformities of it appear—being translations of *camarão* ('prawn'). Ruiters, by the way, gives another Portuguese name for Mount Cameroon, in addition to those already discussed: *Montegos*. Naber interprets this as (I translate): *monte*='mountain', *gos* 'measure of length' (see Naber, 1913b, p. 31, note). Portuguese *gos* derives from India, and ultimately from Sanskrit *gavyuti* (DELP)—a measure of about two miles.
16. Figueiredo (1614, folio 57, reverse).
17. Ruiters (Naber, 1913a, p. 83).
18. Brun's surname is so spelt on the title-page of the German edition (which is also in his own words, from which the Latin edition of De Bry seriously departs). The edition is Naber (1913b).
19. Bouchaud (1952, pp. 82–83) uses the Latin (De Bry) translation of Samuel Brun (1625), which unfortunately tidies up and even misrepresents the German text in many respects. For example, after the passage cited above, the German says in literal translation: 'The which two countries (*Länder*) received their names from the Spanish, since fine rivers or streams there flow down and into the sea'. The former says according to Bouchaud, p. 82): 'These two appellations, borrowed from the Portuguese, were given to the streams which flow into the sea at this place because they are particularly pleasant and salubrious.' *Rio de Anckare* (Bouchaud, *Rio de Anchara*), from Portuguese *Angra,* 'creek' or 'bay' is the usual name of the estuary of Rio Muni. It could also mean the *angra da pescaria* of Rio del Rey. Bouchard states that here it means Ambas Bay. I think it does not: Corisco (see below) was the next land-fall at this time after the Cameroons River. The length of coast concerned is said by Brun to be 'sixty miles'. We must assume sixty Dutch miles, however, which will be more compatible with the distance from Rio del Rey to Corisco. Possibly Brun confused the names of the Pescaria and Corisco but visited both.
20. Naber (1913b, p. 32) gives Brun's words. His statement about the Spanish gives the form *La alt tierra de Ambosy.* Dapper (1668) copies it as *Alta terra de Ambosi,* and Barbot (1732) copies him as *Alta-Tierra de Ambozi.* Burton (1863, vol. II, pp. 235–237) copies this, but quite wrongly attributes the source to 'Mr Grazilhier' whom Barbot uses for a different part of his text. Barbot is cited in the Cameroons Annual Report (e.g. 1958) and has acquired currency locally.
21. In Ardener (1956) and Ittmann (1956, 1957) the local versions of *Bota* probably stem ultimately from a Duala-European source. They are not used

by the inhabitants of the present Bota Island and Bota Land. When *Bota* was applied in the seventeenth century to a point on the coast there is much to suggest that it was at a different point—near Cape Debundscha.

22. Tessmann thought to see Bubi influence on the Bakweri language, although his examples are not convincing (Tessmann, 1932, p. 119). Another etymology for the first element of *Efas'a mote* would be *masa* 'mountain' (var. *basa*). The Bubi call both their own peak and the distantly visible Mt Cameroon by this name, the latter being in Tessmann's time distinguished as *masa mo moa mbola:* 'Peak inside the *moa'* (Tessmann, p. 151) where *moa* is 'the view on the horizon'.
23. I cite the second edition of 1676, p. 137.
24. Dapper, p. 138.
25. In Churchill (1732, p. 385).
26. Barbot, p. 386.
27. Cf. the famous map reproduced at the end of Bouchaud (1952).
28. If they express phonetic care they render almost exactly the Yoruba greeting: *kâbɔ̀ɔ́* (some misunderstanding involving a Benin coast interpreter? That way madness lies!).
29. See Brutsch (1950, pp. 214, 216); Ardener (1956, pp. 18–20).
30. By the omission of Mbedi.
31. The *Kole (Kɔ̀lɛ̂)* offer the best centre for speculative derivations since their usual eponymous form Kol'a Mbedi was actually in use to describe them in the nineteenth century, as *Collambedi* (Hutchinson, 1858, p. 167). Since this would be heard as something close to *Kɔlambɛri,* the likeness to 'Calabar' is striking even if, as is all too possible, fortuitous.
32. Avelot's views may be found in Poutrin (1930, p. 49 ff.).
33. Bouchaud (1952) cautiously suggested Ibo or Abo as etymons. I (1956, p. 22) suggested the present *Bamboko* (through some form as *vato v'Amboko*). Mveng (1963, p. 175) follows me. I rejected the *Mbo* because this very active cluster never reached the coast. It is now possible to think that the name *Mbo* whose full form may appear in Bakossi Mbuog, is basically a place-name of the same origin as Womboko. This matter will be treated elsewhere without prejudice to the question of the origin of the Portuguese *Ambos.* These confusing elements should be noted: According to DELP, *Ambó* 'from the Indo-Aryan' occurs in the Portuguese literature on the Indies as the name of a fruit tree ('. . . *arvores de fruitas . . . ambós fermozissimos . . . de grandes, e saborozos*') which occurred in Amboina. Dr Pocock informs me that *ambó* would be connected with Gujarati *amb,* Skt. *amr:* 'a mango'. The world-wide nature of the 'onomastic reserve' of the Portuguese language should not be lost sight of. Finally, a lady called Ana Ambó gave her name to the bay *(enseada)* at which the first Portuguese settlement on São Thomé was made in 1486, under João de Paiva (Tenreiro, 1961, p. 59).
34. I cite the second edition of 1676, p. 135.

35. There is a reference to Leers' work, the only one which I have seen, in Naber (1913b; see the valuable note to p. 31).
36. There is an error (90 miles for 900 miles) in Bouchards' text, p. 85, for the distance of Cape Mount from Angola, which has misled him, and indeed makes him take the story as evidence of a strong French presence in the Congo area at this early date. Naber's edition is quite clear on the point. Mveng further states this error on his p. 117. The referenee to the *Staden* is also in neither author.
37. Brun's 'uns Teutschen' is translated as 'us Dutch' because he is clearly identifying himself with the Dutch interest. Bouchard, followed again by Mveng, gives 'sixteen years' instead of 'six years'. The latinized text is also inevitably a more polished and over-explicit paraphrase of Brun's rather crude style.
38. Linschoten (1596, p. 1 of the Description).
39. See note 12.
40. Lobato's letter was written only a month before the complaint of Duarte Rodriguez. Lobato is given in MMA, I, 1952, pp. 505–518, and is listed in Ryder (1963, p. 12) as item 40. For a discussion of general reasons why São Thomé and not Fernando Po became the centre of Portuguese power, see Tenreiro (1961, pp. 57–59).
40. The text is in MMA (VI, 1955, pp. 346–350). It is also quoted in Cordeiro (1881, p. 23), and listed in Ryder (1963, p. 79), as his item 965.
41. Leers (p. 304). It is the first Dutch form for the name Old Calabar known to me. It is important to note that Leers' source refers to New Calabar only as *Rio Reaal*. It is Dapper who applies the name *Kalbarien* to both the *Rio Reaal* and *Oude Calborch* (he uses for the latter the alternative *Kalborgh* derived from Leers' source). The Leers' form *Calborch* may not be a folk-etymology (as if ending in *-burg* or *-borg*), but a form coincidentally similar to that of (New) Calabar and which was known first to the Dutch. One would ask the historians of the Delta when the name (New) Calabar (from Kalabari) was first used separately from Rio Real (Simmons gives a reference to 1650). It is certainly separated in the late Portuguese period, e.g. Garcia in 1621 separates a *rei de Calabar* from a *rei do Rio Real* (Cordeiro, 1881, pp. 27–28; Ryder, 1965, p. 79, item 965, says 1620).
43. These MS. charts present some difficulties because both are to some extent collations (Hague, *Rijksarchief:* (1) *Marine* 2334, (2) Leupe 145. No (1) is also incorporated in No. (2), but rationalized, it seems, in the light of a Barbot-type description. No. (1) calls the Dibamba Creek *Monna Base Gat* for *Monnabaes Gat*. The clear parallel with the name of the village (so: Monnaba's Creek) clears up the problems of later forms: *Monambascha* and the like, which have been interpreted as Malimba and Basa in the past. The Basa may be looked for in vain in the sources.[Edwin Ardener gave talks on maps of the coast and creeks. Unfortunately this was never fully written up and published, as intended. Ed.]

44. Dapper, p. 137; Ogilby, p. 483. Ogilby is not a reliable souree to use without reference to the original.
45. Dapper, p. 139. Ogilby more imposingly translates: 'The Town where he keeps his seat royal stands scituate on a Hill, very neatly Hedged about with Trees . . .' (p. 484).
46. Brun (Naber, 1913b p. 32), refers to a drink named *Gayombo* which he says is made from 'a certain root'. He says that the people made it. If, as Naber suggests, this is a reference to Gombo (*Hibiscus esculentus*) from which 'Gomba coffee' is made, the drink would be of West Indian origin and drunk perhaps by the African crew-men when short of palm wine, not by the local people.
47. For the present inhabitants, see: Ardener (1956); Ittmann (1956, 1957); Ardener, E. W. and S. G. (1958).
48. Barbot (pp. 381, 383, 465); Forde (1956); Jones (1963).
49. From 'love'. The reference to 'Portuguese' origin is of no corroborative value in this context. The Portuguese were not at Old Calabar as we have seen. Whatever the implications of the following part of this paper for Efik contacts with Bantu-speakers elsewhere, I suggest that the term Ambo at Creek Town comes from the period of Barbot and later.
50. Mbarakom=Mbudikum, and the like, which meant at the coast the approches to the inland plateau. The name is connected (in a complex way) with that of the Widekum area on the borders of the plateau (cf. Chilver 1961, p. 235). In all the early sources it may be noted that only two purport to refer to any far inland area. The first is the undoubtedly corrupt text of Pacheco concerning Bota. All probability is against the figure '50 leagues inland' being a real one, quite apart from other considerations already cited. For, in the words of Shakespeare's Henry V, 'who hath measured the ground?' We are not dealing then with the Babute (Wute), as Mauny and others speculate (Mveng, 1963, p. 105). The second is Ruiters (p. 83 *et seq.*), who has a section called: 'Of white men, who dwell among the blacks, and continually fight with the *Negros*'. He says that 150 miles to the north-east or north-north-east of the Cameroons River 'live a race of people who in contrast to the *Negros* are not black but pure white'. He adds that they wage fierce war against the Negroes who live there. Their people were so strong (or numerous) that, 'had they all their faculties', they would have overwhelmed all the Negroes. (Ruiters takes them to be albinos, whom he goes on to describe in accurate detail, with their physical infirmities.) There may conceivably be an echo of inland rumour here. The distance was probably inspired by some version of Pacheco's '50 leagues'. It sounds like someone trying to check Pacheco on the spot and getting a vague account of marauding white-men in the interior. At about Ruiters' period of reference, c. 1600, the Sefawa kingdom of Bornu, under Idris Alooma

(c. 1580–1610), had Turkish military instructors, and 'Bornu influence was extended southwards towards the Benue' (Forge, 1962, p. 36). So into the purview of the Cameroon Grasslands: an area easily affected by disturbances on the Benue, and one that may have been at the head of its present dynastic histories at about this time (Kaberry, 1962, p. 285).

51. Kernkamp (1908, pp. 3–21). But the letters of Blommaert to the Swedish Chancellor Oxenstierna, 1635–1641, discussing the openings in Guinea for Swedish copper and iron, omit the stretch of coast between Benin and Cape Lopez, just as do so many other sources of the time (pp. 67 ff.).
52. The Bakoko branch of the Basa people are supposed to have been supplanted by the Duala, but doubtless the fishermen of both peoples had used the estuary for long before that. The sons of Mbedi must have merely jostled out a niche at the most favoured trading post (Dugast, 1949, pp. 11–12).

Annexe

The Leers Vocabulary, 1665 [Additions in square brackets]

Woorden, in de *Cameronis, Rio d'Elrey,* en't hooge Land van *Ambosus.*

[1]	Daby	Schip	[Ship]
[2]	Macrale	Blancke	[White man]
[3]	Inboe	Land	[Country]
[4]	Kende	Gaat	[Go]
[5]	Singa	Komt	[Come]
[6]	Edican	Komt hier	[Come here]
[7]	Ommele	Handelen	[Trade]
[8]	Bange	'k Wil niet	[I will not]
[9]	Jubaa	Stelen	[To steal]
[10]	Nanga	Slapen	[To sleep]
[11]	Tocke Tocke	Kleyn	[Small]
[12]	Ninne Ninne	Groot	[Big]
[13]	Fyne	't Is goet	[It is good]
[14]	Broucke	't Deucht niet	[It is no good]
[15]	Mareba	Water	[Water]
[16]	Amon	Water	[Water]
[17]	Moeye	Vuur	[Fire]
[18]	Masiotje	een Man	[Man]
[19]	Lobbesje	een Vrou	[Woman]
[20]	Oreyne	Vis	[Fish]
[21]	Wynba	Wine	[Wine]
[22]	Bolly	Bananese	[Banana]
[23]	Makonsje	Iniames	[Yams]
[24]	Obre	Iniames	[Yams]
[25]	Corca	Hoendors	[Fowls]
[26]	Jocke	Koebeesten	[Cows]
[27]	Marule	Oly de Palm	[Palm-oil]
[28]	Masange	Koralen	[Beads]
[29]	Malulle	Orangie past	[Orange paste]
[30]	Nigelle	Lavendel q^r	[see notes]
[31]	Poupe	Wit q^r	[see notes]
[32]	Macocke	Ysere staven	[Iron bars]
[33]	Longe	Kopere dito	[Copper bars]
[34]	Mabeusie	Beckens	[Basins]
[35]	Faye, Mes	Mes	[Knife]
[36]	Myse	Oogen	[Eyes]
[37]	Insou	Toebak	[Tobacco]

Tellinge (Numbers)

Moo	Een	[One]
Meba	Twee	[Two]
Melelle	Drie	[Three]
Menaey	Vier	[Four]
Metany	Vijf	[Five]
Metoba	Ses	[Six]
's Jamba	Seven	[Seven]
Lomba	Acht	[Eight]
Sieyte	Negen	[Nine]
d' Jon	Tien	[Ten]

Linguistic Notes

(Efik forms from Goldie (1874); Duala from Dinkelacker (1914); for the latter, double tones only marked; b.a.='borrowed as'.)

1. This first word has no obvious explanation from local languages. Perhaps Duala *ndabo*, 'house'—referring to the ship's superstructure.
2. Efik *makara*, 'white man', b.a. Duala *mokala*.
3. Duala *mboa*, 'home'; Bakweri *mboa*, 'village'; Isubu *mboka*, 'dry land'.
4. Isubu *kɛndɛ*, 'go'; Duala *ɛndɛ*.
5. No explanation (*singome* in Barbot's list means 'show me').
6. Efik *ɛdi ken*, sing. *di ken*, 'come here'.
7. Duala, *ongwɛlɛ*, 'trade with'; *mongwedi*, 'trader'; Bakweri, *umwɛlɛ*, 'show someone (something)'.
8. Duala *banga*, 'to refuse'; *nabangi*, 'I refuse'.
9. Duala *jǐba*, 'to steal, theft'.
10. Duala *nanga*, 'to sleep'.
11. Efik *ɛtük-ɛtük*, 'small, a little', *b.a.* Duala tɔki-tɔki, 'the very first'.
12. Balundu *nɛnɛ nɛnɛ*, 'very big': Duala *ndɛnɛ ndɛnɛ*.
13. Efik *fɔn*, 'to be good'; spelling influenced by Portuguese or Spanish *fino*, or even by Dutch.
14. ? Error for Dioucke=Efik *diɔk*, 'to be bad'. (Too early for English 'broke'!).
15. Duala *madiba*, 'water'.
16. Efik *mmɔŋ*, 'water'.
17. Duala *wea*, 'fire'; Bakweri *mweâ*, 'a lava stream'.

18, 19. These are inexplicable from local languages. Barbot's Old Calabar jargon contains *labouche* for 'woman' which resembles (19). (18) is probably Portuguese *muchacho*, 'boy'.

20. Uwet *ɛrɛnkemu*, 'fish' (Goldie): Andoni *iriŋ*, *iriɛŋ* (Thomas, 1914).
21. Isubu, Bakweri *mimba*, 'wine' [Wynba=Mynba].

22. Bakweri *mbɔ̌*, 'banana', Efik *mburo,* 'ripe plantain'. The Bakweri form implies earlier **mbɔ̀lɔ́.*
23. Not explained.
24. Kwa (Ekoi) *ɔbid, ɔbirɛ* or the like, 'cocoyams' (cf. Crabb, 1965).
25. Kwa *ŋkɔk*, 'fowl'.
26. Duala *nyaka,* 'cow'.
27. Duala *mŭla,* Bakweri *mauja,* 'palm-oil'. A form **màúlá* would lie behind.
28. Duala *misanga,* 'beads'.
29. Whatever 'orange paste' was, its name is only a doublet for 27, 'palm oil', which is also an orange-coloured paste! Dapper mentions both 'orange and lemon pastes' among his trade-goods for Cameroons (p. 139). In Barbot (p. 384) they have become 'presses for lemons and oranges'. The Frenchman Labarthe as late as 1803 was still quoting Dapper for this area and (p. 184) he translates this passage as 'presses to extract orange and lemon juice'. What can be meant? Palm-oil presses? Pomade? Or just palm-oil? Shades of Ogilby's 'Thin beaten Bosses, which they use instead of Money'—to translate Dapper's *Boesjes* (=cowries).
30. This must be in full: *Lavendel Quispel-grein*—the phrase occurs in Dapper (p. 139) and is translated by Ogilby (1670, p. 485) as 'Violet beads'. Barbot seems to mean the same when he talks of 'bloom-colour beads or bugles' (p. 384). Labarthe (loc. cit.) talks only of 'lavender'.
31. This would mean presumably 'white beads'. I cannot offer equivalents for *nigelle* and *poupe* but suspect Portuguese *nigela,* 'black inlay', and *pombo,* 'dove-white' or the like.
32. Duala *mikɔkɔ,* 'iron bars' (sing. *mukɔkɔ).*
33. Unexplained.
34. Unexplained.
35. Bakweri *fao;* Duala *pɔ*, 'knife'. Cf. Efik *faka,* 'long knife' (Goldie, 1874).
36. Duala *misɔ*, 'eyes'.
37. ? Efik *nsuŋikaŋ*, 'smoke' (without *ikaŋ*, 'fire') seems to belong here.

Numerals

DUALA (Class 2/3)		EFIK (Goldie)
mɔ̌	1	*kiet*
mibǎ	2	*iba*
milalo	3	*ita*
minɛi	4	*inaŋ*
mitanu	5	*itiuŋ*
mutoba	6	*itiokiet*
samba	7	*itiaba*
lɔmbi	8	*itiaɛta*
dibua	9	*usukiet*
dôm	10	*duüp*

Comments

Of 28 locally explicable forms, other than numerals: 11 are explicable from Duala, 6 may be from Bakweri/Isubu, 1 from Balundu, 7 from Efik/Ibibio, 1 Andoni, and 2 Kwa (Ekoi). Some of the forms or meanings suggesting Bakweri/ Isubu (e.g. Notes 3, 4, 17) are not inconsistent with true Duala dialect. Nos. 18 and 19 must be interpolations from slaving jargon.

In addition, the numerals with the exception of 'nine' are without doubt Duala. They cannot be Bakweri (e.g. Bakweri: *lisamba*, 'seven', *wambi* 'eight', *liome* 'ten'), or Isubu (e.g. Isubu *Isaka,* 'ten'), or Balundu (all numbers after 'five'). Duala *dôm*, 'ten', with implosive *d* may even be represented by *D'Jon.* The numerals alone are clear evidence for the Duala language, properly so called, on the coast. Basa or the like can be ruled out. For 'nine' an interpolated derivative from Efik is suggested (interpolation of the Spanish for 'Seven' is less likely). It is not a Balundu or Kwa form.

The Leers list shows evidence of printer's errors even in the Dutch. The abbreviation 'q^r' for *quispel-grein* is probably a misprint for 'q^u'.

* * * * *

Postcript

Ardener's analysis of the Leers vocabulary was not the only one: at about the same time, though unknown to Ardener, the linguist historian Paul Hair published his own thoughts on the early word list (Hair, 1969). Hair's article appeared too late to be of use to Ardener in writing the paper above. Linguistic work has continued, most importantly Hedinger (1987), and Kuperus (1985). Connell and Maison (in press) find evidence for migrations associated with the dispersal of the Lower Cross peoples in Ardener's discussion of the Leers vocabulary and elsewhere in the article. The composite nature of the early wordlist is a theme which is explored in greater depth in Connell (in press), where Ardener's reservations (expressed in footnote 1) as to the use of 'Efik' to identify the non-Bantu elements of the list are confirmed. Ardener's passionate interest in language, especially of this region, also led him to prepare an annotation of John Clarke's Specimens of Dialects *for a Gregg Press reprint of the 1848 original (Clarke, 1972 [1848]).*

B. Connell

2

Kingdom on Mount Cameroon: the Bakweri and the Europeans*

1. The Ethnography and Oral History of the Coast

Introduction

It was once suggested that a monument to the *Anopheles* mosquito should be built in West Africa: for this carrier of malaria had prevented European settlement. The Bakweri people of Buea lacked that ally—for it was the supposed absence of malaria there that concentrated the attention of colonial interests upon their settlement. Its situation on the well-watered section of the Cameroon Mountain, made it appear suitable for a health station. Also unless it was conquered it would have been a hindrance to the establishment of plantations. As a health station in the German period, however, it was only a partial success. The effective plantation centres also are elsewhere—at Bota, Ekona and Tiko. It is perhaps unlikely that anyone with today's experience would have chosen this mountain site as a place to build an administrative headquarters. Buea is a product of Bakweri and German friction in the nineteenth century.

This story covers the documented history of Buea from 1844, the time of the visit of the missionary Merrick, to 1898, the date at which independent Buea finally vanished. One section contains a verbatim extract of Merrick's account of his tour. Burton printed the account in his book *Abeokuta and the Camaroons Mountains* (1863), but his version contains many printing errors in the important names Merrick records. Here, therefore, I have had recourse to Merrick's original text, printed in 1845, which I have given a detailed commentary. Most of what follows has never before been fully published in English. The course of the German conflict with Buea has been derived from the official reports in *Deutsches Kolonialblatt,* some of which are given here in translation. The material for the sale of Buea is totally new. In discussing the sources I have related them to Bakweri traditional material, including the work

* *Written 1969*

of local antiquarians, and to my research since 1953.

For the general student of African history the climax of the story is a remarkable one. Its outline has been generally known, but it has lacked detail. The Cameroon Mountain was for a decade effectively denied to a modern European power by a people with a population of no more than 1,500. This resistance was both political and military, and the documents make it clear that it was led by a Cameroon ruler of remarkable acumen: Kuv' a Likenye. He was remembered by his own people, but after the collapse of the mountain population under the impact of the plantation economy, his historical contribution came to appear retrogressive and barbaric. Unlike some other Cameroon kings, Kuva received a totally hostile press from the German officials. Missionaries hated him. Thus he alienated Christian Cameroonians.

This study also throws further light on the way German land acquisition in the Cameroon Mountain area proceeded. The tale of the purchase of Buea by Governor von Soden, in a private capacity, must rank as one of the most extraordinary episodes in a train of events which already has more than its share of grotesque incidents.

This historical study is complete in itself. It follows on logically, however, from *Eye-Witnesses to the Annexation of Cameroon 1883-1887* S.G. Ardener), which covers related events at the Coast. It is contemporary in part with *Zintgraff's Explorations in Bamenda* (E.M. Chilver). The Battle of Mankon described there, which defeated Zintgraff, occurred in the same year, 1891, as the Battle of Buea, in which Gravenreuth fell. Both defeats delayed German colonial penetration for several years, and increased official coolness to expeditions. The remoter repercussions of the Gravenreuth expedition even rippled on until the Treaty of Versailles.

Spelling

Certain names occur in several different spellings, according to the renderings of the different sources, which are cited as found. In general, the town of Douala is given its modern spelling. *Duala* is used for the people and language.

Acknowledgements

The Baptist Mission Archives, London, and Regent's Park College, Oxford, kindly allowed access to the *Missionary Herald* and other documents. The Royal Geographical Society, London, and Mrs E. M.

Chilver, made possible lengthy consultation of the volumes of *Deutsches Kolonialblatt*. The late P. M. Kale kindly made available copies of some pages of his *Brief History of Bakweri* for inclusion, before his death. Chief Endeley III, Mr Esasso Woleta, and members of the Martin and Steane families, have frequently discussed their genealogical records with me, over a number of years. Mr Esasso Woleta for long preserved copies of two letters from the German period, which he kindly sent to me. Mr Kalle Njie also kindly made enquiries on certain doubtful points. The work of these and other students of tradition receives important vindication from the foreign sources. It is a pleasure to dedicate this study to them.

Edwin Ardener
Buea, 1969

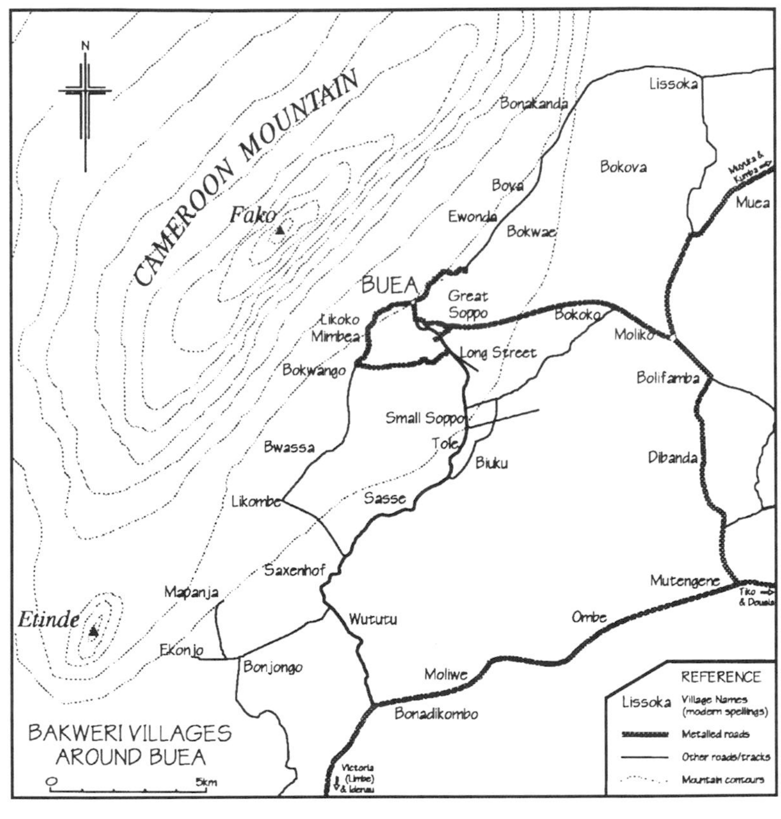
N
CAMEROON MOUNTAIN
Fako
Etinde
Lissoka
Bonakanda
Bokova
Boya
Muea
Ewonda
Bokwae
BUEA
Great Soppo
Bokoko
Likoko Mimbea
Moliko
Long Street
Bokwango
Bolifamba
Small Soppo
Bwassa
Tole
Biuku
Dibanda
Likombe
Sasse
Saxenhof
Mutengene
Tiko & Douala
Mapanja
Wututu
Ombe
Ekonjo
Bonjongo
Moliwe
Bonadikombo
Victoria (Limbe) & Idenau
BAKWERI VILLAGES AROUND BUEA
0
5km
REFERENCE
Lissoka
Village Names (modern spellings)
Metalled roads
Other roads/tracks
Mountain contours

Nineteenth Century Buea

The Mountain Population

The Bakweri people occupy the south-eastern slopes of Mount Cameroon (Fako). Buea is one of their settlements lying at about 3,000 feet, in a relatively densely populated belt of the mountain. The Germans thought the Bakweri numbered about 25,000 in the 1890s. Probably it was less. Buea seems to have had a population of between 1,000 and 1,500 Bakweri (more or less) for probably a century. Bakweri villages are fenced and the fence of Buea, as we shall see, once rambled around a considerable area—210 hectares in 1897.

In 1841 the Niger Expedition Captains visited the coast, and rendered the name of the mountain people as *Bakwileh*. The Bimbia people (Isubu or Isuwu) were a small coastal group who spoke a language similar to Bakweri, but they had become differentiated through their development as a trading people in contact with foreign ships. In the 1840's their chief was known to Europeans as King William (from his name *Bile*).[1]

The Chiefly Line of Buea

On 23 April, 1844, the Baptist Missionary Merrick left Bimbia and reached Buea (Bwea), thus for the first time bringing information to the outside world concerning the Bakweri settlement which was later to become an important colonial capital. Merrick spent much of the time on his journey preaching to the people, and most of his account, published in the *Missionary Herald* of February 1845, is filled up with pious reflections. Nevertheless he is very helpful in many ways. We are able to plot with some accuracy the positions of a long list of Bakweri villages, and we have the names of large numbers of quarterheads. He reached Buea through Moliko and Wokpae, and arrived at what is clearly Lower Buea or Mokunda, behind the present Buea Stranger Quarter. This he called 'Dickenye's Town'.

The mention of 'Dickenye' as the chief of Lower Buea is of especial interest, for the spelling refers accurately to the Duala pronunciation (*Dikenye*) of Likenye, the father of the two famous Buea chiefs, Kuva and his successor Endeley I, who clashed with the Germans in 1891 and 1894. The final subjection of Buea occurred almost exactly fifty years after the first recorded foreign visit.

The Buea chiefly line is therefore firmly fixed historically from 1844 down to the present day. A few further speculations may be made on the basis of the available dates. Kuva died in 1895 after the second German attack, reportedly as an old man, although how old cannot be securely stated. Eye-witnesses reported him as active and in full possession of his faculties, and it is probable that he was nearer sixty than eighty, and born about 1835. This would have made him already nearly ten years old when Merrick visited his father. If Kuva, the eldest son, was born in 1835 it is unlikely that Likenye, his father, would have been born before 1810. Indeed, given the early age of marriage which is probable, he could have been born as late as 1815. If Kuva died at an age somewhat older than sixty, or if Likenye had daughters or dead children before Kuva, we should expect an earlier birth date.

Reasonable indirect estimation would then place Likenye's birth with good probability between 1805 and 1815. Merrick does not guess at Likenye's age, but the Chief's entourage does not seem to include any grown sons. His 'brother', who was probably a lineage elder, seems to dominate the proceedings. Likenye could be under forty therefore, even about thirty-five years of age. So a date of birth about 1810 is probably not far out. Although this is not an 'historical' date, it is probably the earliest one that can be tied in to the documentary evidence relating to Buea.

We have no record of Likenye's death and the succession of Kuva. We know only that Kuva would not have been likely to succeed before 1855, when he would be about twenty. He would even have been thought too young then, in all probability. But any date is possible in the next thirty years. In the 1880's Kuva himself comes into the view of witnesses, and is already referred to as a well-known chief by Europeans, and it does not therefore seem likely that he had only recently succeeded as Chief. One suspects a minimum tenure of ten years. Although we are totally in the realm of guesswork, the least unlikely period for the death of Likenye, and the accession of Kuva, lies somewhere in the decade 1860-70.

After that the succession is plain sailing:[2]

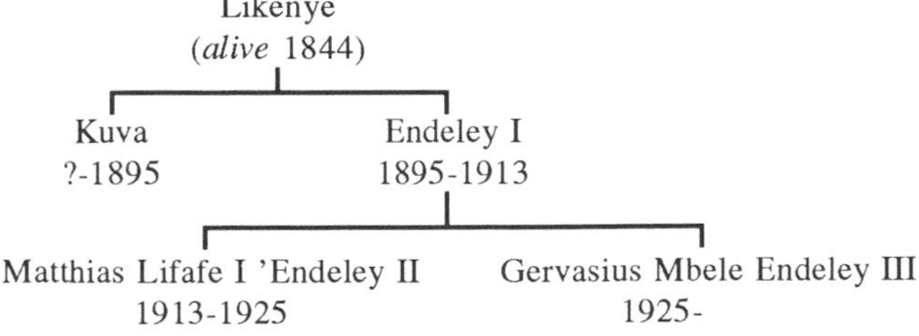

As the Chiefship of the Lower Buea area, this succession is not controversial. Its status as the Chiefship of Buea as a whole was briefly challenged by the line of Upper Buea.

The succession of Upper Buea was as follows:

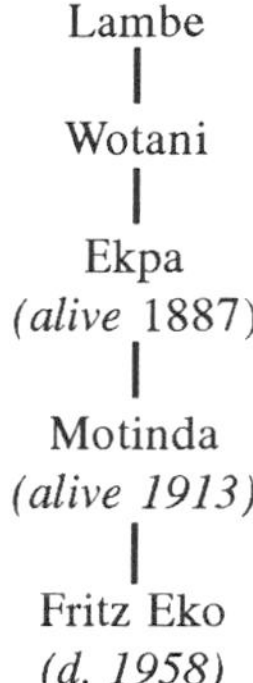

We know from documents that Ekpa was contemporary with Kuva, and chief of Upper Buea in 1887. This area was destroyed for the Station in 1895. The people moved into the present area called Wondongo, which is geographically part of Lower Buea. When Endeley died Motinda was appointed by the colonial government to act as paramount of Buea. He died too and his son Friedrich (Fritz) contended for the post with Endeley II before the appointment was confirmed in favour of the latter.

Conflicting Traditions

Our materials for traditional Buea, as for the rest of the Bakweri area, consist almost solely of genealogies. These are very often in conflict, and they represent, in the versions we have, important vested interests. In the last forty years at least three schools of thought have grown up deriving from the work of literate persons. They may be called a Bimbia school (associated with the work of Charles Steane and Manga Williams), a Buea school (associated with the Endeley family), and a Soppo school (associated with the Bakweri antiquarian Esasso Woleta). Mainly, the Soppo school have objected to the prominence given to Buea in histories of the Bakweri, and particularly to the line of the Endeley family. They and the Buea school have both objected further to the dominance of the Bimbia view of history, which they feel has over-stressed the role of certain Victoria families. These controversies have resulted in distortion and counter-distortion of the tradition by members of each camp.[3]

At the time just before the annexation of Cameroon in 1884, the political balance on the West Cameroon coast was in a flux. The mercantile power of Bimbia was in decline, as the Isubu historians themselves concede. In 1858 King Bile (William I) had been able to cede to the Baptist Missionary, Saker, coastal territory for the settlement of Victoria, with no effective opposition from the inland Bakweri settlements. But in 1882 King Bile's son and successor Ngombe (William II) was murdered, it was believed at the instigation of Soppo, in a village on the very coast where Isubu traders had been predominant for so long.[4] Inland, Buea and Soppo both involved themselves in control of the access to the mountain hinterland. By 1891 Buea appeared to the Germans to be the more dangerous of the two, while Soppo appeared to be a possible ally on the German side. After the final defeat of Buea it seemed to many an injustice that Buea, and not Soppo, should have arisen again as an administrative centre. The re-establishment of Bimbia influence in the twentieth century in the person of Chief Manga Williams of Victoria was no more welcome. The source of the conflict in the colonial period lay in the belief that certain villages were being put 'under' others when the Native Authorities were set up. The belief took root when the Bakweri area was divided into two Districts with capitals at Victoria and Buea.

Since the dust of these controversies is now beginning to settle, it should clearly be said that there is no evidence that any one village had primacy in the settlement of the mountain by the Bakweri. Furthermore, in the settlement of all the larger villages people of various Bakweri origins participated at various periods. The present Buea, for example, contains lineages of several origins. The main tradition, however, relates to the branch of the Wonyalionga lineage from which the line of Kuva sprang.

How correct is it to regard the Kuva line as always having provided the chiefs of all Buea? As we shall see, the treaty with Valdau in 1887 was signed by two Buea groups, representing Upper Buea and Lower Buea. The former party was relatively small. The latter was numerous and was headed by Kuva, and there is no doubt that at least by 1891, Kuva, militarily, was Buea. After the German conquest, Upper Buea was destroyed to make the station, and its people scattered. When we trace back to Merrick's visit in 1844 the pattern is already one in which Likenye (Dickenye) of Lower Buea looms largest, with other chiefs also important. The picture in the nineteenth century thus shows Lower Buea providing respected chiefs throughout. We need not doubt that other lineages had their own heads, but that of Lower Buea was still a significant one. The question of real competition between chiefs became serious only when there were important things to compete over. In particular, the arrival of European goods provided such grounds. Later the question of Native Court membership and District Headship gave others.

The Pre-Nineteenth Century Period

How far before 1800 can any light at all be thrown? Recent research has shown the date of the arrival of Bantu-speaking people in the Cameroon Mountain area to be much earlier than was thought possible a decade ago. The evidence is intricate and can only be touched on briefly here. In a Dutch vocabulary of the Cameroon Coast dated 1665 there are words of Duala form, together with some of Bakweri and Isubu appearances.[5] It now seems probable that there was no great difference in the ethnic pattern in 1600 from that of the present-day. Precisely how detailed and dense the mountain settlements of the Bakweri would have been in the early period is not clear. One thing is certain: the settlement pattern of the 1840's was not recent. We can trace some Bakweri settlements, even quite tiny ones, back to 1844 as a result of Merrick's report. Nearly all are named in a report of John Clarke of 1848.[6] The relatively large population of Buea in 1895—at least 1,000, perhaps 1,500—suggests that it may have been one of the older settlements, although possibly its population was built up by being continually swollen by immigration from less hospitable parts of the mountain. The same would apply to Soppo. This is a well-watered stretch of Mount Cameroon which would attract population. The introduction of the *xanthosoma* cocoyam at the coast by the missionaries improved the food supply out of recognition.

A further factor is the name Buea itself. From purely linguistic analysis it can be demonstrated that the name represents an earlier **Bo-Eya* or 'people of Eyé', which gives by regular derivation Duala *Bwe(y)a,* Bakweri *Gbeya.* In this respect the name follows the pattern of the majority of Bakweri villages, which are named after founders in this way. In confirmation of this a founder of the name Eyé, son of Naliomo, is recognized in the Buea story of origin. Now this Eyé is accepted as ancestral to the Kuva line among others. The mode of descent is, however, contested. All sources agree that the father of the historical Likenye was Lionge, from whom the whole lineage of Wonyalionga descends. Lionge's father was Vefonge. Beyond Vefonge the many variants suggest that 'telescoping' has taken place (that is: generations have been omitted), and Vefonge has been attached in various different ways to the founder Eyé. In the standard Lower Buea version, which was written down by the Endeley family as long ago as 1929, Eyé is given as the father of Vefonge. If this were correct the founding of Buea would have occurred in the eighteenth century. In this version Eyé's father Naliomo is also called Njie. However, in another version, Njie is given as the son of Eyé and brother of Vefonge. In yet another version Vefonge and Njie are both said to be the sons of Tama son of Lifanje, who has further ancestors going back five generations. Njie is widely believed to have founded the Buea settlements outside Wonyalionga, and thirty years ago Ittmann was told that Njie founded Buea.

It should be said, at once, that none of these versions but the first is accepted by the elders of Wonyalionga. It is important to note that variants do occur, however, and they derive from the fact that, despite belief, no village is directly descended in the male line from one founder. Many individuals and some lineage units may have different origins. They are probably all by now interrelated, but ancestors can be traced in many different ways. Many people who live in Bakweri villages are related, for example, through matrilineal ties: sisters' sons and daughters' sons (*valalo*). As we shall see later, even at Likenye's level some difficulties occur. Some of his 'brothers' seem perhaps to have been cousins.

It is unnecessary here to become involved in controversies about the descent from Eyé. We know from the name Buea that an Eyé probably existed, and that whatever other men came to live there the whole settlement continued to keep his name.[7] After Eyé then came Vefonge, whose supposed brothers—Mowale, Iwange, Motande, Wotumbe, Wolongo, Mokumbe and others— are all ancestors of lineages connected in some way or other with Buea.[8] At this level we are probably dealing with figures who lived in the eighteenth century. From one or another of the whole group many Upper and Lower Buea lineages were derived. After Vefonge came Lionge and his supposed brothers. Lionge was the ancestor of the main Lower Buea group of Wonyalionga. He was a figure of the last quarter of the eighteenth century and the father of the historical Likenye of 1844. It is with Likenye that this account begins.

Merrick and Likenye

The Baptist Missionaries, on their arrival on Fernando Po in 1841,[9] soon turned their interest to the mainland. Joseph Merrick, a Jamaican of mixed Afro-European ancestry, arrived in 1843, and established a station at Bimba in 1844. He made his journey to Buea almost at once. The trade up the mountain, from Bwenga on the creeks, was in the hands of King William's relative, John King, who acted as guide.

Introduction

Merrick sailed from Clarence, Fernando Po, for Bimbia on 10 April, 1844, and stayed at King William's Town (Bonabile). On 23 April he set off on a trip up the Cameroon Mountain, accompanied by eleven attendants and carriers, Copper his interpreter, his Isubu guide John King, and a deacon of the church at Clarence, John Smith. On that day they reached 'Bwengga' market by sea, a position not far from the Bwinga beach of Pamol Ltd. The Bakweri village now spelled Bwenga (or Gbenga) consisted then of isolated homesteads spread over a very great area.[10] Merrick was surprised to note that the territory of Bwenga spread from the beach as far inland as the escarpment above the present Mutengene. The scattered nature of Bakweri villages in the forest made him prefer to use the word 'District' to refer to them. The separate homesteads he called 'Towns', naming each one after its headman. Thus he stayed on the first night at 'Ebore's Town' in the 'Bwengga District'. Ebore lived well inland near the present Dibanda. Merrick stayed in the settlement the next day, visiting other notables.

On 25 April he was intending to visit 'Sofo' (Soppo), but he was told that the headman Manja of 'Moriko' wanted to see him. Merrick's party therefore set off in that direction, passing first the 'Bori-pamba district'. This is the Bakweri Wolifamba, but from Merrick's account it is clear that the village territory then included the plantation land behind Ekande and Wokova, villages which Merrick does not mention. The travellers then passed through the 'Bakuku district' which was so close to the 'Moriko district' that he says they were really the same place under different names. Bakuku was clearly Bokoko (Wokoko), and it is interesting to note that to this day strangers still confuse Bokoko and Moliko. Indeed the two villages now form a continuous settlement.

At 'Moriko' (Moliko) they stayed at 'Manja's Town'. Two men from Bwea came to see Merrick there, since John King had put it about that the purpose of the visit was to go up the mountain. It was locally believed that there were 'treasures' up there for which he had come to seek.

Merrick, who was largely concerned with his preaching, was thus directed up the mountain to some extent against his will.

The next day, 26 April 1844, they set out for Buea, passing through 'Bokwei district' (Wokpae), until they came to 'Dickenye's town' the homestead of Likenye in Lower Buea. We take up the story in Merrick's own words.[11]

Merrick's Visit to Buea

Friday, April 26 [1844]

> We were to have left Manja's Town early this morning, but were detained by heavy rains till twelve o'clock, when we proceeded on our journey. At twenty-five minutes after twelve we entered the Bokwei district, and at the same time passed Morio's Town. At one o'clock the country became very hilly. We arrived at Dickenye's Town at half-past one, which is situated in the Bwea district. I was kindly received by Dickenye, who appeared very happy to see me, and like Ebore, dwelt for a long time on the great honour bestowed on him by the visit of a white man. I however soon discovered that great suspicions were entertained respecting my intended visit to the mountain, and John King, in order to learn the real object of my visit, took Smith aside and questioned him closely on the subject.
>
> Shortly after my arrival Dickenye told John King that there were immense treasures on the mountain, that on the death of any influential person in the Bwea district they had frequently seen cloths of every description spread out on the mountain;[12] that there was a great deal of gunpowder, salt, and dollars on the mountain, and they thanked John King for bringing me to show them how to obtain the treasures. There was also a 'large water' on the mountain, where a white man was often seen, and which no black man could pass; that they sometimes heard the report of guns fired by the white man; that the white man was my brother, and I had come to see him, and fetch him down from the mountain. In vain I endeavoured to persuade them that the sole object of my visit was to impart the knowledge of the true God, and to learn whether they were willing to receive religious teachers. During the day I embraced every opportunity of declaring the gospel, but like those of Manja's Town, the Bwea people were more desirous to sing, and dance, and make a noise, than attend to what I had to say.
>
> In the afternoon several chiefs came to see me. After they had listened to the truth a short time, Dickenye, who is an incessant talker, began to address the people, after which he danced about, and endeavoured to appear very great. He was followed by another man, who wore a sort of tippet made by himself. He also delivered an address, and like Dickenye, danced and sung, and capered about amidst the applause of the surrounding

multitude. As evening approached John King informed me that all the gentlemen of the district were to assemble after dark in order to come to some decision respecting the charge they were to make for allowing me to visit the mountain. Accordingly we had a meeting in one of Dickenye's houses in the evening, when all the gentlemen strenuously maintained that there were incalculable treasures on the mountain, and that John King had brought me to obtain them. I replied that many of them would on the morrow accompany me to the mountain, and would have an opportunity of seeing all it contained, and that whatever I might bring down they were at perfect liberty to retain. During my short life I have met many great talkers, but never before heard so garrulous a man as Dickenye. He seems never tired of chatting, and will scarcely allow any one else to speak a word.

None but those who have been engaged in an African palaver[13] can form a correct idea of its tediousness. When you imagine that the subject in debate has been brought to a close, and about to be settled, all on a sudden you find yourself at the point from whence you started, and the objections which you had before answered again brought forward as if they were entirely new. This was the ordeal through which I had to pass at Dickenye's place, and what rendered it more trying was my ignorance of the language, and consequent dependence on John King and Copper for an interpretation of all that was said. The palaver being closed I retired to rest after commending myself and our party to the divine protection, and as usual slept well.

Saturday, April 27

We were to have started before daylight, but could not manage to get away before fifteen minutes before seven. It is very difficult to get an uncivilized African band to travel early. On my arrival at Dickenye's I was informed that his town was the nearest to the mountain in the Bwea district, but I discovered this morning that my information was not correct. Shortly after leaving Dickenye's we passed three towns, all near each other, and arrived at the last town on the way to the mountain at a quarter after seven. At this time we saw a road to the south, which I was informed leads to Rumby. At fifteen minutes to eight we arrived at a river flowing from the north-west in a south-westerly direction. At this point there was a sensible change in the atmosphere. I drank of the water of the river, whose bed was very rocky, and found it delightfully cool.

Near the river is a small abandoned farm, which was formerly cultivated by some of the Bwea people. Before visiting the interior I thought the people spent a great deal of their time in agricultural pursuits, but was surprised during my journey to see so few farms, and those so much neglected. All the plantain farms I saw were covered with grass and bush. Like those on the coast, the people in the country live a life of almost absolute idleness. They do not set the smallest value on time, and prefer spending days and weeks in hunting (though they not infrequently return home as empty as they went out) to cultivating the soil. May they soon come under the influence of that gospel which so strongly condems idleness and inculcates the necessity of industrious habits.

But to resume our narrative. At eight o'clock the Bwea men who accompanied me stopped to perform a ceremony called Mosere. Dickenye's brother, Bunggome, with a mug of water in his hand, delivered an address to the following effect: 'That the Moriko and Bwengga men were unwilling that the Bwea people should engage in trade with Bimbia, but that John King had kindly brought a white man to see them, who he hoped would open a communication between the coast and the Bwea district.' After the address a libation was poured out on the ground, and the remainder of the water in the mug drank by all who had engaged in the ceremony. I requested John King to say to them that the good word which I had spoken to them was calculated to unite all people in one common bond, and if they and the Moriko and Bwenga people attended to it, instead of opposing each other in trade, they would live as brethren, and do all in their power to promote the welfare of one another. They appeared quite pleased with my remarks, and proceeded on the journey with smiling countenances.

A few minutes before the Mosere ceremony was performed, we crossed a fine stream whose water was very cold. At twenty minutes before ten we arrived at another river-course destitute of water, except a small portion (rain water I suppose) in hollows of rocks, and which reminded me of the pools of rainwater from which the Israelites were wont to refesh themselves on the journeys to the holy city. Our whole party took a long draught of water here, as we were given to understand that we should meet with no more during the remainder of our journey. Ten minutes before ten we had an excellent view of the sea. Perhaps it is necessary to observe that the whole district through which we passed is very well furnished with hardwood. The wood is so hard that the Bwea men, not possessing proper axes, are unable to fell the trees for the purpose of making farms. Eight minutes after ten we passed the last farm of the Bwea people on the way to the Cameroons Mountain. On this farm is growing the finest piece of cocoa I have seen since my arrival in Africa. I was rather surprised that the Bwea people should cultivate farms so far from their towns, and thought they must have good reason for doing so, and on inquiry found that they were in the habit of spending whole weeks in the woods hunting the ngika, or buffaloe, and during that time cultivated the soil in the vicinity of the chase.

Twenty five minutes before eleven the brother of Dickenye perceiving that we were drawing near the mountain, broke a small bush, and holding it in his hand, prayed aloud to his dead father and mother to protect him from danger in approaching the mountain. I directed John King to tell him that Obassa-Luba (the name by which the Deity is called) alone could afford him help, and that his petitions should have been presented to him. On hearing this he began to cry to Obassa-Luba for help. The evident fear of the people as they drew near the mountain led me to conclude that they had never before travelled so far, though they wished to make me believe that many of them had before ascended the mountain. At twenty minutes before eleven we arrived at a beautiful plain, extending along the base of the mountain a considerable way. This plain is covered with a fine wing-grass, some of which I brought down as a memorial of my visit. A quarter before eleven we had an extensive and splendid view of the sea, rivers, and lowlands from the plain at the base of the mountain. We saw very distinctly Balimba Point and River, and a little eastward the Bakuku, Munggo, and Bunji rivers and country.

At ten minutes after eleven our band sat down on the grassy plain to hold a consultation as to whether they should ascend the mountain at whose height and majestic aspect they were manifestly alarmed. While with wonder and awe they gazed upon the grand and lofty fabric, Smith observed that if they were so alarmed at beholding the works of the Almighty, what would be the state of their mind when they beheld the Almighty himself on the judgment day? John King, who had all along spoken of his determination to go to the very apex of the mountain, now declared that he could not proceed further; while the Bwea men said it was useless to accompany me if no treasures were to be obtained. I reminded them that I had agreed to pay them to go with me, and if they broke their engagement they could not expect payment. At length ten of the Bwea men made up their minds to accompany me, and with Smith, Copper, and myself started for the much dreaded Munggo, as mountain is called in the Isubu tongue.

With much difficulty we ascended about a third of the mountain at six minutes after one, where it was so cold that I judged it unwise to proceed higher with men who had only a piece of cloth around their loins. This, with other reasons, induced me to descend the mountain before reaching its apex, though I must confess I did so very reluctantly. At the elevation on which I stood I experienced all the sensations produced by an English winter. My nostrils ran copiously, my eyes were much affected, and my fingers stiff. The faces of my attendants were covered with a sort of white incrustation, such as may be seen on the skins of black men in England during winter; their eyes were also much affected, and Dickenye's brother had a fit of ague, and trembled like an aspen leaf. The mountain after a certain height (perhaps from about the sixth of its altitude from the base) is entirely covered with a fine and beautifully green grass, with here and there a few shrubs. The soil is composed of small pieces of soft stone, which have evidently been subject to the action of fire, and which frequently crumbled or resigned their places as the weight of our bodies rested upon them in ascending. From the point on which we stood we had an excellent view of the lowlands and the different rivers in the Bight of Biafra.

We began to descend the mountain about a quarter after one, and arrived at the grassy plain at ten minutes before three, from whence, though much fatigued, we immediately proceeded homeward. When we had nearly reached our resting place the Bwea men assembled, and agreed to tell the people on their arrival that there were immense treasures on the mountain, but that I had resolved on not taking them away till my return, when I would bring another white man with me. On hearing this I requested John King to undeceive the people, and let them know the truth.

At fifteen minutes after five we arrived at the last town on the way to the mountain, and eight minutes after six reached Dickenye's Town, our resting place. In returning the Bwea men sang the greater part of the way, and seemed very glad that no harm had befallen them on their way to the mountain. One of their songs was to the following effect: 'The white man cut down the grass[14] and told it to stand up. The grass replied, how can I stand; you have cut me down.' My feet ached so much at my long and difficult journey that I could hardly stir, but a good night's rest refreshed my wearied frame and rendered me strong again for duty.

Lord's-day, April 28

I spent a pleasant time this morning in instructing several children and young people from my Isubu lesson. They exhibited considerable pleasure in spelling the words of their language, and though they spent more than a quarter of an hour at their lesson, did not appear tired. Finding that the adult people were more inclined to drum and dance than listen to the gospel, I left Dickenye's Town after breakfast, and accompanied by John King went to see a very old man named Ibungge, who has been sick for a long time, and intelligence of whose death arrived at Bimbia a few days ago. I endeavoured to preach salvation by Christ to him and his people, but fear the old man did not comprehend what was said to him.

I saw a woman this morning with her face besmeared with dirt, and a band of the fibre of the plantain-tree round her forehead, which I learnt is the usual badge of mourning of the people of the district. The Bimbia women do not wear the band round their foreheads, but besmear their faces for several months with a mixture of dirt, lamp-black, and palm oil.

About two o'clock today a man from the Boba[15] district came to see me, and listened very attentively to the truths which I declared to him. Dickenye introduced him to me, and sat for a short time. I had not, however, spoken long before he began to interrupt me, but finding that I would not attend to him, and was determined to go on conversing with the Boba man, he left the hut, and called away his friend, but he would not go. As the Boba man defended the practice of polygamy I dwelt much on the evils of it, and assured him it was very offensive to God. After the departure of the poor man I learnt that he had recently shot a man for seducing one of his wives, and had in consequence to desert his house, and hide himself in the woods. According to a rule, or law, called Dibumbe, every man, from

Bimbia to the Camaroons Mountains, and I believe at other places, who commits murder is given up by his town's-people to be hanged. While speaking to the Boba man little did I think I was pointing out the evils of the very sin which had compelled him to leave the few comforts of his home to wander in the woods.

As in South Africa, there are men in the Bwea district, and in other parts of the country, who profess to be able to produce rain. John King firmly believes in the pretended power of the rain-makers, and strenuously maintained that they did possess the power notwithstanding all I could say to convince him to the contrary.

I understood this afternoon that the Chief men of Bwea, and especially Dickenye, are entertaining large expectations respecting the presents they are to receive before my departure. They told John King that he, King William, Dick Merchant, and the other traders of Bimbia, had received large presents to allow me to visit the interior, and now I had seen their mountain, John King did not wish me to give them any thing. The covetousness of the people is exceedingly trying and distressing, and, with vain glory, exhibits itself in almost every word and action. Oh, that the time may speedily come when their selfishness will be subdued and their hearts renovated by the divine Spirit!

About three o'clock Smith and I sang a hymn, read a portion of Scripture, and engaged in prayer, in which we specially implored the Lord to visit the dark places of the earth with the light of his glorious gospel.

Smith and I conversed much with Copper today about the necessity of a change of heart. It is very gratifying to me to be able to state that light seems gradually shining upon this man's mind. He has already abandoned a few of his country practices, and will I hope be given to us as the first fruit of our labours.

When resolved on visiting the Camaroons Mountains I fully expected difficulties on the way. True I did not entertain the slightest apprehensions of personal danger, yet I by no means imagined that my path would be a smooth one. Indeed from the day of my arrival at Bwea I plainly foresaw that we should meet with opposition before our departure. It was not to be expected that Satan would sit quietly and see one of his strongholds attacked without retaliation. But greater is He that is for us than they who are against us. The prey of the enemy will yet be plucked from his teeth, and the kingdom of Christ established where Satan's empire now raises its proud and lofty head.

Monday, April 29

I arose unusually early on Monday morning, and spent a sweet season in prayer. My soul was much drawn out in behalf of the heathens in general, but more particularly for Africa. I felt while supplicating the mercy-seat that the Lord was preparing my mind and strengthening my spirit for some trial. When our baggage had been packed up, and we were ready to leave, I presented Dickenye and three of the chief men of Bwea with cloth, garments, and other things, but they were quite dissatisfied, and said they would not allow our boxes to be taken away unless I gave them more cloth. I knew well that if I yielded to their unjust exaction, instead of being satisfied, they would be encouraged to make other demands, and consequently declined giving any thing else. On hearing this they made a great noise, and seemed determined to detain us. Several of the men were armed with cutlasses, and during the palaver flourished them about (not however in a threatening manner), but the Lord graciously preserved me from fear, and kept my mind in perfect peace.

Oh, what a blessedness to be able to rest on the arms of Him who is powerful to save. Not one of our party had a weapon of any description. On leaving Bimbia I strictly enjoined John King not to carry guns, swords, or cutlasses, assuring him that the God whom I loved and served, and whose truth I was going to declare, would protect and preserve us; and I have no doubt that our defenceless state tended more to disarm the Bwea people than any thing else. I do hope that all our missionaries who may come to Africa will be members of the Peace Society. After a long and noisy discussion, in which John King, Copper, and a few others of the men who conducted me, nearly talked themselves out of breath, the Bwea men withdrew, and held a private consultation. At this juncture Smith became alarmed for our safety, and on my return from the mountain told Mr Ducket that he was just waiting to know the result of the conference of the Bwea men, and if they had resolved on killing us he intended to request them to destroy him first, that he might not endure the pain of seeing me put to death.

Smith's fears were, however, quite groundless. I do not think that the people had the remotest intention of hurting a hair of our heads. All they wanted was the contents of our boxes, and not being able to frighten me into submission, they withdrew to come to some decision respecting the mode of bringing the palaver to a close. They soon returned, and said that as I was unwilling to give them more cloth, they would be satisfied with a book (certificate) stating that I had visited the mountain from their district, in order that they might show it to any white man that might come after me. I very soon furnished the 'book', when our carriers were permitted to leave; but we had only walked a short distance when one of our people was stopped by Dickenye's brother because he said he had not received a shirt. The fact is, this man took a fancy to Smith's flannel shirt, and requested me to give him one like it. On leaving I borrowed Smith's flannel, and gave it to him, but after receiving it he was quite dissatisfied, and said he wanted a shirt similar to those the other chiefs had received; but as all of that description were distributed I could not comply with his request. He was, however, determined to get a shirt, and therefore followed us after we left his brother's town, and stopped one of the boxes. Copper directly drew off his shirt, and gave it to Bunggome, but took good care to secure for himself the flannel shirt, which is of more value than the one with which he parted.

We left Dickenye's Town at twenty-five minutes before eight, and after passing a town in the Bwea district, entered the Bokwei district at half-past eight; and after leaving the towns of Morio and Namunde entered the Bakuku district at five minutes before nine, and arrived at Junge's Town at two minutes before nine. We again reached Manja's place at seven minutes after nine. The old man appeared happy to see me, and pressed me to remain over the night, expecting no doubt another present in the event of my doing so, but I told him I could not by any means stops as I was anxious to get down as early as possible.

***

Thus ends Merrick's account. On the same day (29 April 1844) he made his way through the villages of 'Bunjoku' (Wonjoku), 'Bunjumba' (Wonjamba) and 'Minyali Munggo' (near Wonya-Imali), back to Ebore's place in Upper Bwenga. The next day he visited another homestead in the area, 'Madiba's Town', and passed out of Bwenga into 'Bunjo district'. This was Wonjo, a settlement on the Ombe river which was still in existence in 1899, but was later destroyed to make the Moliwe plantation. He stayed with one Mekwalle, and on 1 May set off again, passing extensive farms in Wonjo territory, and then crossed into 'Mobeta district'. This was on land in the lower stretches of the Ombe River which is now covered by plantations. After Mobeta they entered 'Gyangu' (Jange) a village, now vanished, on the coast just north of 'Dick Merchant's Town' (Dikolo). From Jange, Merrick went by canoe to 'King William's Town' (Bonabile) and was home at 4.15 p.m. the same day.

Historical Significance of Merrick's Account

Merrick's trip in general provides extremely valuable information on the condition of the Bakweri in 1844. For example it shows that the distribution of villages in this important central zone from Buea to Bwenga was already much the same as at present. The present Moliwe estate was, however, covered by the very large village territories of Mobeta, Wonjo and Bwenga of which only Bwenga now remains, in much reduced form, although Mobeta survives as a plantation name in the form of Mabeta.

The Buea of Merrick

The trip from Manja's homestead in Moliko to Buea was very short. Merrick left at 12 noon, crossed Wokpae boundary at 12.25, passing Namunde's settlement at the same time. 'Shortly after' he passed Morio's Town. He reached Dickenye's Town at 1.30. On the way back he mentions that another Buea settlement intervened between Dickenye's and the Wokpae boundary. Morio's Town is the first settlement in Wokpae. As it happens, there is now a Wonya-Molio which is a Buea settlement, according to the Buea tradition, the first reached from the Wokpae side. It is descended from Moli' a Monyoke, the brother's son of Likenye. It may be that Morio's settlement in Wokpae was of Buea origin and later was attached to Buea again. For the traditional relationship to be genuine, if that was so, Monyoke would have had to be a considerably elder brother of Likenye (possibly deceased), if his son Morio was to have had his own homestead in Wokpae. The two settlements may of course be unconnected.

It is evident from Merrick's description that Likenye's settlement was more or less in the present area (Mokunda) where his descendants live—the Lower Buea referred to by later travellers. His son Kuva lived in 1894 below the hill on which Chief Endeley III made his home. In Merrick's time there were three more settlements in Buea 'all near each other' after Likenye's on the way to the mountain. They were traversed in half an hour. These settlements can be guessed at. Most of the present Wonyalionga are descended from brothers of Likenye. The first 'town' mentioned by Merrick might contain some nucleus of this group. One 'town' would be the nucleus of the present Wondongo then situated near the centre of the German Station, in the area of the Bismarck Fountain. In 1887 this was the leading settlement of Upper Buea. It was dispossessed in 1895, as has been said, by the Germans, and re-established close to the descendants of Likenye, an arrangement becoming the cause of later friction. The headman in 1844 was, to our loss, not named by Merrick, but was probably Wotani, son of Lambe la Ndonge the founder of the settlement. The third town was situated above the area of the Bismarck Fountain and near the Mosole stream, some of whose descendants were moved from the area of the present Lodge in 1895. This group was descended from Motande, supposedly a younger brother of Likenye's grandfather Vefonge. By 1895 this group had divided into sections each containing the descendants of different grandsons of Motande, before they were disastrously scattered by the Germans, the inhabitants fleeing in several directions. From those who

Joseph Merrick at an Isubu Funeral (*Missionary Herald*, 1845)

settled in Lower Buea came P. M. Kale, the late Speaker of the West Cameroon House of Assembly.

Such a pattern of settlement is plausible and Merrick's route would not be very different from the present one up the mountain *via* Upper Farm. At the uppermost settlement Merrick saw a path going south (i.e. approximately along the mountain) said to go to 'Rumby'. This path would in fact pass above Wokpaongo along the mountain descending to the coast west of the present Victoria. 'Rumby' itself was used at that time to refer to the coast north of Idenau.[16]

The climb

At one point in the forest above the town the Buea men performed a ceremony which Merrick says was called *Mosere.* This term is now unknown. Such a libation is usually called *lisomelele* nowadays. The ceremony was also evidently intended as a kind of oath and resembles the water oath (*vê ve maliva*) of Bakweri tradition.[17]

There are various hints on the way of life of the Buea people. They farmed plantations and 'cocoa' (cocoyams). The latter were probably of the kind called *lende* (*Colocasia esculenta*), not the more prolific *makawo* (*xanthosoma*) which were introduced to the coast by Merrick's fellow Baptists soon after his time. The Bakweri hunted in the forest, which then was thought to contain buffalo. They did not, however, seem at all familiar with the mountain above the level at which the grass begins (6,000 feet). The belief that the lava-strewn summit contains 'treasures' still survives at the present time in that story of *Efasamote*, the mountain deity, half man, half stone, whose sugar cane may be eaten on the spot, but if taken away, vanishes in mist through which the traveller is lost. This story still persists even though Bakweri hunters travel on the summit area regularly. The belief in the 'treasures' on its own, therefore, need not suggest unfamiliarity with the summit. A careful reading of the account does, however, suggest that the upper slopes were a novelty to Bakweri members of the party. It should be noted that they conspired to tell their people in the town that there really were treasures on the mountain.

Furthermore, the modern story of *Efasamote* is more consistent with knowledge of the mountain than was that told to Merrick. We are not nowadays asked to believe in piles of cloth, gunpowder, salt and dollars, but in magic farm-plots in the mist—something which the imaginative traveller could even now still find a possibility. Merrick himself provides a clue to the ignorance of the summit. He seems to have led his party up to the 10,000 foot ridge: the top of the main grassy slope visible above Buea, but was defeated by the cold. It is, in fact, very unlikely that 'men in loincloths' would have voluntarily braved the summit temperatures very often, if at all. With the advent of more shirts, singlets and wrappers, and the incentive of explorers' expeditions, times would change.

In the fashion of travellers of the day with their hosts, Merrick feels free to refer to Likenye as an 'incessant talker', 'garrulous', 'never tired of chattering', and as scarcely allowing anyone else to speak. Merrick does not, however, reflect on the impression he himself made. Merrick admits that during the day 'he embraced every opportunity of declaring the gospel', but the Buea people, not unnaturally perhaps, preferred to sing and dance. At the meeting with Likenye on 26 April, the chiefs had again 'to listen to the truth' from Merrick. It was when Likenye interrupted that he was dubbed an 'incessant talker'. Nevertheless, Merrick was a good observer, and what he saw as garrulousness, can easily be recognized as the Bakweri debating procedure known as *veleke.*[18] The principal speakers dance out their points, singing their arguments with a great show of power. Likenye could not have maintained his position without this skill. I have witnessed this musical rhetoric, and found it both dramatic and impressive and considerably less tedious than the conventional procedures of modern courts and debating chambers. Similarly, Burton, in his account of the mountain in 1862 scornfully dismisses the dance of the chief of Mapanja.[19]

When Merrick departed there was certainly some argument over the presents that he was to leave. Although this was worrying, it turned out to be harmless enough. The political structure of Buea is confirmed by the distribution of gifts. Likenye and 'three of the chief men' appear to have been treated as of approximately the same standing. The three would presumably be the headmen of the other three 'towns': the Upper Buea of Motande, the Middle Buea of Wotani, and the settlement of Likenye's collateral relatives. In the end they let Merrick leave when he had given them a certificate that he had visited the mountain from Buea, to show to any later white man. Their purpose is obscure. It is likely that they were asking for the same kind of 'book', or Treaty, as that which they had probably heard had enabled King William to become so rich on the coast.[20] It is possible that John King had told them it was an IOU for more goods. Whatever it was to be used for, it did not survive the decades before the next white man arrived.

The final palaver with Likenye's brother arose because he felt that his gift should have been of chiefly status. This man 'Bunggome' has left no echo in the genealogies of Buea, and he is no longer remembered by the Chief and elders. The answer can only be that he left no male descendants into modern times, or that they migrated elsewhere.

In sharp contrast is the case of the 'very old man' Ibungge, who lay seriously ill, and to whom Merrick preached on Sunday, 29 April. This must be Ewung' a Lionga, the father of that Mosisa Ewunge who signed Valdau's treaty in 1887. Ewunge is given as a brother of Likenye in the Buea genealogy. It is perhaps unlikely that 'a very old man' could be Likenye's full brother, unless Likenye himself was one of the youngest children of a large family. But if Likenye was a late child it is unlikely that he would have acquired the chiefly position, since even if Ewunge was too old, there would surely have been other brothers older than Likenye. Or, if we guess that Likenye had set up his own settlement separately from his brothers, we must wonder how his settlement had become so important that he was the leader of the chiefs of Buea. There are many possible ways of explaining such a situation. The most likely is that Ewunge was a cousin, not a brother. It is necessary, however, to have some respect for tradition that has preserved Ewunge's name, that of a person who must, if Merrick was right about his age, have been born in the eighteenth century. Ewunge's descendants lived near Wotani's descendants in the area of Buea cleared by the Germans. He was a member of Wonyalionga lineage, and Ewunge himself probably lived in that first settlement after Likenye's, which I have suggested was the site of the future Wonyalionga.

Bakweri Beliefs

On the same Sunday, Merrick conversed with a man from Wova, a village north of Buea (rendered by him in the form 'Boba'), who was said to have shot his wife's lover, and was subject to the rule of 'Dibumbe' (Bakweri *luumbe*). Merrick sees this as a secular law of banishment to the forest. In fact it was a spiritual effect: an inevitable fate or doom which overtook anyone who had killed by intention or accident.[21] Warriors had to be specially immunised against it. The sudden decline of the Isubu of Bimbia in the 1880's was blamed by them and by their neighbours on the accumulated *dibumbe* of many deaths and killings. Many have continued to believe this to the present day. It is of interest to see this word (in Isubu form) recorded by Merrick, in the heyday of Bimbia, before its commercial supremacy had withered.

In general, the religious ideas recorded by Merrick are little different from those observable in the recent past. Bunggome prayed to his deceased parents to protect him as the group were about to move out of the forest zone. This is still the normal procedure of hunters. The divinity name Obassa-Luba which Merrick records (as usual in coastal form) is still that used by the Bakweri for God (*Ovas'a Lova*). The woman seen in mourning was following well-known traditional rules.

In addition, on his way back from Buea, Merrick gives an account of a funeral rite at 'Minyari-Munggo'. It was performed for a man called Dibutu Lanja, and is of great interest because it is an account of the traditional *eyu* ceremony. For this reason it is treated in Annexe A.

Trade

The question of the trading position of Buea in 1844 now arises. The remarks of Likenye's brother at the libation throw light on one trade route. He complained that trade with Bimbia had to pass through Bwenga and Moliko. This route avoided Soppo, and it is interesting that Merrick's intention to proceed there was diverted by the need to visit the 'influential and wealthy old man' Manja of Moliko. In 1844 there was, of course, as yet no settlement at Victoria and all contact with the Bakweri would be from the Mungo River estuary across the Tiko Plain. The use of Bwenga as the trade outlet for Buea continued until 1894, when Kuva threatened to attack it.

Manja was wearing a large greatcoat (so large indeed that Merrick had to shake Manja's sleeve, as his hand was invisible), showing that trade clothing was already familiar to senior men on the route Merrick followed. It should be remembered that Bimbia had been in direct contact with foreign traders since the eighteenth century, and the whole Cameroon Coast had had moderately close contact with the outside world since 1826 and the arrival of the British interest at Fernando Po. One lesson of Merrick's account is that John King of Bonabile was still able to lead the party of travellers into the heart of Bakweri country, with no serious hostility being shown to any of them.

After Merrick

Nevertheless, this route was not used again by outsiders for forty years. After the establishment of Victoria the mountain dwellers were approached only through the Boana route. It was this way that Burton passed in 1862 to the top of the mountain *via* Mann Springs. Inner Bakweriland lay closed from view. The Baptist appetite for exploration wilted after Merrick, for some twenty years. The missionaries and Creole settlers at Victoria seemed to dread the interior, and looked towards

Douala. Quintin Thomson's trip in 1872 as far as Wonjongo was treated as something of a revelation.[22]

Some time in the period after Merrick's visit Likenye of Buea died and was succeeded by Kuva. We know that during the same time the agricultural economy of the area was transformed by the *xanthosoma* cocoyam (*makawo*), introduced by the Baptists at Douala and Victoria. It was cultivated by the women and flourished in the Bakweri area on the Buea side of the Mountain to such an extent that it overshadowed the men's plantain crop.

Livestock also benefitted from the cocoyam waste. The establishment of Victoria brought a market for food-stuffs, and the growth of trade. Gunpowder and muskets travelled up the mountain. By the 1870's the hold of Bimbia traders on the coastal access to the Bakweri had begun to weaken. The interior villages began to send men down towards the coast. About 1880 it was Soppo which seemed to be leading the movement. Woloa wo Fike, one of their chiefs, was thought to be behind trouble on the Bamboko coast in 1882. That it was Buea that later clashed directly with the new colonial power, and not Soppo, was probably a result of a combination of factors. Soppo and Buea were, as now, settlements of about the same size (although Buea was probably slightly bigger), but Buea had the advantage of an extra 300 feet of altitude overlooking Soppo, with the whole mountain at its back. Soppo always ran the risk of being squeezed between the coast and Buea. In addition, by the 1890's Great Soppo had a new chief, Sako. Kuva of Buea was probably the senior in age, and he had taken on the role of main threat to the coast.

2. Swedes and Germans 1886

External Influences

It is not generally remembered today that the earliest modern commercial enterprise on the Cameroon Mountain was Swedish.[23] The Swedes, Knutson and Valdau, arrived at the end of 1883. Making Bibundi on the Bamboko coast their base, they explored the whole mountain area. In the course of their journeys they discovered the presence of wild-rubber vines, and even trained Bakweri to collect the latex. They established a trading factory at Bibundi and visited most of the Bakweri villages including Mapanja, Buea, Soppo and Lisoka. After the Germans annexed Douala in 1884, the knowledge gathered by the Swedes in the hinterland was invaluable. In the months of the 'scramble', when the rival treaty-making activities of the German Zöller and the Pole Rogozinski (on behalf of the British) nearly led to clashes, the Germans were greatly assisted by Valdau and Knutson. They were officially accredited to represent Governor von Soden in a letter of 14 October 1885 to the President of the Court at Victoria.[24] During this period the route from Victoria through Boana, Likombe, Bwasa, and Mimbia-Wokpaongo to Buea became fairly well-trodden, and reports of the bargaining at Buea even reached the German and British press.[25]

It must have been at this time that the people of Buea, through exposure to new riches from the competing Europeans, began to develop a certain self-confidence. Owing to the continued British occupation of Victoria itself until 1887, the mountain remained virtually isolated from German official power. At the end of 1886, however, the Chancellor of Kamerun, the second in command to Governor von Soden, made a tour of the mountain. The Chancellor was Jesko von Puttkamer, then aged thirty-one, who was himself to become Governor nine years later. He had represented von Soden in the inquiries into the precise boundaries of the Victoria settlement, during the rather wretched negotiations for the sale of the Baptist territory. [26]

Puttkamer's expedition included Dr Krabbe, an official who was soon to be the first German District Officer at Victoria. They left from Victoria on 11th December, and went via Bonjongo, passing the ruins of the English Mission established by Comber and Quintin Thomson in the 1870's but abandoned for some years, and reached Mapanja. There they stayed in 'the hospitable house' of the Swede Valdau.[27] The village had some 400 inhabitants. Next day, 12 December, they set out 'for Buea, the chief village of Bakweri country'. They passed a fine market-place at Lekumbi (Likombe). This village had had a brief notoriety in the treaty-making months, but Puttkamer reported: 'the still flourishing village of the time of Zöller and Rogozinski has been burnt because of a tribal feud, and the inhabitants have fled. Every week a big market still takes place here.'[28]

He continued: 'After a march of one hour, through a strikingly fine landscape on good forest paths, we reached the little village of Lower Buassa, then, after two more hours, Mimbia. The expedition went through a deep forest valley, and climbing again, marched through a flourishing high forest. After crossing the Mossola, a rapid mountain stream with crystal-clear water, we reached the long stretched-out village of Chief Betongo of Upper Buea, and soon the expedition was in the big palaver ground in Lower Buea of the paramount chief (*Oberhäuptling*) Kuwa [sic], one of the most respected men of the mountain.'

The old crossing of the Mossola (Mosole) stream to which Puttkamer refers lies just below the Secretariat. However, there seems to be a misunderstanding about the chieftaincy of Upper Buea. *Betongo* is first of all a printer's error for *Letongo* who signs later documents with Kuva and the chiefs of Lower Buea. This man was, furthermore, Lotonge Molie, the son of the Molio who founded Wonyamolio in Buea near to the main Lower Buea settlement. By now, however, Kuva's name clearly outshone those of other chiefs in the eyes of foreigners, and possibly Lotonge, who as we shall see appears to have been second in seniority to Kuva in Lower Buea, had been sent to meet Puttkamer in Upper Buea, and thus, by chance or design, the error arose.

We know nothing more about this meeting between Kuva and Puttkamer, the two most famous names in Buea's history. The Germans stayed over two full days, and left again for Mapanja on 15 December, 1886. On the 17th, they climbed *via* Burton's route to Mann Springs; on the 19th down to Mapanja again; finally on 21 December, 1886, they returned to Victoria.

After his trip, Puttkamer reported on the Bakweri in less contemptuous terms than those he maintained later in his official life, which at the time of his removal from office in 1906 had become the standard German view, and which were transmitted into our own days. But here for the first time we read of 'degeneration', a term too often used to excuse the dispossession of the people. Like Burton, Puttkamer came to regard the mountain as wasted on the Bakweri. To these European travellers of the nineteenth century, sudden death from malaria was a constant reality. Their covetous eyes on the supposedly 'fever-free' slopes thus had a certain life-or-death quality. In addition, Puttkamer was to be stirred later by the economic possibilities. As far as the Bakweri are concerned Puttkamer was always a hostile witness. Thus his remarks on the Bakweri situation in 1886 are very informative, and his praise of the Buea people was praise indeed.

Puttkamer on the Bakweri

The text follows in translation:[29]

> The Bakwiri tribe, the most populous on the Cameroon Mountain, are bordered on the north west by Bumboko country with its chief village Bomana, where the western and north-western slopes of the mountain descend. Northward begins Bakundu country. South-east of the Bakwiri are the Bimbia people, who form the transition to the Dualla of Kamerun.

> The Bakwiri all speak the same language, which together with that of the Bumboko is related to the Asubu [sic] spoken in Bimbia, and to Dualla. The Bakwiri were cut off from the coast by the Victoria people who immigrated from Fernando Po, and they are at a lower level of civilisation than the coastal dwellers. Lack of water, and the uncleanliness connected with it, cause a frequently recognizable physical degeneration. Dreadful superstition is common, with its frequent bloody consequences. In the lower-lying villages, bananas are cultivated principally, and in the higher ones, cocoyams. Pigs, dogs, goats and fowls are abundant, and in certain places cattle also. The Bakwiri have only in recent years begun to exploit the basic products of their country: wild coffee and rubber. This trade is completely monopolized by the markets of Bimbia. A notable trade route (on which the Bakwiri villages are merely staging posts) runs via Buea and Sopo [sic] in a north-easterly direction to Bakundu ba Nambele on the Mungo [= Banga]. The centre of the country in every respect is Buea village which can, on its own, muster 400 armed men. Its inhabitants stand out from their fellow tribesmen through their powerful, well-built bodies, their courage and their skill in hunting, as well as through their cleanliness. The latter is probably due to the excellent mountain water that flows in plenty through their country. Although still in the forest, the settlements stretch for a kilometre over open, undulating, grassy slopes (*Matten*), which provide rich fodder for the astonishingly fine cattle. This place, being, as it is, nearly always subject to mountain breezes, without the detectable cold and tiresome mist of the higher mountain sites, appears to beg an especially favourable field for a Mission. If a European settlement were once established here, a health station for convalescents would also develop. Buea is most conveniently reached *via* Mbinga [Bwenga] and Soppo.

Puttkamer's view of Buea testifies to the excellent topographical conditions which made this settlement already so populous. The contrasting waterlessness of the north-eastern Bakweri area (to which he refers) remains a problem even today.[30] His view of the Buea climate, however, was that of a December tourist. Later he was to experience the rain and mists of most of the year, which led his subordinates to refer to the Schloss he built as the Cloud Throne (*Wolkenthron*) and the Realm of mists (*Nebelheim*).

The overland trade route to Bakundu-ba-Nambele (Banga) on the Mungo had been developed only since the Baptist Comber had reached that place in 1877.[31] This led to the establishment in 1879 of a Mission station, in the charge of a couple called Richardson. From there, the way through to Buea *via* Lisoka had been travelled to provide a land route to Victoria.[32] Puttkamer shrewdly noted the effect of Victoria and Bimbia in blocking off the Bakweri from contact with the coast. The increasing pressure of the big villages of Buea and Soppo upon the coast routes was, in fact, already under way.

The Sale of Buea 1887

Valdau and Soden

Two months after Puttkamer's visit there occurred the extraordinary episode of the sale of Buea. The Swede, Valdau wrote from his station on the mountain to Governor von Soden at Douala as follows:

> Mapanja, 15th Feb. 1887.
>
> Your Excellency!
>
> Yesterday I succeeded in buying whole Bwea for you. As the trade within Victoria and the mountain-towns since long time is cut off by the fight within Bonjongo and Bosumbo I got it to good price...

With his letter he enclosed agreements signed by the Chiefs of Upper and Lower Buea, apparently selling their lands for a total of £28. This remarkable document was confirmed by a further agreement at Buea on 4 March 1887, which was written in German. From these papers flowed all subsequent German claims in the Buea area, and from von Soden's title, all others have been derived. These documents are printed in full in Annexe C, to which reference should be made.

The arrangement between Soden and Valdau was clearly the first step in the implementation of the plan for a convalescent station that Puttkamer had embodied in his reports. This was, however, also the time of the first acquisition of plantation lands, and later von Soden was directly involved in plantation investment. The project of buying Buea was certainly a bold one. The Bakweri area was not even under administration as yet. Victoria itself was not officially handed over by the British Consul to the German Governor until 28 March, 1887. Valdau was the person best placed to negotiate a sale.[33] He had the trade network. He also had the confidence of the people, whom he had turned into tappers of wild rubber and gatherers of forest products. For a brief period rather merry gangs of Bakweri swelled Valdau's fairly informal labour force. He and Knutson had been back to Europe in 1886, and had obtained a home-based partner and further capital. The firm of Knutson, Valdau and Heilborn was established as a result with its head office in Stockholm. The two active Swedes on the spot established factories on the Meme at Lobe, and palm-oil was brought to their Bibundi factory. Valdau was the first commercial man to use Cameroon labour in his enterprises, rather than Kru or Gold Coasters.

The critical date of 17 February 1887 was to set in motion the forces which ended Bakweri independence, although it could not have seemed like that at the time. No certain recollection of the event remains in the traditional memory: all was wiped out by the disaster of 1894. A detailed consideration of the documents follows.

The Document of 17 February, 1887

Valdau's letter and agreements are handwritten in an English heavily affected by pidgin. There is a covering letter and two agreements of sale signed respectively by the chiefs of Upper and Lower Buea. There is also a list of the trade-goods required by the people. Valdau notes the significant fact that Upper and Lower Buea were enemies, and had to sign separately. The identities of the two sets of signatories can for the most part clearly be established, and they throw considerable light on the structure of Buea at the time.

Valdau makes the further significant statement that a fight had broken out between Bonjongo and Bosumbo (Bufumbu) blocking the trade between Victoria and the mountain villages. As a result, Valdau says, the Buea chiefs were prevailed upon to sell their land for a relatively cheap price in goods. The Governor was to send the goods to Mokundange at the coast. Valdau would transfer them to Mapanja, where the Buea people would come down to receive them. Valdau adds items of miscellaneous news for the Governor, mainly about the misdemeanours of other traders. A Calabar firm had employed a dismissed Cameroonian as a clerk at Bibundi, and was selling rum there. More seriously, Edgerley, the Victoria trader, had been selling arms of precision (Snider rifles) to Buea for cows. The Germans, like the other colonial powers, were always opposed to the sale of modern weapons to people under their jurisdictions.

What did Valdau really buy? He was convinced it was, in his words: 'whole Bwea'. A study of the texts of the two contracts shows that the two groups of Bakweri signatories each sold 'our part of the territory of Bwea' to Governor von Soden, and declared that from the day's date (17 February, 1887), he was 'the legal and legitimate owner of the named territory'. This statement is quite unequivocal. The next sentence then states that 'the houses, palmtrees, farms and other private property' of the people of Buea should be 'possessed of further on [sic] as they have been up to this day'. To Valdau this private property would no doubt seem easy enough to determine. For the people of Buea, 'our part of the territory of Bwea' and their 'private property' could not be so easily distinguished. The broad statement and the exception would almost appear to contradict each other: they were taking back with one hand what they were giving with the other. Here was their trading friend Valdau offering goods for something which was unsaleable. No interpreter could have translated such an idea into Bakweri. Valdau and the Governor would not be able to make use of all that land. The white men could build or hunt or collect rubber; in time the effect of the goods would wear off, and a new contribution could be made. If the chiefs were aware of what they were doing, they must have felt like those legendary tricksters who, after the Second World War, had offered to sell the Eiffel Tower or the Tower of London to American tourists. To sell Buea was inconceivable, and so they signed it cheerfully away for £28 sterling.

The actual cost to Valdau and von Soden was much less. The document is obscure, but the arrangement was apparently that Upper and Lower Buea each signed as agreeing to receive £14 before 1st June, thus making up the total of £28. Then the chiefs and Valdau worked out a list of goods which would be equal in value to this sum, not at coast prices but at the inland prices. This list totals, in fact, only £25 13s 24d. It is possible, of course, that they had already had £2 6s 8d worth on account. In addition the sum has included in it £1 5s 0d worth of cloth to pay Valdau's ten carriers to bring the goods up to Mapanja, as well as 15 shillings worth for only three carriers to accompany the Buea people from Mapanja to Buea, and come back again. The interpreter also got blue baft out of it to the value of £2. The payment for the land itself turned out therefore to be assessed at only £21 13s 4d. Of this the 'people' were to get 11 kilograms of tobacco, worth 110 shillings, and eight fathoms of cloth, worth 13s 4d (nine pence per yard), totalling the sum of £2 3s 4d.

The kings and chiefs, of whom fourteen signed, were to get goods worth £19 10s 0d in all. Their modest needs on this momentous occasion were ten pieces of striped satin, ten kegs of gunpowder, five cap guns,[34] two demijohns of rum and one kilogram of tobacco. King William of Bimbia, as long ago as 1858, had sold his not very clear title to Victoria, where he did not live, for £2000.[35]

The Document of 4 March 1887

Valdau's letter about this bargain did not leave Victoria by sea (as his postscript shows) until 24 February, 1887. Next day Governor von Soden had already registered it in Douala. There is no record of the Governor's reply, but he must have set off almost on receiving the documents, for on 4th March, he was signing an official contract with the chiefs in Buea. It was written first in pencil on his headed paper, with *Kamerun* (Douala) crossed out and *Buea* added. It was then written over in ink. This time Sam Steane of Victoria was the interpreter. Valdau and the trader Vanselow were also present. The new text in German states that the chiefs have received 'the contracted purchase price' from the Governor 'for all the land in Buea (Upper, Middle and Lower Buea) in so far as it is not cultivated and inhabited by them'. The chiefs agreed, however, that they would not sell any of the exempted cultivated or inhabited land to anyone else, without reference to the Governor or his successors. No other land transactions would now be valid without such reference. They signed also that the agreement had been translated and that they had understood all its provisions. The text ends in a strange manner saying: 'The first chief of Buea Kuba expressly declares that he takes full responsibility on behalf of those of his subchiefs who have not appeared today and have not signed, and will see to it that they receive their share of the price'. Yet among the list of signatories for Upper and Lower Buea which follow, Kuva's name is itself absent.

Then come the signatures of the interpreter Sam Steane, and the witnesses Valdau, Vanselow and von Soden. Underneath was written (in German): 'A copy has not been left in Buea for lack of time', and then: 'The going over with ink was done later'. These notes are in Soden's hand and signed again by him.[36]

A suspicious element of haste appears in this agreement. It does not mention the amount of the selling price again, and it is to be assumed that the £28 of Valdau's first agreements still stood. It appears, however, that the goods were paid over on this occasion, since Kuva was to pass on shares to certain of his chiefs who had not been present. Yet Valdau and Soden omitted to get Kuva's signature. Lower Buea's senior representative was Letongo (Lotonge). This could hardly have been a mere oversight. It seems to be fairly clear that Kuva was not even present. The reference to 'der erste Häuptling von Buea' the 'first chief of Buea' is to be noted, since the usual term for a 'paramount chief', as the Germans considered Kuva to be, was 'Oberhäuptling'. In the pencilled text the name 'Kuba' is added above the line. In the inked-over text the-name is fully incorporated. One wonders if the term 'first chief' was intended to refer to Lotonge. Perhaps the final clause was originally drafted to bind Kuva in his absence. Then perhaps it was felt necessary to put in Kuva's name since he could not be classed as a subchief. The deed is worded so that one would expect to find Kuva's mark and few or none for his subchiefs. Yet the facts are the exact reverse. Most of his subchiefs signed (all were important people) but Kuva did not.

The ambiguity of this document suggests an awareness in Buea that the simple contract with Valdau had become a serious and possibly troublesome matter. The trade goods were too tempting to be refused, but Kuva somehow did not sign. The German Governor still had Kuva's mark on Valdau's first document. The new contract merely cleared up the question of the exact reversionary rights over the inhabited and cultivated areas. The wording also gave a slightly more strict interpretation of these areas than did Valdau's agreement. The difference must have been almost impossible to render in the necessarily free translations of the interpreter, Sam Steane, but it may have begun to raise doubts.

The Governor left Buea. The official handing over of Victoria by the British Consul occurred on 28 March. Von Soden wrote to Bismarck in Germany on 14 April that he had bought the 'greater part' of Buea for 'about 6–800 Marks in money'. He went on to say that the land was at the disposal of the Imperial Government at cost price. From now on, Governor von Soden in person was treated officially as the owner of Buea. In 1888 he tried to exchange it for a piece of Government land at Bota. By 1890 he had given a piece of it to the Basel Mission to set up a station, a gift on which the legal title of the Mission came to rest.[37] None of this could have been realised by the chiefs of Buea, to whom we now turn.

The Buea Signatories of the Documents of Sale[38]

The identities of those who put their marks to Valdau's document of 17 February for *Lower Buea* were as follows:

1. *Kuva*—Named 'King' by Valdau, this was, of course, the son of Likenye and great-uncle of Chief Endeley III of Buea.
2. *Letongo*—This was Lotonge Molie, head of the settlement of Wonyamolio. This man is also styled 'King' on both the treaties of sale. The line of Molio was, as we have already seen, collateral to

that of Kuva, and was descended from Likenye's brother Monyoke, The Wonyamolio lineage now lives near Kuva's descendants, at the Buea *Mbando* stone. One of their elders, Kulu a Njome, whose grandfather was a brother of Lotonge, died in December 1968. Lotonge's importance at this period is clear, not only from his receiving the title 'King', but because Puttkamer had already, as we saw, erroneously mistaken him for Chief of Upper Buea. There is no reason to think that he was in competition with Kuva. The title of 'King' is discussed later. He would seem to have been the most senior of the Lower Buea elders.

3. *Molue*—This was Molu' a Lionge and thus the brother of Likenye, and an uncle of Kuva. He was styled 'Chief' as were the remaining signatories. The problem of Likenye's supposed brothers has been touched on already. One (Ewunge) was 'very old' in 1844, and yet here is one able to make a mark on an agreement in 1887. Molue's survival is quite plausible. He could have been much younger than Likenye, who would himself (had he lived) have been only 77, on the most plausible dating. To have produced the old Ewunge as well, Likenye's father would have needed a child-begetting life of 40 years (say from the age of 20) or younger, to about 60 which in polygamous chiefly families, even today, can hardly be said to be unheard of. Molue lived at the upper end of Lower Buea, near the Upper Buea settlement by the present Prime Minister's office area.
4. *Ndele*—This was Kuva's brother and successor: Endeli a Likenye (Endeley I, 1899-1913), father of Matthias Lifafe (Endeley II, 1913-25) and Gervasius Mbele (Endeley III, 1925-). Endeley II was the father of Dr E. M. L. Endeley, Leader of the House, of Justice Sam Endeley, and of Mr David Endeley.
5. *Mesombe*—This was Mesomb' a Likenye, another brother of Kuva.
6. *Motutu*—This was Motutu Ekombe of Gbefofo. This settlement was founded behind Lower Buea proper by Motutu's grandfather Efofo a Jonde, who came from Ewongo village.
7. *Name*—This was Nam' a Molie, brother of Lotonge, whose son, Evamb' a Name died in 1967.
8. *Metumba*—This was a sister's son of Lotonge. He was Metumbe, son of Mwende of Bulu village. His mother was Namondo mo Molie. Metumbe's own daugher, Susannah Nanyonge Metumbe, who still lives in Buea, became second wife of Endeley II and mother of Mr David Endeley.
9. *Mosokko*—Mosoke came originally from either Ekonjo or Gbasa

village, but lived in Lower Buea. His grandson, Sergeant Sam Mbomb' a Linonge la Mosoko, is married to Anna daughter of Chief Endeley III

10. *Kange*—This was Kang' a Mosisa, whose further relationships are not known.

Of these ten men of Lower Buea, only Lotonge, Molue, Endeli and Metumba also signed off the second contract of 4 March. In addition, two people also signed this second document:

11. *Njaki*—who cannot be identified under this name; and
12. *Ewokise*—who was Evakis'a Manga, and who eight years later, on Kuva's death in 1895, was to go with Endeley I to negotiate peace with the Germans. Evakise came from an influential family of independent origin. His descendants live in the Vasingi-Moli area.

For *Upper Buea* only four people signed. They did so on both agreements. They were:

13. *Epa*—who is styled 'King' on the documents, the other three being called 'chiefs'. He was Ekpa Wotani of Wondongo, a settlement then in the area of the Bismarck Fountain. His son Motinda Ekpa was, as has been already noted, appointed chief of Buea for a while by the Germans, on the death of Endeley I. The destruction of Upper Buea was a bitter blow to the family, for Wondongo was joined with Lower Buea. Its foundation went back to a daughter's son who had returned to Buea from Soppo: Lambe la Ndonge.
14. *Manga* or *Manja*—was Meange me Lambe, an uncle of Ekpa.
15. *Mosissa*—was Mosis' Ewunge, the son of that Ewung' a Lionge who, in 1844 as an old man, had been visited by Merrick. Mosisa had built near Ekpa.
16. *Dingundu*—was Lingondo la Ekambi, of Gbekambi. His brother Isoli built at the site of the Prime Minister's Lodge.

The Structure of Buea

To summarise the position in 1887: Ekpa Wontani signed as 'King' of Upper Buea; Kuva and Lotonge signed as 'Kings' in Lower Buea. The remaining men on both sides were listed as 'Chiefs'. Kuva was, however, as all sources agree, the senior 'King'. These titles are not indigenous. They are symbols in English of the rights these men claimed when dealing with Europeans: the right to 'dashes' of a special size. We learn from Valdau that in 1887 Upper and Lower Buea were at enmity. The fluctuations in the numbers of Lower Buea signatories between the two agreements could suggest that Lower Buea was less keen on the sale than Upper Buea. Their £14 was also apparently divided among many more people.

The relationships between the various elements which made up Buea can be explained as follows. There were, on one side, Kuva and his brothers, together with most of his collateral relatives. They were descended from Kuva's grandfather Lionge (Wonyalionga), and, apart from Kuva himself, Lotonge was the most influential of them. Then there were certain people who had settled in Kuva's area from elsewhere. This includes the Gbefofo people. On the other side, there was Ekpa and his relatives (Wondongo) in Upper Buea in the present station, whose ultimate Buea ancestry was independent of Lionga's group, and who had also strong connexions with Soppo. In addition there were the groups (of which Gbekambi was one) along the Mosole stream from the present site of the Prime Minister's Lodge down to the House of Assembly. All these were descended from Motande, a supposed brother of Vefonge, and thus an ancestor separate from that of Wonyalionga. The two blocs were very blurred however. Thus Mosisa Ewunge lived in Upper Buea although he was Kuva's cousin.

On the second agreement Kuva, as we saw, did not sign, but his brother Endeli did, as well as Lotonge and Lotonge's sister's son. Those who did not sign the second time were mostly hangers-on, or perhaps (for example, Molue?) old. The notable absentee was Motutu of Gbefofo. The appearance of Evakise on the second occasion is of interest in view of his later historical importance.

The division between Upper and Lower Buea was, then, not a sharp one geographically or genealogically. To some extent it was, no doubt, exaggerated by competitiveness in seeking gifts from Europeans. Geographically one could better speak of an Upper, a Middle and a Lower Buea, and some travellers did so. Since Ekpa's place was in Middle Buea this adds a further confusion. For practical purposes geographical 'Middle Buea' was included in political 'Upper Buea'. We cannot find evidence of all the present sections of Buea in these documents.[39] We shall deal further with the pre-conquest Buea later. It is sufficient here to note that from the ravine on the road to the Mountain Hotel to the end of the present Stranger Quarter, Buea stretched in a continuous line of small settlements.

Interpreters and Others

Valdau's interpreter was Mbua Moki of Mapanja. His reputation as an elephant hunter is remembered. No doubt he sold ivory to Valdau. He died in the first decade of this century. Valdau's witness was Ndive Eko of Wonjongo, in the time of the late Chief Efesoa. The interpreter for the second document was the Victorian, Sam Steane. The Edgerley of Victoria who was illegally selling arms of precision in Buea was Samuel. His father, Samuel Eyamba Edgerley was a Calabar man who married Julia Wilson, from one of the original families that settled from Fernando Po. The original Joseph Wilson of Popo went to Fernando Po with Captain Owen in 1826 from Sierra Leone. The younger Sam, seller of arms, was a successful trader. His elder sister, Rose Edgerley, had married the Missionary George Grenfell, and moved with him to the Congo.[40]

Finally, we may note that Bonjongo and Bussumbu near Victoria were in conflict. Six years later a conflict between Bussumbu and Boana was still in existence. It may be that this was the same one. The area had been disturbed at least since the death of Ngomb' a Bila at Mokundange in 1882. Kuva was soon to be accused of meddling in events of this kind. We begin to hear of his misdeeds from Lisoka almost to the coast. During his eight more years of life, he was to become an especially hated name to the missionaries and Christians at the coast. He was to see a German Governor, in person, visiting Buea after suing for peace. Yet it could already be said of Kuva, as of Richard III of England, 'Dickon, thy master, is bought and sold'.

The Defeat of Gravenreuth

Preliminaries

In order to understand the lull between the German occupation of Victoria in 1887 and their first attempts to administer the mountain area, it should be remembered that the new Protectorate of Kamerun was very short of money. Governor von Soden's tenure of office (1885-1890) was marked, as far as the interior was concerned, by the dispatch of a number of partially independent expeditions, subsidized by the home government, which were not easy for the Governor to control. In West Cameroon, the expedition of Dr Schwartz passed up the Mungo to Mundame at the end of 1885, went overland to Mambanda and Kumba, but turned back at *Kimendi* (Ikiliwindi).[41] The expeditions of Dr Zintgraff were more extensive: in the hinterland of Douala in 1886, then to the Ndian side of the Cameroon Mountain in 1887. He did not, as a result, pass through the Buea area, and in January 1888 he set up his station at Kumba. From then on he was preoccupied with his explorations north to Bamenda.[42] Soden had no resources for the opening up of the Mountain.

Soden went on leave in 1889, and various people acted as Governor through 1890: the Commissioner for Togo, von Zimmerer, then von Puttkamer (now the Lagos Consul), then Government Assessor Leist. In April 1890 Dr Preuss, a botanist, arrived at Douala, on his way to join Zintgraff's expedition, and to take charge of the Barombi Station at Kumba. In that year, Captain the Freiherr von Gravenreuth, returned on leave from the East African Protectorate Force, prior to taking up special duties in Kamerun.[43] Both men were now on the first steps of the course which would bring them finally to Buea: the botanist was to bury the soldier. Knutson and Valdau had been flourishing, and they now had palm-oil collecting points at Lobeland in the Meme area, with their main factory still at Bibundi. Swedish scientists were to come out to their trading zone, among whom would be a botanist. In July, Valdau reached the lake north of Kumba, which he named Lake Soden.[44] On 2 December 1890, Zimmerer returned as full Governor of Kamerun. 1891 began with the news of Zintgraff's disastrous Battle of Mankon which took place on 31 January, the first of many catastrophes of Zimmerer's term of office, which he came to blame on the irresponsible leadership of the subsidized expeditions.[45] The year ended with the first Battle of Buea.

The course of events in Buea began with the establishment of the Basel Mission there at the end of 1890. Soden had encouraged the Mission to settle, and gave them the land out of his supposed ownership of the town. Soden was not even in Kamerun when the Mission representatives went there. Kuva and the chiefs let them have ground on the present site of the old church and Mission buildings. The Mission may have mentioned Govenor Soden's name: in later years the chiefs said that this piece was the only land they had given the Governor.[46]

Building of the Mission compound must have begun quickly, for next year it was properly laid out. It was founded specifically as a health and convalescent station, and the Douala firms contributed 'considerable amounts'.[47] In July 1891 the mission reported that already a little house was ready for convalescents (*Erholungsbeduerftigen*). The people were still reluctant to attend school and church.[48] No permanent missionary was established yet, although one called Scholten had visited. There was, however, a lay teacher from Victoria there, the treacherous 'catechist' of Bakweri legend. The catechist showed a righteous zeal in castigating the disrespectful heathen.

On 1 January 1891, the botanist Dr Preuss arrived, having left Kumba and stayed in the Mission House. Dr Preuss noted: 'relations with the natives are satisfactory, although a little caution is required, given the rough (*rauhen*) character and forward behaviour (*dreisten Benehmen*) of the populations'. He found meat and cocoyams plentiful, but few plantains and no fruit. He concentrated on his studies. Insects were scarce, and there were no butterflies, due, he thought, to lack of sunshine. Lizards were rare, but snails were numerous, and chameleons abundant. He began sending off specimens. After 19 February he made weather observations.[49]

Buea, he further reported, was about 950 metres in altitude and stretched in an arc for four kilometres along the mountain. He estimated that there were 1,500 inhabitants, with 600 men capable of bearing arms, of whom 400 had guns. 'They busy themselves enthusiastically with hunting and palavers, and wage wars with their neighbours at every opportunity. In their relations with the white man [i.e. himself] they are impudent and unashamed in their confidence in their superior numbers, and they make continual vexations for him, although they are quite glad to have him, or rather his tobacco and his cloth, in the village. They have not as yet learnt his power.'[50]

Meanwhile von Gravenreuth had arrived at the coast in charge of an expedition.[51] It was intended to strike north from Douala, even to the Chad. Gravenreuth had recruited troops along the coast. Some he got from Togo, but a high proportion were obtained by calling in at Whydah in Dahomey and purchasing slaves from King Behanzin: 300 men and 100 women. The men were then bonded to serve as soldiers for no pay until the 'redemption price' had been paid off. They may have welcomed this novel arrangement at the time, although some years later they mutinied. The arrival of Gravenreuth's expedition at Douala must have seemed to officials there to be a useful way of pacifying rebellious tribes. Governor von Zimmerer was away, and the Acting Governor was von Schuckmann.[52] In February, the Abo people of Miang above Douala had blocked their river to Chancellor Leist. As a kind of exercise, therefore, Gravenreuth and his two fellow-officers, von Volckamer and von Stetten, set out in October to punish the Miang people. The expedition was a great success. On its return Leist and Gravenreuth recommended sending the expedition up to Buea. The excuse given after its unexpected disaster was that disturbing reports had come from Dr Preuss, and that Kuva's people were becoming a dangerous threat to peace. Von Schuckmann's report follows, in translation, without quotation marks, until the end of the chapter.[53]

Report of Acting Governor von Schuckmann, 18 November 1891

According to news reaching Kamerun in the middle of last month [October, 1891] the Buea people had burnt the big village of Momange [Lisoka], killing five men, and had laid waste other smaller villages. Chancellor Leist found the rumour confirmed in Victoria. Dr Preuss reported to him there the further news that the Buea people frequently disturbed the peace of the mountain, and had instigated an uprising among the mountain tribes. Some men from Buea had already come down to Mokundo, [Mokunda] or Boando near Victoria, in order to catch Victoria people there. The Buea people had even threatened to attack Victoria.

Freiherr v. Gravenreuth, who had accompanied Chancellor Leist to Victoria, was likewise of the opinion that something had to be done forthwith to restore peace in the Mountain, and above all to put a stop to any spread of the movement. After consideration I decided to set out with a strong detachment in order to calm the people by the *demonstration* of our existing power *in a peaceful Palaver,* and to warn them by the imposition of not too severe a punishment. The Buea population were to be informed of my peaceful intentions by the Missionary Scholten, who had formerly been active for some time in Buea. Herr Scholten promised me to go up to Buea for this purpose from the Möwe-See [Mungo estuary] and to reach there before the expedition.

As I did not underestimate the strength of the powerful Buea people, I ordered Fhr v. Gravenreuth to provide for all contingencies. He declared that with 150 men and a Maxim gun he was quite strong enough to crush any opposition. The expedition of v. Gravenreuth, together with v. Stetten, v. Volckamer, Dr Richter, myself, 150 expedition personnel, and 10 Kru policemen, were brought to Victoria on 3 November by H. M. Cruiser Habicht. N.C.O. Szcadock being ill I had Gardener Pfeil take part in the expedition.

Relying on the effect of the missionary and of our peaceful intentions, we marched off; and at 3 p.m. on the 5th November we reached about 1,500 metres from Buea. We heard hunting horns and drums, and Gravenreuth had the flag unfurled as a sign of our peaceful intention.

After taking a few unoccupied obstructions, the column reached a double barricade of stakes with stones piled up two feet high. The leaders were without weapons, when suddenly a hail of fire burst out against us from the palisade. The blacks in front of us scattered to the sides; the Maxim gun was to be fired; it didn't work. Dr Richter and Lt v. Stetten were slightly wounded. Fhr v. Gravenreuth sent Stetten's detachment on a flank attack through the bamboo thicket that surrounded us, and had them fire a salvo from the path. This resulted in such firing that it was very dangerous for us whitemen on the road. For the black soldiers had pressed into the thicket on the side, and although they could not see five steps, they were firing in all directions. Only a few of my Krumen stood firm under the heavy fire on the path with the whites, firing calmly. Then, as Stetten's detachment under Gardener Pfeil began to fire vigorously from the flank, Fhr v. Gravenreuth gave the order to charge. Gravenreuth, together with myself, five Krumen and some expedition soldiers broke out: the best Kruman fell, the headman collapsed wounded. About twenty yards in front of the barricade we had some slight cover, and we reloaded. The shooting from the barricade stopped for a moment. We leapt out of cover for the last run up, and were met with terrible fire. Fhr v. Gravenreuth collapsed, hit in the chest, fifteen yards from the barricade. As I took hold of him he received a second shot in the back. I dragged him back. Ten yards behind us I found my servant, one Kruman, and an expedition soldier, cowering on the ground with no other black soldier near by. The men helped me bring Gravenreuth back. His head had hung as if lifeless immediately he received the shots, and in my opinion he was already dead. Hardly had Dr Richter confirmed the death, than Stetten's detachment appeared from the flank on the barricade. They took it by storm and pressed on. The black soldiers from the thicket now plunged forward. As no other European was available I ran forward, halted them at the barricade and stopped them from firing indiscriminately ahead on the Stetten detachment. We had begun up-rooting the barricade when Lieutenant v. Volckamer, who had been in the rear with the baggage, appeared with his men at the run and drove forward in a spirited manner. The objective was the Mission House where Dr Preuss was living. Contact was quickly made with the advance detachment. The bodies of Gravenreuth and two black soldiers, and the baggage, were brought up later. The column retreated to the Mission House which was 20 minutes away. Its surroundings had been already scoured by the advance detachment. Von Volckamer and Dr Preuss were there. Von Stetten had meanwhile gone back to lead the rearguard. The baggage arrived in an orderly march. All round licked the flames of burning huts.

Next day [6 November] the two kings' compounds, which were further on, were burnt down under the supervision of Lt v. Stetten, without serious opposition. On the return march v. Stetten received at point blank a shot that wounded him in the upper arm. The military command then passed to Lt v. Volckamer. On the 7 November various patrols were sent out to conduct further operations, and to capture enemy stragglers. The town was completely in our hands. We seized a lot of cattle, barrels of gunpowder, and other supplies. Dr Preuss estimated that we had 600 guns against us at the barricade.

The old bridge over the ravine where Gravenreuth was killed.
Site of the Battle of Buea.

Apart from the tragic loss of Frh v. Gravenreuth and the wounding of v. Stetten, we had only lost three black soldiers. I cannot estimate the enemy losses, but they are in any case slight. Various bloodspots were visible, and today the report came in that a 'big chief' has died from his wounds.

[In the expectation that everything would go off peacefully, Gravenreuth had left part of the ammunition in Victoria. There were only sixty rounds per man.] We had to think of the return march. With Gravenreuth killed, and the second-in-command out of action, I dared not take the previous route, which could have been designed for ambushes. After the behaviour of the Dahomey men at the battle, it was to be feared that the loss of one or other of the whitemen on the way back would jeopardize all order. To return via Soppo to the creeks, as I originally envisaged, also seemed inadvisable. In Dr Preuss' opinion Soppo, which was protected by fences, was not safe, and we would have been between two fires. So I ordered the return march over the mountain. Guided by Dr Preuss, who led the advance guard, the expedition set off at daybreak on the 8th November, and reached the grass unmolested. We stayed overnight at the caves (2,300 metres). Gravenreuth's corpse was decomposed already to such a degree that it was impossible to transport it. So we took the head and heart with us and buried the rest deep under the cellar of the Mission. We took about twenty small loads of Dr Preuss's collections of specimens. In addition every man carried meat for three days from captured cows. Each European carried a light load.

On the night of the 9th November, we slept at Mann Springs. On the next day we were to go down to Victoria *via* Mapanjea [sic]. But the path regrettably could not be found. The Expedition had to return exhausted to the Springs. As Dr Preuss, who was in the lead, came near the Springs again, a shot passed so close to his ear that he went quite deaf. His men were somewhat in the rear, and so could not catch the enemy, who were sheltered in the bush. This demonstrated once more the cunning way of fighting of the Buea people. Soon after, a patrol met some Buea people on the path from Buea to the Springs and shot one of the enemy. Nothing more was seen of the Buea people.

As the paths were overgrown and the right way to Mapanjea could not be found, we decided to descend *via* the Levin Springs at 2,700 metres to Bibundi. After a stiff march and after an uneventful descent the expedition camped in the forest without tents in the pouring rain.

On the 12th, we had largely to cut our way with matchets, and we stayed yet another night in a tornado in the forest. Next day at noon we reached Bibundi, and on the 14 November we were already back in Kamerun [Douala] on board H.M. Habicht.

As regards the result of the Buea Punitive Expedition, it is certain that it has instilled in the Backwiris [sic] respect for the power of the Government. There has been no punitive expedition in the Protectorate so far which has been so thorough. Buea is regarded in the eyes of the natives as heavily punished, especially as it has suffered great losses in cattle [five days' food for 150 men] and supplies. The people were so confident of their strength that they had evacuated only a small amount. They believed they could withstand any attack at the strong palisade. The Buea people were the terror of all other villages on this side of the mountain, as they began disputes and wars at every opportunity, confident in their supremacy. It will surely have a good effect that this very powerful people have been punished, their stronghold taken, and their royal compounds reduced to ashes.

The building of a road to Buea, and the establishment of a station or plantations on the mountain, could not have been considered until the inhabitants had learnt to know the power of the Government, which they have never recognised. As the impudent attack on the peacefully marching column shows, a demonstration of strength was urgently necessary, if only to achieve one thing, which it surely has: to put a stop to open breaches of the peace. The Buea people will feel no further inclination to attack Victoria.

Our arrival meant liberation for Dr Preuss, who had already decided to flee by night with his seven people into the Mountain, as he had already been closely guarded for several days. The missionary had not arrived, having turned back, as he was told that the Buea people would cut his throat.

I would like to emphasise the calm and circumspection of Lt v. Stetten, the liveliness and daring of Lt v. Volckamer, the steadiness of Dr Richter under fire, the calmness and energy of Dr Preuss, and the brave conduct of Gardener Pfeil. All of those named did their duty in an outstanding manner.

The earthly remains of Gravenreuth which we brought with us were yesterday consecrated by Rev. Father Walter of Sanaga, and ceremonially interred by the Nachtigal memorial.

Post Mortem

The report put a good face upon the unexpected outcome of Gravenreuth's expedition, but the Acting Governor could not hide his evident shock. The supposed 'peaceful intentions' of the marching column, with its banner waving, hardly carried conviction. Nor did the comment that, apart from the loss of von Gravenreuth and the wounding of his second-in-command, casualties had been light. They had of course rescued Dr Preuss, although he would not have needed rescuing if they had not attacked his hosts—if indeed he needed it then. Dr Preuss as a man of scholarship had a proper sense of priorities. What reflections must have passed through the minds of citizens and officials alike, when the expedition stumbled soaking wet to the coast, from the wrong direction, and bearing the head and heart of von Gravenreuth and twenty boxes of scientific specimens?

Von Stetten

Von Stetten was convinced that the failure of the Maxim gun accounted for the disaster. In his own fuller military report[54] annexed to that of the Acting Governor, he confirmed that on hearing the drums and horns of Buea, von Gravenreuth had the flag unfurled (in sign of peace again), and also had the Maxim gun brought out. When they reached the firing, von Stetten was sent to operate it, and found Dr Richter, a hundred metres from the barricade, trying to feed in the ammunition belt. It was jammed, and the two of them tried to find the defect under a rain of fire, while von Gravenreuth and the Acting Governor fired back. Bakweri guns were loaded with miscellaneous small shot, and von Stetten was hit in the belly, and the doctor in the face, with bits of stone and iron, which put them both temporarily out of action. 'The failure of the Maxim gun', reported von Stetten, 'had an extremely depressing effect on our black soldiers, who had learnt to esteem it highly at Miang' (on the Abo expedition). They ran into the bush, while von Stetten and the doctor pulled the gun out of range of the shots. Even if the gun had worked, it was now masked by von Gravenreuth and the Acting Governor, who charged on with two soldiers. Von Stetten now went after his own detachment and saw no more of Gravenreuth.

It is possible to reconstruct the events, although the reports are not models of clarity. Lieutenant von Volckamer drew a sketch which is very useful. Looking towards Buea, the Germans were faced with a ravine, dry at this season, *in front* of which was a palisade of stakes barricaded with stones. [This is the Namonge watercourse close to the present Parliamentarian Flats Hotel - Ed.]. It stretched about seventy metres, ending in bush at either end. Behind it there was the ravine (which is better described as a gulley), about 10 metres broad and perhaps 5 metres deep. Behind it again on the further rim was the Buea town fence which ran in an unbroken circuit around the whole settlement for several kilometres. The stretch along the ravine was part of that which enclosed the Upper Buea area. The fence was not a strong defensive structure: examples can be seen around many villages today, including the present Buea 'Native' area. The effect of the double row of defences combined with the hail of fire was nevertheless demoralizing. The Dahomean troops, hiding in the bush each side of the road, fired indiscriminately. Von Stetten's detachment of Togo troops had gone off with Gardener Pfeil to the left of the road, in order to outflank the front palisade on the uphill side. Von Stetten followed after them. He and his men got around the end of the structure, and descended on the defenders, who retreated over the ravine and behind the fence. While this operation was under way Gravenreuth made his frontal charge. Acting Governor von Schuckmann complained that the Togo troops, as well as the Dahomeans, were also firing indis-criminately. It is obvious that the road was raked from the front by Bakweri fire, and from both sides by the fire of the panic-stricken soldiery.

These circumstances raise the serious possibility that at least one of the shots that hit von Gravenreuth might have come from his own men. He was hit in the chest as he charged, and in the back as von Schuckmann 'took hold of him'. He died at once. Yet von Stetten and Dr Richter had been peppered with shot, and had been only lightly wounded. It is no diminution of the Bakweri achievement to suggest that Gravenreuth may have been helped on his way by a bullet from his own men. The shot in the chest (possibly the fatal one) Buea may claim with high probability; there will always remain a marginal doubt about the one in the back. [In 1996 the fatal shot was attributed to Mondinde Mw Ekeke of Wonya Lionga - Ed.] The only responsible German witnesses, the Acting Governor and the doctor, may well have shared this doubt, and perhaps with better reason than we now have. If so, no better lips could have been chosen by fate to remain sealed. The troops stayed three days in Buea. No attempt was made quickly to enclose the corpse in a wooden coffin: although those twenty wooden boxes of Dr Preuss were lovingly transported. Dr Richter, as surgeon, was no doubt the one to certify that the corpse was decomposed. Certainly he (aided perhaps by the scientific Dr Preuss) must have removed the head and heart. An examination of the wounds would be natural, convenient, and even desirable. Dr Richter was no doubt satisfied that the bullets were from Bakweri guns.

Whatever happened, the surgical intervention had made future autopsy much more difficult. The death of von Gravenreuth is already sufficiently extraordinary, perhaps, to be left as it stands. His remains, covered by the Maxim gun, were left buried, still uncoffined, deep under the Mission house, until they were disinterred by Dominik, three years later.

Von Volckamer

The capture of the forward barricade by von Stetten and Pfeil, and the arrival there of Acting Governor von Schuckmann, was followed by the arrival of young Lieutenant von Volckamer, who had been with the baggage in the rear. His own report[55] is full of simple enthusiasm. With commands of 'loads down' and 'march, march' he ran to the barricade, where the Governor revealed that the now lifeless Gravenreuth was 'seriously wounded' (*schwer verwundet*). He penetrated the gaps now broken in the main defence, but Kuva's men were now behind the town fence, firing down into the ravine. The Lieutenant complains that the four Europeans now had to cover a Bakweri firing line 200 yards long. Finally he leapt into the ravine and up the opposite side, and ran into a hail of aimless cross-fire from all directions, 'so that their own troops seemed to be endangered'. He seems to refer here to the Bakweri, but by this time, once again, the Togo and Dahomean soldiers were also firing away. The Lieutenant broke through with his men, and the defenders gave way.

So it was that young von Volckamer, with fifty men and his interpreter Pelegrin, appears to have restored the situation. Leaving thirty of them ranged in two lines on a clearing near the foot of the Prime Minister's hill, he pressed forward with twenty men, this time taking the Acting Governor's servant, Fulzu, as an interpreter. He followed the line of the old path past the 'Holt's Store' houses, crossed the Mosole stream, and on a cleared space with a hut nearby, almost exactly at the present Old Secretariat, he met Dr Preuss, apparently on his way to meet them. Together they hastened up to the Basel Mission compound. The Lieutenant sent out two patrols to burn down the neighbouring huts, in the course of which one of his men was shot dead. After half an hour, von Schuckmann finally arrived, followed soon after by von Stetten with the loads. The Acting Governor then sent the Lieutenant to get Gravenreuth's corpse, which he did, with 'a small rearguard' against attack. On its return the party was fired on at fifteen yards range, as it reached the Basel Mission ravine, five minutes from safety. On that day young von Volckamer lost one soldier dead, two wounded, and three missing, two of whom, it was later discovered, had deserted fully armed to Victoria.

Buea and the Aftermath

Next day, von Stetten set off with Dr Preuss along the village fence, which then ran along the upper boundary of the Mission compound, until they reached the 'extreme western edge of Buea', and from there inwards they began to burn down the village. Von Stetten reported: 'Thus both royal compounds were destroyed. There was no opposition, only isolated shots now and then, which, in order to save our very scarce ammunition, I rarely allowed to be returned. In the destruction of the last complex my upper arm was smashed by a gun-shot at close range'. So the second-in-command was out of action.

Some of the houses in Upper Buea are shown in von Volckamer's sketch. Just over the Gravenreuth ravine inside the town fence on the left of the road was a cluster of huts with a separate fence round them. Then on the lower slopes of the Lodge hill to the left of the existing short path which climbs it, was a cleared area with huts scattered up the slope. This zone was part of the area of Gbekambi. Another hut was marked opposite the present Secretariat, and another group overlooked the Basel Mission ravine in the area of the old Public Works Department and the Old Government School. Then came the Mission Station. These were clearly the habitations visible from the road. The two royal compounds mentioned were presumably those of Ekpa and Kuva. In moving from west to east the 'last complex', from which the shot came which disabled von Stetten, would have been Kuva's own Lower Buea.

The extensive destruction of Buea, and the seizure of the people's cattle and other supplies, was the Acting Governor's chief reason for reporting that Buea had been thoroughly punished. It was, however, wishful thinking to say, as he did, that the population of the mountain regarded Buea as having been taught a lesson. No doubt it was a consoling thought in Victoria and in villages opposed to Buea, but the story could hardly have rebounded to the Goverment's military credit. The huts could be rebuilt rapidly. The other losses were no doubt regrettable. It is clear that the Germans were harassed in Buea until the very end, and all the way to Mann Springs. Nothing could disguise these events as anything but a retreat.

The waste of von Gravenreuth's expedition had serious repercussions. It should have been used to go far into the interior to counteract French movements. In March 1894, Germany signed an agreement with France which fixed the eastern boundary of Kamerun far more narrowly than once had been hoped for. The official memorandum on the Treaty contained a withering catalogue of the ineffectiveness of German colonial expeditions compared with those of the French. The home negotiators had, as a result, no serious territorial claims in north and east to offer. The Zintgraff and Gravenreuth expeditions were singled out as failures in this respect.[56] Furthermore, Gravenreuth's Dahomeans were turned into a police force at Douala. There they experienced indignities at the hands of Chancellor Leist, when he was acting for Governor Zimmerer in 1894, and mutinied, almost destroying Douala.

Kuva's Victory: The Bakweri View

The cause of the war of 1891 is easy to seek: it needs no other explanation than the desire of the colonial government to occupy the Mountain as quickly as possible, a step which was already long overdue. The Gravenreuth expedition came to hand very conveniently. The increasing disturbance on the Mountain seems, however, to have been real. Fights in the Lower Bakweri area near Victoria had been common for some years, as we have seen. The novel feature appears to have been Kuva's intervention in them. The raid as far as Lisoka would give Buea control of the mountain trade route. Kuva was related to the influential Bonjongo chief Efesoa: a well-placed ally among the Lower Bakweri. The scale of the military defence of Buea was remarkable.

The Victors

The Bakweri of Buea in their recollection of the time, and their attempt to explain the German expedition, singled out the role of the Basel Mission catechist. They believed that the attack was the result of their practice of hanging witches after making them drink sasswood: that it was Bakweri 'wickedness' which had brought the German intervention. The names of two women who were hanged are known. It should be remembered that the role of Victoria Christians on the mountain was an equivocal one. They were the medium through which allegations of savagery came. The probability is that Kuva's rule was marked by an increase in witchcraft allegations. His reign marked a progressive period for the Bakweri. Such periods have, they believe, been made possible by the clearing out of witches. The existence of Victoria meant that many people suspected or accused of witchcraft fled there for sanctuary.

The story is told that the Basel Mission catechist who lived in Buea before the German attack was known as *Chicha* ('Teacher'). He was not popular because of his activities on behalf of condemned witches, whom he sent off where possible to Victoria. Many versions of the story circulate. To the true Bakweri he is an Iago-like figure. Later on many saw him as a heroic Christian. The version recorded by P. M. Kale in 1939 preserves an ironical balance, and gives the nearest thing available to a description of Kuva. The account of the Gravenreuth expedition shows some hostility to the Bimbia interest, a prejudice which is to be expected in a tale of Kuva.[57]

The First German War

For quite a considerable period, according to Kale, the Mission succeeded in saving a number of innocent souls who would have otherwise been hanged, and easily converted them to Christianity. Nevertheless, trials by ordeals and hangings continued in Buea as the means of identifying and punishing witches. The catechist was aware of this and many a time interceded to plead for doomed victims. He tried to convert this warlike people to Christianity, but had many disappointing failures. As long as the Buea people remained heathen it was difficult to convince them of the evil of killing people for witchcraft alone; but they treated him with the greatest scorn whenever he attempted to preach the message of Christ. He found that while their ruler detested the introduction of a new faith in their midst no person in Buea would dare to be baptized. In fact no one even showed curiosity about this new belief. It was now regarded as the strange faith in which witches found favour. The poor catechist was very sorry to discover this misrepresentation of the Christian religion among the very people whom he was struggling to deliver from heathenism. At this rate the mission would never make a foothold among the Bakweri people who regarded it with contempt, because it had started by sheltering people who to them were only fit to die. Kale (1939) continues:

> This contempt became more intense when the Catechist, with the usual outspokenness of a missionary, openly denounced all Bakweri beliefs and customs as being evil before the eyes of God. Here comes the use of force, when blind pursuit of faith becomes absolute. This blunder struck the final blow of his failure, so he continued only to intercede for condemned witches. Many, however, were quietly hanged in his absence.
>
> The climax arrived when a certain woman, who had been found guilty of witchcraft, was handed over for execution. *'Chicha'* pleaded in vain for the victim, but he was not heeded. A quarrel arose, and he went and reported to the headquarters at Victoria.
>
> The Mission appealed to the German Government,[58] which had by now been established at Victoria, and they resolved to tame the Buea people. This did not prove to be an easy task, as was imagined, for the people of Buea under their fearless and witty leader Kuva-Lykenye repulsed the first German attack successfully.
>
> *The First War*—The method by which Dr Gustav Nachtigal claimed the Cameroons for the German Reich, particularly the Bakweri area, was no more than a witty design of securing at midnight the signature of chief

Bille of Bimbia who after this assumed the title of king Williams [sic] of Bimbia.[59] In his behalf, let it be said, that while he was giving the German his signature and acknowledging them rulers of the near coast region, he did not fail to mention with emphasis that all was not well with them, because up the mountain there was a monster who was a terror to him in particular, owing to the wonderful way in which he (the monster) made use of the 'Spear'. This monster, he mentioned further, would undoubtedly resist the white man's entrance into his area, except force was used. The monster, he said, went by the name of Kuva-Lykenye.

Now that the Germans had seen the catechist's report, they were not lost in wonder. To them a king whose method of punishing his people for crimes like witchcraft was to kill them in cold blood, as the Catechist's report read, whether for any other reason or not, would surely not be a friend to the whiteman, except he was tamed.

Veiled by this, they then agreed to test the situation. Drastic measures were not taken immediately, but a spy was sent, piloted by one of those subjects whose chief had been deceived by a couple of bottles of rum, some heads of tobacco and a few bags of rice and stock-fish.

One cold morning, as Kuva-Lykenye sat with his bodyguard, beating his bare chest, stretching his sinewy arms, and with his deep audible voice recounting reminiscences of his encounters, he was disturbed by the appearance of a European. The European introduced himself through an interpreter in cordial terms saying that he had come to befriend him much, as he had heard of him as a brave and kind king. Without waiting for an answer, he produced some spirits, the usual article of deception, set now to stimulate friendship. Kuva looked at his feet, drew his long beard, and ordered that the drink should be served. He sipped long shots, and his eyes sparkled. Then he replied to the whiteman, through the same interpreter, that he was glad to have him as a friend, and that they could discuss matters. But before that, as a mark of gratitude for the drinks the friend gave him, he was asking his people to give him a dance. This was done and the whiteman thanked him.

At the time of exchanging friendly thoughts, the whiteman, in a most cunning way, asked Kuva to give him a portion of land on which to build. By this he said, they would live at close quarters and meet at any time. Kuva sternly refused, telling the 'spy' that the area of land that he ruled came under him through the 'Spear'[60] and if he (the whiteman) wanted to get a share of it, he would better not pretend any diplomacy, but get ready with his own 'spear', and that would decide the issue.

This was just the kind of answer the spy expected. He nodded his head, as much as to say: 'you've struck the right note'. This ended the intercourse, and he returned to Victoria. Getting there, he hastened to narrate what the monster said, and the Germans got ready, for the first time in their lives perhaps, to meet African warriors. Kuva, knowing what would follow, had got his 'braves' encamped in a barricade of stones. They knew that they were nearly safe in a fortress of nature, and the only way unsafe was the side through which the enemies were coming, and at this they set their guns ready to fire.

Quite ignorant of what was before them, the Germans marched up to meet the mountain tribe, with the confidence of cutting all to the throat, and taming them once for all. After some hours of climbing, they reached a spot where guns were fired at them without break from the front. There was no other way opened to them for escape, save this from where the gun powder was being smoked at them. How it happened that they could not see spears as they expected was a surprise. They were in a great dilemma. They ran helter-skelter, and in their confused state shot at random. And as my father, who took an active part in this war, related to me, the enemies' guns were so powerful that as they shot up the trees, twigs were falling on the heads of the Buea people, but strengthened with the memories of their past difficulties they loaded their guns in turn and never looked behind until the Germans retreated. This ended the first war.

Comment

The account of the 'Spy' must refer to Dr Preuss, yet it is possible that this tradition contains some blurred memory of the land negotiations. It certainly suggests that by now Kuva was aware of the claims to the land of Buea. If the Europeans who came after the Valdau-Soden Purchase made reference to it as their basis for settlement (as was very likely) Kuva's hostility would have been aroused. The bitterness of the Buea defence can thus be partly accounted for. Nevertheless, the story as told by Kale seems much closer to an event that occurred with Gardener Pfeil, as we shall see, before the second German expedition.

The father of Kale was Kal' a Monyonge of Gbekambi, Upper Buea, and his account of the fire-power and panic at the barricade confirms the German account in a remarkable manner. Another traditional account names certain Bakweri at the barricades. It was also believed that a 'war dog' was shot with Gravenreuth, although the German accounts say nothing about it. According to another story I received in 1953, the Germans left a gramophone playing as they evacuated the Mission, to confuse the Buea people. (Whose? Dr Preuss's? The old cylinder-type record would allow only two minutes grace.) Kale's account does not mention Gravenreuth, although others do (*Galáfalot*). No traditional version mentions the burning of Buea. It has always been remembered as a complete victory, a rout at the barricade: the famous *nguva*. The news of the German departure from Victoria was known because Buea people had been there buying goods. The complete preparedness of Buea is further explained by the fact that precise warning of the German advance was sent up to Kuva by his sister's son Efesoa, Chief of Bonjongo. Not only was the *nguva* constructed on the Wokpaongo road entrance to Buea, used by the expedition, but the road itself was blocked by frequent felled trees. A look-out sounded a slit-drum when the troops were in sight.[61]

The Defeated

Chancellor Leist wrote the Annual Report for 1891.[62] The Expediton of Zintgraff had, he noted, restored order at Bali after the unlucky fight at Mankon. The Gravenreuth expedition had punished the Abo people and the rebellious people of the mountain village of Buea, bringing 'a greater respect for German power'. Sadly the expedition leader 'lost his life on this occasion'. The Acting Governor's role was marked up considerably: 'Freiherr v. Gravenreuth died a hero's death before the palisade of Buea. Legationsrath v. Schuckmann dragged the dying man out of reach of enemy fire and guarded his corpse throughout from the desecrations of the rebels.' Dr Preuss had to move his residence to Victoria as a result of the Buea fighting 'as the Government was not in a position to place a strong security guard on the said investigator'. Progress in Victoria had gone on. Among the notable additions was 'a roomy dwelling for workers (cement and pan) with prison attached'.[63] Dr Preuss now devoted himself to the new Botanical Gardens at Victoria, where, after leave, he took over in April 1893.[64]

Gravenreuth became a colonial hero. His fellow officers of the 3rd Royal Bavarian Infantry Regiment, at Augsburg in Germany, published a mourning notice on 20 November 1891.[65] On 11 December a Mourning Ceremony (*Trauerfeier*) was held at the Architect's house in Douala for the colonial dead, which 'relatives and friends of the fallen' attended. Pictures of Gravenreuth and of other officers dead in colonial wars were displayed in front of myrtles and palms. Woeful music and speeches marked the occasion.[66] By August 1892 a national collection had gathered 7,725 Marks for a fine memorial at Douala. A Bronze Lion was cast at Munich to surmount it. Among the contributions were: 2,000 Marks from nineteen branches of the German Colonial Association, 2,000 Marks from Freiherrin Marie von Gravenreuth, 300 Marks from the Gräfin von Gravenreuth (both at Munich), 75 Marks from the 'Viktoria-Klub'. The Kolonialabteilung (the Colonial Department of the Foreign Office) in Berlin gave 190 Marks. Adolf Woermann, the German

Reburial of Gravenreuth in Douala, 1895

Drawing of monument on Gravenreuth's grave in Douala

trader, gave 200 Marks, yet Woermann opposed expeditions. From Lagos, Eduard Schmidt, who for little reward had in 1884 obtained Kamerun for Germany, sent 30 Marks. Later other sums were contributed. The monument was not unveiled until 27 January, 1894.[67]

Acting Governor von Schuckmann handed over to von Zimmerer again in January 1892 and returned home. There, in recognition of his services at Buea, he received from the Kaiser the Order of the Red Eagle, 4th Class (with Swords).[68]

Uneasy Peace

For the whole of 1892 the Bakweri of Buea remained undisturbed. Governor von Zimmerer was occupied with the results of other expeditions. He was becoming increasingly cool towards Zintgraff's operations on the route to Bali. The expedition inland from Douala to Yaounde, which von Gravenreuth should have conducted, continued first under von Stetten and then under Captain Ramsay, who both reported difficulties with the dead officer's 'ill disciplined' Dahomean troops.[69] Von Stetten himself went up to report on Zintgraff's work at Bali in September. His own experience with the Dahomeans, and the slapdash organization of his own former leader von Gravenreuth, were not calculated to make him favour Zintgraff's idea of arming the Bali as auxilary troops. His report was critical.[70] Official feeling against the policy of expeditions was hardening. Peace was signed with various peoples: the Bakoko in December 1892, and the Abo people of Miang in early 1893.[71] It was now the turn of Buea. A formal peace was signed with Kuva, followed by an unarmed visit of conciliation from the Governor in person.

Peace Treaty

On 4 February 1893, the Gardener Pfeil was sent to Buea with a Peace Treaty, which was announced in these words, in translation:

> By the Bezirksamtsmann [District Officer] of Victoria (Kamerun) v. Alvensleben and the Chief of Buea, Kuba, a peace treaty has been concluded as follows:
>
> Kuba, Chief of Buea, recognizes the protectorate of his Majesty the German Emperor Wilhelm II over his whole territory on behalf of himself and his subchiefs, and engages:

> 1. To give effect to all orders of the German Government, especially to all requests for the execution of judicial orders, and for the surrender of criminals.
> 2. To provide warriors in numbers demanded, in case of need.
> 3. To permit all whites, especially missionaries, the right to stay in his territory, and to guarantee personally their lives and property.
> 4. Not only to permit his subjects to visit the coast unhindered, especially the market of Victoria, but also to encourage the trade with the coastal places in every way.
>
> The treaty was signed by both sides and a number of witnesses on 29 January and 4 February, 1893. Besides Kuba and his son, four other chiefs signed. It is indicative of the present mood of the Buea tribe that when Gardener Pfeil, who undertook the peace negotiations, visited Buea on 4 February, and explained the peaceful purpose of the visit, he was received with jubilation by the inhabitants and conducted into the village.[72]

It seems that the Treaty must have already been signed by the Government in Victoria on 29 January, and carried up to Buea by Pfeil on 4 February. The original treaty is not available. It is not possible therefore to confirm whether Kuva's 'son' signed, rather than his brother. The arrival of a peaceful mission must have been a relief, as well as a surprise to the people, and their delight was sincere enough. Here at least was further evidences of their victory. From the Government's point of view the treaty had its face-saving features, but it was an agreement merely re-establishing relations between Buea and the coast. From Kuva's point of view, acceptance of the Kaiser's protectorate was a recognition of a remote paramount chieftaincy. He may also have hoped that it would wipe out the deed of sale of 1887. The Basel Mission was already destroyed. Little did he know that von Soden's 'purchase' was now in the provisional *Grundbuch* (Land Register), and its partition was still being argued over in Douala.

To Kuva the Government's request for future military assistance from Buea must have loomed larger. In view of the recent trouble over Zintgraff's Bali troops it is impossible to imagine that this was a serious proposition. This clause may have masked some vague plan to entice the Buea warriors out one day, and to isolate and disarm them. On the other hand, in the recent Bakoko and Abo treaties the chiefs had undertaken to supply a number of labourers for Douala and for the plantation at Bimbia of Herr Teuss. By now the 'labour question' was a burning one in the Protectorate. But these were defeated peoples. It is possible that such a clause was included in the Buea treaty, and that this was amended from 'labourers' to 'warriors', when it became apparent that no labour agreement would be forthcoming. The request for a raising of Kuva's embargo on trade with Victoria was a sign that Bakweri foodstuffs were now in short supply at the coast. The resumption of trade was also in Buea's own interest, if the property destroyed and the gunpowder consumed in the war were to be replaced. The war itself seems to have had the notable result of placing Kuva firmly at the head of Buea. Upper Buea must have suffered most from the German expedition. It is possible that von Stetten had not been able to reach all the isolated huts of the more populous Lower Buea before he was wounded. The generally suspicious attitude of Kuva to the Germans over the sale, which perhaps some of the other chiefs had not shared, would now be clearly vindicated.

In March the Governor visited Buea in person, and after initial coolness was well received. He seems to have gained the confidence of Buea, and while there he arbitrated over the longstanding war between Boana and Busumbu. His report does not note that his very presence at Buea, arbitrating over such matters, would be interpreted by Kuva as an increase of his own prestige.

Official Report of the Visit of the Governer of Kamerun to Buea (Translation)[73]

> The Imperial Governor of Kamerun, Herr Zimmerer, paid a visit in the second half of the month of March (1893) to the Buea tribe, with whom a formal peace treaty had been concluded shortly before and he stayed nearly fourteen days on the Cameroun Mountain.
>
> From his communications, the losses suffered by the Bueas in the battle of November 1891 have been determined, and it is evident that they were very serious. The Buea tribe lost not less than forty dead including two chiefs, as well as numerous cattle.
>
> The present state of affairs on the Mountain is related to the vigour of the punishment: security, calm and peace have been reestablished, and the status of the Government is unreservedly recognized.
>
> The Governor was able to make his way there with a few companions, and without weapons. Although he had at first to move forward by a closely overgrown bush-path, when he passed the boundary of Buea he found it was cleared to a breadth of four or five metres. The reserved attitude (*Befangenheit*) which there was among the Buea people on the first entry of the Governor very soon gave way to great joy over the visit, which manifested itself in play, dance etc.
>
> The Governor took the opportunity on various occasions during his time there to arbitrate in old tribal feuds, and his judgment was unhesitatingly accepted by the parties.

While he visited different villages, observing the life and livelihood of the inhabitants from dawn to dusk, and spending the nights among them, he was able to form observations on the character and ideas of the natives. In this connexion his report states:

> The Buea people, in their unfeigned joy over the peace which had been concluded and over the visit of the Governor, which was certainly unexpected, sought to show publicly their most pleasant side. However it is clear, as may be conveniently discovered from these 'palavers', that the mountain folk are of a far wilder disposition than the surrounding tribes of the lowlands, and bloodshed is almost an everyday matter. The so-called palavers are not only lawsuits, but also peace negotiations, in which there comes into consideration not only destroyed huts and plundered cattle, but also a greater or lesser number of killed or injured people. The tenet that blood can only be expiated by blood corresponds exactly to the view of law of these mountain folk. Hence follows, of course, the difficulty of coming to a truce; since the party who is in the wrong must pay for his guilt with blood, and no tribe agrees easily to that; also it is very difficult to bring together the hostile parties, as this can only take place in a neutral village which each can reach without passing hostile territory. I did manage to settle some old feuds in this way, and I believe that it would not generally be hard for a white man who was known and liked by the natives to settle disputes, since both parties are happy to be able to go about their affairs without the fear of death.

In order to illustrate the pettiness (*Geringfügigkeit*) of the causes of bloodshed, I will only mention here the feud between the Boana and Busumbu people. The latter had arranged a festivity with wrestling matches, at which Boana people also turned up, most of whom, however, were thrown. This caused a scuffle without significant consequence, and it ended with the Boana people leaving Busumbu. However, some of them lay in wait and, when it was dark, cut down with their matchets two children four or five years old, without killing them. As a result of this the Busumbu people marched against the Boana, to punish them. The outcome of these hostilities was several dead and wounded on both sides, and they continued for two years, during which the number of mutual outrages steadily grew. I held the Palaver in neutral Buea. After both parties had fought their cases with great vigour, I gave judgement against the Boana people, since they had given the grounds for hostilities by maltreating little children. This decision was immediately accepted, and the discussion was now concerned with the fixing of the penalty or compensation. The Busumbu people naturally immediately demanded that some Boana people should be killed. When however I told them that enough people were already dead on both sides, and that they could only claim compensation, the parties came to an agreement on the payment in a very short time. It consisted mainly of a fixed number of livestock, such as oxen, goats and pigs.

A chief cause of disturbances of the peace and bloodshed comes from the sorcerers (*Zäuberer*) who are everywhere in the mountain. For a couple of pence (*Groschen*) they are ready to attribute the guilt for the occurrence of natural events, or of natural deaths, to innocent people, who are then punished with death and the confiscation of their property. The superstition and fear shown towards these swindlers is so great, for example, that the Buea people did not have the confidence in themselves to bury such a sorcerer who died on the day of my arrival, and chief Kuba paid five Kru goats for my interpreter, helped by my carriers, to bury the corpse two hours from Buea.

It is impossible to seek to root out these abuses with force, and it could cause complications for the Government which would delay the opening up of the mountain.

In order to increase the influence of the Government, and to achieve a further strengthening of the peaceful conditions on the Mountain, frequent contact of officials in the District Office in Victoria with the inhabitants of the Mountain is necessary. To this end the laying out of a road from Victoria to Buea, as one of the most important villages, has been planned and started. When a labour force of adequate numbers is available, the Governor hopes that the road will be completed in the not too distant future.

Kuva's Peak

This visit marks the zenith of Kuva's true power. Kuva himself in 1893 and 1894 was in a position of unchallenged supremacy on the mountain. He began to claim to control his trade-route to Bwenga. Yet he was fighting a losing battle. The advance of the road from Victoria to Buea was slow, but it posed an unavoidable threat. His main weakness lay in the minds of his followers. His fight against Mission intervention in Buea was a wise instinct for a man who wished to preserve his independence. The fight was in a sense ideological: Kuva's obsession with witches was a recognition of this. He must have felt that the run of luck could be destroyed at any time by any false step, such as involvement with the burial of an important diviner. This obsession was no more barbarous than others which leaders in his comparative position have shown. Victoria was, however, full of Christianised Bakweri who saw Kuva as aligned with the forces of savagery. The long legacy of Baptist rule at Victoria now had its effect. In addition the plan to alienate the mountain for plantations was now coming to fruition. While German power gathered strength Kuva began to find arms difficult to get. On 16 March,

Governor von Zimmerer had already signed an Ordinance to control the importation of firearms into Kamerun.[73] He went on leave on 29 June 1893.

3. Beginning of the End

Plantations

The Acting Governor of Kamerun, who was now Chancellor Leist, reported in September 1893[74] that Buea would be profitable as an area for coffee plantations. There had been consultations with Spengler, a German planter on the Portuguese Island of Sâo Thomé. He was the German Vice-Consul there and his hill plantation, Monté Café, was a favourite resort for Kamerun officials, 36 hours by steamer from Douala. His contacts with his fellow Germans made known his view that the Cameroon Mountain could be planted in the same manner. Leist made a visit to Sâo Thomé and saw the profitable coffee, cocoa, cinchona and vanilla.[75] Spengler was asked to visit Cameroon.

Meanwhile the case for using the mountain as a health station was officially reopened.[76] From 1885 efforts to avoid malaria had been unceasing. First, an old warship in the Douala estuary was tried, then the Suellaba Peninsula, then Mondoleh Island, off Victoria. Dr Zintgraff had favoured Man-o'War Bay, and a few houses were in fact built there. In 1892, the hospital was at last built in Douala itself. Dr Plehn, the surgeon in charge, still pressed for a convalescent station. Monté Café was suitable but on foreign [Portuguese] soil. Burton's old views on the Cameroon Mountain were cited with approval. The experience of the Basel Mission and Dr Preuss at Buea was drawn on. Governor Zimmerer also supported the use of Buea to Monté Café as it was only six hours by steamer, or fifteen by canoe, from Douala to Victoria. Then a road would be necessary. Leist thought the road should go as far as Soppo at least, 'broad enough for two ox-waggons, each with four oxen, to pass each other.' This would transport produce, as well as plantation products. He took as a model the road on Sâo Thomé to Monté Café and other plantations.

Dr Preuss wrote a special report on 3 December 1893.[77] He said that Buea, or possibly the neighbouring Soppo (which he thought had a slightly better climate, although rather surprisingly he had not visited it) were the only two villages suitable for a convalescence home. All the others he knew were too low, or too far from the coast, or were short of water (Bonjongo and Mapanja), and were, besides, 'the very homes of sandflies'. The advantages of Buea were many. Fowls, eggs, pigs, sheep, goats and cattle were available. European cattle should also do well. Preuss had himself grown lettuce, endives and other vegetables. Potatoes thrived. The cocoyams and yams were of high quality. There was not much fruit as yet. He thought grapevines could be attempted. There was good water available: a mountain stream which he says (referring accurately to the Mosole) disappears from view in Buea and reappears in Soppo. A good walker reached Buea from Victoria in eight hours on the footpaths, sometimes his men did it in less, even with loads. The road from Victoria had begun, but it was costly and slow. Between Victoria and Boana the land rose in 'the form of terraces', and between Boana and Buea there were ravines. On a good levelled road a fit walker could reach Buea in six hours. The road should be wide enough to take wagons.

There was good building stone and timber in Buea. Preuss thought the station should not be for the seriously ill: they should stay in Douala. Convalescents could go up to Buea for four to six weeks. The difficult question of 'relations with the natives' was referred to briefly: 'The Buea people will not permit any armed person to enter their villages nor allow any Kruboys, that is foreign workers, into their village. When the first plantation undertakings have taken sites in Buea, and all efforts should be based on this at first, it will be better if first one or more Europeans with 100 or 200 blacks were to be in the village, thus breaking the power of the Buea people.'

It is probable that a second expedition to Buea might have set out quite soon. On 15 December 1893, however, the Dahomean soldiers revolted in Douala and seized the arms magazine, including guns of all kinds and vast quantities of ammunition. At that very time, Dr Plehn and Dr Preuss were on a trip to Sâo Thomé, no doubt gathering fresh hints on convalescence stations and plantations. They arrived back as passengers on the German warship 'Hyäne' on 20 December, which was greeted with some relief by the beleaguered Acting Governor Leist. The Dahomeans had revolted against their peculiar semi-slave status, whereby they had to work off their redemption money. The precipitating cause came on 15 December when Leist had the women stripped and beaten. His career ended in ignominy.[78] The Leist case became the most well-known German 'colonial scandal', and twenty-five years later at Versailles was given as one of the detailed reasons for the removal of Germany's colonies by the Allies. Thus finally ended the curse of the grotesque Gravenreuth Expedition.[79]

Leist in his report on the uprising (1 January, 1894) had a thought for Buea. He asked for a further warship: it was necessary to have bigger forces for German prestige. 'Also there is the imminent possibility that the building of the Buea road will lead to some developments with the Bakwiris—especially the Buea people'.[80]

The versatile Dr Preuss and Gardener Pfeil played their roles at Douala. Pfeil, now more suitably promoted to *Polizeimeister* in the Police Gendarmerie, arrived from Victoria in a sailing ship with forty of Dr Preuss's labourers and the new Gardener, Scholz. Together they all 'did good service' as patrols, and in the recovery of the Douala Government Station from rebel hands.

On 8 January Regierungsrat Rose of the Berlin Kolonial-Abteilung set out for Kamerun to enquire into the mutiny, followed two days later by Governor von Zimmerer returning to take over from Leist.[81] He did so on 17 February 1894. At the same time Vizefeldwebel Biernatsky set out from Germany to enter the Police Gendarmerie (Polizeitruppe). He was to end his colonial career in charge of Buea, being shot there by a crazed subordinate in February 191 1.[82]

Meanwhile up at Buea Kuva had had another visitor. In February 1894, the Apostolic Prefect Vieter of the Roman Catholic Pallotiner Mission arrived in order to look for a site for a Sanatorium. He was accompanied by ex-Gardener Pfeil. On his return from Buea on 14 February he wrote a letter to the Governor.

'Cuba' [Kuva] was clearly reluctant to offer any land to the mission. He probably could not yet understand why more than one Mission should want land. For as long as anyone could remember Missions meant Victoria and the Baptists, and the Basel missionaries were their successors. This seems to be the explanation of the first obscure refusal to grant land to the Prefect. Furthermore Pfeil had broken Kuva's rule and entered Buea armed. Kuva did not like it, however, when Vieter and Pfeil went to Sako of Soppo. Vieter's letter follows in translation.

Letter of Apostolic Prefect Vieter to Acting Governor Leist

To Chancellor Leist
Acting Governor
Kamerun

Yr. Excellency,

Victoria, 14 February, 1894

Being returned this morning from my journey, I hasten to report to you as following upon my reception and success among the Buea people.

King Cuba did not indeed receive us in a very welcoming manner, but still well enough. He brought a few fowls as a gift, and provided us with a house as lodging, but concerning our intentions, i.e. the establishment of a convalescence station and a Mission station, he explained that he would first have to hold a Palaver with the subchiefs, and he fixed for this purpose Sunday morning, 11th inst. Unfortunately, not all the chiefs appeared at the Palaver, and so he invited us for Sunday afternoon to Soppo to the 'play'.

After that was over, a Palaver about our affair would then take place. Unfortunately, after the very interesting 'play' was over no Palaver took place. That was postponed until Monday morning. My guide and companion, Herr Pfeil, and I looked round on Monday very early for a suitable site, and we appeared about 10 a.m. when the chiefs were assembled. After long negotiation and much shouting it was reported to me that the Baseler Mission had bought, so there was nothing against my coming, but it was impossible to cede me another piece of land. Herr Pfeil immediately left the meeting, and I had no better alternative than to follow his example. We went straight to Cuba's, quickly packed our things and went to Soppo to King Sako, who received us in a very friendly manner, and at once killed a sheep so as to be able to entertain us decently. Before our departure, Herr Pfeil had taken the firing pin from Cuba's rifle, which was booty from the Gravenreuth Expedition. Cuba soon sent his nephew, who asked us to come back, which we flatly refused to do.

Various other messengers had no better success. Again his nephew Heinrich received the answer: Cuba had insulted us and he should come himself to us to show he was sorry for his behaviour. Cuba then came himself in fact, and asked us to pardon him. He had been afraid, as Herr Pfeil had brought a shotgun with him this time. He would give for nothing a place in his 'town' to build a house; however, I explained to him that I did not want to live in the town, but outside it, and I asked for two hills, which lay opposite his dwelling, of which the lower one was not much further from Soppo than from his dwelling. He and the chiefs with him at once said that they agreed. They would not hear of any payment but would make a gift of the hills, and I accepted and concluded. I intend to build at first on the lower of the hills. It is somewhat higher than Cuba's residence (Lower Buea), not very far from the stream and has the advantage that in case Cuba and his supporters were to become unpleasant, Soppo stands open to me. I must further note that Cuba had looked for his gun after our departure, and also correctly realized that the firing pin was missing (for which he blamed his 'boys'). In a test the spring flew back and injured his hand, which will soon heal, however, with his tough constitution.

The Buea people did not make a bad impression on me as a whole. A few showed themselves somewhat defiant, but many were timid. Cuba, as well as his subjects, seems to wish to avoid a Palaver with the Imperial Government if at all possible.

Your Excellency, I would like to request you to refrain from sending a military expedition to Buea. Such would indeed show the Buea people the power of the Imperial Government, but would probably also involve losses. It is my conviction that I can make a beginning with the establishment of a convalescence station. Meanwhile I request Your Excellency to communicate to me whether any obstacles lie in the way of my intention.

[etc.]
signed
P. Vieter, A.P.[83]

The picture of Kuva is of a man clearly disturbed by the problem of European visitors. Ever since the War they had been received coolly at first, but always it had seemed impossible to do anything but entertain them and hope they would go away. He must surely have guessed who had disabled his gun. Pfeil and he were old acquaintances. Vieter is probably right that the Buea people did not want another head-on clash if they could help it. The danger that Sako of Soppo would ally himself with the German interest was certainly the reason why Kuva came down and so rapidly granted Vieter's wishes.

Sako of Soppo was Sak' Ewumbue the nephew and successor of Woloa wo Fike, the Soppo king known to the travellers of the 1880's. It is probable that Buea and Soppo had usually been in uneasy alliance. Both had been hostile to the Bimbia coastal dominance, and Woloa wo Fike, it will be recalled, had been blamed for instigating the death of Ngomb' a Bila, King William II of Bimbia in 1882. Since then it had been Kuva's turn. Within Buea, however, it was Upper Buea which had closest relations with Soppo, and so Kuva was always careful about his neighbours. The hostility later between elements in the two towns mainly turns on certain disputes of the colonial period, which derive from the wedge driven into the alliance by German negotiators of the type of Vieter and Pfeil.[84]

The two hills between Soppo and Lower Buea were not made over to the Pallotiner Mission, as we shall see. It eventually settled at Bonjongo (the 'Engelberg'). It is, however, interesting to note that seventy years later the Buea Roman Catholic church was at last built on what appears to be one of the hills, although the Mission was unaware of its significance.[85]

Vice-Consul Spengler

Soon after, more travellers appeared. At long last Vice-Consul Spengler made his visit. In company with the Acting Governor Leist (who had just handed over to Zimmerer) and Dr Plehn, he made an extended visit to the Mountain from 24 February to 10 March, 1894. They passed through Boana, Soppo, Buea, Mapanya [sic] and Bonjongo, going up to 10,000 feet but not to the summit, because the carriers were ill with cold. Spengler's subsequent report on this trip[86] was the go-ahead for the plantation industry on the mountain. His eyes were on soil, crops, and geological formations: he hardly noticed the people. He noticed that the forest was no longer primary in wide areas round the villages because of shifting cultivation. The villages were made up of scattered compounds. They had fences round them made of stakes and living trees. Although the individual farms might be 'a couple of plantains and a cocoyam field' there was as a result lots of overgrown land. Thus in the inhabited zone the mountain was not, as the unpractised eye might judge, mainly untouched forest. It was a man-made landscape, the soil, to some extent, then depleted. But the advantage for new plantations would be that it was much easier to clear. The area of the two adjoining villages of Buea and Soppo was not less than sixty square kilometres.

Spengler's report in general was highly favourable to the idea of plantations, and especially for cocoa and coffee. Coffee was already growing on the mountain and seemed to be doing well. At Bonjongo he saw cocoa plants damaged by cows. He did not favour tobacco.

The water resources were not fully known. For example, no-one knew the source of the Limbe River at Victoria. Similarly no-one knew exactly the course of the Buea stream (the 'Mosoli'), although it rose somewhere above Middle Buea, and was thought to drain into the Bimbia River. He measured its volume of flow in cubic metres per minute at a spot 'eighteen minutes distant from King Kuba's residence'. Thus science passed through Buea: indeed Spengler remarked that the Cameroon Mountain ought to-be called the 'Mountain of Science' (*Gebirge der Wissenschaft*) rather than the 'Mountain of the Gods' as he had heard the natives did. He asked the people about volcanic outbreaks. He heard there was one above Buea thirty to fifty years before. He found little trace of such an eruption, and thought it might have only been a show of fire and smoke. Another was thought to have occurred above Mapanja eighty to a hundred years before (he does not explain how these figures could have been calculated). This, he thought, was in fact 200 years old. The dry season just finishing, he recorded, was the longest in recent memory.

The End of Kuva

In November 1894 the *Kolonialrat* (Colonial Council) met in Berlin to discuss the Kamerun budget.[87] Adolf Woermann 'vigorously attacked' warlike expeditions into the interior: they disturbed the population and the welfare of the colony. The Chairman, Dr Kayser (Director of the Colonial Department) said that now the boundary agreements had been made with England and France only peaceful penetration was necessary with purely economic and scientific aims. In December that policy was to be put into operation against Buea. The second Buea Expedition was one of the last acts of Governor von Zimmerer's personal administration: he went on leave on 5 January 1895. But it was historically appropriate that on the 3 December Jesko von Puttkamer, the final dispossessor of Buea, set out from Togo to relieve him. He was to remain in an acting, and then a substantive, capacity as Governor of Kamerun for the next twelve years.

The end of Kuva's rule was a stubborn rearguard action, an anticlimax to the war of 1891. He was hemmed in by the growing influence of the Government. To the end he fought the establishment of the health station: the arguments must have been put to him in terms of sick and helpless patients but he must have sensed the plans for the dispossession of land. His continual efforts to reach trading points outside Victoria made him threaten Bwenga. His position had been weakened since 1 January 1894, by the establishment of a Native Court at Victoria, whose bench was composed of five members: one Victorian, two Bakweris, and two Isubu (of Bimbia).[88] The government therefore acquired legitimacy in some Bakweri eyes, especially among those tired of the continual inter-village wars in the Lower Bakweri zone. At length he was prevailed upon to visit Victoria. This was obviously a mistake for he was exposed to questions in front of the despised Victorians.

The expedition when it came was led by von Stetten, who was now the commander of the *Schutztruppe* (the Protectorate Force) assisted by Lieutenant Dominik, a new officer long to be associated with the opening up of the Yaounde area.

The official report follows, in translation:

The Military Occupation of Buea

> After the peace treaty of 7 February 1893 with the Buea people, the prospect of peace and calm seemed to open in this part of Kamerun. Governor von Zimmerer stayed several days among them, and had the chance to convince

Von Puttkamer in full Dress, 1895

Von Puttkamer and Dominik on horse by the Bismarck Fountain

himself of the wild character of the mountain people. Hope of a peaceful outcome was still not excluded. Not long after, however, the situation visibly worsened again, in that Chief Kuba did not carry out his obligations under the peace treaty, but on the contrary re-established his former reign of terror [*Schreckensherrschaft*] in a wide circle round Buea. As a result of many irregularities and outrages, Governor von Zimmerer decided therefore to take a stricter line with Kuba, and if necessary make use of the military power at his disposal.

Before the beginning of the action in question, the Governor made Polizeimeister Pfeil lay various questions before Kuba (who had withheld himself for a long time) at a Palaver held in Victoria, and received answers characteristic of Kuba's viewpoint.

For example, he declared he would only permit the erection of a health station in Buea on the condition that the purchase of flint-locks should be freed.

On the establishment of plantations he stated that he would permit it on condition that the whitemen lived in Buea village itself, i.e. as prisoners.

The Buea people flatly refused to come to Victoria court sessions. This is the more remarkable as Kuba intervened in all Palavers, even of the coast population, and claimed that everyone killed or wounded was a close relative of his. The perpetual disputes of Bota and Boando could never come to an end because of Kuba, and the threatened destruction by him of Mbinga [Bwenga] on the Bimbia Creek was only prevented by the personal appearance of Assessor von Saltzwedel, as Kuba had up to then shrunk from using force directly against whitemen. In view of these facts, the Governor instructed the Commander of the Schutztruppe to establish a military station at Buea.

The latter, Rittmeister von Stetten, was transported for this purpose with the Schutztruppe to Victoria on the Government steamer 'Nachtigal', and set off for Buea on 21 December, 1894 at 6 a.m. with 7 whites, 190 soldiers and 64 carriers.

In Likumbi, the last watering place before Buea, a camp was made on the night of 21/22 December.

At 6 a.m. on the 22nd the troops continued their march, and at about 10 a.m. appeared quite by surprise in front of the old fortifications, which the Buea people had only just begun to improve.

They offered little resistance to the soldiers as they came swarming out, although they received the troops with horn-blowing and cries, and fell back at first on Lower Buea. The first shot came from the enemy side, in fact against Polizeimeister Pfeil.

The Schutztruppe then established themselves between the old Mission land and the stream, on a site which was suited for the establishment of a Government station, because of its unimpeded view and wide extent, combined with a fairly gradual slope.

> While Rittmeister von Stetten had been engaged in erecting a temporary station, the war is continued by daily sending out stronger troops. Kuba, who was at present at Ebunda [Ewonda] about an hour distant from Lower Buea, refused to accept his overthrow and sent people to Momongo to buy flint-locks. The losses of the Buea people numbered twelve dead, while the Schutztruppe had only two wounded.
>
> If a good basis for further action is created by the speedy capture of the whole widely extensive site of Buea, the war may still take several weeks, in view of the difficult conditions of terrain, before the complete subjection of the Buea people is achieved.
>
> The erection of a temporary station is provisionally envisaged, as the troops are to remain together for any possibly bigger undertaking in Buea. As numerous cattle were captured and most farms are not harvested, the troops are still in a position to maintain themselves completely.
>
> The soldiers have shown themselves without exception to be energetic and resourceful in the bush.
>
> As a result of the complete subjection of Buea, and the impression which the punishment of this feared tribe will make in a wide area, security on the Cameroon Mountain will soon be all that is desired. The plan of the Basel Mission to erect a health station in Buea will now be able to be executed without danger. Also one of the principal obstacles to the extension of plantations in the Victoria hinterland is removed, and it is to be hoped that the military operation will bear rich fruits also for the economic revenue of the protectorate.

The account of Dominik confirmed the general picture.[90] He it was who described the visit to the Mission, and the digging at Gravenreuth's grave. The tools hit something hard: the Maxim gun. This was lifted out, and Dominik describes with somewhat gruesome emotion the sight of the ragged remains, with their long, yellow-leather, nail-soled, marching boots still unaffected by a three-year interment—a true advertisement, he almost seems to add, for German industrial products. For Dominik, however, Gravenreuth was a colonial hero worthy of emulation, and his emotion was sincere. The body was sent to Douala, to be re-interred with the head and heart in the new Gravenreuth memorial.[91]

Kuva moved from Ewonda to Wonyamokumba, a village related to Buea, near Muea. The guns never came. There, some time in January 1895, he died, and with him ended all armed resistance to German rule among the Bakweri. He was secretly buried on the border of Buea and Wokpae, where his grave remains hidden and unmarked until this day.

The Fall of Buea

The German sources seem to make clear that Buea was undefended because the attack was unexpected. Probably the peaceful nature of recent German visits had lulled the population into complacency. It seems likely that they had heard of the attack only on the very morning. The angry reception given to the column as it entered, and the stiffening of resistence as the troops reached Lower Buea seem to confirm the theory of surprise. We do not know whether the Buea people were deliberately deceived as to the nature of the expedition. As with the trickery of the ex-Gardener Pfeil, these matters were not always reported. The shortage of ammunition probably accounts for the relatively sporadic defence. The concentration of fire against white officers, which had worked against Gravenreuth and von Stetten was tried against Pfeil and failed.

The Buea tradition sees their evacuation of the town as voluntary, as in a sense it was. Even in 1891, they had left the town to the Germans: the only effective policy. This time however, the Germans were not a group of flamboyant amateurs, short of ammunition, and at the mercy of the massed firepower of Bakweri flintlocks. Von Stetten's Schutztruppe were experienced in long expeditions, and it was the Bakweri who were short of ammunition. This time the Germans simply did not go away. Middle and Upper Buea were already no more, and a station was being built in the area of the present Bismarck fountain.

Here finally then is a Bakweri version of the events as recorded in the words of P. M. Kale:[92]

Of the evacuation:

> A well equipped army was therefore sent out to conquer the Buea people and their heartless leader Kuva-Lykenye. But before the army reached, some friends from Bimbia and Victoria came up to Buea and advised Kuva, having of course ascertained from him that he had run short of fighting materials, to give up fighting. They made him to understand that Europeans were to a certain extent good people, and he should therefore allow them to settle down. But now that he had fought and conquered them for the first time, it was evident that for the second time they would come with an army ten times stronger and better equipped than his own and they would not give up fighting until the whole Bakweri land was devastated. In order to save this situation, therefore, it were better if Kuva and his men leave Buea for other surrounding villages, before the Germans arrived. In the event of his doing so, and the Germans not meeting with any opposing army,

they would burn down the houses, and later on call the Buea people for settlement.

Acting on this advice, whether for lack of ammunition, or for fear of Bakweriland being annihilated, brave Kuva called his people together, and with the words of a leader bade them to leave Buea for a while, until the Lord called them back again. This land, he told them, had been 'their ancestors' for generations, and it would be theirs forever, and so no fear should be entertained as to their coming back to it again. Thus came another movement of the Buea people into different homes and villages.

Of the German arrival:

Not long after this the Germans arrived, red-eyed, almost rabid to quench for the final time their opposers, but to their bewilderment only thatched houses greeted them. They marched this way and that, not a soul was found. They could only hear the singing of the birds of the air, and the droning and humming of beetles, and swarms of bees from the high Cameroon Mountain. Once again they were in a great consternation.

Of the end of Kuva:

King Kuva himself and his bodyguard went to a village called Wonya-Mokumba, where after a short stay he unfortunately caught ill and died. News of his death quickly echoed all around the jungles and mountain plains of Bakweri land, bringing dismay and sorrow to the Buea warriors. This was in itself, a sufficient cause of their not continuing the war. The giant's body was removed to Buea, and with due burial performances of a hero, it was laid to rest for eternity.

Lo! the hands that waved the spear
And loaded the gun,
Lo! the dreadful voice that roared,
And scattered the multitude,
The hero remains immortal.

Peace

At the end of January 1895, peace negotiations were already under way. Sako of Soppo was the German intermediary, and the Schutztruppe were at this time already first established in Soppo, and later built their permanent headquarters there in buildings which were taken over after the First World War by the Roman Catholic Mission. Once more a document preserved by Mr Esasso Woleta of Soppo throws extra light on this period. Sako was called to Victoria by the Acting District Officer, who was the Customs Officer Scheffler:

Agreement with Sako[93]

Victoria, 21 January 1895

Supplementary Negotiation

> Sopo promises this afternoon at Victoria District Office, and in the present of Lieutenant von Stein of the Imperial Schutztruppe, to serve as intermediary in the peace treaties with the Buea people, and to procure some Chiefs of the latter for a peace negotiation.
>
> Sako further declares himself ready to receive a detachment of the Imperial Schutztruppe temporarily in his village, in order to render harmless the Buea people who are roving about.
>
> X Mark of the Chief of Sopo
> The Acting District Officer,
> [signed,] Scheffler
> Customs Director
>
> Copy of the same sent to Herr von Stetten [signed] Scheffler.

Once more negotiations appear actually to have been opened by the Germans. The proposed meeting did not take place, however, until March, as a report of 3 April 1895 says:

> The Buea people have in the middle of last month asked for peace through the chief *Ndeli*, and for permission to be able to settle again on their old site. Ndeli is the brother of the late Paramount Chief Kuba, and appears to have been entrusted with the chieftaincy on the death of the latter. Ndeli presented himself with some forty Buea warriors at Chief Sacco's of Sobbo [sic], the neighbouring tribe and village to Buea, and asked him to mediate with the German authorities.
>
> Chief Sacco brought Ndeli and his following to the Buea military station, whose head (*Vorsteher*), Sergeant Siebert, sent him to Victoria. The peace negotiations have begun before the District Officer von Saltzwedel. As I hear, the Buea people will be granted settlement near their old site, when they have sworn to keep the peace and have paid a war contribution of fifty head of cattle.[94]

Peace Terms

The terms of the peace at Victoria were as follows:

> Between the Imperial Government of Kamerun and the peace negotiators of Buea at the District Office, Ndeli, Ngaueli, Ebakise, peace has bean concluded under the following conditions:
>
> 1
>
> The Buea people are deprived of their former territory and are charged to establish for themselves a new dwelling area in formerly ownerless land.
>
> 2
>
> Until the completion of their new dwelling the Bueas are free to use a measured area of their cocoyam farms in the former Buea territory for food.
>
> 3
>
> As war indemnity, the Buea people are to give the Imperial Bezirksamt fifty head of cattle or their value.
>
> 4
>
> Rights of peace and war, legal jurisdiction and Palaver competence are taken from the Buea people and are transferred to the Imperial Government and to the Sopo people.
>
> 5
>
> The Buea people engage, at any time, to put at the disposal of the District Office, Victoria, 400 labourers against a monthly pay of seven marks and free maintenance.
>
> 6
>
> The Buea people promise in future to obey the orders of the German Government and to keep the peace.
>
> 7
>
> For the validity of the foregoing peace the ratification of the Imperial Governor of Kamerun is necessary.[95]

The two main Buea signatories were Endeli (Endeley I) brother of Kuva, and Evakis' a Manga. The latter was among those totally dispossessed by the Station. In the final arrangements (years later) the area of Lower Buea was not vacated, but resettled. The raising of Soppo to the paramountcy of the area, seems to have been based on a legalistic view of Buea's influence. Kuva's supremacy had not been 'legitimate' in that it was based on alliances, raids, and personal influence. It could not be transferred. To the Germans Kuva had for so long been the enemy that they may have felt his passing left a vacuum. Thus they replaced Buea by Soppo.

What the German records do not say is that Endeley and Evakis' a Manga were transported from Victoria to Douala, as hostages until the indemnity was paid. Elders say that Buea men sold their daughters in marriage to amass the amount. The troops had destroyed their original livestock. Finally the number was still not complete, and the account was settled by an ivory tusk. The labour of the Bakweri was used to build the Station.

On 28 April, 1895 Acting Governor von Puttkamer reported that the new Buea station had two N.C.O.'s and fifty soldiers.[96] In September the English traveller Mary Kingsley arrived, and had a meal with Puttkamer who was on his yacht 'Nachtigal', steaming in Victoria Bay. She set off up the new road to Buea which was as wide as a London street for the short distance it went. She then passed through Boana to Buea, where she found Sergeant Siebert and his half-completed station. The house had no windows as yet, but had blankets nailed to the windows. She had a very wet trip up the Mountain and returned to the coast.[97] Puttkamer reported on 19 October, that a *Stationschef* (Station Officer) would be coming from Togo. This man, Leuschner, would be able to solve the technical difficulties of the road, and proceed with the new station.[98]

Puttkamer went on leave, and a new official Dr Seitz, (the Acting Chancellor), was left in charge. Seitz, who was himself to be Governor in the future, visited Buea on 19 and 20 November, 1895. The officer's report of this visit follows.

Buea Mountain Station[99]

Dr Seitz visited Buea 19/20 November 1895.

> The Station is managed by Stationschef Franz Leuschner, with Assistant Overseer Robert Schut. A unit of the Polizeitruppe serves there to preserve peace and order on the mountain. The Station makes a thoughly good impression.
>
> Round the station a big square of forest is cleared, so that from the Station House there is a completely free view of the Kamerun basin and up the mountain. The station house is made of wood and corrugated iron,

> in very good condition. In the absence of window panes these are nailed over with gauze; the inner wooden cladding is complete. There are four fine big rooms, so that there are two spare rooms for whites. Convalescent Officials will be able to stay. It is as good as summer air in the German mountains.
>
> On the mountain side of the Station house is a spacious, levelled yard round which the Soldiers houses lie in a square. They are of native type, soon to be renewed. There are sheep, goats, hens, ducks. Experiments with mountain cattle will be soon made.
>
> Two gardens are in operation, a smaller and a bigger. There are vegetables. Potatoes are grown both by the station and by the Basel Mission in Buea. In the bigger garden is some mountain rice.
>
> The Station will not only feed its own men [thirty] but in the foreseeable future it will export, especially potatoes, elsewhere.
>
> During the presence of the acting Governor, the chief of the Buea people, Endeli, and the Chief of Soppo appeared at the station. Both promised to support the Station with manpower; Endeli will soon deliver the remainder of the war indemnity laid on him to Victoria.
>
> The question of the erection of a Sanatorium in Buea is undergoing examination at present.

The Basel Mission had already begun to rebuild their station under their missionary builder Schmid.[100]

Dispossession

The arrangements for the resettlement of Buea were based ultimately on the rights conceded to Valdau by the Buea Chiefs, to which we must retrace our steps.[101]

The Soden Negotiations

Soden's purchase was entered in the form of an extract from the Grundbuch (Land Register) on 8 April 1890. The Grundbuch has a number of vertical columns. The plot is No. 1 on folio 2 of Vol. 7. The land is described as 'Territory (*Landschaft*) of Upper, Middle and Lower Buea'. Added subsequently and underlined there follows: *'with the exception of the land belonging to the Basel Mission'*. The columns referring to the area were left blank. The owner was given as 'Freiherr Julius von Soden, Imperial Governor, in Kamerun'. The force of the last two words and the comma is: 'at Douala'. Under 'Time and Basis of

Acquisition' is written: 'Acquired by Treaty of Purchases of 17 February, 1889. Registered on 8 April 1890. Signed Gf [*Graf*=Count] Pfeil, Chancellor [not to be confused with the lowly Gardener], Wallmuth, Secretary'. The date of the purchase is wrongly given as 1889, instead of 1887. Under the column 'Value, is written: 'Fourteen English pounds in goods, about 280 Marks'. Once more an error due to a hasty reading of only one of Valdau's agreements. Upper and Lower Buea each got fourteen pounds. Later it was argued that the regulations through which land claims could be registered had not been observed (especially that there had been no survey). This entry was eventually to be referred to as in the 'provisional Land Register'.

At the time of the registration von Soden was on leave, and still talking of exchanging his Buea claim for Government land at Bota. However, he was transferred to the Governorship of East Africa. He wrote to the German Chancellor Caprivi from Dar-es-Salaam on 29 August 1891.[102] Soden explained that he himself had made a decree in Kamerun that land purchased in the colony should revert to the Government if it was not cultivated within a certain time. Partly to comply with this, and partly in the interests of the country and the Mission, he had therefore transferred two hectares of his Buea land free to the Basel Mission, for a Mission building and a Sanatorium. Now he had learnt lately that a Botanical Research Garden had been laid out in Buea, which he welcomed, but it must, he wrote, be 'on my land and soil', and he would have thought the Government in Kamerun would have let him know where on his land it was, and its size.

On 25 September the Foreign Office copied it to von Schuckmann the Acting Governor of Kamerun, noting that the letter seemed to refer to the vegetable garden of Dr Preuss, and so was probably on the land given to the Mission.[103] Von Schuckmann must have received it at about the time he set out on the Gravenreuth Expedition. Afterwards, Soden's query must have seemed academic.

On 20 January 1894, Soden wrote to the Foreign Office again, from retirement at Vorra in Bavaria.[104] Once more he referred to his own decree that unexploited land should revert to Government after, he thought, five years. This, he noted, was to stop 'unhealthy speculation' in land. He thought this time limit had been exceeded in the case of his Buea land, and he was asking for an extension of the time limit. He gave as a ground that he had already ceded a plot to the Basel Mission for nothing, and he believed that Dr Preuss also had a research garden on it. This might, by a benevolent interpretation be considered exploitation of land, especially since in Germany there was now a prevailing mistrust of big colonial enterprises, which made it difficult to get capital. Also, if he was correctly informed, it would have been impossible to start any such enterprises in the Buea area because of the insecurity there. Even if the land did revert to Government, he didn't think this would make its development any more likely.

On 4 April 1894 Zimmerer sent a copy of this to Leist, who was in Victoria, for a report.[105] On the 7th Leist wrote from the District Office that the Soden purchase was still not registered in the *Grundbuch* of Kamerun, since it was not feasible to apply the Grundbuch regulations to Buea, due to the political conditions there.[106] As things were at the moment, he added with some irony, he did not think Chief Kuva would give his consent to have the land registered in the name of Baron Soden, especially (Leist noted) since Kuva had omitted to sign the declaration of 4 March 1887. And even if his consent were replaced by a legal declaration, execution of the judgement would be impossible with the Government's present resources. Kuva would never permit the boundaries of the land sold to his Excellency von Soden to be fixed, and without their being so fixed no registration (according to paragraph 87 of the Imperial Chancellor's enactment of 7 July 1888) could be undertaken. In the circumstances, Leist recommended that Government should take up Soden's original offer to sell the land at cost price, estimated at 600-800 Marks. It was clear, wrote Leist, that the Buea country had a great economic future.

Leist, who had just been in Buea with Vice-Consul Spengler, was clearly out of sympathy with Soden's fantasy landlordism. In the end a non-committal reply was sent to Soden.[107] Berlin told him on 7 June 1894 that judgement on reversion would be made when the property was registered. Leist's realism over the Buea land is refreshing, but his legalism was inconsistent. Basically Leist did not see why Soden should benefit from the new developments which would soon come from Vice-Consul Spengler's report. His recommendation .to accept Soden's offer of 14 April 1887, still assumed the legality of the original purchase.

On 15 December, 1894, the Imperial Chancellor wrote to Zimmerer (who was on leave in Berlin), noting that since Soden bought the land in 1887, the purchase preceded the Ordinance of 27 March 1888, establishing the time-limit. Soden's rights could be proved by showing that Soden's land was entered in the provisional Grundbuch. Von Soden could then be recognised as owner.[107]

Thus, before the second Buea Expedition took place the land was already decided to be von Soden's. When his old friend von Puttkamer was Acting Governor things were easier still. Puttkamer wrote to Soden in Bavaria on 6 April, 1895 from Spengler's plantation at Monté Café, São Thomé, enclosing the following:

Certificate

> It is hereby officially certified that His Excellency Freiherr Julius von Soden is the owner of the territory of Buea, on the basis of the Agreements of 17 February and 4 March, 1887 to be found in the files of this country, and in virtue of the entry in the former provisional Land Register of the Protectorate.
>
> Monté Café, São Thomé, 6 April, 1895
> [initialled] v. P.[109]

Next year, on 30 March, 1896, Soden complained that the Roman Catholic Mission now claimed some of his Buea land.[110] Seitz wrote a letter from Kamerun to the Imperial Chancellor on this subject, on 20 July, 1896, in which some light is shed on Bakweri reactions to the whole topic.[111] Seitz remarked that he had recently visited Buea to determine the boundary between the area allocated to the Bakweri and the Station. He went on:

> In the negotiations, there were discussed among other things, various claims raised by whites to the territory of Buea. The brother of Kuba, the present Chief Endeli, stated that the Governor von Soden had only acquired the plot belonging now to the Basel Mission. The Catholic Mission had certainly not acquired any land. Some years ago a member of the Catholic Mission had been in Buea—from the description it was Father *Vieter,* who is at present on home leave—in order to negotiate a purchase of land with Kuba. Kuba had refused any sale, but had declared he would make no difficulties if the Mission wanted to settle on his own land. Later Kuba had, however, thought better of it and refused the Catholic Mission the settlement in Buea.

For the rest of 1896, the correspondence dealt with the question of a survey of the Buea boundaries, so that the Government Station and the Basel Mission land could be set against Soden's own land. The Mission wanted their title made clear. On 10 May, 1896, the Berlin Foreign Office informed von Soden that von Puttkamer wanted about 10 hectares for the Station.[112] The military was to be moved away, and F. Leuschner would be in charge with a small detachment of police. Soon it would be a health station. Extensive land would be needed for gardens and parks, cattle pastures, and so on. As a result the land should be surveyed. Soden agreed, and appointed a representative on the spot. When Seitz saw this he minuted on 31 July that 10 hectares was not enough for the Station. Puttkamer noted: 'Preuss is to survey Buea and report.'[113]

On 4th September the Acting Stationsleiter Bittner of Buea wrote to Seitz that Preuss had already surveyed the boundaries of Buea before it was taken by von Stetten. This was when Dr Preuss had been acting as District Office. Bittner was saying that he himself did not need to survey them again since Preuss had used instruments. He had, however, already marked the boundary with the Bakweri.

> I have marked the boundary on the Buea side (Endeli) with a pyramid 1 metre high, which naturally evoked the displeasure of Chief Endeli. He declared that the Buea people who had fled after the war wanted to settle again in the old territory, and thus the area measured was too restricted. Also he wanted the boundary moved, which I refused in accordance with my instructions.
>
> Also according to the opinion of Dr Preuss, who viewed the area of the territory fixed, it is sufficient for the time being for the small population increase of the Buea people.[114]

On 24 December, 1896, Puttkamer settled the matter in advance:

> 1. Dr Preuss is authorised to measure out 1,000 hectares for His Excellency von Soden, 25 hectares for the Government Station, and to fix the area of the Mission land.
> 2. Bring up to me on my return from Yaounde. (Report to the Foreign Office and inform Soden).
>
> I have unofficially informed His Excellency von Soden privately.[115]

Preuss's Report

Dr Preuss conducted his survey, and reported on 10 January, 1897. The report is the record of a piece of gerrymandering in the interest of the new owners. It gives us the last picture of old Buea before it vanished, to be transformed as von Puttkamer's *Wolkenthron.*

Preuss left Victoria on 22 December, 1896. The government road now reached Boana. From 23-27 December he surveyed the boundaries of Buea with the neighbouring territories of Mimbia, Soppo, Molyko and Ewunda, and fixed the position of streams in the Soppo area, which might be of importance to the plantations. On the 27 December he returned to Victoria, surveying the part of the road from Soppo down to Boana.

In his survey of Buea, Preuss made a distinction between a narrow and a broad definition of the territory of Buea. The *narrow* definition was the land enclosed by the old village fence. Its course was broken only at two places by very deep ravines. These were, it seems, the Mosole and Mission ravines in the uphill part of the fence. The area enclosed was not more than 210 hectares. Of this the Government station now occupied sixteen hectares. The Basel Mission claimed six hectares. This left about 190 hectares over for Freiherr von Soden.

The exact course of the fence was as follows: From the bridge over the Gravenreuth ravine on the Mountain Hotel road, uphill along the ravine to the level of the Pr[esident's] Lodge then behind the Lodge grounds to the Mosole ravine, upstream from the Lodge bridge. Then came a break. Then from the other side of the ravine, but slightly higher up, it ran along well uphill of the Office in the grounds of the Lodge but below Upper Farm, until it reached the upper part of the Mission ravine. It was again broken, and on the other side it ran along the present upper boundary of the Mission land, and straight on until it met the present town fence, which is beyond the football field. The fence around the present Buea 'Native' follows approximately the old course, cutting the Bova road, then turning south and cutting the road to Wokpae, and turning north again. In 1896, however, the fence then enclosed the present Stranger Quarter and 'Bonaberi', so that the main Stranger road was inside the fence.

It then cut below the stadium, and behind Houses 39, 37 and 38, and passed the Mission Ravine again lower down. It curved behind the Magistrate's Court and the House of Assembly, and along the boundary between the Federal Rest House and houses 49, 52 and 48. It then crossed the present main road, and passed parallel to it, but a little below it, to cut the road to Small Soppo somewhere below the junction and above the Education Office, probably going through the garden of House 19. It then followed the general course of the road of the Federal Quarters, until it reached the Gravenreuth ravine lower down. It turned uphill again along the bank, coming up through the Development Agency workshop to cross the road, where we started, at the bridge on the way to the Mountain Hotel on the Mimbia-Wokpaongo road,[117]

This territory swung almost in a semicircle so that from Lower Buea, near the present Stranger Quarter, one could see right across to the lowest point of Upper Buea above the Education Office. Thus inside that semicircle was all Soppo 'bush' land. The whole lower boundary of

Buea, Preuss found, was in fact the fence itself on the south with Soppo, on the east with Wokpae and Moliko, and on the north-east with Ewonda on the road to Bova and Bonakanda. Preuss's *broader* definition of Buea included the land outside the fence on the Mimbia side. The boundary of Buea territory with Mimbia here was a '*mumangi*' tree (an iroko), about 1600 metres from the Station House, and at that spot indeed is the present boundary point. Preuss then determined an arbitrary boundary which ran from the 'mumangi' and behind the present Hotel and Federal house, to link up with the fence below the Gravenreuth bridge. On the uphill side he drew a straight line to the north-west, and then made it turn along the mountain to include all the Upper Farm area, to join the fence again on the side nearest to the Ewonda boundary. Preuss admitted that this area was approximate only.

As far as the 'narrow' area of Buea inside the fence was concerned, Preuss had allocated the area between the Mosole and the Mission ravines to the station. The Basel Mission received less than their present plot. Soden's 190 hectares then consisted of the area between the Mosole and the Gravenreuth ravine—that is, the present Prime Minister's Lodge area, and all that part of the present station down to the Mountain Club. In addition he had the whole of the present station and town from the Basel Mission onwards. In the future this allocation was totally lost, but its sweep today seems astonishing. Preuss was uncomfortable about the whole business of Soden's land. The Buea people were crowded into the Lower Buea part, and Station Officer Leuschner was already complaining that he should also have land on Soden's side of the Mosole. So much for the supposed extensive plantation lands that Soden was dreaming of.

Preuss then took into account the 'broader' area of Buea on the mountain and Mimbia sides. First he took the best piece for the Station, part of the Upper Farm area. The area on the Mimbia road side he allocated to Soden. This also seemed rather steep and mountainous. So as a final piece of jigsaw puzzling, he took the quite arbitrary step of annexing the whole stretch of uninhabited Soppo bush from the present stranger quarter to the Buea boundary along the Mimbia road, and adding it to Soden's allocation. This zone became the present West Farm and Lower Farm areas. Thus Buea was enlarged at Soppo's expense in order to give Soden his supposed rights. Soppo, with a detachment of Schutztruppe stationed there, would be in no position to object.[118]

As finally allocated, Preuss's survey thus gathered together 1000 hectares for von Soden. He was, however, critical of the Basel Mission's claim. He said the mission's land at Victoria was unused and in a 'scandalous' condition. He awarded 4 hectares. The Station had now got a total of 50 hectares. On 13 February 1897 an official noted that the survey should only have given the Government 25 hectares, and he asked Dr Preuss to amend the plan and cut out some government land. Von Puttkamer firmly minuted: 'Not my opinion. It remains the present size, about 50 hectares'. Later on, when Preuss had amended his map, von Puttkamer repeated: 'It remains 50 Hectares.' [119]

On 24 March the Governor wrote to Berlin explaining that the 'broader' area of Buea had been taken, to Soden's benefit, so that he had received, instead of 'unfruitful' Buea land, a 'very fruitful piece of Soppo land'.[120]

Meanwhile the commercial plans of Soden were moving to fruition. On 17 February 1897, a newly founded company made an agreement with the Colonial Department of the Foreign Office at Berlin to develop certain lands as plantations. Thus appeared the great *Westafrikanische Plantagengesellschaft Victoria* (W.A.P.V.) with its Headquarters at Bota. Certain old acquaintances appeared at its birth, as the following extract shows:

> The conditions of the treaty refer to the property authenticated in Kamerun of the Westafrikanische Plantagen-Gesellschaft Victoria, which consists of the following lands:
>
> 1. The lands at Buea formerly belonging to Governor (Retired) von Soden, of an area of 1,000 hectares.
> 2. The lands at Buana sold to Herr Scholto Douglas by a contract of 4 June, 1896, of an area of about 3,000 hectares.
> 3. The lands south of Buana sold to the Vice-Consul Spengler by a contract of 2 April 1895, of an area of about 2,000 hectares.
> 4. The Bota area transferred to Dr Zintgraff by a Land Concession of 5 January 1896, of an area of some 2,000 hectares.
> 5. The lands of Ngeme sold by a contract of 10 February 1897, to the Westafrikanische Pflanzungsgesellschaft Victoria, of an area of some 2,000 hectares.[121]

On 7 August Preuss's assessment of Soden's land was confirmed by the Colonial Department to the W.A.P.V. headquarters in Berlin, who replied (10 August) requesting that the Buea property should be registered. A certificate was issued on 21 August. Finally Buea was entered in the Grundbuch as belonging to W.A.P.V. on 24 September, 1897, ten years and seven months after Valdau's original words 'Your Excellency! Yesterday I succeeded in buying whole Bwea for you'.

In the future, W.A.P.V. gradually ceded the area between the Mosele and the Gravenreuth Ravine, for extensions to the station, and, in time for von Puttkamer's Schloss. Other adjustments were made over the years: in particular Lower Buea, the present Native Area, was finally recognised as a 'Reserve'. The Mimbia Road (West Farm) and 'Soppo Bush' (Lower Farm) areas passed from W.A.P.V. ownership after the two World Wars, into the hands of the Cameroon Development Corporation, who finally conceded them to the Government of the South Cameroons in 1955. The vegetable gardens still survived for some years after.[122]

Conclusion

Von Puttkamer

During 1897, the layout of the new Buea was well advanced. Puttkamer reported[123] that several missionary families were already living in the new Basel Mission dwellings. The gregarious Puttkamer wrote appreciatively of the new life in Buea. The house of the Stationschef was 'friendly', small, with four rooms on pillars. 'Since Stationschef Leuschner has brought out his young wife with him, to the benefit of the station and its hospitality, I have allocated him this house permanently'.[124] The road from Victoria was on its last stretch from Boana to Buea. Villagers cleared the trace to the breadth of four metres; horses and hammocks could traverse it. Puttkamer had Leuschner begin upon a Governor's Residence in January 1897.[125]

Plantation companies now at work included not only W.A.P.V., and its old-established rivals at Debundscha (Jantzen und Thormählen) and Bimbia (Kamerun Land-und-Plantagen-Gesellschaft), but also the estate of Günther and Rausch (Günther-Soppo) on Soppo and Moliko land.[127] Valdau (now using the German spelling of his name) was in the Rio del Rey area with the Deutsch-Westafrikanische Handelsgesellschaft.[128] By 10 December, 1897, W.A.P.V. alone was employing 1,150 men. Zintgraff had recruited 431 Bali. There were also 151 Kru, 317 Yaounde, 15 Banyang, and 8 Bakundu.[129] The arrival of the Günther-Soppo plantation was not popular. Acting Governor Seitz reported (23 May 1898) that 'at first' it was difficult to get labourers for it. Roses were being planted in Buea.[130]

In 1898 the new Government House was finished.[131] From now on von Puttkamer lived regularly in Buea. He immediately set in motion his plans to build his impressive chateau—the present Pr[esident's]

Minister's Lodge—on the other side of the Mosole stream. The spread of plantations up on the mountain now continued unimpeded, and for ten years the upheaval was unabated. In those years, missionaries were the main spokesman for the villagers, as the plantation managers moved settlements about to make room for their plantings. In the end, Land Commissions established reserves for the Bakweri, but their work was still not completed by the First World War.[133]

Von Puttkamer, to whom West Cameroon owes the rapid establishment of the plantation industry, was ready with replies to all criticism. Already as early as 10 January, 1899, the Kolonialabteilung in Berlin was writing to him, as a result of petitions from the Basel Mission about his land policy. On 30 May, 1899, Puttkamer, enthroned on the lands of Gbekambi and Ekpa Wotani, replied from Buea in a surprised and reasonable tone. He wished the Mission would abstain from general accusations like: 'suppression', 'violation', 'exploitation' and 'ill treatment'. These were big words, easily said. As for the Bakweri, this was the picture he painted (one that must be a classic of disingenuousness):

> This people, who were so accustomed to free movement, have so far adjusted to the quite changed conditions of life, that they gladly work on the new plantations, and thereby they are able to earn a more than adequate living, while the women and children work their own farms, as formerly, or go as carriers between Victoria and the stations on the Mountain. They still cultivate not a twentieth of the land allocated to them, and they are still ready to sell any plot of their land, and constantly seek an opportunity to do so. I once, in fact, thought of forbidding them to sell any more land (except of course to Missions) to preserve their tribal situation, but I think the measure is no longer necessary. More intelligent chiefs like the well-known Efesua of Bonjongo (a Baptist Christian) are planting rubber and cocoa in their village areas.
>
> An increase of population is not to be thought of; on the contrary, the population numbers on the coast are steadily declining, and on the mountain they are, at the most, remaining stable. Fifteen *ares* (of land) per head are quite plentiful enough, and this is exceeded everywhere, except at Bota where they are fishermen. Almost everywhere the people have two *hectares* per hut, an amount of land they will not now, nor ever be able to cultivate.
>
> The only difference is that formerly the people planted petty plots all over the forest, often far from their compounds, with maize, beans and the like, while now they have to plant directly next to their huts, and thus to follow an orderly mode of agriculture, which there was no thought of formerly. Some have seen the advantage of the thing: thus Soppo, a village formerly scattered over an endless area, willingly had itself collected into

> a big village with a regular village street. The huts stand in rows on both sides of the street, numbered, and surrounded by gardens in which are grown the above-mentioned foodstuffs. The *Soppo* people are proud of their new fashion, and from all sides petitions come into Buea to make other villages as beautiful. It only lacks the postman hurrying from house-number to house-number. That will not be long to wait for: the mission schools will take care of that.[134]

From the world of Merrick to Puttkamer's utopian fantasy was a great step in forty-five years. P. M. Kale may be excused a temporary lapse from impartiality when he wrote in 1939:

> The Germans had cleverly taken the mind from their subjects and like the sorceress Circe turned them into swine. It is not strange, therefore, that the poor victims were blind to their plight.[135]

Kuva's Policy

From the vantage point of the present day, the rise of the small kingdom of Buea was remarkable. When it was in alliance with Soppo and Bonjongo a mountain political system came into being which began to look towards the coast and the creeks. This 'imperialistic' period was very short lived. It occupied the time-gap between, on the one hand: the decline of Bimbia, the inaction of the Baptists at Victoria, and the ending of the British Consular control; and, on the other: the full growth of German power. It was a phenomenon therefore of approximately 1880-1895. It grew up on the very eve of colonial rule, and came to its peak when that rule was officially in existence. It was a small-scale political movement, but one which, aided by the strategic possibilities of the Mountain, was for a brief period actually equal in scale to the amount of German power that could be deployed from Victoria.

The personality of Kuva, throughout, must be accounted unusual, for it makes itself felt through the reports of his enemies. By chance, perhaps, he had acquired the leadership, but one cannot fail to be impressed by the way he preserved a consistent policy. This can be expressed as the search for a way to outflank the traders of Bimbia and Victoria, and the building up of a supply of arms on the mountain. The year 1891 represents a brilliant success for this policy. By 1894 it was impossible to maintain. The German pygmy was suddenly a giant. Zimmerer deprived Kuva of arms at the stroke of a pen. That his policy should have had a 'reactionary' appearance at the time was inevitable. To him Christianity, the hated Bimbia, and the Germans, were linked together. The weakness of his ideological position defeated him as much as his lack of arms. He was, he thought, fighting witches as well as whitemen. He cut himself off, therefore, from educated support at the coast. When the mountain villages were dispossessed some, in the naive fashion of the day, saw it as divine retribution.

Nevertheless, Kuva's case is of more than local interest. This remote and ideologically merely intuitive tribesman held up the march of events, by an unexpected veto on the foreign economic exploitation of the mountain. The veto only ended with his death. During its existence, it revealed serious weaknesses in German colonial administrative and military practice. He was successful at a time when individual agents of the Government were working with obscure responsibility, and when money was scarce. Corners were cut, and risks were taken. The irresponsible recruiting methods of Gravenreuth were typical of the period. Any serious setback could mean that the whole ramshackle structure was seriously shaken. The resistance of the mountain people provided one of the important shocks to the early colonial system in Kamerun. As a resistance movement it was before its time; as a micro-imperialism of the Buea kingdom it began too late. But Kuva must receive the credit for diverting the curse of Gravenreuth and his slave-troops upon the colonial masters themselves.

Bakweri Buea still exists behind its restored fence, now restricted to the zone of the pre-conquest Lower Buea, which it shares with the Stranger Quarter. Fortunately even W.A.P.V. balked at swallowing all this inhabited area. The village was rearranged round a stony ring-road, and it too must have presented a suitably tidy appearance to the German Governor. The passage of time has, however, reduced the visible effects of this regimentation, and has begun to efface even its memory.[136]

Annexe A

Merrick's Account of a Bakweri Rite

On the way back from Buea, Merrick gives an account of a funeral rite at 'Minyari-Munggo'. The name of this village presents problems. It is, in my view, a name beginning with *Wonya,* 'children of'. The present village in the area is called Wonya-Imali. Merrick does not make any other error of such a scale, and in additon Wonya-Imali is said to be a relatively recent settlement. The recency of settlement may, however, refer only to the present site. Merrick's *Minyari* could perhaps represent *Wonyimali.* The ending 'Mungo' possibly misspells *wongo:* 'that is, over there'. Thus the sentence *Wonyimali wongo:* 'that is Wonyimali' might account for Merrick's form. The settlement of Dibutu Lanja lay in this village area. Merrick says:

> At half-past four, arrived at a town whose chief, Dibutu Lanja, had died three days ago. The usual funeral ceremonies were being performed when we arrived, which were exceedingly ill adapted to the occasion. From five to six hundred people were assembled on an oblong piece of ground, and amidst the noise of drums and the greatest confusion, danced up and down in the most ludicrous manner. A group of ten met together, and raising up their right hand struck it against the hand of each other till the ceremony of striking hands had been performed throughout the whole group.
>
> On my arrival I was conducted to the house of a man named Foke, a short distance from the scene of the funeral ceremonies, lest, as I was told, my presence should attract the attention of the people, and thus put an end to their mirth. Many followed me, to whom I showed letters of the alphabet and my Isubu lesson. My watch as usual was quite an object of wonder and amazement. Unable to obtain a sight of me, some of the boys, Zaccheus like, climbed on trees to gratify their curiosity. Being anxious to see the whole of the funeral ceremony, I got up to walk to the place where people were dancing but Foke would not allow me to go. However, shortly after Madiba, whose town I visited before going to the Cameroons Mountains, and to whom I have already alluded, came up, and taking me by the hand, conducted me to the scene of action, and thus afforded me an opportunity of seeing all that was going on. I had not sat long before the man who was to succeed the deceased chief made his appearance in a soldier's coat. A man held an umbrella over his head, and followed wherever he went. In a stooping posture the new chief ran among the crowd amidst the caressing of several young women, striking hands with all who presented theirs to him.
>
> After a great deal of noise and dancing, silence was commanded, when

> Madiba, being master of the ceremonies, arose to speak; but before he commenced his address he picked up a pebble, and spitting upon it, placed it under his foot, and then walked up and down the avenue speaking as he walked along. He said that Dibutu Lanja had died three days ago, and left so many pieces of cloth (I do not recollect the number), pigs, sheep and goats; and that during his illness two of his goats had been killed for him. Madiba having finished his address several of the people exclaimed 'He, he' (Yes, yes); shortly after which the party began to disperse.
>
> I understand that on the death of a chief or master of a town, all his property, which generally consists of cloth, pigs, goats, and sheep, are distributed among his relatives and friends, and nothing is thought so honourable to a man as to be able on his death to leave a great deal of property for distribution. All the cloth which Dibutu Lanja possessed was on his death exhibited to the public for inspection, but was taken in before my arrival. I however saw his pigs, sheep and goats all of which were tied to stakes placed in the ground for the purpose.
>
> (*Missionary Herald,* 1845, p. 146.)

***

The Bakweri ceremony three days after death is called *sasa.* The display and distribution of goods after death is called *eyu.* This rite nowadays, if performed at all, is performed some time after death in order to allow time for the collection of the necessary goods. At an *eyu* in Wova in 1960, an umbrella was carried over the head of the heir just as Merrick describes for 1844. (See also Ardener, 1956 pp. 87-89.)

Annexe B

Bakweri Villages 1848

John Clarke lists (*Missionary Herald.* 1848, July, p. 101) what he calls '125 towns or districts in which the Isubu, or a dialect of the Isubu is spoken'. The source of this list is almost certainly Merrick. The list consists, in fact, of Bakweri and Womboko villages, and some others. The identifiable Bakweri villages are shown here. Nowadays, some Bakweri villages are known in Bakweri spellings, some in Duala-type spellings, and in a mixture of the two. For convenience I list the Clarke/ Merrick names with the modern names in two columns (a) the Duala-type spellings (b) the Bakweri spellings. When there is no difference, only column (b) is filled. This list will not have been exhaustive so that modern villages missing from itmay nevertheless have been in existence.

Clarke 1848	*Spelling* (a)	*Spelling* (b)
Babengga	Babenga	Vavenga
Bagpogko	Bokwaongo	Wokpaongo
Boandu	Boando	Gbando
Boana	Boana	Woana
Boba	Boba	Wova
Bokuku	Bokoko	Wokoko
Bokiri	Bokeli	Wokeli
Bokum [Bokwei]	Bokwae	Wokpae
Bolu	Bulu	Wulu
Boksulu	Bokulu	Wokulu
Bonjongo	Bonjongo	Wonjongo
Borunggu	Bolongo	Wolongo
Boyoke	Bojoke	Wojoke
Buripamba	Bolipamba	Wolifamba
Bwea	Buea	Gbea
Bwengga	Bwenga	Gbenga
Dibanda	Dibanda	Livanda
Dikoko	Dikoko	Likoko
Diebo	Diebo	Liewo
Ebonggo	Ebongo	Ewongo
Ebonji	Ebonji	Ewonji
Ekona		Ekona
Manum [Maumu]		Maumu
Matanggo		Matangu
Mokunda		Mokunda
Momanggi		(=Lisoka)
Mouko [Moriko]		Moliko
Owe		Owe
Sofo	Soppo	Sofo
Ikatu		Ikata
Mobeta		[Mabeta]
Monjangge		Monyange
Mosuma		Masuma

Annexe C

The Agreements of 1887

Buea File IV B 34i, Vol.2. Created on 11.1.1911 and closed 11.8.1911, it contains a compilation of the following agreements, together with the correspondence discussed previously.

1. The Agreement of 18 *February, 1887.*

[The text which follows was handwritten in ink, totally in English, with the spellings as printed.]

Mapanja, 18th Feb., 1887,

Yours Excellency !

Yesterday I succeeded in buying whole Bwea for you. As the trade within Victoria and the mountain towns since long time is cut off by the fight within Bonjongo and Bosumbo I got it to good price. I could not get all the kings an [sic] chiefs together at one time because the Upper and Lower Buea are enemies and must therefore make two contracts. The prices on the contracts are after the account of the people—not the prices of the factories. The Bwea people will come to Mapanja and receive the payment. If you send the payment to Bokundange I will forward it to Mapanja and pay the people there.

At the enclosed note you will found the goods which is to be send. The people want that kind capsgun Mr Allen sell in Cameroons.

It will need about 10 carriers to take the goods to Mapanja.

Yesterday a black trader Edgeley and a man from Victoria sold Snider in Bwea for cows what, I believe, not is allowed.

With kind regards to you and Mr von Puttkamer.

I remain
Yours Respectfully

George Valdau

P.S. As I here [sic] you don't know that the small Calabar steamer has sold rum in Bibundi, I have to report that we have bought from him 2 barrels, and some demejons Rum the first time he was in Bibundi.
The former captain for the cutter, Henry, who has been punished of you for steal has the same Calabar firm out as clark in Bibundi. I suppose he is not allowed to stop in German territory.

D.S.
[=Derselbe]

Note

Payment to the Kings and Chiefs of Buea:	£	sh	d	£	sh	d
10 pieces Satin-Stripes	10	—	—			
10 kegs Powder	5	—	—			
5 Capsguns	2	10	—			
2 demjons Rum	1	—	—			
1 km. Tobacco	1	—	—	19	10	—
'Dash' received by the Bwea-people:						
10 km. Tobacco	1	10	—			
8 fath. f-Madras à 1/8d	—	13	4	2	3	4
Payment and Dash to the Interpreter:						
2 pieces Blue Baft	——	——	——	2	—	—
Three carriers from Mapanja to Bwea and back to Mapanja:						
12 fath. C-Madras à 1/3d	——	——	——	—	15	—
Payment for 10 luggages from Bokundang [sic] to Mapanja:						
20 fath. C-Madras à 1/3d	——	——	——	1	5	—
				25	13	4

We the undersigned herewith declare that in conformity with the wish of the people of Bwea, we have sold to His Excellency the Governor of Cameroons Sir J. von Soden our part of the territory of Bwea and that from the day of date he is the legal and legitimate owner of the named territory. The houses, palmtrees, farms and other private property the people of Bwea shall be possessed of further on as they have been up to this day. The payment been fourteen Pound Sterling (£14) in goods shall be paid to the first June this year.

Done in two copies this seventeenth day of February eighteen hundred and eighty seven at the town of Bwea.

	Their	
King	X	Epa
Chief	X	Manja
Chief	X	Mosissa
Chief	X	Dingundu
	Marks	

The sign of the King and the Chiefs confirm at the same time present witnesses.

		Interpreter
(*signed*)	(*signed*)	(*Signed*)
Ndibe Ekoa	Georg Valdau	Mbua Moki

We the undersigned herewith declare that in conformity with the wish of the people of Bwea we have sold to His Excellency the Governor of Cameroons Sir J. von Soden our part of the territory of Bwea and that from the day of date he is the legal and legitimate owner of the named territory. The houses, palmtrees, farms and other private property the people of Bwea shall be possessed of further on as they have been up to this day. The payment being £14 shall be paid to 1st June.

Done in two copies this seventeenth day of February eighteen hundred and eighty seven at the town of Bwea.

	Their	
King	X	Kuva
King	X	Letongo
Chief	X	Molue
Chief	X	Ndele
Chief	X	Mesombe
Chief	X	Motuttu
Chief	X	Name
Chief	X	Metumba
Chief	X	Mosokko
Chief	X	Kange
	Marks	

The sign of the Kings and Chiefs confirm at the same time present witnesses

Moesse from Bonjongo		Interpreter
His	(*signed*)	(*signed*)
X	Georg Valdau	Mbua Moki
Mark		

2. *The Agreement of 4 March 1887.* (Text in German, in ink over pencil, except for headings as shown)

Kaiserlicher Gouverneur von Kamerun (*Printed letter-head*)	Kamerun (*Printed and crossed out*) Buea den 4 März 1887 (*ink over pencil*)

Die unterzeichneten Häuptlinge von Buea bescheinigen hiermit von dem Kais, [sic] Gouverneur Herrn von Soden den verbundeten Kaufpreis fuer das sämtliche Land in Buea (Ober- Mitterl- und Unter-Buea) sofern(e) es nicht von ihnen bebaut und bewohnt wird, erhalten zu haben. Auf an dem derzeit von ihnen bewohnten und bebauten Grund & Boden räumen die Buea-Leute dem Kais. Gouverneur bezugsweise dessen Rechtsnachfolger ein unbedingtes Vorkaufsrecht ein, das heisst: sie werden von diesem Grund & Boden ohne vorhergehende Benachrichtigung des Gouverneurs nichts an dritte Personen verkaufen. Jeder Landvertrag ohne Vorwissen des jetzigen Käufers oder seiner Rechtsnachfolger geschlossen, soll somit kein Gültigkeit haben. Vorstehendes ist den unterzeichneten Häuptlingen von dem Dolmetscher Sam Stien [sic] übersetzt & von alle, Anwesenden ausdrücklich erklärt worden, dass sie Alles wohl verstehenden hätten & dem Vertrage ihre vollständige Zustimmung ertheilen. Der erste Häuptling von Buea Kuba (*on the pencil script underneath, 'Kuba' is interpolated*) erklärt ausdrücklich, dass er für diejenigen seiner Unterhäuptlinge, die heute nicht erschienen & nicht unterzeichnet hätten, die volle Verantwortung übernehmen & dafür Sorge tragen werde, dass sie ihre Antheil am Kaufpreis erhalten.

My translation:

Imperial Governor of Kamerun	 Buea, 4 March. 1887

The undersigned Chiefs of Buea certify herewith that they have received from the Imperial Governor Herr von Soden the contracted purchase price for the whole of the land in Buea (Upper, Middle, and Lower Buea) in so far as it is not cultivated or built on by them. The Buea people confer upon the Imp. Governor, or his successors in law, an unrestricted prior right of purchase to the land which is at present cultivated and built on by them, that is: they will not sell this land to third persons without prior notification to the Governor. No land contract concluded shall be valid without the foreknowledge of the present purchaser or his successors in law. The foregoing was translated for the undersigned chiefs by the interpreter Sam Stien [sic] and it was expressly stated by all present that they had understood, and they gave their complete consent to the agreement. The first chief of Buea, Kuba, expressly declares that he takes full responsibility on behalf of those of his subchiefs who have not appeared today and have not signed, and will see to it that they receive their share of the price.

From here the pencilled text is in English with German written on it in ink. The English follows:

			(Handzeichen) Their	
	King Epa	X His Mark	King	X Letongo
(Häuptling)	Chief Mosissa	X His Mark	Chief	X Mollue
—	Chief Manga	X His Mark	Chief	X Ndeli
—	Chief Ngondo	X His Mark	Chief	X Metumba
			Chief	X Njaki
			Chief	X Ewokise
			Marks	

(*English pencilled text:*)

The sign [sic] of the Kings and Chiefs confirm at one time present witnesses.

(*Written over in German in ink:*)

Die Handzeichen der vorstehenden Häuptlinge und Unterhäuptlinge werden hiermit durch die Dolmetscher und die Zeugen begläubigt

Georg Valdau (*ink over pencil*) Sam Steane (*ink over pencil*)

Vanselow (*ink over pencil*) Der Kais. Gouverneur v. Soden (*ink only*)

(*From here the writing is in German, in ink only, in Soden's handwriting*)

Eine Abschrift ist in *Buea* nicht zurückgelassen worden mangels an Zeit.

(*My translation:* A copy was not left in Buea for lack of time.)

Die Übermalung mit Tinte hat nachträglich stattgefunden.

(*My translation:* The inking over was done later.)

Signed
Soden
Gouverneur

Annexe D

Selected Genealogical Tables

These selected tables are merely illustrative of the descent of certain individuals mentioned in the text. Many important Buea descents are excluded.

1. Among the supposed sons of Eyé Naliomo are named:

   Vefonge, Lifanje, Iwange, Motande, Wotumbe, Motumbe, Movale, Wolongo, Mokumbe.

2. Part of the descent from Vefonge:

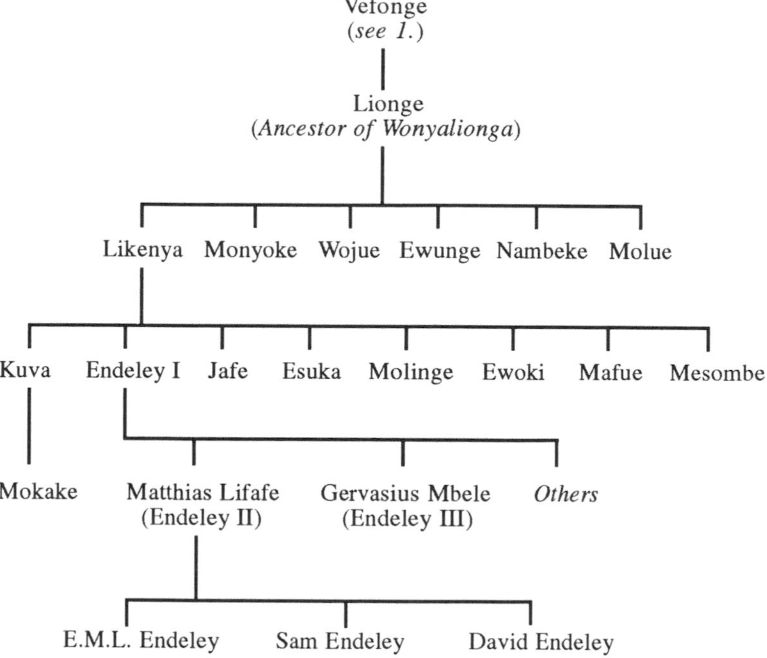

From Ewunge came Mosisa mo Ewunge.

3. The descent of Lotonge Molie:

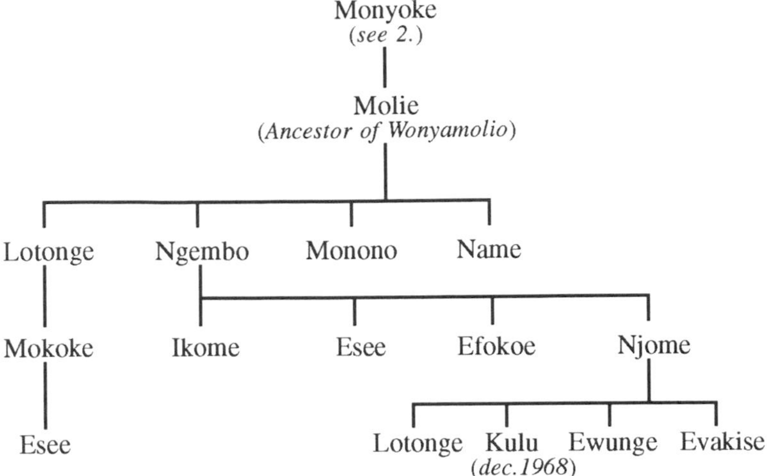

4. The descent of the Kale Family, formerly of Upper Buea:

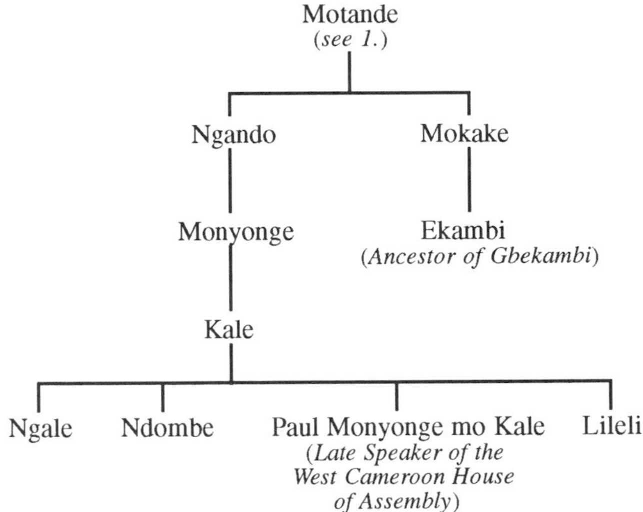

5. Some descendents of Ekambi, formerly of Upper Buea:

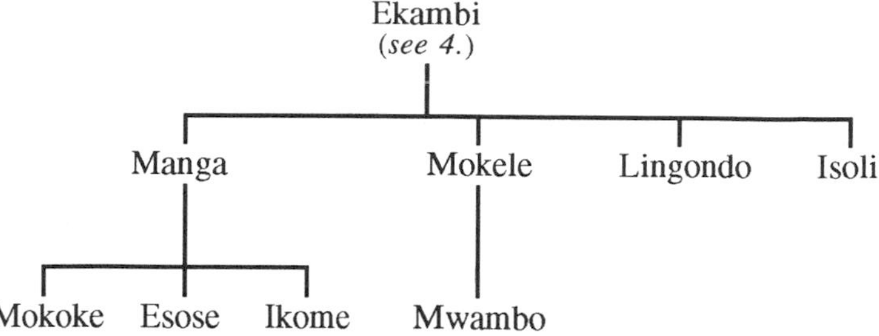

The descendants of Motande lived in 1894 in an area which stretched along the Mosole River, on both sides from the Lodge to the House of Assembly. Isol' Ekambi lived on the Lodge Hill. His group fled to the Bova-Ewonda boundary. The families of Lingondo and Mokele fled to Mimbea-Likoko, where the Muambo's still live. The descendents of the Manga family went to live in Lower Buea, as did the descendents of Ngand' a Motande—the Kale family.

6. The descent of Epka Wotani of Upper Buea:

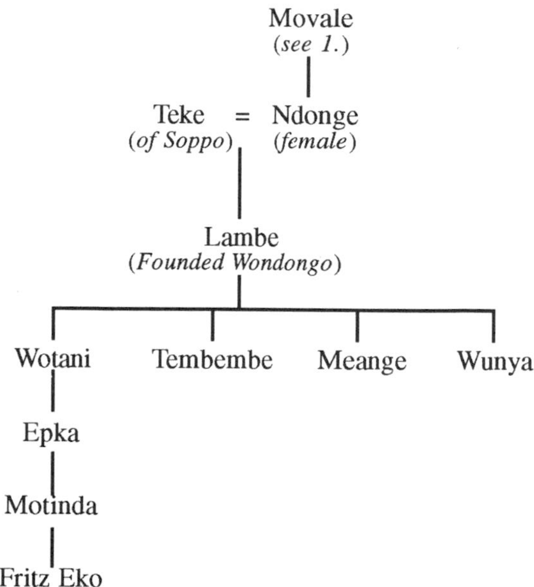

Some derive Ndonge from Lifanje, another of the supposed sons of Eye Naliomo. Wondongo was an extensive area about the Bismarck fountain.

After the destruction of 1895 the Wondongo people were settled in their present site near Wonyalionga.

7. The line of Evakis' a Manga

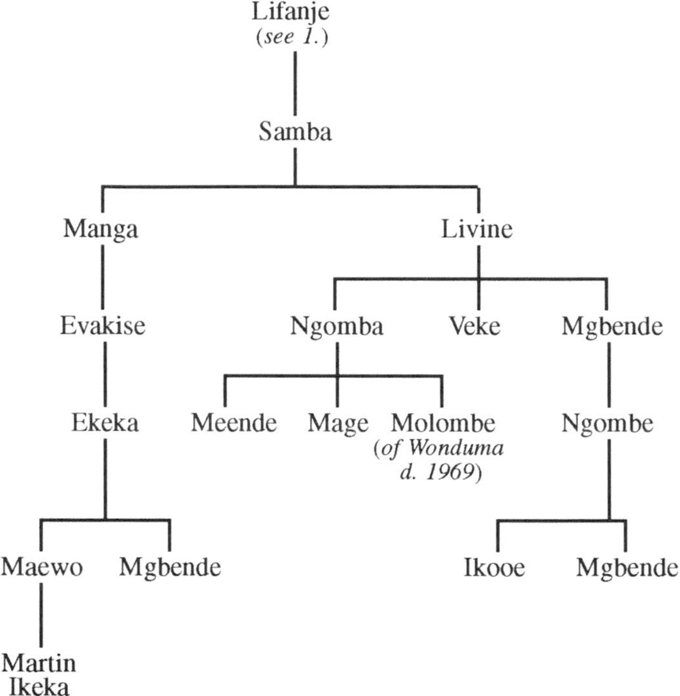

This influential Buea group has connexions also with Moliko.

8. The Descent of Motutu:

Efof' a Jonde was connected with Ewongo village.

Notes

1. See Ardener, E. W., *1956. Coastal Bantu of the Cameroons;* Ardener, S. G., 1968. *Eye-Witnesses to the Annexation of Cameroon, 1883–1887.* The Bakweri call themselves *Vakpe* (sing. *Mokpe*). In various sources used in this volume their name is spelt: *Bakwiri, Bakwili, Backwiri.* [See note to Editor's Introduction above. Ed.]
2. The name *Endeli* is spelt *Endeley* by the family. This spelling is therefore used throughout, except when quoting from texts. *Kuva* is the extended form of *Kuve.* In various sources quoted in this study the forms *Cuba, Kuba* and *Kuwa* appear. Generally I have used the non-extended forms of Bakweri names: e.g. *Likenye,* not *Likenya,* but there are exceptions, of which *Kuva* is one. To follow strictly the Bakweri naming usage would confuse the general reader. See Ardener, 1956, pp. 84–85.
3. Steane and Manga Williams made available material to administrative officers; in addition Steane wrote manuscript notes in 1928. The contribution of Charles Steane to the study of Bakweri folklore was outstanding. The Buea school was represented by material given to officials in 1929. In that year also Chief G. M. Endeley III compiled a genealogical volume of remarkable range. Furthermore P. M. Kale published *A Brief History of Bakweri,* Lagos, 1939. Mr Esasso Woleta of Soppo compiled a genealogical volume over a number of years, from which he has issued frequent extracts in lively and polemical style. Also, since 1953 I have myself collected versions from elders. None of the traditional schools have been aware of the documentary material published here. The identifications of individuals named in texts were often confirmed from written versions first made long ago.
4. Quintin Thomson, 'A Native Court or Palaver at Victoria, West Africa,' *Missionary Herald,* 1 December, 1882. This is quoted in Ardener, S. G., 1968, p. 58. The murder was at Limbola (Ardener, 1956, p. 29). The dates of the Bimbia succession are not clearly established. King William I of Bimbia died before 1877. In that year Comber, a missionary, refers to King William as 'a quiet, well-meaning, young man'. This must be Ngombe, whom we may call King William II. (Myers, J. B., *Thomas J. Comber, Missionary Pioneer to the Congo,*1889, p. 54).
5. Ardener, E. W., 'Documentary and Linguistic Evidence for the Rise of the Trading Polities between Rio del Rey and Cameroon, 1500–1650' in Lewis, I., (ed.), 1968. *History and Social Anthropology.*
6. Clarke, J., in *Missionary Herald,* July, 1848, p. 101; see Annexe A.
7. I have not dealt with Eyé's traditional origin from Womboko (a version is in Ardener, 1956, pp. 23–24).
8. Mokumbe, for example, was the ancestor of the village of Wonyamokumba, near Muea, to which Kuva moved before he died.
9. See Ardener, S. G., 1968, pp. 6–11, and Note 11, p. 52.

10. Apart from Merrick's spelling *Bwengga,* the Duala *Bwenga,* and the Bakweri *Gbenga,* the estate of Pamol Ltd. is written *Bwinga,* and that of the Cameroon Development Corporation is written *Buenga.* In addition, we shall see that in the 1880's the Germans called the village *Mbinga.*
11. The text is cited without quotation marks. I have introduced certain paragraph divisions for ease of reading.
12. 'Whenever an Isubu man dies all the cloth he possesses is spread out on the house-top; and exposed to public view. In accordance with this custom the Bwea men think that the genii of the mountains entertains so much respect for their chiefs as on their death to exhibit a variety of cloths' (Merrick, *note*).
13. 'Conference' (Merrick, *note*). Merrick tended to find 'tedious' most of the occasions on which he was not himself preaching.
14. 'Alluding to the plants which I brought down with me' (Merrick, *note*).
15. 'This district is some distance to the north of Bwea.' (Merrick, *note*). The present Wova.
16. Ardener, 1956, p. 21.
17. Ardener, 1956, p. 72: 'The water oath would be sworn by the whole village. . . on some highly important occasion, such as in the threat of war. All would wash their hands together and swear not to harm each other or to run away.'
18. Ardener, 1956, p. 72.
19. Burton, R., 1862. *Abeokuta and the Camaroons Mountain.* Vol. II.
20. King William had only just signed (on 24 February 1844) an anti-slave-trade treaty with Lt Earle. By Article V the Chiefs of Bimbia promised to allow the British to have access to trade 'throughout the whole of their dominions'. (Hertslet's *Commercial Treaties;* text also in Ardener, S. G., 1958, pp. 63–64). John King may well have thought that Merrick's visit had some connexion with this.
21. Ardener, 1956, p. 78.
22. For the treaty between the Chiefs of Bonjongo and Quintin Thomson, see Ardener, S. G., 1958, p. 62.
23. 'Swedische Ansiedler im Kamerungebiet', *Deutsches Kolonialblatt* (*DKB*), I, 1890, pp. 25–26. Other accounts appeared in the Swedish journal *Ymer.*
24. *Foreign Office Confidential Print* (*5303*), *July 32, 1886. Africa 21.* This is quoted in Ardener S. G., 1958, p. 45.
25. See *Pall Mall Gazette,* 10 March, 1885. The account of an abortive attempt to sign a treaty with Buea is given in Ardener, S.G., 1968, pp. 44–45.
26. Ardener, S. G., 1968, p. 50.
27. 'Reise des Kanzlers von Puttkamer durch das Bakwirigebiet im Kamerungebirge', *Mitteilungen aus den deutschen Schutzgebieten,* 1, 1888, pp. 35–37.
28. *Mitteilungen aus den deutschen Schutzgebieten,* 1, 1888, p. 35. The Zöller episode is in Ardener, S. G., 1968, p. 44.
29. *Mitteilungen aus den deutschen Schutzgebieten,* 1, 1888, p. 37. All names

are cited in the spelling as found.

30. Guillaume, G., and Bedermann, S. H., 1967. *Subsistence Activity in Five Villages on and around Mount Cameroon in Victoria Division, West Cameroon.*
31. Comber, T. J., 1879.'Explorations inland from Mount Cameroons, and Journey through Congo to Makuta', *Proceedings of Royal Geographical Society.* p. 233. (He called it Bakundu-ba-Namwidi).
32. Woloa of Soppo supplied carriers to the Baptist Missionaries on this route (Ardener, S. G., 1958, note 70). For Calvin H. Richardson's mission see *ibid* p. 62, note 121; *Missionary Herald,* 1879, pp. 252–53.
33. Similarly the traders Schmidt and Voss had been used to negotiate treaties with the Kings of Douala in 1884.
34. The cap guns wanted were like those Mr Allen sold in Camerooons (Douala). This was presumably Dr George Allen, English physician and trader at Douala 1880–89. For references see Ardener S. G., 1958, p. 55, note 34.
35. The Buea Chiefs had, however, unlike those of the coast, no direct experience of signing treaties backed by strict legality. Fifty years of British Consuls made Douala and Bimbia fully trained in these matters. Even the browbeaten Bell and Akwa sold their freedom dearly. Unfortunately, the Buea chiefs only knew the mass-produced treaties of Rogozinski, Zöller, and the rest, two years before—mere tickets to receive trade-goods.
36. There must be an element of doubt as to whether Soden was actually present. He may have signed the inked-over document, and made his additional notes, somewhere else. The failure to leave a copy in Buea does not help in assessing the facts.
37. The correspondence and the agreements were recorded in Akten IV, B. 34i, Vol. 2, Buea (see Annexe C).
38. The basic identifications were suggested by the elders of Wonyalionga. These were checked against Chief Endeley III's genealogical book, in which the relevant portions date from 1929. No serious discrepancy was found with other sources. The points about which there is a serious residual doubt are No. 10, Kange, and No. 14, Manga. The connexions of Kange a Mosisa are obscure. He was not apparently related to Mosis' Ewunge. Mr Kal'a Njie made enquiries about No. 11, Njaki. An old man who was a boy in Kuva's day told him he remembered an Njako Ewunge. Chief Endeley had heard of an Njako Wokome of Wondongo. Njako is a well-known name in Muea village. See Annexe D, for selected genealogies.
39. The present Vasingi and Moli sections may have been represented by Evakise.
40. The Steane-Martin records explain the Edgerley relationship. For Rose Patience Edgerley (she was known in the Congo by her second name) see Johnston, H. H., 1908. *George Grenfell and the Congo,* p. 239.
41. Schwartz, B., 1886. *Kamerun: Reise in die Hinterlande der Kolonie.*

42. Zintgraff, E., 1895. *Nord-Kamerun.* and Chilver, E. M., 1966. *Zintgraff's Explorations in Bamenda, Adamawa and the Benue Lands, 1889–1892.*
43. *DKB,* I, 1890, p. 72;
44. *DKB,* I, 1890, p. 113; II, 1891, p. 266.
45. Zintgraff, 1895; Chilver, 1966, pp. 26–29.
46. *DKB,* II, 1891, p. 398. For full details see below.
47. *DKB,* II, 1891, p. 398.
48. *DKB,* II, 1891, p. 520.
49. *DKB,* II, 1891, pp. 155, 276, 471.
50. *DKB,* II, 1891, p. 517.
51. *DKB,* II, 1891, pp. 513–517.
52. Von Schuckmann was a member of the permanent staff of the Colonial Department (*Kolonialabteilung*) of the Berlin Foreign Office. The circulation of colonial and home officials was quite common. Von Schuckmann sailed from Germany on 5 July, 1891, with von Gravenreuth.
53. 'Bericht des stellvertretenden Kaiserlichen Gouverneurs in Kamerun Legationsrath von Schuckman vom 18 November, 1891 betreffend die Bestrafung von Buea'. *DKB,* III, 1892, pp. 14–18. In the following translation the italics represent the German typographical emphasis. I have not followed its practice for personal names for which it seems superfluous in English. *Buea* is spelt with a diäresis over the *e* in this and some other texts, but this has been omitted. All other spellings are as found. The translated text is restricted to von Schuckmann's own report. The two annexures by von Stetten and von Volckamer, are discussed in the next chapter.
54. 'Anlage I . Bericht des Premierlieutenants von Stetten über die Buea-Expedition vom 18 November 1891', *DKB,* III, 1892, pp. 16–17.
55. 'Anlage 2. Bericht des Premierlieutenants von Volckamer über die Buea-Expedition am 18 November 1 891', *DKB*, III 1892, pp. 17–18.
56. 'Abkommen zwischen Deutschland und Frankreich vom 15 März 1894, Denkschrift', *DKB,* V, 1894, No. 8, pp. 165–176.
57. Kale, P. M., 1939, pp. 18–21. This extract is cited as printed with certain amendments of punctuation and the correction of printing errors. Mr Kale permitted this and other extracts to be made before his death in 1966. This pioneering work was originally edited by the well-known politician Eyo Ita. P. M. Kale was prominent in Cameroon politics and ended his life as Speaker of the House of Assembly. Although originally criticised by the Soppo school as representing the Buea view of history, his book is impartial in tone, with a lively style.
58. 'Appeal of Christian Missionaries to Government to use armed force to subdue primitive unbelievers, and to the traders to bribe them has led many to associate the Bible with the machine gun and with gin'. (P. M. Kale, *note*).
59. Kale is here mixing several incidents. King William I (Bile) of Bimbia received his title from treaties with the British, of which the first official

one to use the title was in 1841. The German Treaty with Bimbia of 11 July, 1884 (F.O. Papers, 403/32, Letter 22, encl.) was signed by the traders Schmidt and Voss for the Germans, and by chiefs headed by Quan, of the line which descended from the brother of William I, Makaka ma Kwan. In Bimbia the direct line of Bile was in decline. In Victoria the family of Edward Nambeke Eyabe Williams came to the fore. No doubt Kale is referring to him or his son (the later District Head Manga Williams). Kale's humorous strictures should not be the cause of offence: Kuva's own view of Victoria must have been much like this.

60. 'Kuva's spear was said to be a magic one, which if pinned into the ground in the battle-field, fighting would go on equally on both sides, but at the moment he removed it, the enemies would scatter in confusion running here and there, throwing their war materials, and the battle was won.' (P. M. Kale, *note*). The symbolic nature of the 'spear' in Bakweri is shown in the phrase *mot'a maongo,* 'person of spears'. This is used of a man known to be ruthless in fighting, and no respecter of persons or laws, an asset in war but a trouble in peace. The term *maongo* has the sense of 'war' or 'violence', a violent death from any source being known as *kpel'a maongo* ('death of spears'). *'Maongo, e!'* is the standard cry of calamity given when there is fire, theft or murder'. (Ardener, 1956, p. 78). Kale further remarks, 'Note the value of land to the African'.
61. Ardener, 1956, pp. 24–25. Of Efesoa, who was educated by the Baptists, it is said, more accurately, that his mother and Kuva's mother were related. It is probable that Efesoa and Kuva belonged to one *litumba la mbus'a nyango* or matrilineage (for the Bakweri double-descent system, see Ardener, 1956, pp. 53–54)
62. 'Jahresbericht, betreffend die Entwicklung des Schutzgebietes Kamerun im Jahre 1891' (Leist), *DKB,* III, 1892; pp. 198–208.
63. *DKB,* III, 1892; p. 205.
64. Preuss reported in 1892 on experiments he made at the Government Garden in Victoria (*Mitt. aus den d. Sch.,* II, 1892) and recommended the expansion of the Garden to a research plantation, to try out crops for the future. The Kolonialabteilung agreed in principle (*DKB,* III 1892, 1 May, p. 266).
65. *DKB,* III, 1891, p. 525. Due to a telegraphic error, they thought he died at 'Buka'. Karl, Freiherr von Gravenreuth (b. 12 December 1858, d. 5 November 1891, aged 32) was the son of Royal Bavarian *Kämmerer* (*Chamberlain*) Freiherr von Gravenreuth. He entered his regiment in 1877, and became a 2nd Lieutenant in 1879. He went to the Reserve in 1885 and into the service of the East African Company. In 1888 he was awarded the Order of the Red Eagle 4th Class with Swords, and the following year became a 1st Lieutenant in the service of the Imperial Commissioner. He served in East Africa and gained further decorations. In 1899 he rose to Captain, and became Leader of the Southern Expedition of Exploration into the Kamerun Hinterland. (*DKB,* II, 1891, pp. 506–507).
66. *DKB,* II, 1891, p. 541.

67. *DKB,* III, 1892, p. 452; IV, 1893, pp. 154, 321.
68. *DKB,* Ill, 1892, p. 102.
69. *DKB,* III, 1892, pp. 391–400.
70. *DKB,* IV, 1893, pp. 33–36.
71. *DKB.* IV. 1893, pp. 80–81, 182.
72. 'Friedensvertrag mit dem Bueastamm', *DKB*, IV, 1893, p. 231.
73. 'Besuch des Gouverneurs von Kamerun in Buea', *DKB*, IV, 1893, pp. 288–89. I have translated this fully save for two references to earlier issues of *DKB*. The diäresis has been omitted from the e of Buea.
74. 'Eine Anregung zur Errichtung einer Kaffeeplantage bei Buea auf dem Kamerungebirge', *DKB,* IV, 1893, p. 434.
75. *DKB,* IV, 1893, pp. 501–2.
76. 'Die Sanitären Einrichtungen und die Anlage einer Gesundheits-station im Kamerungebirge'. *DKB,* V, 1894, pp. 69–74.
77. Ibid., pp. 72–74.
78. 'Über die Unruhen in Kamerun', *DKB,* V, 1894, pp. 89–98. The rebels captured 2 Maxim guns, 2 quick-firing guns, 600 Model 71 rifles, 20 Model 88 Carbines, 40 Model 71/84 rifles, 80 Remingtons, 18 revolvers, 400 shells for 3.7 guns, 15 chests of 100 cartridges (Model 71) and 100 chests of 600 cartridges (Model 88). They besieged the Europeans. Part of the time Herr Vanselow of the firm Randad and Stein was trapped in the Doctor's house where he had gone as a patient. (Vanselow had witnessed the agreement for the sale of Buea in 1887). The damage to property was 20,000 Marks. Assessor Otto Julius Reibow was killed. He was the author of the compendium of colonial law: *Die deutsche Kolonial-Gesetzgebung*.
79. Leist's behaviour was one of the cases raised in the Reichstag during the 1906–07 colonial controversies in Germany, which resulted in the well known liberalisation under Dernburg. These debates later provided the material for Allied charges of German colonial misrule.
80. *DKB*. V, 1894, p. 93.
81. *DKB,* V, 1894, p. 44.
82. *DKB,* XXII, 1911, p. 160; Ardener, E. W., 1965. *Historical Notes on the Scheduled Monuments of West Cameroon.* p. 14.
83. Most of the German text of this letter was published in *DKB,* V, 1894, pp. 212–13. It omitted, however, the three sentences referring to Pfeil's trickery over Kuva's gun. These have fortunately been restored from a typewritten *copy* of the letter which came into the hands of Mr Esasso Woleta of Soppo. Mr Woleta sent me a copy of this copy in 1957. Its authenticity, despite the circuitous route of its preservation is undoubted. It does not exist in any official source in Buea. Mr Woleta kindly showed me his records and only two German letters were contained in them: this one, and one other. However they came into his possession, they owed their preservation to his industry. It was, nevertheless, fortunate indeed that I was given copies by him; for in a disastrous fire at his house the 'original' copies were later totally destroyed. The 'Heinrich' mentioned in this letter is unknown. He

may have been a matrilineal relative of Kuva, since the Bonjongo connections had been in an educated background consistent with acquiring Swiss or German names.

84. There was a petition in the 1920's about the District Headship, in which Thomas Nganjo argued that Soppo had been accorded certain rights of general jurisdiction in Native Court matters by the Germans. Such things dragged on for years.
85. The discrepancy between the statement that these hills belonged to Buea, and Preuss's survey of 1898 which ascribes them to Soppo, is discussed later.
86. 'Bericht des Kaiserlichen Vizekonsuls Spengler über die Anbaufähigkeit des Gebietes des Bezirksamts Victoria der Kolonie Kamerun', *DKB,* V, 1894, pp. 282–288.
87. *DKB,* V, 1894, pp. 569–570.
88. *DKB*, V, 1894, pp. 104–105.
89. *DKB*, VI, 1895, p. 134.
90. Dominik, F. W. H., 1901. *Sechs Kriegsund Friedensjahre in deutschen Tropen.*
91. It was not finally done until 15 June, 1895—six months later. The monument was about 3.6 metres high and was described as follows. It had a Carrara marble pedestal raised on two steps, with on one side a plaque of Gravenreuth in bronze. 'On the pedestal there rests a lion, in a seated position, with raised head looking into the distance, and with the forepaw guarding a German war-banner, which is partly draped over the pedestal'. *DKB*, III, 1892, p. 425; VI, 1895, p. 383.
92. Kale, 1939, pp. 22–23. I have quoted the text in three parts: the evacuation, the German arrival, and the end of Kuva, in their actual historical order. Kale put the end of Kuva before the German arrival. He likens the evacuation, in a note, to the Russian defeat of Napoleon, although possibly this would be more appropriate to the war of 1891. The man who advised Kuva to retreat is said to have been Efesoa of Bonjongo, who no longer favoured resistance.
93. This second document, translated by me, has a similar history to the Vieter letter (see above). The *Supplementary Negotiation* refers to the separate negotiation with Sako. The main negotiation was with Buea. Once more the document is clearly a genuine copy.
94. *DKB,* VI. 1895, p. 321 (translated).
95. *DKB,* Vl. 1895, p. 382 (translated). *Ngaueli* cannot be identified, despite repeated enquiries.
96. *DKB*, VI, 1895, p. 296.
97. Kingsley, M., 1964. *West African Studies,* (reprint). *DKB,* VI 1895, p. 655.
98. *DKB,* VI 1895, p. 619.
99. *DKB,* VII 1896, p. 158–159. The translation is condensed and paraphrased, in parts, for brevity.

100. 'Basel Mission Annual Report', 1 July, 1896 (*DKB*, VI 1896, p. 560).
101. The material for this chapter comes from 'Grundstücksangelegen-heiten im Bezirk Buea', Akten IV B 34, Vol. 2, Buea.
102. Soden/Caprivi (copy: K8650), 29 August 1891.
103. Rettich/v. Schuckmann (Auswärtiges Amt, Kolonial-Abteilung, 2066, Az 72), 25 Sept. 1891.
104. Soden/Caprivi (Copy: KA1079), 20 Jan. 1894.
105. Zimmerer/Leist, 4 Apr. 1894.
106. Leist/Zimmerer, 7 Apr. 1894. In the following paraphrase, Leist's spellings are retained.
107. Marschall/Zimmerer, 7 Jun. 1894, encl. Marschall/Soden 7 Jun. 1894.
108. Schwartzkoppen/Zimmerer, 15 Dec. 1894.
109. Puttkamer/Soden, 6 Apr. 1894.
110. Soden/Schwartzkoppen, 30 Mar. 1896 (copy).
111. Seitz/Reichskanzler, 20 July 1896.
112. Schwartzkoppen/Soden, 10 May 1896 (copy).
113. Kayser/Puttkamer, 9 Jun. 1896, and minutes.
114. Bittner/Seitz, 4 Sep. 1896.
115. Minute on Folio 38.
116. 'Bericht des Dr Preuss über die Abgrenzung des Buea-Gebietes' (Report of Preuss as Acting District Officer, Victoria, to Hauptmann von Kamptz, Acting Governor of Kamerun, 10 Jan. 1897).
117. This description is based on a close collation of the Buea terrain with Preuss's sketch map.
118. The question of 'Soppo bush' has certain obscurities. Preuss's report is our prime source for pre-conquest Buea. If the fence to the south abutted straight onto Soppo land, then the two hills sought by Vieter for his Mission were not on Buea land at all. Yet Kuva allocated them to him, or so Vieter thought. The 'Soppo bush' area must have been a sort of no-man's land between the two settlements. The picture of an originally fairly close alliance between Soppo and Buea tends to be confirmed by these circumstances, especially taking into account the Soppo ancestry of the Wondongo part of Upper Buea. Kuva's mother also came from Soppo.
119. Minutes, Folios 41 and 43.
120. Puttkamer/Reichskanzler, 24 Apr. 1897.
121. Folio 44. The W.A.P.V. was formed on 21 January 1897 (*DKB* ,VIII, 1897, p. 76). it must have been well-bruited in Cameroon by the preceding 7 November (1896), for Dr Preuss then, in a report on the prospects of plantation undertakings on the Cameroon Mountain, speaks of the W.A.P.V. as recently founded. 'Two years ago I recommended the establishment of plantations, but then the Bakwilis, with the Buea people at the head, were masters of the country. Now they were defeated by the Schutztruppe and the trade in arms and ammunition is ended', and the mountain people 'are turned into peaceful labourers' (*DKB,* VIII, 1897, p. 45).

122. Upper Farm still has some farm produce. Lower and West Farms are gradually being used as building land.
123. 'Ueber die Station Buea', *DKB,* VIII. 1 Mar. 1897, pp. 133–134.
124. This house was on the site of the present Archives Office, exactly opposite the fountain. A new house was erected for two other Europeans on the upper part of the old square.
125. *DKB*. IX, 1898, p. 410.
126. Both established in 1885 by the two firms that were instrumental in annexing Kamerun. The Bimbia plantation was owned by Woermann (see Ardener, S. G., 1968). In 1897 the Bimbia agent for Woermann's retailing activities was 'Calla Quan', that is Kal' a Til' a Makaka ma Kwan, a member of the line that became village-heads in Bonabile (King William's Town). His grandson is Eric Likoko la Kwan (Quan), the civil servant (*DKB*, VIII, 1897, p. 541; Ardener, 1956, p. 28). In January, 1899 the Tiko store of Woermann's was in the charge of 'Manga William' [sic], the future District Head Victoria, then aged 22 (*DKB,* X, 1899, p. 403).
127. The basis of the C. D.C. Moliko estates.
128. Later the owners of Ndian, Bavo and Lobe estates (*DKB*, X, 1899, p. 849). Valdau (Waldau), who bought Buea, worked in Cameroon into the British period. He was a plantation manager in 1922, when he witnessed, and wrote a report on, the 1922 eruption of Mount Cameroon.
129. *DKB*, IX, 1898, p. 96.
130. *DKB*, IX, 1898, p. 411.
131. This structure was in the grounds of the present Prime Minister's Office (Ardener, 1965; Puttkamer, J. von, *Gouverneursjahre in Kamerun,* 1912).
132. Field, M., 1969. *The Prime Minister's Lodge,* Buea, and Puttkamer, 1912.
133. It makes a suitable postscript to note that the vast area of Merrick's 'Bwengga district' was remarked upon by the Land Commission of 1903–1904. It spoke of the 'concentration or gathering together of very scattered villages, as for example, the village of Buenge [sic], which was scattered over the areas of the Moliwe Plantation and the Kamerun-Land und Plantagengesellschaft (Likomba Plantation), and which with 250 families covered an area of nearly a German square mile.' Since a German mile was about four English miles, the area of Bwenga was nearly twenty square miles, ('Bericht über die Tätikgeit der Landkommission für den Verwaltungsbezirk Victoria in der Zeit vom 1 Juli 1903 bis 31 März 1904', *DKB* XVII, 1906, p. 37).
134. Buea, I C 15 sp. a, Vol. 1. Puttkamer/Buchka, 30 May 1898, in *Anlage* 11, to *Anträge zu den Land-reservaten an Kamerun Plantagengebiet,* Berlin (Land Commission Report), p. 25. Part of this was also published in *DKB*, X 1899, p. 513. Lest the letter be thought to be a persuasive representation of the facts it should be remembered, in order to put the arguments in perspective, that the Günther-Soppo plantation had been opposed by the people, not welcomed. Also Puttkamer's concern that the

Bakweri should not sell their land (except to Missions) accompanied the expropriation of some 300 square miles of it. Puttkamer, furthermore, shows himself unaware of the staple crops of the area. Bakweri worked on the plantation as forced labour. Finally, he presents the decline, or at best the stagnation, of the population as benefits, and speaks with equanimity of the use of women and children as carriers for distances of 20 miles on mountain terrain.

135. Kale, P. M. 1939, p. 41.

136. Secure conditions did not exist until 1900. A section of the Buea people was deported in 1899, for remaining obstructive after the peace conditions were fixed, and were sent 'to settle ownerless land behind Massuma village'. This may perhaps be the present village of Lio-la-Buea, although the latter claims an older ancestry. The land they had occupied in Buea was allocated to 'younger Buea people' who were 'permanently in the Station service' (*DKB,* X, 1899, p. 276). Road building was part of this 'service'. The Victoria-Buea road had still as many as 200 men on it, while the 'Buea-Tiko' road (the present Buea-Mutengene stretch) was already begun. A Buea-Lisoka bridle-road, along the old Mountain trade-route was already completed, and it linked the new Esser-Oechelhäuser plantation (now Ekona estate) with the capital. Further away, connection was made between Victoria and Boniadikombo, and on to Buenga market aiming to reach Tiko (*DKB,* X, 1899, p. 561). In Buea, the Schutztruppe planned a mutiny in January 1899. They were mostly Wey (Vai) men from Liberia. Leuschner heard, on 26 January, that twelve soldiers had planned to shoot all the Germans, break open the safe, and flee to Calabar. On 29 January, Leuschner assembled them outside his quarters (the site of the present Archives Office), and disarmed them by a ruse, telling them to collect uniforms in the Palaver Hall. (This building is to be the surviving structure upon the new Square, once part of the Post Office.) The ringleaders resisted, and were wounded or killed. The leader was N.C.O. Johnson (*DKB,* X, 1899, p. 235).

3

The Plantations and The People of Victoria Division*

Land Agriculture and Subsistence in Victoria Division

Some problems of land use and other features of the indigenous economies are often summed up in the phrase: 'the Bakweri Land Problem'. This phrase is misleading, since such problems as exist are only incidentally of land and are not restricted to the Bakweri. The historical background of the problems specifically relating to land is given below, followed by a discussion of the special demographic conditions of Victoria Division[1] and of the indigenous agricultural and social systems.[2]

German Land Policy

On the establishment of the German Protectorate at Duala in 1884, Bimbia was immediately annexed, while the English Baptist settlement at Victoria was bought out by arrangement with the Basel Mission in 1887. The German Victoria District (*Bezirk*) eventually included the whole area of the Cameroon Mountain, and consequently territory occupied by the Bakweri, Bamboko, Balong, Isubu and Wovea. The Bakolle and the Fish Towns were included in the separate District of Rio del Rey.[3] Rudin states that in 1884 the exploitation of the country by plantations had not been the primary intention of the Germans. However, beginning as early as 1885, under the initiative of the two major German trading firms, Woermann and Jantzen und Thormählen, plantations were founded at Bimbia[4] (Kamerun Land- und Plantagen-Gesellschaft) and Bibundi (West Afrikanische Pflanzungsgesellschaft Bibundi), a Bamboko settlement on the coast to the west and north of Victoria.[5] In the next ten years, concessions were obtained by plantation companies over the greater part of the southeastern, southern and southwestern slopes of the Cameroon Mountain. In these early years,

---

* *Edited from Part III (Chapters X, XI and XII) by Edwin Ardener in Ardener, Ardener and Warmington, 1960.*

largely covering the governorships of Soden and Zimmerer, the acquisition and tenure of land by German interests were based on no definite system. In the case of the Kamerun Land und Plantagen-Gesellschaft, title to ownership appears to have been established by direct occupation, which the German Government later acknowledged when the question of title was raised. The West Afrikanische Pflanzungsgesellschaft Bibundi, on the other hand, obtained their tract of land by purchase from the native chiefs, and there was the inclusion of a clause in the agreement recognizing the rights of the natives.[6] Later, the Government vested the freehold of the land in the company. Again, various individuals purchased from the Government tracts of Crown land of about 2,000 to 3,000 hectares (5,000 to 7,500 acres) at an average price of five marks per hectare. In one such case Crown land was created to make the transaction possible. These properties and interests were later amalgamated into the West Afrikanische Pflanzungsgesellschaft Victoria (W.A.P.V.) which was to become the most important of the companies, with its headquarters at Bota. In another case, four individuals founded a company with privately acquired land, which was registered in the Government land register (*Grundbuch*), and later, although it was found that no deed of purchase existed, their title was confirmed. In these years occupation and direct negotiation with native chiefs and elders would appear to have been the typical means of acquiring land titles. W.A.P.V. purchased several farms which formed enclaves in its land, a transaction which was sanctioned unconditionally by the German Government. The holdings of the Deutsche Westafrikanische Handelgesellschaft (D.W.H.) amounting to more than 50,000 acres on the Meme and Ndian Rivers around the Rio del Rey were based on undocumented transactions of this type, which, however, were eventually questioned by the German Government.

The extension of German civil control in the Cameroon Mountain area appears to have met no serious resistance from any tribe except the Bakweri in their settlement at Buea. In an expedition sent against them in 1891 the German commander, Gravenreuth, was killed when attempting to storm a barricaded watercourse. By 1899 almost all the settlements of the Bakweri south of Owe had been enclosed within the boundaries of plantation concessions. The map overleaf illustrates this. Generally the concessions were of geometric shapes which took little or no account of the extent of native land needs.

In the concessions near the coast, which were first developed, villages were confined to small rectangular enclaves, and it was here that the reciting of villages became most common (e.g. Wokeli, moved

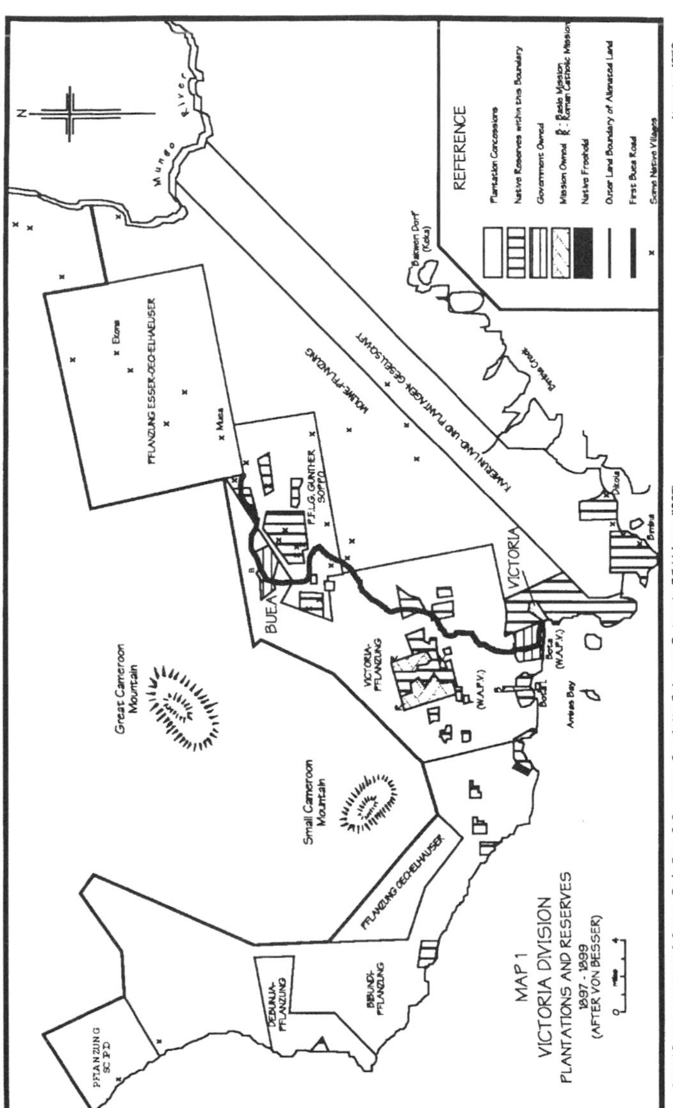

The Plantations and the People of Victoria Division 1897–1899

to found the Sachsenhofen plantation of W.A.P.V.). The extensive Günther concession at Soppo, however, contained so many Bakweri villages that its boundaries had little significance, and its fragments were eventually merged with W.A.P.V. as the Tole and Molyko plantations. The Esser-Oechelhäuser (Ekona) and Moliwe concessions also contained all the Lisoka, Muea and several other groups of Bakweri, as well as the Balong of Mpundu. At this time no other concession had been obtained on what is now known as the Tiko plain except that of the Kamerun Land und Plantagen-Gesellschaft (of which Likomba now forms a part). Von Besser's map of 1899 does not show Tiko, indicating only a 'Bakwiri Dorf' on Keka Island.

In 1894 Governor Zimmerer began to urge stricter supervision of land transactions, and in 1896 an imperial decree was enacted which with its later interpretations remained the basis of land policy for the remainder of the period of the German Protectorate. These laid down the conditions which were in future to rule land transactions between natives and non-natives, including the marking of boundaries and the presence at each transaction, which was to take place on the land itself, of an administrative officer, a missionary (as 'Guardian of the Natives') and responsible members of the village concerned, as well as the buyer and seller. The administrative officer was to ascertain that the natives retained sufficient land for their own use and that all present agreed to the disposal of the property. At the same time all unoccupied land in the Cameroons was declared Crown land, the boundaries of which were to take into account both present and future needs of the native population, and provision was made for the establishment of Land Commissions to determine these needs. Crown land could be sold to private individuals or corporations on condition that the purchaser surveyed the land and that specific areas were developed within specific periods. Crown land could also be leased, in which case there was an obligation to cultivate or otherwise utilize the land, and the lessee had the right to purchase during the currency of the lease land taken into use. When one half of the leased land had been taken into use, the lessee had the option of purchasing the whole.

Although the 1896 decree should have safeguarded native interests, in actual fact its provisions were weakened by the *laissez-faire* policy of Governor Puttkamer, and the first land commission was not actually created until 1902, and then largely as a result of an active campaign by the Basel Missionaries who claimed that the administration had tolerated abuses in the movement of Bakweri into reservations. At Muea, the Mission station as well as the native village was ordered by the plantation authorities to move. After the beginning of the work of the land commission there was closer regulation of all land transactions. Reservations were founded on the basis of a minimum allotment of six hectares (about fifteen acres) per hut in addition to a domestic plot,[7] although it was still policy to move villages into the reservations. From 1903 the land commission always contained one missionary member.

By 1914 there had been many modifications of the boundaries of the reservations, and the situation at that date is shown in Map 2 (over). In addition, further plantation concessions had been granted, chiefly on the Tiko plain, including a small British concession (Ambas Bay Co.). These concessions resulted in the creation of the Tiko reservation and the movement of the Bakweri village of Keka to make way for wharf facilities.[8]

There seems little doubt that the early land policy of the German protectorate subordinated native interests to those of the concessionaries, and the practice of moving villages must have caused a great deal of dislocation of tribal life, accompanied as it was by the repressive measures at Buea and the widespread use of forced labour. Missionaries protested that the owners of plantation concessions considered the populations of native enclaves within their boundaries as private sources of labour. The contribution of this policy to the decline that took place in the indigenous population was probably considerable. Later, genuine efforts appear to have been made to enlarge the native reservations. By 1914, however, immigration had already created an additional problem. The influx of Africans of other tribes into the Division, some indication of which has been given in previous chapters, gradually resulted in the settlement of large immigrant populations in many reservations. Overcrowding of the small reservations near the coast was particularly common since these reservations had often received their restricted boundaries precisely because of their location in the most intensively worked plantations, a location which also attracted immigrants.

Immigration and the Population Structure in Victoria Division in 1960

The Victoria Division Tribes

Most of the estates of the Cameroons Development Corporation lie among or next to the lands of the Bakweri, Bamboko, Isubu, Mongo and Balong tribes of the Victoria Division, while outlying plantations lie in the territories of the South Balong (Mukonje Estate), the South Bakosi (Tombel Estate), the Balundu (Boa Estate), and the Mbonge (Mbonge Estate) of Kumba Division. In Victoria Division besides the C.D.C. plantations, the Likomba Estate and (since 1958) the Bafia-Bavenga concession of Elders and Fyffes Ltd. and the small Bwinga Estate of Pamol Ltd. also fall in the Bakweri area. In Victoria Division, where the plantation system has been of longest standing and where the greatest concentration of estates is to be found, many social problems have arisen in an acute form, and it is with the people of this Division that the following section is concerned. The indigenous peoples are now the responsibility of the Southern Cameroons Government which is mainly elected by them, and therefore many matters discussed in this chapter fall within the purview of various ministries. On the other hand, the problems discussed also concern the Cameroons Development Corporation.

The present territory of the Bakweri is now largely broken up by plantation lands, the stretch of country between the villages of Membea and Lisoka being the most populous block. Since 1937 this block has been connected with the Muea-Wonganjo enclave, which was formerly completely surrounded by plantation land. The villages of the Bakweri north of the Ekona plantation were, until the Bafia-Bavenga concession of 1958, still completely unaffected territorially by plantation concessions. The rest of their settlements are to be found in enclaves completely or largely bounded by plantation lands. The largest of these, containing 22 villages, is the Wonjongo (Bonjongo) enclave occupying the southern foothills of the Cameroon Mountain and overlooked on the west by the Small Cameroon Mountain. Other completely enclosed reservations are those of Mutengene, Likomba, Dibanda (now uninhabited), Lower Ekona and Mundame. The outermost ring of settlements are generally bounded on three sides by plantation lands and on one side by the sea like the Ngeme, Bota and Victoria enclaves, by the creeks like the Tiko and Ebonji enclaves, or by the Mungo River

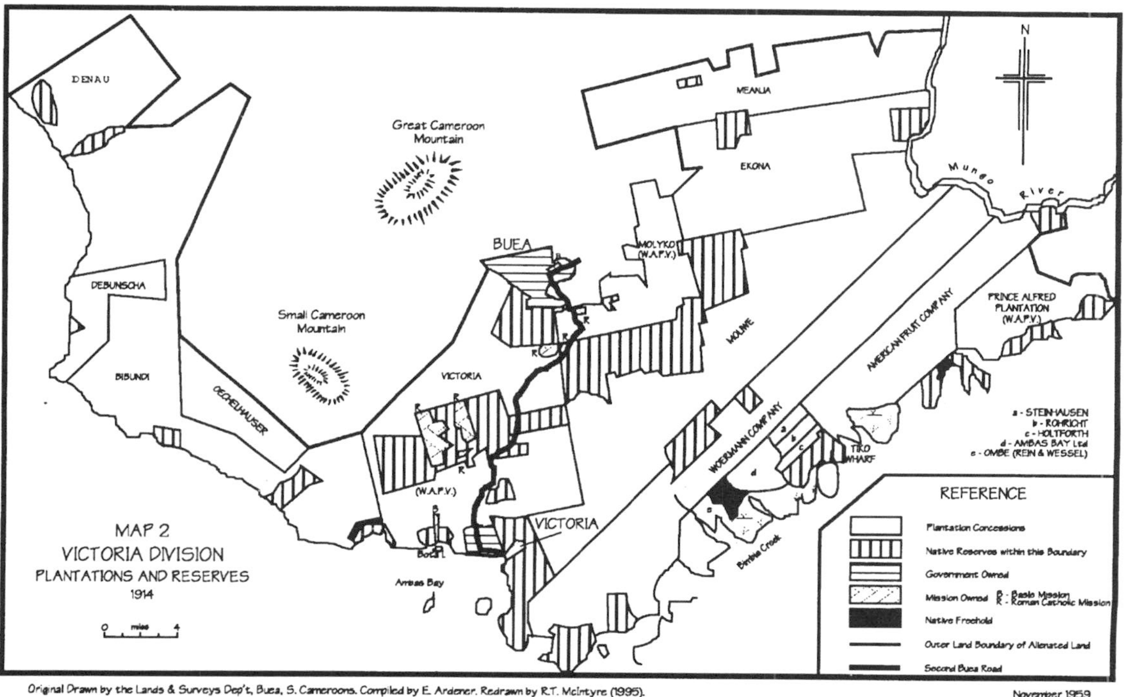

The Plantations and the People of Victoria Division 1914

like the tiny Likoke enclave. Mondoni reserve is bounded on one side by the Mungo River, on one side by plantation land and on two sides by territory of the Mongo tribe. In the Bota enclave only two of the villages, Kie and Mokindi, are strictly Bakweri, the Bota mainland and island settlements being of different origin. The indigenous population of Victoria is also only partly of Bakweri origin. The original territory was Isubu, and the population also includes descendants of liberated slaves brought to the site by the Baptist Missionary, Alfred Saker. Tiko and Ebonji also contain persons of the Mongo and Duala tribes.

The broken territory of the Bakweri has made grouping for administrative purposes difficult. At one time only the inner block of Bakweri were administered together, as the Buea District, the outer enclaves being administered together with those of the Bamboko, Mongo and Isubu as the Victoria District. After a reorganization before the war, all the Bakweri settlements except those in the Ngeme, Bota, Victoria, Tiko, Likomba and Ebonji reservations formed part of the Bakweri Clan Native Authority divided into five 'Village Groups', each of which had its own Native Court. The remaining settlements formed two 'Village Groups' of the composite Victoria Federated Native Authority. In 1958 an elective local government system was introduced, in which 'strangers' were represented. The Bakweri Council superseded the Clan Native Authority, and the Bakweri areas of Tiko and Mutengene Village Groups and Mondoni village came under the Tiko Area Council.[9] The Bakweri settlement of Buea (Gbea) is the headquarters of the Bakweri Native Authority. Buea also provides the administrative capital of the Southern Cameroons.

The total population of the true Bakweri in Victoria Division excluding the Bota mainland and island settlements (Wovea) may be calculated at 15,714, and including these settlements at 16,209. Of the total, 2,312 Bakweri, male and female, live on the plantations.[10]

Bamboko. The Bamboko (more correctly *Womboko,* singular *Momboko*) inhabit the opposite segment of the Cameroon Mountain to that of the Bakweri and from Sanje to Mokundange have reached the coast. This coastal strip is included in Victoria Division, and is largely occupied by plantation concessions. The remainder of the tribe inland is included in Kumba Division, where the only estate established in their territory (Mongonge) is not in operation. The Bamboko, from whom the Bakweri appear to have migrated, seem themselves to have moved southwards along the coast from their own side of the mountain at some period before the Bakweri reached the coast on their side. It is not known exactly when this occurred, but villages of this or of some previous tribe are noted as early as the seventeenth century.

All the Bamboko villages in Victoria Division are now included within six reservations, each bounded on one side by the sea and on the other by plantations. Four of these reservations contain only one village each: Sanje, Bibundi (Vewonde), Njonje and Bakingili (Vakingili). The larger of the remaining two reservations includes two villages (Etome and Mbase) of Bakweri origin. The Bamboko form a Village Group under the jurisdiction of the Victoria Area Council to which they elect five native members. The Victoria Division Bamboko number 795 (there are 983 in the Bamboko territory included in Kumba Division).

Isubu. This tribe (which calls itself *Isuwu* or *Isu*) is now confined to three villages in two enclaves on the coast of Bimbia promontory surrounded on the landward side by plantations, but it was formerly of great importance. The tribe is of mixed origin, the main body being descended from an early migration along the coast from Bamboko country. In the last quarter of the eighteenth century their chief was *Mbimbi a Mbela,* and from about this period Isubu territory became known to English merchants as Bimbia, a term still in use in the Division, which is corrupted from his name. The Isubu became prominent in the slave-trade at this time, and in the early nineteenth century Nako, a grandson of Mbimbi and the chief of their settlement at Bonangomba, was noted by Europeans. After his death, however, the strongest element in the tribe was to be found at Bonabile, a settlement founded by Bile, who was the child of an Isubu mother and a Duala father. Bile himself was recognized as 'King William' by the British Consuls from 1826 and received support from them in his clashes with neighbouring tribes. In 1858 King William ceded land to Alfred Saker, the Baptist missionary, on which he founded Victoria. Since the establishment of the German Protectorate, followed by the alienation of lands for the plantations, the Isubu population must have greatly declined, until in 1953 only 140 persons were enumerated.[11]

The three Isubu villages make up the Bimbia Village Group, under the Victoria Area Council, to which they elect four native members. The Isubu Chief Manga Williams, a descendant of the household of Bile, was President of the Victoria Divisional Council, which is elected from the area councils. Chief Manga Williams was always, until his death in 1959, closely associated with the administration of Victoria Division from his first appointment by the German Government in 1908.

Mongo. This tribe, sometimes termed *Mungo,* is situated on the lower reaches of the River Mungo which is named after them, and in Modeka and Missellele villages on the edge of the creeks. Part of the tribe is found on the French-administered side of the river. The origin of the tribe is not clear, but appears to be closely associated with the migration that brought the Duala to the coast some time in the eighteenth century.

Only Modeka and Missellele villages are hemmed in by plantation lands, in this case those of the Missellele Rubber Estate. The population of the British Mongo can only be conjectured as approximately 600. The Mongo elect five native members to the Tiko Area Council.

Balong. The Victoria Division Balong are related to other segments of this tribe in Kumba Division and on the French side of the River Mungo, and occupy four villages bordering the river in the northeast corner of Victoria Division. One village, Mpundu, is bounded on one side by the Mungo River and on the others by the Ekona plantation. Muyuka is bounded by plantations in the south. Malende village is adjacent to the narrow strip of Malende plantation, but in this case the plantation is small enough to be regarded as an enclave in native land rather than the reverse. Formerly Otto Holtfoth owned a tiny plantation at the Balong village of Yoke (German *Njoke*). Part of this land has been returned to Yoke village. Since 1956 Muyuka and Yoke have been the headquarters of timber extracting firms.

The Balong formerly constituted a separate Clan Native Authority. They now fall within the jurisdiction of the Balong Council, which also includes the Bakweri village of Owe. Their population is probably not more than 400.

Bakolle. This tribe inhabits a stretch of coast north of the Bamboko towards the Rio del Rey area. They are descended from a branch of the migration that brought the Duala to the coast, the founders of these two groups being brothers. No plantations are found in this area, but their territory is an important route by which Nigerians migrate into the Victoria Division. The tribe now falls in the Bakolle Council Area. Their population is about 300.

Fish Towns. In the Rio del Rey area, north of the Bakolle coast proper, are numbers of fishing settlements inhabited by Nigerians, largely from Calabar. Most of these settlements would appear to be more or less permanently occupied, although the population is unstable owing to periodic returns to Nigeria. The population of 907 persons recorded in the 1953 census is certainly an understatement. They elect three members to the Bakolle Council.

Wovea. Usually included with the Bakweri tribe, partly because of their small numbers but chiefly because of their present-day similarities in custom and language, is a group inhabiting one of the rocky Pirate Islands in Ambas Bay and the village on the mainland opposite. They call themselves Wovea (Duala *Bobea*) and are descended from an ancestor of Bubi (Fernando Po) origin. Formerly they inhabited the two larger islands in Ambas Bay outside the Pirate group: Ambas (Ndame) and Mondole, vacating the former during the nineteenth century and the latter under compulsion in 1905 when the German government used the island as a leper settlement. The Mondole islanders were resettled on the opposite mainland on the coast of Monkey Point (Affen Halbinsel), where they have since lived. The Wovea community were known by the Bakweri as 'Ewota' and by the Duala as 'Bota'. In the last form they gave their name to the headquarters of the former German West Afrikanische Pflanzungsgesellschaft 'Victoria' (W.A.P.V.), which is now the headquarters of the present-day Cameroons Development Corporation.[12]

In 1957 the younger part of the population of the island requested to be established at a locality on the mainland known as Isokolo. Negotiations were still uncompleted by 1958. They did not elect to go to the original Bota Mainland settlement which is situated in the same enclave as the two Bakweri settlements of Kie and Mokindi. This enclave with Bota Island and the separate Ngeme enclave is administered as Bota Village Group, which elects four native members to the Victoria Area Council, two of whom are Wovea. The Wovea of the mainland and island numbered 495 in the Census.[13]

In the following sections of this chapter most attention will be paid to the problems of the Bakweri and less to those of the Balong, Bamboko, Isubu and Wovea. This block comprises the majority of the indigenous population and includes almost all of it that is affected most directly by the plantation economy. The problems of the Mongo and Bakolle are of a different order. The former have a portion of their tribe domiciled on the French side of the Mungo River and are thus orientated both towards Duala and towards the British sphere. The latter are an outlying group of fishermen. Since both these tribes are, however, heavily affected by the immigration which results directly from economic conditions in the Victoria Division, they will be considered in that context.

Population problems are given prominence next, since they are largely responsible for the special conditions in Victoria Division. Next the problems of prostitution and the instability of marriage are discussed. A review of land policies since German times is followed by a discussion of the problem of indigenous agriculture and lastly conclusions summarised. Ethnographic material has had to be restricted to that directly relevant to the purposes of this study, some of a more specialised nature being published elsewhere.[14]

Population - Introductory Remarks

A basic problem of the plantations in Victoria Division has always been an inadequate local labour supply. In German times, the first labourers on the plantations were people of the Bakweri, Bamboko and Isubu tribes, in whose territory the estates had been established. Labour from these sources was inadequate, and in the earliest years when German rule was confined to the coast, workers were recruited from neighbouring parts of West Africa. When the hinterland was opened up, defeated tribes were required to supply workers, or private recruiters contracted with chiefs to supply workers for specified periods. Labour continued to be a problem, and administrative officers were led to protest against the depopulation of villages.[15] In 1913 all private recruiting was ended and became the responsibility of the German Government, who also decided to allow tax delinquents to be used as workers by private employers.[16] By various means, therefore, people from other areas of the Cameroons, originally notably Ewondo from Yaounde (now in French Cameroon) and the Grasslands, were introduced into the plantation areas. Dependence of the plantations on the labour of immigrants into Victoria Division has continued ever since, and they have never ceased to come in large numbers, even though direct recruitment has been abandoned, except for one brief experiment, since the British administration was set up forty years ago. The latter half of this period has been notable for the large increase in the numbers coming from Nigeria. Although immigrants working on the plantations have been largely housed on the estates, a very great proportion of the total number of immigrants has always tended to gravitate to the native reservations, where they have taken up land. In addition, the large proportion of males in the immigrant population soon resulted in a drift of the women and girls of the indigenous tribes into prostitution and other irregular liaisons.

An attempt is made here to assemble and interpret some of the demographic data available from the Census of 1953 and other recent sources which bear on the two related problems of immigration and the structure of the indigenous population. It will be seen later that in many respects the basic data must be treated with caution, and the analysis cannot attempt to be conclusive. Special access was granted by the Cameroons Government to the Schedule 1 (Group Count) Census sheets before these left the Cameroons. This made it possible to obtain figures at a more detailed level of breakdown than the published bulletins allow. The Schedule 1 forms which were made available account for 99 per cent of the African population of Victoria Division.[17]

Immigration into Native Areas

Immigrants into the Division come from many different tribes of the Cameroons under both British and French Trusteeship, Nigeria and some other African territories, and while many seek and obtain work on the plantations and live in housing provided on the estates, many others at some time or other reside in the areas reserved for the indigenous tribes. In this analysis, all Africans resident in the Division who do not belong to the indigenous tribes are termed 'immigrants', whether they live on the plantations or in the native areas. The term 'native' is correspondingly restricted to members of the indigenous tribes of the Division, defined as the Bakweri, Bamboko, Bakolle, Balong, Isubu and Wovea. The 'native areas' are those parts of the Division reserved for the indigenous tribes as opposed to plantation estates. The term 'local unit' is used for convenience to describe the groups, often of no ethnic significance, into which the indigenous people are divided for administrative purposes (e.g. 'Village Groups', 'Clans'), The term 'native' has no derogatory significance in the Southern Cameroons; non-African immigration is confined to transient European officials and employees. There is no Levantine or Indian commercial element.

The total African population of Victoria Division is 85,504, of which 84,689 individuals were enumerated on Schedule 1 and 815 on Schedule 2. Of the Schedule 1 population, 50,651 persons were living in the native areas, and this population of whom only 16,059 (or 32 per cent) belong to the indigenous tribes of the Division, while 34,592 (or 68 per cent) are immigrants. Of the latter, 17,532 are Nigerians and 16,802 are members of other Cameroons tribes (including the French Cameroons).[18] In the local unit with the most favourable proportion of indigenous tribe to immigrants (the Bakweri Bonjongo Village Group), immigrants still form 29 per cent of the population, while in Tiko Village Group they form nearly 92 per cent. The percentages of natives and immigrants living in the native areas are set out in Table 1.

As the figures show, no local unit is without immigrants. On the ground, however, the differences in distribution are clearer. In Bonjongo, Muea, Buea, Bamboko, Bota and Lysoka Village Groups their numbers are concentrated in specific localities, leaving others almost free. In the Bimbia and Victoria areas, and probably also in the Mongo area, this is

Table 1

Immigrants in native areas by local unit

Local unit	*Indigenous tribe*	*Natives*	*Percentage of population* *Other Victoria Division tribes*[19]	*Immi-grants*
Bonjongo Village Group.	Bakweri	71·0	—	29·0
Muea Village Group	Bakweri	67·0	—	33·0
Buea Village Group	Bakweri	64·0	—	36·0
Bamboko Village Group	Bamboko	51·4	—	48·6
Bota Village Group	Bakweri and Wovea	50·7	—	49·3
Lysoka Village Group	Bakweri	48·4	—	51·6
Mongo Clan	Mongo	20·7	6·1	73·2
Bimbia Village Group	Isubu	17·0	—	83·0
Victoria Village Group	Bakweri	16·1	—	83·9
Mutengene Village Group	Bakweri	12·4	—	87·6
Balong Clan	Balong	9·7	4.4	85·9
Tiko Village Group	Bakweri	8·3	—	91·7
Bakolle Clan	Bakolle	6·0	0.2	94·0
All local units		31·7		68·3

no longer so, while in the Mutengene, Balong and Tiko areas the indigenous population is confined to what are virtually tiny quarters of sprawling immigrant settlements. The figure for immigrants in the Bakolle Clan area in Table 2 below (4,779) includes Nigerians in the Fish Towns area of the Rio del Rey. But even without these, there are 3,872 immigrants in the Bakolle area proper, or 92·7 per cent of the population, giving the Bakolle the highest proportion of immigrants in the Division.[19]

Where immigration is confined to urban or quasi-urban centres, the problem, although serious, is of a different order from that arising from mass immigration into the villages and onto village lands, since this process tends to disrupt indigenous tribal life. For this reason, the situation of the Isubu tribe in the Bimbia Village Group, where immigrants form 83 per cent of the total population, must be regarded as graver than that of the indigenous population in the largely urban Victoria 'Village Group' where immigrants form a similar proportion of the population. The Balong tribe can hardly be regarded as an effective entity, being outnumbered by ten to one in its own villages. Individual villages in different parts of the Division show even higher proportions of immigrants, as, for example, the Bakweri village of Mondoni, which occupies a small enclave on the Mungo River, in which natives (15 persons) make up 4 per cent of the population of 379, and immigrants (364 persons) make up 96 per cent.

Immigrants on native lands occur in two main geographical concentrations: in the native enclaves along the coast and creeks on the one hand (accounting for the numbers in the Tiko, Victoria, Mongo, Bakolle, Bimbia and Bamboko areas), and on the other in those along the main road from Victoria to Kumba and the branch to Tiko (accounting for those in the Mutengene enclave, in the Likomba enclave of the Tiko Village Group, in the Balong area, and partly for those in the Bonjongo Village Group, in the Muea Village Group and the Lysoka Village Group). In addition, Buea contains a localized concentration, and others are found wherever native lands lie next to plantation estates. From a tribal point of view, the greatest absolute number of immigrants (22,905) is to be found on Bakweri land, while the highest proportions are found on Balong and Bakolle land. This will be seen from the following table in which the Bakweri groups have been combined.

Table 2

Immigrants in proportion to indigenous tribes

Indigenous tribe	*Natives in tribal areas*	*Immigrants in tribal areas*[21]	*Total population in tribal areas*	*Percentage*	
				Natives	*Immigrants*
Bamboko	788	744	1,532	51·4	48·6
Bakweri and Wovea	13,490	22,905	36,395	37·1	62·9
Mongo	600	2,293	2,893	20·7	79·3
Isubu	140	680	820	17·0	83·0
Balong	381	3,544	3,925	9·7	90·3
Bakolle	307	4,779	5,086	6·0	94·0

The figures show that all the smaller tribes in the Division except the Bamboko have been more affected than the Bakweri as a whole.

Immigration to Plantation Lands

Since immigration receives its stimulus from the presence of plantations in the Division, it is interesting to compare with these figures the population, living entirely on plantation lands and outside the native areas shown in Table 3. The figures for this population refer to all persons living in accommodation provided by the Cameroons Development Corporation and other plantation organisations except the small number counted in Schedule 2, and therefore comprise not only *bona-fide* workers and their wives and children but also workers' friends, relatives, concubines and lodgers, and exclude such plantation workers as live in native areas. There is a total population of 34,038, of which only 2,312, or 6·8 per cent, are identifiable as members of tribes indigenous to the Division.[22] The remainder, 31,726, are immigrants into the Division, of which 24,313 come from the British and French spheres of the Cameroons, a figure representing 71·4 per cent of the total plantation population in the Division and 76·3 per cent of the immigrant plantation population. The balance comes from Nigeria and elsewhere.

Immigrants living in the tribal areas are in fact slightly more numerous than immigrants in the plantation areas (34,602 and 31,726 respectively), but there is some difference in their composition.

Table 3

Immigrants in Victoria Division by origin

Ethnic Origin	*Total immigrants Victoria Division*	*Immi-grants, native areas*	*Immigrants plantation areas*	*Percentages* Native areas	Planta-tion areas
Other Cameroons tribes	41,115	16,802	24,313	40·9	59.1
Nigerian tribes	24,564	17,532	7,532	71·4	28·6
Others	639	258	381	40·4	59·6
All tribes	66,318	34,592	31,726	52·2	47·8

Thus, while a higher proportion of the whole body of Cameroons and other immigrants is to be found living on the plantations than on native lands, 70 per cent. of Nigerian immigrants are to be found on native lands. Part of this effect is due to the numbers of Nigerians in the Bakolle area, where many of them are fishermen. Even if the Bakolle area is excluded from the figures, 64·5 per cent of the Nigerians are still to be found on native as opposed to plantation lands (Table 4).

These figures appear to reflect the tendency of Nigerian immigrants, especially Ibo, to be primarily interested in establishing themselves in trade and other activities (in the immigrant quarters of native villages) and only secondarily in plantation work. On the other hand, even among immigrants of Cameroons extraction, who are generally recognised as being primarily attracted to the Division by the opportunities offered for work, over 40 per cent are domiciled on native land.

Table 4

Immigrants in Victoria Division excluding Bakolle area

Ethnic Origin	*Total immigrants Victoria Division*	*Immi-grants, native areas*	*Immigrants plantation areas*	*Percentages*	
				Native areas	*Planta-tion areas*
Other Cameroons tribes	41,103	16,790	24,313	40·9	59.1
Nigerian tribes	19,820	12,788	7,032	64·5	35·5
Others	623	242	381	38·8	61·2
All tribes	61,546	29,820	31,726	48·5	51·5

Total Immigration Further Analysed

Of the total Group Count population in Victoria Division of 84,689 no less than 66,318 or 78·3 per cent are immigrants from outside the Division, only 21·7 per cent being identifiable as members of the indigenous tribes. This represents a ratio of 3·6 immigrants to each native of the Division.

The evidence leaves the scale of immigration quite clear, and a striking feature is, of course, the high proportion of immigrants—over 50 per cent—who live in the native areas. These immigrants fall into a number of broad categories, which despite their tendency to overlap can be fairly easily distinguished on the ground. There are no direct data concerning the relative proportion of each category in the whole immigrant population in the native areas: the estimates given below and based on various sources of information should be treated with caution. They are applicable to the period roughly from 1953 to 1955.

(*a*) *Plantation workers without accommodation on the estates.*

This group includes workers dissatisfied with their housing because of overcrowding or dilapidation. In 1955 it seemed likely from current estimates that this group is about 7,500, or perhaps 7,000 allowing for workers and dependants who were native to the Division.[23]

(*b*) *Plantation workers' dependants with farms.*

There will always tend to be a number of workers living in native areas in order to grow food so long as opportunities for gardens are limited on the estates. Such workers would be included in the estimate for the previous category. Some workers establish their wives and children in native settlements while they reside in plantation camps for the working days of the week.[24] Their wives normally look after farm plots or engage in trade. A proportion of these were Bakweri and others native to the Division. It seems certain that the total migration into native areas represented by plantation workers or their dependants in both categories may be reasonably taken as no more than 8,000-10,000 persons.

(*c*) *Other employees and their dependants.*

Numbers of immigrants work for other employers than the plantation organisations. These either do not provide special housing or, when they do so, provide it inevitably in non-plantation areas. At the time of the Census immigrant employees and their families did not exceed 2,000. 500 convicts and secondary schoolboys from outside the Division may also be mentioned here.

(*d*) *Fishermen and their dependants.*

A great deal of the total immigration into native areas of the Division is accounted for by fishermen of Duala, Ibibio, Ijaw and other non-native origin. These immigrants and their dependants can be fairly accurately assessed at about 7,500 since almost all the immigration in the Bakolle, Mongo and Isubu areas is of this type.

(e) Traders, craftsmen and their defendants.

The greater part of the African retail trade in the Division is in the hands of immigrants who live in the native areas and distribute all kinds of goods. Probably the largest proportion of these traders, male and female, are Nigerians. Many immigrants also engage in tailoring, shoemaking and other skilled occupations. Nigerians are also prominent in these fields, and some, such as tinkering and bicycle repairing, are especially associated with members of the Ibo tribe. Probably the majority of the Nigerian immigrants on native lands outside the Bakolle area represented persons in this category and their dependants, in round figures perhaps between 6,000 and 8,000 persons.

(f) Farmers and their dependants.

Some immigrants are purely subsistence farmers who gravitated to the native areas after having come to the Division to work. Many such persons are retired plantation workers who have settled in native villages. Some have wives and children, others are unmarried. Such immigrants are commonly also casual workers or odd-job men in the native communities. Most of these quasi-settlers tend to come from the Grasslands of the British and French Cameroons. Other immigrants also farm for market or export. These have often, but not always, previously worked on the plantations, and many have dependants and are long-established. These men are industrious and grow and sell yams, plantains and other subsistence crops and to an ever increasing extent since about 1955 export crops like cocoa and bananas. They are also often engaged in other forms of trade. Both Nigerians and Cameroons tribes are represented. In addition, however, almost all other categories of immigrants on native lands are engaged in farming to a greater or lesser extent as well as their other pursuits. Using the estimates of the numbers of immigrants in other categories as a guide, those engaged entirely or primarily in agriculture may have numbered, with wives and children, between 4,000 and 6,000, in 1955, but by 1959 were probably increasing rapidly in number.

(g) Visitors.

This term covers the floating populations always present in the native areas and comprises fellow tribesmen of immigrants of every other category living with the latter, as a preliminary either to finding work or to returning to their home areas. On the plantations one worker in eight had a lodger, and the proportion is likely to be greater among house-holding immigrants in the native areas. This floating population can hardly have been less than 2,000, but the upper limit cannot be determined with any accuracy, these people being found among the dependants of immigrants of all other categories. Most would appear to be young males. Although most immigrant women resident in the native areas are the wives or dependants of male immigrants, there are some who have entered the Division to take up prostitution. These are largely from the Southern Cameroons, and should possibly be numbered in hundreds rather than in thousands.

This rough breakdown of the immigrant population shows that plantation workers and their dependants may at the time to which the figures refer have accounted for as much as a quarter of the immigration to native land. The importance of adequate housing and access to food plots on the estates is thus clear. Although the immigrant populations in the native areas form centres of labour supply to the plantations, quite a large number of persons seem to be engaged in agriculture and fishing or in providing goods and services. Some of this activity, notably fishing, would probably continue if there were no plantations, but much of it provides goods and services to other immigrants which would not be provided by natives for lack of numbers. Immigration into the Division, therefore, may be said to produce 'working immigrants' and 'supporting immigrants', although the personnel of these two groups often interchange. It is probably the growth of the population of supporting immigrants together with the fact that not all working immigrants and their dependants are housed on plantations, or indeed are plantation workers, that has helped to produce the situation in which half the total immigrant population live in the native areas. But permanent settlement is still the exception. The only group who have shown any consistent tendency to settle for a lifetime have been men of some French Cameroons tribes who arrived in the German period.[25] There is little difference between immigrants living on and working for the plantations and those in native areas: some stay for years, some for a few months, many make regular visits to their home areas, and most expect to return home sooner or later. Urbanization is also still on a small scale, the three main centres, Victoria, Tiko and Buea, having total populations of only 8,000, 5,300 and 3,000 respectively. Of these, only Victoria is at all urban in layout with some hard-surfaced streets and considerable numbers of permanent houses. Its development is still continuing in an orderly manner. In comparison, Tiko is little more than an overgrown immigrant settlement, and Buea a fenced Bakweri village with a moderate sized immigrant quarter, and Government offices and housing scattered over a considerable area outside it.

Because of the small size of the native population immigrants are only absorbed by the indigenous societies where they come as individuals or in small numbers. Otherwise immigrants usually tend to live alongside the native villages in long untidy 'stranger' settlements, in contrast with which the former, which are typically enclosed within a fence, often appear secluded and quiet backwaters. Where immigrant settlement is densest, as along the main roads, this relative isolation breaks down, and the indigenous area is submerged and can barely be distinguished.

Since the period to which the figures refer, the distribution of immigration may have begun to change radically for the first time for half a century. The entry of large timber firms into the formerly undeveloped part of the Division north of the plantations, combined with the startling success of banana cooperatives, are now making their mark. By mid-1958 the K.C.B. timber group were employing about 1,300 men in Victoria Division who were largely immigrants. In addition, with the clearing of forests, immigrants were entering the land and planting bananas. The timber group operates from Muyuka and Yoke (Njoke) in the Balong area, but most of the forests are in the Upper Bakweri area. It seems certain, with a smaller plantation labour force and the new economic factors, that immigration onto native lands far exceeded that on the plantations by 1959 and was entering a new phase of growth. Total immigration into the Division appears to have remained fairly stable for a time.

The Local Land Use Problem

The problem of the allocation of land to immigrants by the indigenous peoples in the already small reservations has repeatedly disturbed the United Kingdom, since it became responsible for the area, but at first it was primarily concerned with the conflict of interest between the natives and the plantations.

The majority of the plantations were bought back into German hands at the second of two auctions in 1922 and 1924. Soon plantation managers exercising their rights under their land titles claimed that in many areas Bakweri farms and villages formed encroachments on their concessions. The Nigerian Government opposed any measures to remove these settlements, and a report of one of its officers pointed out that to compel their return within the reserve limits 'would be tantamount to approving their extinction', adding that it was essential that increases in the reserve areas should be made. The chief company involved was W.A.P.V., and the Government proposed in 1929 to purchase a 5,000-acre property of the Kamerun Eisenbahn-Gesellschaft in Kumba Division, then still unliquidated as a result of delay in clarifying the title, and to offer it to W.A.P.V. in exchange for an equivalent area of W.A.P.V.'s holdings in Victoria Division, including all areas of native encroachments. This proposal was accepted by the company, but was made impracticable by a decision at The Hague that any ex-enemy property remaining unliquidated in the hands of mandatory powers should be returned to the original owners. It was therefore decided instead to purchase the required land in Victoria Division outright from W.A.P.V., and negotiations continued until 1933, eventually also involving the Moliwe Plantation, resulting in the purchase from both companies of a total of 6,698 acres at a cost of £9,202 to the Nigerian Government.[26] The companies were naturally reluctant to surrender any of their freeholds, and acquisition by negotiation was preferred by the Government to compulsion. If agreement had not been reached, it would have been necessary to expropriate the land under the Public Lands Acquisition Ordinance, but it would have been for the Courts to decide whether the Ordinance was intended to apply to the extension of native reserves.[27]

The enlargement of the reserves did not, however, solve the problem of the taking up of land by immigrants, and the land question has been further complicated in the postwar period by its revival in another form. From 1946 a Bakweri organisation (the Bakweri Land Committee) made several requests to the Trusteeship Council of the United Nations for the return of all alienated lands to the indigenous inhabitants. Since 1947 the former German estates have been leased by the Nigerian Government to the Cameroons Development Corporation and have been reclassified as 'native lands' utilised by C.D.C. in the interests of the Southern Cameroons as a whole, and the Trusteeship Council therefore noted that ultimate ownership was in fact vested in the people. In 1948 a senior administrative officer, Mr. W. M. Bridges, was asked by the Nigerian Government to inquire into the whole question of the land needs of the Bakweri and other peoples in Victoria Division. Part of his extremely competent report was summarized for publication in 1949.[28] The inquiry was conducted on the basis that fifteen acres per household would be adequate for the needs of the inhabitants, a basis, it should be stated, that in many areas errs heavily on the side of generosity. As a result, it was discovered that, while the more fortunately placed communities possessed between them 6,453 acres in excess of the amount of land calculated on this basis, the remainder would require additions of land amounting altogether to 25,000 acres. However, it is significant that the reporting officer stated that 'in nearly every case in which a local shortage of farming land was observed it was found to be due in the main to the fact that immigrants, taking advantage of the widespread breakdown in the control of land-use, had obtained the use of farm land which the local community could ill spare'. It was maintained by the administration that the indigenous peoples tended to leave agriculture in the hands of immigrants and that the further enlargement of the reserves would only result in more land being taken into use by immigrants. The Nigerian Government therefore proposed that excisions from the plantation lands leased to the Cameroons Development Corporation be made on the basis of fifteen acres per household to members of the indigenous tribes, but under safeguards. The excised lands should be controlled by public bodies on which the people, the administration and the Cameroons Development Corporation would be represented to ensure sound use of the land, with the provision of technical advice and a guaranteed market for the surplus agricultural products of the settlers. These proposals were rejected by the Bakweri Land Committee who claimed nothing less than the return of all alienated lands to the Bakweri tribe. At the time of writing, the proposals still stand, and the Trusteeship Council has urged the Bakweri to accept them. The issue has faded into the background during the recent period of constitutional change.

The 'Bakweri land problem' had its roots in the methods whereby lands were alienated to plantation interests in the period of the German Protectorate. In the early days the problem was one of reconciling the needs of the indigenous population with the excessive claims of the plantation concessionaries. However, by the time of the British Mandate this clear-cut problem had been partially resolved by the activities of the German Land Commissions, a process continued by the later enlargements of the reserves by the Nigerian Government, and was already giving way to the problem of the taking up of land in the reserves by immigrants. Even at the present time, it would be hard to maintain that there is insufficient land in the reserves if the indigenous people only were taken into account. The land problem is an aspect of the whole problem of immigration.

Land Tenure - Rights and Bakweri Practices

The legislation governing land transactions in the Southern Cameroons is the Native Lands and Rights Ordinance,[29] which, at the time of writing, also applies to Northern Nigeria and to the Northern Cameroons. This legislation declares all lands in those areas to be 'native lands' vested in the Governor-General of Nigeria, and that no right of occupancy is valid without his consent. Rights acquired by native law and custom are automatically recognised by the definition of the purpose of the ordinance. The legislation provides strict controls over the alienation of land to non-natives and, despite its peculiar features[30] has succeeded in its main aim. At the time of its first application to the Southern Cameroons the freeholds granted to the German estates were specifically excluded. Since their purchase these lands have also come under the ordinance, from which the Cameroons Development Corporation derives its right of occupancy. Only a few estates and 'native freeholds' now remain outside the ambit of the legislation. Unfortunately, the drafters were primarily concerned with the prevention of acquisitions of land on the German model, and the ordinance is weak on the subject of alienation to African immigrants. In Section 2 a 'native' is defined as a person one of whose parents is a member of any tribe or tribes indigenous to the Northern Provinces or the Cameroons under United Kingdom Administration, and the descendants of such a person. The provision in the Third Schedule that 'it shall not be lawful for any native holding a right of occupancy to sell, transfer possession, bequeath or otherwise alienate his title to a non-native except with the consent of the Governor' therefore does not apply to any inhabitant of Northern Nigeria or the Southern Cameroons who happened to be living in Victoria Division, although it does apply to inhabitants of the Eastern and Western Regions, unless they make a statutory declaration of permanent residence in the Division. In fact this is not enforced.

Even the right of a 'native' to alienate title to another 'native' is not absolute. A native may sell, transfer possession or bequeath his title (subject to any native law or custom to the contrary) 'to a blood relative being a native' provided that the change of title is registered within six months. Subject again to any native law or custom to the contrary, he may alienate his title to 'any other native permanently resident in the same district, with the consent of the district headman and the approval of the head chief, subject to registration'. The first of these provisions has never been enforced and would swamp the small Buea land registry if it were. The second, which would be of value in regulating alienation of land to immigrants whom the law recognises as 'natives', embodies terminology which is not directly applicable to Victoria Division. One conclusion seems clear: that probably no transactions involving alienation of land by a native occupier to an immigrant, whether classified as a 'non-native' (like an Ibo or a French Cameroonian) or a 'native' (like a Bamenda man or Fulani), have been legal for forty years; this is tantamount in practice, however, to saying that they have all been legal.

The ordinance sets great store by native law and custom, and presumably in any contest the sanction of native law and custom would be strong evidence of legality. Unfortunately the determination of the custom ruling land tenure in the special conditions of Victoria Division is no easy matter. In the writer's six or seven years' acquaintance with the Bakweri it has not remained unchanged. The basic system is as follows. Among the Bakweri generally the landowning unit is the lineage (*litumba*), which is a small close kinship group whose men are all directly descended from a common ancestor.[31] Theoretically the land of each lineage is in the control of its senior surviving member, but each adult male has the usufruct of parcels of land in his own lifetime. On a man's death, the land he had used was customarily divided with his other goods by a senior surviving member of the kin-group between his sons and brothers. Nowadays, it is general for control of land to pass to the deceased's eldest brother if he leaves no sons or if the sons are young, or to the eldest son if he is of responsible age. Sons of sisters may acquire rights to plots of land under certain circumstances, as recompense for services performed at the funeral, and sometimes this occurs nowadays owing to the dying out of all male succession in a lineage. Women could not own land, but when married they had the right to land from their husbands on which to grow cocoyams and other crops. This was a right of usufruct only, and the right lapsed if, for example, the marriage ended in divorce. A woman could not inherit land, nor could land used by her be inherited by anyone other than a male member of her husband's lineage (this person might, of course, be her son). This is still the normal practice, but again the shortage of male heirs in a lineage has sometimes resulted in the *de facto* inheritance of land by a daughter who then passes it on to her son. Such inheritance by women was regarded as anomalous by the Bakweri, and in theory the women may still be said to be entitled only to the usufruct, the land itself only being held in trust for male offspring. On the other hand, *de facto* ownership by women is so common that they now undertake to sell land.

There was formerly no transfer of land rights by sale. In strict custom, within the village individual males possess established rights to the use of land, but its allocation and disposal rests with the lineage. In indigenous circumstances the question of alienation would only arise when a Bakweri of another village wished to live in the village and farm. Such a person would ask the chief and elders (who would themselves be the responsible members of their lineages) for permission to settle. If this was agreed to, it followed naturally that the stranger would be given land to build and farm on, and he would kill a pig for the villagers as a sign of goodwill. This was not a purchase. If the settler proved to be obnoxious and was expelled, he lost all right to the land he was using. Nor at any time could he alienate this land to another without the consent of the village.

It should also be noted that while the settlement of complete strangers was not unknown, the commonest applications for land were from persons related to natives of the village, often by marriage but most typically because their mothers had been born in the village. The pig was in a sense a payment for a lease on the land, but such terms are misleading, since the use of land was regarded as being dependent on residence in the village, and the grant of land to a stranger followed automatically on granting him residence. Independent transactions solely in land were unknown.[32] Attitudes of this type to land can only exist where land is not a scarce commodity. It is only when resources are likely to be insufficient that the close regulation of alienation becomes necessary.

Neither the outright sale of land to the German plantation interests nor the tremendous influx of non-Bakweri immigrants were therefore envisaged in custom. In the case of the former, elders in many villages willingly conceded the use of large tracts of land to the early concessionnaires when offered what to them were unusually high inducements to do so. In one sense they knew clearly what they were doing. There cannot be any doubt that they knew they were conceding rights to land use and, as they thought, profitably. On the other hand, the only precedent for such concessions was the settlement of strangers of the same tribe, and therefore they were not prepared for the rapid development and transformation of such extensive areas, with the concomitant need for labour and the introduction of an economic system completely foreign to them. Later, the alienation of land to the plantations was controlled by the German Government through the creation of reserves and of Crown land, and direct negotiation between natives and planters ceased. The postwar claim for the return of the plantations to Bakweri ownership is an expression of a feeling that, as the late Chief Lucas of Wonjongo put it, 'for a jar of brandy we lost all'. The impracticability of this claim, however, at a time when not only the Victoria Division tribes but the people of the Southern Cameroons as a whole contribute to the exploitation of the plantations and depend on their profits to a large extent for the economic stability of the territory, is apparent to the majority of the Bakweri; on the other hand, they may be able to satisfy legitimate land needs by taking up the offer of the Government made in 1950, perhaps along the lines recommended later.

When African immigrants first came into the native areas and asked for land, the immediate effects were not so quickly apparent. Originally, immigrants (like stranger Bakweri) did not pay rent, and in many villages this is still so. Later it became common to ask for sums of money, but even in 1955 the system was still informal. One Bakweri allowed a native of the Bamenda area to use land after an initial payment of five shillings and a bottle of kerosene. In the next ten years the landlord received further payments amounting to £1. 5s. The landlord then died, and his son received five shillings from the tenant towards his funeral expenses. In eleven years the tenant had paid a little over £2 or about 3s. 6d. per year. In many cases immigrants are expected to provide recompense in kind. For example, at the Balong village of Yoke an Ibo immigrant contracted to cook a meal of rice for the landlord, to buy him a hat, waistcloth and shirt and to build him a house; in actual fact, however, the tenant continually postponed payment, and none of these things were ever received. Landlords tended to regard tenants rather as they did sons-in-law, to be approached at various times for money, although with no assurance of receiving it. However, in many native areas immigrants were and remain so numerous that they were squatters rather than tenants, and they paid rent to no one except, more often than not, to each other. Such payments as were received were generally for roadside sites which are always in great demand by trading immigrants and which are therefore hard to come by. In the case of farmplots on some reserve land the natives had and still have very little control. In the Mutengene enclave, for example, there are large immigrant settlements off the road in which no rent has ever been paid to a native and the same is true of many immigrant districts. It would be very wrong to believe that immigrants were originally allowed to take up land because the natives wished to profit from rent, and even nowadays it is often doubtful whether the indigenous inhabitants derive much direct benefit from their presence. Plantation workers sometimes claim to pay high room rents when they live in some native areas, often more than 10s. per month. Renting of rooms by the month is a feature of predominantly immigrant centres, and the landlords are almost invariably themselves immigrants who may or may not be paying any rent themselves. This is so in Tiko, Likomba, Mutengene and other main road centres.[33]

A frequent problem due to the use of land by immigrants is the ownership of permanent improvements to the land such as buildings and tree crops. Immigrants are customarily regarded as having a right to any subsistence crop they may grow, but they should not grow any permanent crop. In the Balong area, however, it is said that if an immigrant leaves, the standing stems revert to the landlord. Similarly, any house built by an immigrant should be left to the landlord when he leaves, since in the absence of any system of ground rent if an immigrant sells the house the landlord loses effective control of the land. An Ibo immigrant quoted in a previous example absconded, selling a house he had built to a Bakoko from the French Cameroons for £50, also having failed to make the landlord the contracted payment in kind. In another case, a more complex example of the same type of problem was illustrated. In one area thirty years ago a Bakweri allowed another man the use of land without payment. On this land the latter built a permanent house which he eventually sold to a third person, who rented out the house and also allowed others to build on the land. The family of the true landlord recently claimed their land; native custom as it existed in former times could not envisage such a situation. In such cases there would seem to be no doubt that the land still belongs to the indigenous owner, but where improvements are extensive and carried out over many years at no cost to him, it can be argued that the tenant should be compensated on vacation of the land by the market value of any improvements he has made, less a deduction for reasonable arrears of rent for the land if rent has not been regularly paid.

The indigenous tribes have been blamed for the admission of immigrants on to their land, but the pressure of immigration has been such that only an exceptionally single-minded and well-organized people could have resisted it. The numerically small tribes of Victoria Division with their social systems already disorganized were never in a position to do so, and once the first immigrants had been allowed to come in, the situation rapidly passed out of their control in all the popular areas of settlement. Indigenous systems of land tenure were customary usages evolved in a situation of plentiful land in which alienation was uncommon and of a simple kind. The position has changed once again since the competition for land that has grown up among the Bakweri themselves as a result of the development of native banana production. The full effects of this have begun to make themselves felt since about

1955 or 1956. In the report version of this book it was suggested that a growth in indigenous economic activity would tend to increase Bakweri valuation of land. Certainly land is rapidly becoming a scarce commodity, and transactions quite contrary to what has formerly been accepted as native custom have become common. Thus outright sale (rather than transfer of the right of usufruct) between unrelated Bakweri occurs, supported by handwritten documents stating that the sale is 'for ever'. Supposed outright sale of land by women who have children, by elder brothers with younger brothers, both inside and outside the village, have become increasingly common. Lineage elders have been bringing cases to court to have some of these transactions invalidated; some, however, they have been in ignorance of, and some they have connived at. A proportion of these transactions still involves immigrants and this has awakened considerable concern in some areas. It is now true that an immigrant who wants land in a Bakweri community can rarely obtain it for nothing. On the other hand he may now effect a supposed purchase with an appearance of legality. The increased valuation of land has also resulted in land sales of the same type between immigrants. There is no doubt in the writer's mind that none of these transactions are permitted by Bakweri custom as it stood in the last generation and before. Their legality is also, to say the least, questionable. By 1959 it seemed clear that the status of outright sale in native custom was confused, and that the overriding right of village and lineage to veto land transactions was being put to the test in several areas. The peculiar population position in the indigenous areas has often left some lineage lands in the control of youths or women who may dispose of it light-heartedly, while other lineages and the village as a whole may be short of land.

It seems a matter of some urgency that a precise statement should be made of the legal position concerning individual ownership, ownership by women, alienation by natives to immigrants and similar matters. To leave alienation controlled neither by native custom nor by the Native Lands and Rights Ordinance, is to store up yet another body of problems for the future. In certain native enclaves where the immigrant population greatly outnumbers the native inhabitants, no kind of initiative on the part of natives alone can be effective in reducing immigration, and such areas should be kept under review to ensure that uncontrolled immigration does not eventually lead to gross overcrowding.

In 1958 a new system of local government was introduced to supersede the former Native Authority system (Ardener 1960). The important provisions (*Southern Cameroons Legal Notices 31 to 38 of*

25 April 1958) are that immigrants both on and off the plantations in specified proportions are represented as well as natives, and that both native and immigrant representatives are now elected rather than appointed. Power of appointing a very small and specified number of representatives is retained by the Commissioner of the Cameroons to ensure the representation of special interests, such as 'traditional ruling elements' and women. The native representatives are kept well in the majority (for example in Victoria Area Council 23 natives and 7 non-natives are provided for). Both kinds of representatives are elected by both natives and non-natives in the units concerned. Provision is made for (in practice) the senior chiefs of the Division to become ceremonial President and Vice-President of the Divisional Council, but the Chairmen both of Area and Divisional Councils are elected by those councils and actually preside over business. The system has not had time to prove itself, but it could bring two benefits to the Division that are relevant here. It could bring into the councils new native representatives who may, through greater education and experience, be able to help their elders in dealing more effectively with indigenous problems. It could also give immigrants a greater sense of responsibility for the area in which they live, and enable the conflicts as well as the ultimate community of interest of native and immigrant to be discussed together. The integration of the long-established plantation worker into his Division is also a valuable step. The problems discussed here should certainly be on the agenda of the councils.

Indigenous Agriculture

The failure of indigenous agriculture to produce an adequate supply of foodstuffs to support the large working population in Victoria Division has often been remarked upon. The Bakweri and Balong are the chief agriculturalists in the Division, the Bamboko, Isubu, Mongo and Wovea being primarily fishermen. A brief outline of the agricultural methods of these two tribes follows.

The staple crop of the Bakweri is a species of cocoyam (*xanthosoma maffafa*) which is called *likao* in their language from the native name for Fernando Po (*Likao*), from which it was brought by the Baptist Mission. The absence of a very dry season combined with the rich volcanic soils of much of Bakweri territory make the cultivation of this crop relatively easy, as the main underground stem (the corm or 'mammy coco') continues to grow for five or even six years and to develop cormels from itself throughout the whole period. Thus it is not necessary, as in many parts of southern Nigeria and the Cameroons, even among the Balong neighbours of the Bakweri, for the whole plant to be dug up and replanted from seed cormels every year. Instead, it is possible for several years to dig at the base of the plant and cut off cormels which have grown from the main corm and replace the earth. This can be done for the first time about three months after planting, when the young cormels are known as *velongelonge*. About a year after planting the cormels are much bigger and are known as *vetinga*. The 'mammy coco' itself gradually grows into a thick trunk-like stem of about eight inches in diameter which protrudes above the surface, throwing up leaves whose tips are commonly five or six feet above the ground. Such mature cocoyams are known as *mekoko* (literally 'logs'), and at this stage while they are still producing cormels it is also possible to cut out some of the growing points on the main corm for use in replanting without damage to it. After a number of years the cormels produced become big and coarse and begin to throw out their own shoots, when they are known as *vekpali*. At or before this stage the 'mammy coco' is dug up and cut into pieces for replanting and the cycle begins again. Replanting may also be done at any time with large cormels which may also be cut.

There is another species of cocoyam (*Colocasia esculenta*) which the Bakweri sometimes state was the original kind they possessed before the *xanthosoma* came from Fernando Po. It is also planted by the women after the *xanthosoma*, but unlike the latter it must be dug up completely each year in December. The two species of cocoyam are easily distinguished by the point of junction of leaf and petiole. When the term 'cocoyam' is used in Victoria Division, and generally in this study, it may be taken to refer to the species of *xanthosoma*.[34]

After the cocoyam the most important crop is the plantain (*Musa sapientium* var. *paradisiaca*) which is regarded as the men's crop, although many women also grow it. It is most usual for the new plantain suckers to be interplanted between new cocoyams. After about one year the plantain is fully grown with one stem of fruit, and it is then cut down and the fruit removed. New suckers grow from the old root, and thus many plantain farms may be left to propagate themselves. Native bananas are grown, which are smaller than the export variety and are used to make a pounded food known as *akara*. Commercial bananas are discussed later.

Yams (*Dioscorea spp.*) are cultivated but are regarded as a subsidiary crop. They are usually planted by women while men put in stakes up which the vines later grow. Several types of yam are grown of which *yono* is white in texture, *jase* yellowish and *evie* reddish, all being varieties of common West African species, *evie,* for example, being a variety of *Dioscorea alata.* Aerial or bulbil-bearing yams (*Dioscorea bulbifera*) are grown and are called *lioko.* The Bakweri say that only one type of yam was indigenous to them, which they call *lisua* (*Dioscorea dumetorum*). This is of inferior quality and deteriorates quickly unless cooked. All other types of yam are said to have been introduced from the hinterland and ultimately from Nigeria in comparatively recent times.

Maize (*Zea mays*) may be planted between the cocoyams by men or women and is regarded as a reliable stopgap food. Cassava (*Manihot utilissima*) is planted (usually by women), but it is not widely popular. The variety usually cultivated does not need leaching before eating, but after some years in the farm the toxic effects are said to appear. One of various widespread species of melon (*Cucumeropsis spp.* or *Citrullus spp.*) produces the edible seeds usually known by the Yoruba name *egusi.* A species of *Cucurbita* or pumpkin, of which both the leaves and flesh are edible, is also cultivated. Peppers and various leaves used as green vegetables in soup grow partly wild and partly cultivated. Sugar cane and pineapples are planted in small quantities.

There is no rigid system of rotation of crops, and plots are normally left fallow when the cocoyams on them have reached the stage when the main corms must be cut up and replanted. Fallows are not short by the standards of some parts of Eastern Nigeria. In the Bonjongo reserve land is rarely left for less than from four to six years, and ten years or longer is common even near the village. Young women are sometimes cultivating plots never used in their own lifetimes. In the Lisoka area 10 years' fallow was regarded as the minimum, before the recent banana boom. Bridges in 1948 found only a few areas in which soil could be termed exhausted or partly exhausted. A survey of soils in selected native areas would be essential to form any reliable idea of the adequacy of fallow periods. On the whole, from a superficial impression it would seem that actual soil exhaustion has not been one of the most pressing problems of Bakweri agriculture. The commercial production of bananas for export, as is mentioned later, may of course change this situation.

Men mark out any new farmplots to be used in the farming season in January and do the actual clearing with machetes. All planting is done between February and May. Women plant cocoyams and generally all the subsidiaries including yams, but plantains are usually planted by men, who also put in the stakes for the yams. Plantains need no special planting season and will grow and come to maturity at any time of the year, but special plantings are usually made at this season. Maize may be planted by men or women. By the end of this period the women have already begun weeding, which is done with machetes or by pulling the weeds out by hand. In June and July maize and pumpkins are ready, and in August and September first diggings of young cormels from the same year's planting of cocoyams may be made.

At this time also the tubers of some yams may be cut without disturbing the plant, leaving the growing point to produce further small tubers which are harvested at the end of the year for seed. From October to December the uncut yams come to maturity and are dug, and further harvests of cormels from the cocoyams may be made. The plantains are ready from ten months to a year after planting. After the time of planting, weeding and most of the harvesting is done by women, although men take an interest in the yam crop and cut down the plantains. Men rarely tend or harvest cocoyams, which are regarded as a women's crop. Men are responsible for the cutting of palm fruit, but the Bakweri are not great oil-palm cultivators and are concerned only for palm-oil for domestic uses. Oil is normally not expressed in quantity for this purpose, enough nuts with pericarp for the meal being simply boiled in a pan of water. Large numbers of Bakweri, if not most, nowadays prefer to buy locally sold palm-oil, largely marketed by immigrants. The oil-palm is tapped for wine by some men, but not in large enough quantities to satisfy the great local demand: palm wine is scarce and expensive.

The most characteristic domestic animals are goats, sheep and pigs, but cattle and horses are common. Fowls and ducks, dogs and a few cats are all found. Pigs and goats are a great danger to cocoyam farms, the former actually rooting out the main corms, thus destroying several years' potential production of cormels. These animals, together with all other livestock, are therefore strictly kept within a fence surrounding the village, the upkeep of which is the responsibility of all the men in the village, each of whom is allotted a section. Cattle belong to a common dwarf breed of West African short-horn, but are in excellent condition and appear to grow to a larger size than is usual in many areas. Pigs also grow relatively fat and are fed on cocoyams and their peel. They are very often kept in the house, usually sleeping by the fire. Horses, where owned, are never eaten and only rarely ridden. Large numbers were purchased in recent years by Ibo for export to Nigeria for ritual purposes. Dogs and cats are never eaten. Livestock was the indigenous form of wealth, and the Bakweri word for wealth (*woli*) actually means 'livestock'. There are complex grading systems for each type of animal. Six or seven sizes of pig alone are recognised. As has been stated previously, marriage payments were calculated in goats.

Ceremonies performed to establish a man as wealthy involved the exhibition and subsequently the dispersal by gift and consumption of large numbers of livestock of all kinds. Until recently it could still be said that the older generation of Bakweri regarded the possession of livestock as the truest form of wealth. This tradition undoubtedly retarded the entry of Bakweri men into trade, in the absence of any strong economic pressure to do so.

Bakweri cultivation methods are not more inefficient, taking into account the difficulties of a terrain with little level ground and many volcanic boulders, than those of most forest tribes. The fact that the *xanthosoma* cocoyam continues to produce cormels for several years means that the Bakweri are not dependent for each year's crop of their staple food on the planting of the previous year. The adequacy of the cocoyam crop for subsistence provides the men with no special incentive to the development of other subsistence crops. It is a common misconception, however, that the Bakweri had no agriculture. They always in historical times lived in settled communities with agriculture and some livestock and resemble numbers of Cameroons forest tribes in their basic economy.[35]

The fact that the women do most of the day-to-day work of agriculture again does not make the Bakweri unique. This is a feature of many Nigerian and Cameroons tribes, including those of the Bamenda plateau where women generally have a harder life than among the Bakweri. The product of women's agricultural work is sufficient for normal tribal needs as well as some surplus for sale, but no real expansion is possible without enlisting the full-time activity of the men. It is rare for men to fail to respond to such a ready economic incentive as exists in the large market for foodstuffs in Victoria Division due to the large working population. Unlike their neighbours, the Balong, the Bakweri have only recently turned with any enthusiasm to export crops. Surpluses of (subsistence) agricultural products are at present sold chiefly at the markets of Victoria and Tiko. The Bakweri formerly had no internal markets, and all trade was carried on at shore marts at which Bakweri women exchanged agricultural produce for fish with the Isubu, Duala and other fishing peoples. This was the origin of Tiko, the site of such a mart, and the markets of Victoria and Tiko are still referred to as 'the shore' (*liwo*). The system of barter which was once general is still to be observed, as for example at the shore mart of Mosoku, at which women of the Wovea community on Pirate Island exchange two or three *bonga* fish (*Ethmalosa dorsalis*) for five cocoyams or one large stem of plantains. Bakweri men never entered trade in the old days, and the internal markets now found, the largest being at Muea on the main road to Kumba, all date from German times. Women from Buea go down in largest numbers to Victoria on Tuesday and return on Wednesday, selling small quantities of produce, though some Bakweri women may be found in the market on most days. Almost all other trade is in the hands of immigrants. In German times the Duala tribe dominated trade; nowadays Nigerians, especially Ibo, are dominant. At Tiko the few Bakweri women with their heaps of cocoyams are the only native sellers in a large market, almost all other vendors being Ibo. Bakweri men say that they would be ashamed to sit in a market trying to sell goods. Long-continued bargaining and sharp practice are distasteful to them, although their standards in these matters are not perhaps as high as they imagine. They are often genuinely amazed at the way immigrants make profits from petty trade. This attitude has acted as a further drag on attempts to stimulate Bakweri interest in agriculture, and at many gatherings at which we discussed the entry of men into food production the men expressed aversion to marketing the products themselves. It is therefore of special interest to review the most striking development in Bakweri agriculture, which has been the recent rapid and indeed startling growth of cooperative societies for the production and marketing of bananas, a development which appears to have completely bypassed traditional Bakweri attitudes.

Between 1950 and 1952 suggestions were made to the Cameroons Development Corporation that it might market bananas produced by local farmers, but the Corporation was not entirely in favour, objecting that there was no evidence of existing native plantings or of any adequate organisation, and that concentration of farmers on bananas might be detrimental to food production. In addition, the Corporation foresaw the danger that native plantings might form uncontrolled centres whereby Panama disease might spread to its own estates. It was also feared that the existence of native plantings might lead to the pilfering of the Corporation's own bananas. Eventually agreement was reached on the arrangement, and in 1952 the Bakweri Cooperative Union of Farmers Ltd. (B.C.U.F.) was formed with an initial membership of 100 individual farmers, making its first shipment of 835 stems of bananas in September of that year.[36] In June 1954 the Union was reconstituted to contain four affiliated primary societies, which by late 1958 had increased to seventeen, with in addition three affiliated secondary societies in Kumba Division. At first the Union confined its activities to Victoria Division, but by 1959 its operations had spread to the accessible parts of Kumba Division along the Mbonge and Tombel roads, so that the Union had partly ceased to be Bakweri. The Union is directed by its own committee and executive staff, including three experts seconded from Elders and Fyffes Ltd., and supervised by three African inspectors, under the guidance of the Southern Cameroons Registrar of Co-operative Societies. Together with the cocoa, coffee and palm kernel co-operative (the Cameroons Co-operative Exporters Ltd.), it has established a separate transport society (the Cameroons Co-operative Engineering and Transport Union) to evacuate produce. Capital of about £60,000 has been invested in the latter, with a fleet of over fifty vehicles and a well-equipped garage.

The progress of the Union was remarkable: in the first year (1952) it shipped 8,000 stems valued at £2,500; in 1958 it was able to ship 1,350,000 stems valued at over £900,000. The organisation, which has now some 4,000 members, has signed a separate marketing agreement with Elders and Fyffes Ltd., who have placed advisory and technical resources at its disposal. Some idea of what this great access of income has meant to Victoria Division is shown in the following table:

Table 5

Average gross income per member of co-operatives
(Year ending 31 March 1958)

Society (Victoria Division only	*Member-ship*	*Value of produce sold* £	*Average per member (nearest £)*
Ekona	84	50,971	606
Mutengene	145	71,186	491
Muea	230	63,220	275
Muyuka	241	61,703	256
Maumu	90	19,512	217
Lisoka	182	39,301	216
Bolifamba	125	24,903	199
Victoria	314	62,470	199
Tiko	96	18,405	192
Bonyadikombo	135	11,250	83
Soppo	200	15,118	76
Bokwae	152	6,563	43
Total	1,994	444,602	223

The net income after the necessary deductions to cover the Society's operations, and after provision for tax, is approximately 66.6 per cent. of the gross. This represents a net influx of nearly £300,000 or nearly £150 per member into the villages of the Division. In Muyuka, Tiko and Mutengene most of this goes to immigrants, but in the others the indigenous people are the chief beneficiaries. Some individuals achieve incomes of £2,000 per year. By 1959 the effects of this income were gathering momentum. The 'carraboard' and mat structures typical of village housing for half a century were rapidly being replaced by plank houses with metal roofs. This process was encouraged by the introduction by the Union of a compulsory deposit scheme in June 1957 whereby two shillings in every pound payable to farmers was deducted and at the end of a year became convertible, plus 2.5 per cent interest, for the purchase through the Union of building materials. By the dry season of 1958 a sum of £76,000 was available for this purpose. In addition money from this fund could be used to purchase agricultural equipment, fertilisers, fungicides and sprays.[37]

This explosive growth and the scale of the indigenous response have surprised and gratified many observers, and the system appears to have overcome the Bakweri antipathy to agriculture and trade. The profit motive alone does not account solely for this; Bakweri have consistently avoided many avenues of profit. Important features of Bakweri acceptance of this innovation are the assured market and the collection of bananas by lorry which relieves farmers of the responsibility for marketing. Under these conditions, banana production has a prestige quite different from that of subsistence agriculture; farmers feel that they form part of an organisation comparable to a plantation company, as indeed they now do. Banana production is also a field in which the younger generation takes an active part. The degree of efficiency achieved in organisation was made possible by the large number of Bakweri with experience gained on the plantations. On the whole the objections raised to the native production of bananas have not yet proved justified. Panama disease has spread in native plantings at no greater rate than in those of the Cameroons Development Corporation. On the other hand Leaf Spot disease (Sigatoka), against which C.D.C. is now compelled to use expensive aerial and ground spraying methods, also occurs in native plantings. Clearly the disease must be attacked wherever it occurs. The cooperatives should be in a strong enough financial position soon to develop their own spraying programme, and this deserves every encouragement.

The effect of banana production on the production of food is difficult to assess, as subsistence crops are often interplanted with the bananas. It is our opinion that so far detrimental effects on food production have been delayed, as subsistence farming remains in the hands of the women, and the proportion of land given over entirely to bananas has not been sufficient to encroach on food production. It will be recalled that the *xanthosoma* cocoyam produces cormels from the same plot of land for several years. In some areas however fallows have now been shortened to provide banana land. The problem is likely to grow in the future if banana development should continue in an uncontrolled fashion. The alienation of fallow land to other natives and to immigrants has helped to produce the land tenure problem already discussed. The success of the B.C.U.F. is however most encouraging and is a vindication of the possibilities of peasant agriculture.[38]

The *Balong* villages are situated on more level terrain than those of the bulk of the Bakweri, near the Mungo River to the northeast of the Cameroon Mountain, in its rain-shadow, and a distinct difference in rainfall is noticeable. The staple food of the Balong is not the cocoyam but the plantain which is a man's crop. Farms are cleared by men from January or earlier if primary forest is involved. From March women plant subsidiaries such as maize and two species of yam—*disu* (equivalent to Bakweri *lisua, Dioscorea dumetorum*) and *ngumbu* (*D. bulbifera,* the Bakweri *lioko*). These are followed by *xanthosoma* cocoyams, normally all in the same farm. Men may then plant suckers of plantain also in the same farm. The women may also plant some groundnuts, cassava and the colocasia type of cocoyams. Weeding is done by women with hoes. In June and July maize is harvested, and some cocoyams are dug. In August a few *dumetorum* yams are dug without disturbing the plant to help with food. In November and December the remaining cocoyams and yams are dug. Among the Balong it is necessary, however, to dig up the whole plant of the *xanthosoma* cocoyam as the main corm will dry up if left in the ground and will not continue to produce cormels as in the Bakweri area. The 'mammy cocos' are kept and later cut up for replanting. The *dumetorum* are cooked soon after digging and eaten or sold within a few days. Here as among the Bakweri, the poor keeping qualities of this yam were stressed. The main tubers of the bulbil-bearing yams are stored and heaped in the house and eaten as needed. The bulbils themselves are not edible, however, as they are among the Bakweris but are planted as seed. The *xanthosoma* cocoyams are similarly stored in the house, but the colocasia are heaped under grass in the farm as they are said to deteriorate in the house. The plantains are cut by men when ready, about a year after planting. As among the Bakweri, plantains may grow and mature at any time of the year, and new plantains grow from suckers from the roots of a cut plantain.

Whether from differences in soil or rainfall or both, Balong agriculture does not have the same favourable conditions as that of the Bakweri, and root crops require more attention. On the other hand, the staple is not a root-crop but plantain, which still requires little attention. As among the Bakweri, farm maintenance and most of the work of harvesting and planting is done by women. Balong men are not so averse to farming as the Bakweri have been, and the Balong do not regard an interest in agriculture as unusual in men. The Balong took very early to cocoa farming, and formerly most of the adult males appeared to be engaged in this, generally using plantains as shade for young cocoa trees and combining cultivation for export with cultivation for subsistence. Now there is a growing interest in bananas. Balong cocoa farmers often make use of immigrant labour to work their farms by a system of *métayage*. For example, one farmer hired three Ibo and allocated them about three-fifths of a cocoa farm of 1.25 acres. They weeded and harvested this plot and in return received half the cocoa crop each year. The remainder of the farm was reserved entirely for the owner's use, although he would employ his labourers to weed it, occasionally for further payment. The three men also received free food and lodging.

The Balong are completely submerged by immigrants, but success in cocoa and banana production together with rents from timber companies has given them economic consolations in recent years.

Victoria Division is at the moment a net importer of food, and it may be that it will always now remain so. Nevertheless, some expansion of food production by the local people is desirable. There are obstacles to such expansion. In some areas the decline of population or local land shortages are limiting factors, but over much of the Bakweri area at least production could be expanded by encouraging full-time male interest in subsistence agriculture. The success of the cooperative movement for the production of bananas in overcoming traditional objections has been described. The lack of male interest in growing foodstuffs for sale was the subject of special inquiries by the writer, and Bakweri villagers often said that they were not prepared to cultivate small plots of cocoyams and sit in local markets with little heaps of produce like women. On the other hand, when it was suggested that land should be cleared on a large scale 'like a plantation' and the produce collected in sacks and by lorries, there was much more favourable response. The men insisted on a guaranteed market, and it was recalled that a scheme in the time of the German plantation managers between the wars (when women had taken produce to fixed points for collection) had eventually stopped without notice. The Cameroons Development Corporation could supply such a guaranteed market.

The time is ripe for the stimulation of cooperative food production. The monetary incentive for food production would be less than that for concentration on bananas, but the two types of activity are not mutually exclusive. As a counterbalance to any excessive use of land for export crops in the future this policy has also much to commend it. The encouragement of yam cultivation would probably be best from the nutritional point of view and would be psychologically more acceptable than cultivation of the cocoyam, a woman's crop. But yams do not thrive everywhere in the Bakweri area; Buea is said to be an area where they do not.[39] Where yams are not suitable to the soil, cocoyams, plantains and groundnuts might be encouraged. Alternatively crops such as tomatoes, onions, potatoes and cabbages might be considered. Cooperative societies would be in a position to advance credit in the form of seed, tools, etc., to farmers. It is suggested that if the question of resettlement of Bakweri from areas of local land shortage on excised plantation lands is reopened, all agricultural enterprise be conducted on such cooperative lines, with the emphasis on the production of food crops. Besides the economic advantages to Victoria Division which would result from the successful expansion of indigenous food production, the further stabilising effects on indigenous village life might well be considerable. Balong agriculture might be encouraged by similar means as a part of the general policy. Their cocoa is already being marketed by a cooperative organization.

The predominantly fishing economies of the Bamboko, Isubu, Mongo, Bakolle and the Wovea deserve stimulation. Fishermen tend to restrict their activities to those sufficient to bring them a small but steady income with the least effort. In actual fact, therefore, fish is more expensive on the coast of Victoria Division than it is many miles inland in neighbouring Eastern Nigeria. The possibilities of organising fishing along cooperative lines could be explored. The advantages of the increased capital outlays possible on nets and on outboard motors (at present unknown here) under a cooperative system would appeal to the tribes concerned. The active Wovea people might be approached first. These people were one of the few tribes of the Gulf of Guinea to hunt whale, although no one now has the confidence or skill to use the necessary gear (still preserved on the island). For the Isubu of Bimbia stimulation of their native fishing industry would be a positive and necessary move to retard the depopulation of their villages.

Marriage and Prostitution in Victoria Division

The Sex Ratio

The most important feature of the population structure of this Division, after the large scale of immigration, has always been the great excess of males over females, and this excess is not by any means confined to the plantation population, as will be shown. Table 6 shows the situation taking Victoria Division as a whole. There is an aggregate deficiency of females which occurs in all age-groups except the youngest (under 2 years).

The low proportion of females in the Division as a whole (35·1 per cent.) is repeated in the native areas of the Division, where it is hardly greater (38·8 per cent.). These represent ratios of 185 and 157 males per 100 females. Table 6 the administrative units are listed in the order of intensity of the phenomenon.

Table 6

Victoria Division population by age and sex

Age Group	*Total Population*[40]	*Males*	*Females*
Under 2 years	4,321	2,056	2,185
2-6 years	8,245	4,489	3,756
7-14 years	10,142	6,555	3,587
15-49 years	59,153	40,571	19,082
50 years and over	2,209	1,314	995
Total	84,689	54,985	29,704
Percentages	100	64·9	35·1

The imbalance in the population is most pronounced in the Bakolle Area, in which only 23 per cent. of the population are female, followed by Tiko, Victoria and Bimbia Village Groups. Only in the Muea Village Group, where females form 48 per cent. Of the population, does the population approach balance. From a tribal point of view the excess of males is less pronounced in the Bakweri, Bamboko, Balong and Mongo areas than in the Bakolle and Isubu areas.

Table 7

Native area population by local unit and sex

Local unit	*Indigenous tribe*	*Total Population including immigrants*	*Males*	*Females*	*Percentages Males*	*Percentages Females*
Bakolle Clan	Bakolle	5,086	3,894	1,192	76·6	23·4
Tiko V.G.	Bakweri	8,334	5,613	2,721	67·4	32·6
Victoria V.G.	Bakweri	7,883	4,981	2,902	63·2	36·8
Bimbia V.G.	Isubu	820	518	302	63·2	36·8
Bota V.G.	Bakweri & Wovea	1,291	779	512	60·3	39·7
Mongo Clan	Mongo	2,893	1,730	1,163	59·8	40·2
Balong Clan	Balong	3,925	2,349	1,576	59·8	40·2
Mutengene V.G.	Bakweri	1,859	1,107	752	59·5	40·5
Bamboko V.G.	Bamboko	1,542	891	651	57·8	42·2
Lisoka V.G.	Bakweri	3,535	1,948	1,587	55·1	44·9
Bonjongo V.G.	Bakweri	3,086	1,681	1,405	54·5	45·5
Buea V.G.	Bakweri	7,745	4,106	3,639	53·0	47·0
Muea V.G.	Bakweri	2,662	1,387	1,275	52·1	47·9
All Native Areas		50,661	30,984	19,677	61·2	38·8

Combination of all the Bakweri areas[41] would obscure the fact that the greatest extremes of variation in the population balance in the Division occur in these areas. It should also be clearly borne in mind that these figures show the sex proportions of the total population including immigrants, and therefore no conclusions may be drawn from them as to the balance in the indigenous tribes themselves; indeed, where a tribe is grossly outnumbered, like the Balong, the proportions in the tables are likely to be more indicative of the structure of the immigrant population than of the indigenous population.

The combined native and immigrant population living on the plantations in the Division shows a lower proportion of females (30 per cent.), but perhaps not so low as might have been anticipated.

The schedule 2 figures for Africans living in individually counted households (excluded from the above figures) showed a low proportion of females (24·7 per cent.) in keeping with the specialized nature of this population,[42] which numbered 815, bringing the total Victoria Division population to 85,504 with 65·2 per cent. males and 34·8 per cent. females.

Table 8

Sex ratios: plantations and native areas

Population	*Total*	*Males*	*Females*	*Males* %	*Males ratios*
Living on plantations	34,028	24,001	10,927	70·5	220
Living in tribal areas	50,661	30,984	19,677	61·2	157
Victoria Division total	84,689	54,985	30,604	64·9	*179*

The Indigenous Population

From German times it has been generally agreed that a decline has occurred in the indigenous population, so that it has been commonplace to speak of the Bakweri, for example, as 'dying out'. Statistical evidence for this contention had, up to the time of the survey, not been produced. The indigenous peoples themselves were convinced that they had dwindled in numbers. Although part of this impression had doubtless arisen from the increase of the immigrant African population around them, there appeared to be some more solid grounds for it. Many villages had found difficulty in finding heirs to village-headships in legitimate lines which were formerly wealthy and flourishing. This is especially true of the Isubu tribe where this had occurred in two of their three villages. Among the Bakweri and Bamboko a number of villages had disappeared completely, and three native reservations instituted by the German Government had lost or had almost lost their indigenous inhabitants. Some large settlements showed evidence from vacant house sites of having been bigger. Other settlements had such small populations that it was ludicrous to believe that they represented the fruit of seventy years of population growth and had such unusual structures that they could not expect to remain stable. As an extreme example Wokpei had in 1957 a population of two elderly men (one the village head) and one elderly woman. At the very least, there have been no signs of any tendency for the indigenous peoples to expand since 1884, the date of the German protectorate, at a rate comparable with that which enabled them to establish themselves in the present Victoria Division during the previous hundred years. The disappearance of some villages or enclaves could conceivably be balanced by an increase in the population of others. Something of this sort has undoubtedly occurred. In those areas or villages now partially or completely depopulated, the last stage has usually been evacuation by the remaining inhabitants to a related group in another village; sometimes, as at Likoke, one or two people remaining behind from sentiment or for other reasons.

Some statistical data have now become available from the discovery of the report of the German Land Commission which sat in 1903 to determine the land needs of the indigenous people. The Commission undertook a census of villages which appears to have been very thorough.[43] Their report says: 'The village population numbers were determined by counting on the spot. Almost all those enumerated were present in person. Isolated cases were missing because of illness, outside work and the like.' For sixteen of these villages, making up the bulk of the Bonjongo Village Group, we are fortunate in having Tax Assessment figures for 1928, as well as the original census sheets for 1953.

We can assume fairly safely that the 1903 figures represent the Bakweri population: the 1928 population includes immigrants, but the 1953 population shows both Bakweri and immigrants and indicates the small scale of immigration into these areas,[44] even in that year. The figures as they stand show a decline of 23 per cent in the first twenty-five years and of 17 per cent in the next; a decline of 36 per cent in fifty years. The usual criticisms of such figures tend to strengthen rather than weaken the inference of decline; earlier enumerations were generally (although not necessarily in this case) underestimates; tax assessment figures tend the same way. Other villages for which the 1928 figures are not available show almost universally the same pattern. To choose villages at random: Masuma (1903) 110, (1953) 28; Wokpae (1903) 630, (1953) 264 and 40 immigrants; Upper Wolifamba (1903) 153, (1953) 65.

Figures for the Balong tribe (see over) also exist (often by name of householder, from which it is clear that the population recorded was indigenous). The 1953 Census did not allow this tribe to be distinguished, but figures for Balong adult males from tax figures may be compared with those for 1903.

There is a heavy presumption of a decline in the *village* populations of Victoria Division in the last fifty years. How far it is due to migration from the villages to Victoria, Tiko and the plantations, how far to a decline in fertility and how far to a high mortality rate these figures cannot indicate. It seems likely that migration would account partly for the figures. The part played by the drift of women to the immigrant centres is mentioned later. High mortality, especially in the first twenty-five years, which included the 1918 influenza epidemic, may well have been an important factor. In addition, a low female net reproduction rate could hypothetically have produced generational declines such as those suggested by the Bakweri figures. The role of infertility is separately examined.

Table 9

Bonjongo Village Group: 1903, 1928, 1953

Village	*1903*	*1928*	*1953* Bakweri	*1953* Immigrants
Wosumbu	238	181	107	2
Masengi	36	61	16	—
Ewongo	134	66	44	1
Livanda	126	29	0	—
Mokunda	459	369	345	2
U. Gbando	158	151	90	3
L. Gbando	61	41	43	—
Ekonjo	34	70	107	—
Mafanja	242	313	301	—
Woana	535	269	207	—
Wojoke	107	76	67	6
Wonjava	113	76	59	—
Wosenge	36	22	23	1
Wongala	61	35	31	—
Wonjongo	672	542	479	13
Wotutu	91	85	56	7
Totals	3,103	2,386	1,975	35

Table 10

Balong tribe: 1903, 1953

Village	*1903* Adult males	*1903* Total population	*1953* Adult males
Muyuka	77	177	46
Mpunda	71	127	18
Yoke	83	200	46
Malende	30	76	17
Totals	261	580	127

Bakweri Fertility

As a result of our interim report on the population problems of the Division, a fertility and morbidity survey was carried out in three Bakweri areas by a Field Unit of the Medical Department in 1954. The unit's findings could not, however, be regarded as reliable, as in none of the areas chosen did the survey represent a census of all Bakweri women, and the sample in each case was determined by the number who chose to come to the unit's centres, while the fertility aspect of the survey was obscured by the morbidity survey carried on at the same time, in which both males and females, immigrants and natives, were examined. The figures were made available to us, however, and analysed by demographers attached to the Population Investigation Committee in London.[45] A gross reproduction rate of 1·72 and a net reproduction rate of 0·65 supposedly applicable to the generation aged 50 and over were derived from the rather imprecise data. These figures were very low, and, because the possibilities of error were considerable, in 1957 the writer undertook a further fertility survey. On this occasion the whole female Bakweri population of marriageable age of four villages and two stranger quarters was interviewed, making a total of 1,062 women. Details of this survey are published elsewhere [Ardener 1958, and below], but the preliminary findings are summarised here.

It was estimated that at the time when the women over 50 years of age interviewed in the sample had been bearing children (about thirty years before) their gross reproduction rate was about 2·13, and the net reproduction rate was approximately unity.[46] This meant that on average each woman then had one daughter surviving to child-bearing age, and that the population was neither increasing nor decreasing. In fact, this estimate (which is already slightly optimistic) has to be based on figures for the daughters of women who were over 50 and survived to be interviewed in 1957, a group very possibly selected for longevity. The true net reproduction rate may well have been, even at that period, therefore, below replacement. After this, however, until comparatively recently, fertility appears to have dropped steadily below replacement level at least to the generation of women who were aged 35-39 years at the time of the survey. Mr. N. H. Carrier of the Population Investigation Committee has suggested a method of assessing current fertility which he has applied to children born to the women of the sample in the period approximately two and a half years before the survey, that is children born in the years 1955, 1956 and up to July 1957. His estimation supplied a gross reproduction rate for this period of 2·04 and (with a calculated survival rate of 583 per thousand up to the midpoint of the child-bearing period) a net reproduction rate of 1·18: that is, just over replacement level.

Bakweri fertility has not therefore remained steady in the last two or three decades and perhaps fell below and climbed back to replacement level in this period. It is quite possible that fluctuations of this sort also occurred in earlier decades, and that the population in this century has been in decline partly for this reason. It may be noted that, even at the highest levels computed from our data, fertility is low by some West African standards. The gross reproduction rate of the Ashanti of Ghana is calculated by Fortes to be about 3·0 (that of the Bakweri about 2·0) and the net reproduction rate about 2·0 (that of the Bakweri about 1·0).[47] Again, a maternity ratio of 6·23 live births per woman living through the child-bearing period is reported for the Ashanti, and of about 6·0 for the Tallensi of Ghana and the Yao of Nyasaland.[48] The comparable Bakweri figure is 4·5. The slump in Bakweri fertility in the last decades shows itself in the figures for sterility in different age-groups. An average of 5 per cent to 8 per cent of married women in Great Britain are usually considered to be involuntarily childless. Of Bakweri women 8·7 per cent over 50 years of age were never pregnant, compared with 15·7 per cent of those in the 35–39 years age-group. It is most improbable that, in the remaining part of the reproductive period, this age-group could reduce its sterility rate to that of the oldest generation.[49]

It remains to be seen whether Bakweri fertility will confirm the recent rise possible from the figures. It may not be a coincidence that it is indicated at the same time as the rapid improvement in village living standards due to the success of cooperatives.[50]

The Sex Ratio in Native Areas

Besides infertility, some decline in village population may be due to the attraction of women away from the villages. The effect of this cannot be assessed. Any attempt to determine the sex ratio in the indigenous population from the census data encounters two difficulties. The first is that of isolating the relevant figures. As the tribal breakdowns in each unit of the Census were confined to the total population involved without classification by sex and age, any analysis of the indigenous population must be restricted to villages or segments of villages in which the only tribe recorded is the indigenous group, this process itself being restricted to those tribes described as 'Bakweri'. The second difficulty is that Bakweri villages are often so tiny that the resulting figures appear ludicrously small by any acceptable statistical standards. It emerges quite clearly that there is, in those native areas with more than 70 per cent of immigrants in the population (Bakolle, Tiko, Balong, Mutengene, Victoria, Bimbia and Mongo areas), a heavy deficiency of females in the total population which must be primarily due to a preponderance of males in the immigrant population. Such areas tend to show most massive excesses of males in the 15–49 years age-group. There is evidence that the biggest imbalances tend to be associated with high proportions of Nigerians in the immigrant population. Thus the six areas with the highest proportions of males in their total population (Bakolle, Tiko, Bimbia, Victoria, Bota and Mongo) are also those with the highest proportions of Nigerians among their immigrants. Balong area, which has the third highest proportion of immigrants in the Division, has only the seventh highest proportion of males, which closely correlates with its ranking of eighth in proportion of Nigerians among its immigrants. The Mutengene area, fourth in proportion of immigrants, ranks eighth in proportion of males and tenth in proportion of Nigerians in the immigrant population. The relative lack of females among Nigerian immigrants is partly because of the difficulties of transport and communications, but partly also because Nigerians on the whole do not intend to stay longer than is necessary to obtain capital with which to return to Nigeria. However, although the imbalance tends to be lower when there are fewer Nigerian immigrants, it is still in such areas a feature primarily of the immigrant population. Although we know little of the sex ratio in the native population, it is generally agreed that there is a considerable flow of native women into unions with immigrants, with destructive effects on the stability of the population of the indigenous settlements. The Bakweri village of Wonya Imali with 17 males and 4 females is an example, or Wokpae Likomba with a population of eleven and no children.

The depopulation of the Upper Bakweri settlements in the Lisoka Village Group shows some evidence of being partly due to a deficiency of females in the indigenous population itself. In these villages it is frequent for deficiencies to occur in the adult 15–49 years age-group, and it is not unreasonable to assume that this represents a loss of women to the immigrant centres as prostitutes.[51] The whole area is affected by the nearness of the concentration of immigrants in the Balong area, especially at Muyuka. The rapid growth of timber extraction here, and the establishment of a new Elders and Fyffes plantation at Bafia and Bavenga, are attracting further immigrants among the Upper Bakweri. It seems unlikely that this will long survive as a Bakweri area.

Demographic factors are clearly important in Victoria Division. With the type of census and other data that are sporadically available, administrative policy can only be based on guesswork. Even if data obtained by censuses and occasional surveys based on sample enumerations could be of a higher standard of accuracy, they would in themselves only show the present state of affairs, and by comparison with previous enumerations, indicate whether the population had changed. They could never show why the state of affairs had arisen or why changes had occurred, and it is precisely in this field of interpretation that error is commonest. There are therefore strong grounds for the introduction of a system of compulsory registration of births, marriages and deaths. During discussions on this subject with Bakweri villagers, it seemed that local support could be obtained by careful propaganda. The Bakweri are genuinely concerned by their low fertility and are able to appreciate the value of accurate knowledge of the numbers of births and deaths in each year as perhaps few other Cameroons peoples are. Whatever the decision, care should be taken that the administration of the system makes it clear that registration is required by the South Cameroons Government and not by the plantation organisations.

As immigration is directly responsible for the greater part of the excess males in Victoria Division, and since this immigration is generally regarded as essential to the economy of the Division, there is little hope of achieving a completely balanced population in the foreseeable future. Whereas some further encouragement for married plantation workers to bring their wives with them may be possible, this is unlikely to have more than a marginal effect, as the considerable excess of males on the plantations themselves at times when employment is at its peak, is due primarily to the numbers of bachelors. The land and economic aspects are discussed later. Development in other areas of the Cameroons would act to relieve the Victoria Division of some of the floating population from these areas. The association of the large Nigerian population with a high proportion of males at least suggests that any policy of actively encouraging Nigerian immigration may tend to increase the problem. One of the most serious consequences of the high proportion of males among immigrants is the part it plays in the break-up of indigenous marriage and the attraction of women into prostitution.

The analysis of village figures suggests that certain Bakweri communities are unlikely to survive as such, although their names may be retained by the immigrant settlements which are supplanting them. For the Bakweri population as a whole, the outlook is not as black as it has been at times in the last twenty or thirty years. If our data are reliable, Mr. Carrier notes that fertility is 'probably high enough in relation to the mortality experienced to ensure the survival of this people if current fertility and mortality experience continues'. The fertility of the rural Bakweri is still undoubtedly low by any standards and only recently may have ceased to be below replacement. An investigation of the causes of sterility, including sterility after the birth of one or more children, which from the data may be crucial to the small family size noted among the Bakweri, appears to be indicated.

The drift of women from the villages into immigrant centres has been suggested to be one of a number of factors contributing to the unsatisfactory population structure of the rural Bakweri, and this is also true of the Balong and other smaller tribes of the Division. Next the problem is discussed in its social rather than its demographic context, but some attempt is also made to assess the place of sociological influences on infertility.

Bakweri Marriage

Among the Bakweri, marriage traditionally consists of three stages: the betrothal, the payment of bride-price and the consummation. In former times prepubertal or infant betrothal was common for girls, as among most neighbouring tribes, although it was unusual to betroth a boy before puberty. Nowadays no girl is betrothed before she is physically mature and without her consent. The initiative in contracting a marriage formerly tended to be in the hands of the parents involved, but nowadays it is usual for a young man to approach a likely girl directly and to discover whether she is agreeable to marriage before approaching her parents. Ideally a suitor looks for a girl whose relatives in the maternal and paternal lines have not included persons suspected of witchcraft and whose womenfolk have shown themselves to be fertile and to have no marked tendency to divorce. If he finds a suitable girl, he is still unlikely to press the matter if there are family objections from either side.

The next step is the payment of a betrothal sum which is taken by the girl herself and was formerly a fathom of cloth. For many years this has been commuted to a money payment now standing at from £2 to £3. The amount is formally bargained between the suitor and the bride's father or elder brother, both being accompanied by a few friends and relatives. The function of the betrothal gift (*ewande,* locally translated 'intendance fee') is to register the intentions of the suitor while he collects the necessary bride-price. Among all the tribes of the Division similar customs prevail, although the amount of the gift varies (Wovea 6s., Balong 10s.), and it is common also to give a gift to the mother or both the parents.

The next step consists of the payment of a proportion of the bride-price. The pattern among all the tribes is much the same. Both the amount to be paid down to the girl's parents and the total amount to be paid may be bargained and fixed, and the suitor and the girl's father or nearest responsible male relative are usually assisted by other close male relatives. The mother receives a special share of the sum fixed, and the other relatives present at the transaction usually receive a gift in money of about £1. A pig may be killed for them by the prospective husband among the Bakweri, or a goat among the Balong.

When the girl's parents have received an adequate portion of the bride-price, the bride is allowed to go to the bridegroom's household. Among the Bakweri this occasion is marked by many customary observances. The bride must not be accompanied by her own parents, and she goes with women of the bridegroom's family and her own sisters and friends. She is given a pullet which has not yet ever laid eggs, by her mother or mother's brother. This is to secure fertility, and the eventual laying of eggs by the fowl is thought to ensure the birth of children to the bride. The first eggs should be allowed to hatch and some descendants of the first chicks should be allowed to reproduce through her lifetime. The pullet is also a recognition of the bride's virginity and is out of place if the bride is pregnant or if it is her second marriage. The assumption of virginity is also contained in the provision that the marriage should not be consummated on the first night, during which the bride sleeps with an older woman who gives her general sexual advice. For about two weeks the bride is supposed to be indulged and to eat well and not to go out or to do any farmwork. During this time one of her girl friends stays with her to keep her company in her new surroundings. Formerly this period lasted three months and appears to have been intended to secure the best possible conditions for conception, forming an extension into the bridal period of the enforced rest and seclusion characteristic of 'fattening' rites performed by girls before marriage.

On the day that the bride goes to her husband, her parents provide her with a number of household utensils or a sum of money with which to buy them.

Bride-price

The marriage payment was originally made in goats. Statements concerning the number of goats previously required vary according to area, but a payment of about 40 goats seems to have been general through most of the Bakweri tribe. This is confirmed by records of 1929 in Buea which state that although payments were by then in cash, 43 goats had formerly been usual and 50 between wealthy people. The bride's mother's share of these would be about five or six. The money value of such a bride-price at the present time would be between £40 and £60. Livestock was the only negotiable form of wealth, and a bride-price of 40 goats must be considered high. In present-day Wum Division marriages involving as few as seven goats are common. The commutation of the payment into cash occurred many years ago, and by 1929 an officer was reporting payments of £35, of which £5 was the mother's share. At that time this was still a high level.

In the 1930s the theory seems to have become widely accepted both by administrators and Native Authorities that adultery and prostitution in the Division was encouraged by the inability of young men to pay the bride-price required. The 1931 Report to the League of Nations spoke of 'grasping parents and guardians', and in 1932 the three native authorities of Buea, Victoria and the Balong promulgated on their own initiative Native Court rules limiting all bride-price claims at divorce. This was intended to limit correspondingly the bride-prices actually paid, in which it was successful. In the Victoria District, comprising the Isubu, coastal Bamboko, Mongo and Wovea tribes and some of the Bakweri, the limit was set at a total of £20, of which £5 was to be the mother's share, and in the Bakweri and Balong areas £25, of which £5 went to the mother. The rule appears to have been confirmed by the then Lieutenant-Governor in May 1932 and must still be in force. Later, however, the status of the limitation as a Native Court rule appears to have been forgotten in the Division, and by 1946 a request for information on the effectiveness of the rule from the then Chief Commissioner at Enugu actually produced the reply based on inquiry among Native Authority officials that no rule had been made. The actual bride-price limits set up by the rule were nevertheless reported back, being described as due to voluntary restriction.

By 1955 the wheel had turned full circle, and one of the common complaints made by Bakweri was, on the contrary, that the bride-price was too low. It was argued that a woman was easily able to obtain sufficient money from lovers with which to refund the bride-price and to divorce her husband. In our inquiries in the Lisoka area chiefs and elders actually blamed 'the Government' for limiting bride-price claims, below a level compatible with stability of marriage. In actual fact, in the Bakweri area bride-prices totalling more than £25 were being contracted where girls were educated and graduation of the bride-price according to education, up to £40 for a girl of secondary education, was already found. The last figure was in 1954 categorically stated to be the highest normally contracted between two Bakweri. However, down-payments of relatively small amounts have always been regularly accepted. Out of a bride-price of £25 most people are said to pay no more than £15 before consummation, the remainder being paid over on different occasions, a few shillings at a time. The reduction of the amount of bride-price if the bride is known to be of immoral character is also normal and common, such girls being regarded as prone to abscond and therefore poor marriage risks. Still operating also is the factor which the original limitation of bride-price claims was intended to combat—the impregnation of girls by young men who cannot afford a higher bride-price.

In the last thirty years, therefore, bride-prices have declined from a high level by West African standards to a low one in relation to the general economic development of the Division. Among the Mba-Ise Ibo of Eastern Nigeria (1951) bride-prices of £50 with down payments of £30 have been usual for an uneducated girl. At present, as Ruel has shown elsewhere, even among the Banyang of Mamfe Division of the Southern Cameroons £50 is a normal bride-price. The establishment of the lower levels in Victoria Division by Native Authority intervention shows that previous bride-prices were felt to be too high. This feeling appears to have resulted from a time-lag in indigenous marriage practice. Formerly fathers or sometimes maternal uncles of young men were responsible for providing the bride-price, then, as has been seen, in livestock. This was usually inevitable, as young men were not generally in a position to accumulate the numbers of goats required. High livestock bride-prices were also made possible by the custom of child betrothal of girls, parts of the payment thus being made in the years before the bride reached the age of puberty. The feeling that bride-prices were too high seems to have occurred at the time when it was becoming common for young men to be required to pay their own bride-prices, and at a time when child betrothal was giving way to the betrothal of mature girls and the requisite payment of much of the bride-price in cash within a shorter period.

The question of the bride-price level illustrates the failure of an attempt to solve indigenous problems by concentration on only one element in the situation. One function of the bride-price in African marriage has often been stated to be the stabilization of marriage, that is: if its level falls below a certain point, it becomes so easy to repay that wives are not discouraged from divorcing their husbands without adequate cause. This point is related both to the general level of wealth and to the attitudes to marriage in the community. Any stabilising function that bride-price has must break down where factors outside the community come into play. In the Bakweri situation the level of bride-price is related to the ability and inclination of young Bakweri to pay. Within a closed community this would make possible a certain definite and related level of divorce. But since Bakweri women are free to enter into liaisons with non-Bakweri who until the last few years have generally had higher cash incomes than the indigenous villager, this is no longer so. Manipulation of the bride-price level is of little benefit. If bride-prices are fixed high, young indigenous males are unable to marry, if low, divorce becomes easy; both manipulations encourage rather than discourage promiscuity in women, if any incentives to promiscuity exist. It is clear that these incentives are the basic element in the instability of marriage; the bride-price level in itself is not therefore a cause of this situation.

Divorce

From our recent figures (1957) 63 per cent of all legitimate unions completed by a sample of 1,062 village women, and 40 per cent of all legitimate unions ever contracted, had ended by divorce. These figures are high: certainly higher than Richards reports from the Baganda of East Africa, whose marriages are generally considered very unstable.[52]

A woman can divorce her husband by returning the bride-price paid at her marriage, or a certain proportion of it. A man can divorce his wife by sending her away and by claiming the refund of the bride-price. While a woman need state only general or even no grounds for divorce, a husband is limited to specific grounds such as the wife's adultery, desertion or venereal disease. In pre-colonial days a woman would, however, not be in a position to effect divorce by herself, since the goats paid on her behalf had passed from her husband to her parents or guardians, and the latter would be unlikely to wish to give back the animals unless the woman had very good grounds. Normally it was unusual for a woman to divorce her husband unless she had another prospective husband who would actually give the amount of the bride-price to the wife's father, who then had the responsibility of passing it to the former husband. Nowadays, the bride-price is refunded when a woman divorces her husband, and paid into the Native Court in cash, like all present-day marriage transactions. The Court then passes it to the husband. Thus the part played by the bride's parents in the transaction is by-passed, and with it much of their former restraining influence. In addition, it is no longer unusual for a woman to collect and repay the sum herself, or with the aid of a non-Bakweri lover who may not necessarily live with her permanently. Divorce is not inevitably linked with remarriage. Divorce of a woman by her husband is relatively rare, and divorce has now become almost synonymous with the desertion of husbands by their wives. There is no doubt that modern conditions have made divorce easier for women than it was under indigenous conditions. However, it should be borne in mind that ease of divorce is characteristic of many West African tribes. The notable feature of divorce among the indigenous peoples of Victoria Division is that it may be associated not with the wife's remarriage but with her entry into some more or less permanent form of concubinage with an immigrant or into prostitution.

Concubinage and Prostitution

If a man lives with an unmarried girl without paying bride-price all children born of the union belong to her father, who exercises legal paternity. Such irregular unions were uncommon in indigenous society and appear often to have been contracted by men of slave status who had not the opportunity to collect bride-price. At the present time, many Bakweri, Balong, Bamboko and Isubu women are living in unions of this type with immigrants, and the customary law governing affiliation of children still applies. In some cases immigrants are prepared to pay bride-price for their Bakweri concubines, but fathers generally refuse to allow this in order to prevent the loss of the children, as they suppose, into the immigrant's tribe. This attitude to the affiliation of children is important in perpetuating illegitimate unions. The attitude of indigenous fathers should not be regarded as primarily conditioned by a desire to profit from the bride-prices of female children of an illegitimate union. It would be most unusual for a bride-price from a fellow-tribesman to be refused.

There are many grades of union between concubinage and true prostitution as it is generally defined, for example, as elsewhere, in such cases domestic arrangements, stability of unions, mutual support between partners, and whether or not children are involved vary but usually all women in illegitimate unions are termed 'harlots' by Africans in this Division. The fact that no distinctions are made is significant, as the important feature of these unions to the indigenous people is their illegitimacy (as defined by the nonpayment of bride-price) and not their degree of transitoriness or mercenariness. In the absence of any elaborate superstructure of sexual idealism, this feature is the socially important one. In the immigrant quarters of the more populous indigenous villages concubinage for periods of years with one, two or three men in succession would appear to be characteristic. In our 1957 sample one in six of village women's extant unions were illegitimate, about equally divided between concubines and prostitutes. Transitory unions and true prostitution are more usual in the congested immigrant settlements on the road from Victoria to Tiko. Bakweri commonly state that their own women and girls are seduced by the offer of sums of money on their visits to market. Tiko and Likomba are the most notable centres of prostitution, where the sex ratio in the resident population is 203 males per 100 females, excluding the large plantation population that visits these settlements (the sex ratio including this population is 237). Natives also complain that their wives are subject to obscene comment when passing plantation labour camps, or when numbers of labourers are about, as at Tiko on banana loading days. Similar complaints were also made by plantation workers with wives in the labour camps, as is discussed elsewhere. Part of the anti-Nigerian feeling which had existed in the Division had its basis in the widespread belief that Ibo were especially responsible for the seduction of women by the offering of money. Many prostitutes seem to be living in the houses of immigrants, but many are married women who deserted their husbands at some time and are living alone, sometimes accompanied by children and sometimes in a group of other such women. The meeting places for prostitutes in some areas are the so called *kpacha* houses where bowls of corn beer (an immigrants' drink originating in the Grassfields) can be drunk. There seems to be little doubt that the shortage of women is so acute in the Tiko area settlements that almost all women engage at some time or another in casual sexual relations for profit. In these areas the seduction of young girls at or before puberty is stated to be common.

The Instability of Marriage

Conditions in Victoria Division tend to favour various types of illicit union. There are sources of tension within indigenous marriage unions which thereby become emphasised. The people themselves are conscious of many aspects of the problem and find it difficult to isolate those which are the most relevant. The subject always gives rise to heated discussion. Thus, in one Bakweri village the Government was blamed (wrongly, as has been seen) for fixing bride-prices too low and also for prohibiting the administration of the sasswood witch-finding medicine to wives. The German Missions were also blamed for suppressing native religious rites. A woman in the same village said that girls went away because they wanted food and clothing. It was maintained by the men, however, that the wives of rich men also ran away. A man actually present was pointed out as having 'many coins' in the house, but his wife had run away that same morning. He admitted this and said his wife gave him no reason. A woman remarked that it was no use if money was in the house if she did not receive any of it. When asked why the Bakweri did not give their wives capital to use in trade as Ibo men did, the men replied that the women would only use the profit to save up to repay the bride-price. Another meeting, in a native reservation in which the Bakweri population has almost vanished, included numbers of immigrants. A Mongo man stated that all the local tribes suffered from the absconding of their wives and particularly blamed the Nigerians. This raised protests from Nigerians present, and eventually an immigrant from Yaounde in the French Cameroons said that Cameroons tribes were also to blame. An Ibo stated that all men had the same desires, including Europeans. The daughter of the Bakweri headman of the village had been herself living for seven years with a plantation worker from Bamenda, much to her father's disgust. She gave as reasons for not marrying a Bakweri that they did not buy their wives clothes and that they did not give wives money for market. This, she said, was not due to lack of money.

Among the Balong, another group blamed immigrants for seducing native women, especially naming the Ibo. On another occasion, a Balong married to a Bakweri blamed Balong men for the same deficiencies for which the Bakweri women regularly blamed their husbands. She mentioned that Balong did not buy their wives enough clothes or give them money for market. She said also that husbands should be considerate to members of their wives' families, should look after their wives when they are ill, and should live in peace with them. The men blamed the women for spreading venereal disease, giving the reason that indiscriminate sexual intercourse represented monetary gain to native women, while to the men it represented expenditure, and therefore they were more likely to abstain. Older native women blamed the girls rather than the men. As one, a Bakweri, typically said: 'Young girls don't obey their mothers. They are headstrong. If they pack cocoyams and say they are going to Tiko market or Victoria market, nobody knows if they will come back. The mother can't scold them or they will take their things and go.' Such women see the chief incentives to prostitution as clothes and money in order to show off (*nyanga*) and 'easy work'. Others, again, blamed the mothers themselves who, they said, encouraged their daughters to go to Tiko because of the gifts of tobacco, cloth and food their daughters would send them. These examples cover the most typical opinions on the subjects of marriage instability and prostitution current among the inhabitants of the Division. To these should be added the common view of official observers that blames indigenous menfolk for making the lives of the women too hard.

There are clearly aspects of native married life which do not compare favourably with life with immigrants. Native men are generally accused by the women of being mean. This is at least partly due to the fact that wives in admiring the smart clothes of prostitutes forget that these are provided not by one man but by many. Some real male meanness is said to be due to a fear that wives with too much money will use it to get a divorce. There is, however, no evidence at all that Bakweri or Balong are in fact meaner to their wives than the men of most of the immigrant tribes are to theirs. Native women have, rather, acquired high standards which their husbands often fail to reach. The contrast between the actual type of life in the villages and that in the immigrant centres is not often mentioned by women, and is perhaps more often stressed by Europeans, to whom the sight of village women carrying large baskets on their backs naturally suggests an arduous life. Comparison with the lives of women in other Cameroons and Nigerian tribes does not suggest that Bakweri and Balong women have the hardest lot. They do not go so far to farm or spend as long there as do, for example, the Grassfields women, and the relative ease of cocoyam cultivation among the Bakweri has been mentioned elsewhere. They are far less busy in housework, farmwork and trade than Ibo women. While the climate of the mountain area in the rainy season makes farmwork and the collection of firewood particularly trying, it is perhaps true to say that the comparative dullness of their lives rather than its harshness makes life with immigrants attractive.

The effect of the instability of marriage on the self-respect of native males is considerable and inevitably affects the attitude of husbands to wives. Many men in villages near to immigrant centres and labour camps cannot discuss the topic without heat. Others appear resigned to the problem and speak of their people as doomed to finish. The tendency to blame one section of the population such as the Ibo has been noted, and this particular case may be due to the fact that Nigerians tend to have fewer women with them than other immigrants. The Ibo have also laid themselves open to special notice by their frequently direct approach to women with offers of money, which appears blatant to members of other tribes.

Social Influences on Indigenous Fertility

The Bakweri and other tribes of the Division, in common with most African peoples, greatly desire children. There is a great deal of attention shown to children in indigenous homes. Babies are passed from hand to hand and admired, and children receive much more individual fondling and affection than is common in many tribes in which children are more numerous. Lack of children was always indigenously associated with witchcraft, and rituals to encourage fertility with both medical and magical elements (*yowo*) were very numerous, the most important of which involved matrilineal kin of the woman. Numbers of these rituals still continue, but the most public of them were suppressed in the early days of mission influence. In addition, puberty and nubility ceremonies existed for girls of a 'fattening room' type common in south-eastern Nigeria [see E. W. Ardener, 1968, 1975]. One of these is associated among the Bakweri with possession by water spirits and entry into a special women's society with a secret language. All these ceremonies involved seclusion for varying periods during which the girl was allowed to eat whatever she liked. Some are still performed, but formerly they were a recognised prelude to marriage. They had the incidental function of providing favourable conditions of rest and nutrition during the maturation period. The 'honeymoon' period after the consummation of a marriage was of a similar type, enabling the bride to adjust herself to her new surroundings during the first three months. If at the end of this period she showed no signs of having conceived, a meeting of the relatives of the wife and husband might discuss possible psychological or physical reasons for this, and if none were apparent, a fertility rite would be performed. Preoccupation with fertility is also characteristic of the other indigenous tribes of the Division. The disappearance of many fertility ceremonies and the spread of witchcraft are often given by Bakweri as the reason for the decline in fertility of the tribe in the last decades.

The effect of prenatal practices on fertility cannot be accurately assessed. Contraceptive practices were unknown in the past, and even nowadays it is likely that knowledge of them is restricted to a minority of prostitutes. Their use can be completely discounted as an element in restricting indigenous fertility. Induced abortion, on the other hand, is believed by natives, male and female, to be common among young women. The commonest method named is the swallowing of washing blue (*mbulu*), which is stated by the medical authorities to have no abortifacient properties. There is no evidence one way or the other that induced abortion is as prevalent as it is said to be, and it is very unlikely indeed that it occurs inside marriage. There is some suggestion that the commonest occurrence of the practice is among young employed females and adolescent schoolgirls—that is, among the section of the female population most likely to experience shame and inconvenience from unwanted pregnancies.

The spread of venereal disease as a result of promiscuity would seem to be the greatest danger to fertility. Gonorrhoea is stated to be prevalent, although reliable estimates of its incidence in the population are lacking. The case-histories of 69 pregnant women who attended the Bonjongo rural health centre between 1951 and 1952 showed that 11 had gonorrhoea and that four others were doubtful cases.[53] This gives an incidence of proved cases of 15·8 per cent. This figure has no representative value, as one would suspect that the sample was biased towards women with histories of reproductive difficulties and that therefore the incidence would be lower among women as a whole in that area. On the other hand, a sample of women in the larger centres would probably show a higher incidence. Testicular lesions due to microfiliariae of *Onchocerca volvulus* have been reported from Ghana, and suggested as a cause of male infertility in areas (of which Victoria Division is one) where onchoceriasis is endemic. It has also been suggested, from cases in Nigeria, that there is an association between frequent abortion and onchoceriasis. We are informed that these suggestions are not widely accepted.[54]

The relationship between general social malaise and infertility has been often postulated but never clearly demonstrated.[55] It may be maintained that the instability of marriage does not provide favourable social and emotional conditions for fertile unions, but there is no direct evidence of this. The rise in living standards in the years 1956 to 1959 may perhaps be correlated with a possible recent rise in fertility.

It is normal in indigenous conditions for Bakweri women to undergo a course of medical treatments under different native practitioners during pregnancy.[56] These treatments have different names, but their general aim is to produce a successful pregnancy. All involve the preparation of an infusion which is taken in an enema. Almost all medical treatment among the Bakweri involves the use of enema medicines, and much of native ritual takes the form of medical treatment of this type. The pregnancy medicines are regarded as especially important, and husbands are obliged to pay for them. It is not impossible, however, that the use of enemas during pregnancy especially of the normal calabash type, may in fact encourage involuntary abortion among women who are especially susceptible. The possibility of peritoneal infection cannot be ruled out. Such questions may well be borne in mind in any medical investigations of infertility among the Bakweri. But since these practices are of some antiquity, dating from the expanding phase of the tribe, it is unlikely that native medical practice is directly connected with infertility.

Conclusions

It has been stressed that behind the marriage problem of the indigenous tribes stands the inescapable fact that there are almost twice as many males as females in the Division. Therefore any measures directed only at symptoms have little hope of success, as has been shown in the case of manipulation of the bride-price level. On the other hand, certain symptoms have been able to flourish without control, the most notable of which is prostitution. Men of the indigenous tribes are fully aware of the problem of an excess male population. One meeting of Bakweri went so far as to say that adultery was inevitable in present conditions, but that adultery was preferable to unrestricted prostitution. Native Authorities have on occasion despatched a lorry to Tiko and rounded up women living as prostitutes and concubines and brought them back to their home villages, but they complain that they lack Government backing in the control of prostitution. Among all sections of the Bakweri and the other most affected tribes there is a remarkable unanimity favouring measures to require prostitutes to be registered and to compel all other women living in immigrant centres without their husbands or parents to return to their villages. The peoples of the Division think that many women and girls would be deterred from prostitution as soon as it came under some degree of control. It is not surprising that, since they rightly or wrongly regard their tribal survival as being at stake, they should advocate clear-cut measures. The arguments against registration with compulsory periodic medical examinations are that it does not in itself limit prostitution, and that as a means of controlling venereal disease it is much inferior to educative measures among the population as a whole.

One of the major problems is not the professional prostitute but the drift of adolescents and married women into casual prostitution. The control of prostitution and the protection of adolescents is a police function but not one that has received a high priority. There are many reasons for this, the most important of which is perhaps that this field is one thought best left to the Native Authorities. In fact, indigenous control lacks effective sanctions, and there is, as a result, almost no restraint on prostitution in the Division. An important part in police control of prostitution is played in developed countries by policewomen, who play a useful role in all cases involving women and children. The possibility of appointing one or two African 'matrons' to work with the police in such cases might be explored. Such appointments would help to provide an experimental basis for the eventual creation of a small body of policewomen.

Apart from the effects upon the indigenous peoples, it is now true to say that the attraction of non-indigenous African girls and women into the Division in order to become prostitutes is also growing. Some tribes have taken measures against this on their own initiative.[57] It is a matter of public concern that some steps should be taken to control prostitution. At the same time a long-term campaign of propaganda against venereal disease in the Division might be set in motion, since here, as elsewhere, ignorance of the seriousness of apparently minor manifestations of disease is an important reason for failure to take treatment.

Direct action of this type can form only a small part of a general policy for the indigenous tribes, other features of which are considered elsewhere. There are indications that a higher standard of living in the villages, such as the success of the cooperative movement is making possible, may lessen the attraction to native women of the immigrant centres to some extent, and heighten the self-respect of indigenous men, and thus work, inevitably slowly, towards greater stability of marriage. This is discussed in the next chapter. The fact that native women and girls must go all the way to Tiko and Victoria to sell their agricultural produce so that they have to stay overnight is an important subsidiary cause of much casual prostitution, and is both a further argument towards an attempt to clear up some of these centres and a stimulus to the encouragement of more local markets.

Bakweri Attitudes

In this final section the place of factors popularly summed up in the phrase 'indigenous apathy' is reviewed.

It was common up to a very few years ago, but less so since the success of the banana cooperatives, to term the Bakweri, Balong and other tribes 'apathetic'; the adjective has been shorthand among both Europeans and non-indigenous Africans to express disapproval of many aspects of native life. Many of their problems were thought to be largely of their own making, and they were considered slow to take such steps as were in their power to improve their lot. They were imagined to have lost all their customs (they have lost remarkably few considering their circumstances) and to be in need of 'social regeneration'. To discuss this matter is to venture into the difficult field of the 'character' of different ethnic groups, but since the actual frame of mind of the native peoples has been so commonly thought to be a contributory cause of their problems it will be briefly touched upon. First of all, the preceding pages should have brought out fairly clearly the whole disruptive pattern of the impact of the plantation economy on the Division. The failure of the indigenous people to deal with at least their basic problems is not surprising in view of the complexity of these problems and the fact that most of them are due to forces beyond their control. They were one of the few tribes of the Southern Cameroons to defeat a German force and kill its officer, and received a heavy punitive expedition as a result. Many of their villages were reorganised and shifted, and they were quickly surrounded by immigrants. Between the wars at least and probably up to very recently their fertility was low, and there has been a net decline in village populations in this century. They have witnessed many attempts to deal with their problems but few have succeeded. The Bakweri, and this is also true of their neighbours in the Division, dislike open quarrels and fighting, and life in their villages is generally quiet. Self-assertion and ostentatious behaviour are not admired. While among the numerous Ibo and Yoruba peoples of Nigeria there is a constant turmoil of activity which does not exist among the Bakweri, so also among the former there are frequent personal clashes and extremes of self-assertion which are lacking among the Bakweri. The quiescence of the Bakweri is quite noticeable, and is certainly one reason for the application to this tribe and its neighbours of the term 'apathetic'. There are little realized demographic factors which bear on this quiescence, for example the small size of villages and, probably, a relatively high average age in the village population compared with expanding peoples.

This is suggested both by the evidence of small family size among the Bakweri and by the fact that a proportion of the younger adult male and female population lives in the immigrant centres and plantation camps as workers, workers' wives, concubines and prostitutes. Certainly, small and ageing village populations are less likely to be active in community development work such as road-digging, especially in the mountain terrain.

At the time that accusations of apathy were commonest the part played by the indigenous Victoria Division tribes, and especially the Bakweri, in the actual work of the plantations was not generally realized. The figures for employment of these tribes by grades in the Cameroons Development Corporation labour force in January 1955 were as follows:

Table 11

Native plantation employees

Tribe	*General labour*	*Special labour*	*Labour grade Artisans*	*Monthly paid*	*Total*
Bakolle	2	2	—	—	4
Bakweri	468	462	116	182	1228
Balong	6	17	1	5	29
Bamboko	14	15	—	—	29
Isubu	13	9	2	9	33
Mongo	—	4	1	1	6
Totals	503	509	120	197	1329

(From tribal analysis)

Thus the ratio of the male population of these tribes employed on the C.D.C. plantations to the total population living at home[58] was something in the order of 1,400 to 16,000 or 1:11. It was 1:10 for the Bakweri alone. These ratios compared very favourably with those for 'active' tribes like the Bali (1:38) or Menemo or 'Bameta' (1:18) The greater skill of workers supplied by the Bakweri is clearly shown in the following table:

Table 12

Bakweri in different grades of plantation employment

Tribe	*General labour*	*Special labour*	*Labour grade Artisans*	*Monthly paid*	*Total*
Percentage of Bakweri workers	38·1	37·6	9·4	14·8	100
Percentage of all workers	71·6	22·4	1·8	4·1	100

(From tribal analysis)

No other tribal contingent in the Corporation's labour force showed higher percentages in the upper grades. These figures taken together do not confirm the common suggestion that the Bakweri have not made a fair contribution to the development of the plantations. This misconception has probably arisen chiefly because of the reluctance of Bakweri to take labouring work in the field of plantation employment. This reluctance is due to the fact that it has become a tradition that men should become skilled workers. This began with the widespread opportunities for training in crafts given by the German Government and Missions.

The basic factors in the Bakweri situation are the demographic ones. The expanding peoples of Nigeria have set a standard which unconsciously affects judgements on the Bakweri, and to a lesser extent even on the Southern Cameroons as a whole, by anyone familiar with the rest of the Federation. Over-small populations have their own development problems as much as the over-large. Many aspects of Bakweri culture reinforce and are reinforced by these problems. They are, as has been said, not strongly competitive. In village life there are various indications of this. There is no elaborate system of chieftaincy in any of the tribes except formerly among the Isubu. Among the others each Village Head, who is in theory chosen from the patrilineal descendants of the founder of the village, exercises supervisory functions with the help of responsible men of the village. The Village Head when chosen receives considerable respect, but he is not expected to be an autocrat. When Bakweri make village laws they are relatively quietly enforced, neither being argued as passionately as they are by the Nigerian Ibo, nor being accompanied by the show of chiefly authority found among the 'Tikar' chieftaincies of the Bamenda Plateau. Bakweri do not like people who try to make themselves appear better than their fellows and who are 'proud'. Thus while mild signs of normal prosperity in a Bakweri villager have not been frowned upon, signs of unusual wealth have been commonly attributed to witchcraft.

The variability of cultural factors is, however, remarkably illustrated by the recent history of the witchcraft beliefs of the people. Various of these are current among the Bantu peoples of the coastal areas of the Cameroons, the commonest of which is one indigenous to the Bakweri under the name *liemba.* Persons with this form of witchcraft are believed to 'eat' the vital principle of their enemies, making them sicken and die unless a special ceremony is performed. Formerly a suspected witch (male or female) would be made to drink a concoction of sasswood (*kpave*), and if this was vomited, the suspect was shown to be innocent. If it was not, the witchcraft was believed to be proved and the witch was hanged. This practice, which was part of the allegations of savagery on which the German Government based its first punitive expedition against the Buea Bakweri, appears to have been completely abandoned. The belief in witchcraft, however, has continued to the present day and has been fortified by the spread of belief in a further special kind of witchcraft also known among the Duala but of Bakossi origin. This witchcraft is called *nyongo,* and it is believed that a person possessing it is able to kill others, especially his own relatives, and to use their bodies to work for him in an invisible town on Mount Kupe in Bakossi country. Persons dying in *nyongo* are believed to call out the name of the person who is taking them. Any excessive material success in Bakweri eyes combined with a dwindling of the successful person's family has been attributed to the possession of *nyongo,* and the belief took such hold that, for example, up to 1955 nearly all persons with houses made of zinc sheets were thought to have this power. People who thought that they were dying from *nyongo* tended to call out the names of such persons.

This belief appears to have entered the Division some time before the 1914-18 war, and its appearance coincides with the building of a number of permanent houses by those successful in the German period. The concurrent decline in numbers of the tribe undoubtedly reinforced the belief. Practical consequences were that there was a reluctance to inherit zinc houses; they were believed to be haunted and were sometimes left empty. Men of standing in a village were very slow to build themselves such houses and were at pains to make the source of their prosperity clear. The belief in *nyongo,* or at least the fear of being considered to possess it, existed in all classes of the population, and it inhibited the demonstration of any conspicuous material progress.

With the success of the banana cooperatives, however, an interesting change occurred. Between 1955 and 1957 a total of approximately £2,000 of banana revenue was spent by Bakweri villages to purchase the secrets of a witch-finding society (*Obasi Njom)* from the Banyang tribe of Mamfe Division. The initiative came almost entirely from the younger men, and lodges were established in most Bakweri villages. These societies are considered to have succeeded in exorcising *nyongo,* and are still believed by the people to be keeping it under control. The building of metal-roofed houses was made possible without danger of accusation; this began rapidly and is still continuing. It is interesting that the improved condition of the villages is attributed by rural Bakweri to the good work of *Obasi Njom* in keeping the villages 'cool'. They also believe that the efforts by witches to kill children have been foiled. This is of interest in view of a possible recent rise in fertility of the tribe. The control of the fear of *nyongo* represents a cultural breakthrough for the Bakweri, but it was preceded by the economic one.

It must be conceded that, for the various good reasons outlined in the preceding chapters, Bakweri morale was low for many years. The introduction of the cooperative movement coincided with the return of educated Bakweri from posts in Nigeria to enter politics after the promulgation of the 1951 Constitution, with the rise of the movement for a separate Southern Cameroons administration, and with the rise of Dr. Endeley, a member of a famous Bakweri chiefly line, to influence in Nigerian politics, and for a time to the Premiership of the Southern Cameroons. These events have all played their part in stimulating that social regeneration which earlier observers thought desirable. In our 1955 report it seemed worthwhile to suggest measures to build up a sense of pride in their history and culture among the Bakweri and their neighbours. Since then interest in these matters has grown considerably culminating in the Victoria Centenary celebrations of December 1958, and such recommendations would now appear superfluous.

The importance of the indigenous value system as an independent factor in the problems of the Division has always been exaggerated. The real problems remain. Proposed remedies for the social problems of Victoria Division must take certain factors as given. The most important of them is the combination of a small native population with a plantation economy. The smallness of the native population is a fact, whether it is at present stable or declining, and it is a physical impossibility for a total population of both sexes and all ages of 18,000 to supply the 18,000 adult male workers required by the plantations alone in Victoria Division. If the population were to double itself in a generation by attaining a net reproduction rate of 2·0, a figure, as has been stated, found in West Africa, but, on the present evidence, unlikely in this Division), it would still be inadequate. Therefore, even if the need for labour does not grow, immigration is likely to remain a feature of the social and economic life of Victoria Division, certainly until the end of this century and probably for much longer. By that time, some sort of social adjustment will have occurred for better or for worse, and it is preferable for the adjustment to be guided by administrative policy. The problems of the indigenous population are directly related to immigration, beside which many other factors, even the possible physiological causes of low fertility in the population, dwindle in importance. This does not mean that certain problems would never have existed without mass immigration, nor that the form the problems have taken is not shaped by pre-existing social factors, but that all problems, major and minor, in the Division are exacerbated and rendered only partly remediable by the effects of immigration. For this reason, measures suggested in previous chapters are generally palliative rather than curative. Taken as a whole they may make it possible for the native peoples to become, while still a minority, a healthier minority.

Some of the complex interrelationships of the problems facing the indigenous peoples have been outlined above; they are summarised in crude but convenient form in the diagram on the following page. In this diagram, the direction of the arrows roughly indicates the general relation of cause to effect, and evidence for the assumed links is set out in the sections numbered. No two-dimensional drawing can represent all the elements producing a single situation, and it is not therefore intended as a substitute for the detailed analyses given above. The method suffices, however, to illustrate the difficulty of dealing with one problem without dealing with many others. To avoid complicating the diagram one minor reciprocal effect is not included: that is that a probable decline in the village population itself has accentuated the need for immigration owing to the smallness of the native population. If the decline is to be halted, measures will be necessary against its contributory causes—low fertility and small family size, instability of marriage, and lack of amenities in the villages. Infertility may be associated with venereal disease or other causes which require investigation. Venereal disease and the instability of native marriage are closely related to the incidence of promiscuity and prostitution in the Division, the last three elements continually reinforcing each other.

Fig. 1.

Some interrelated features of the population

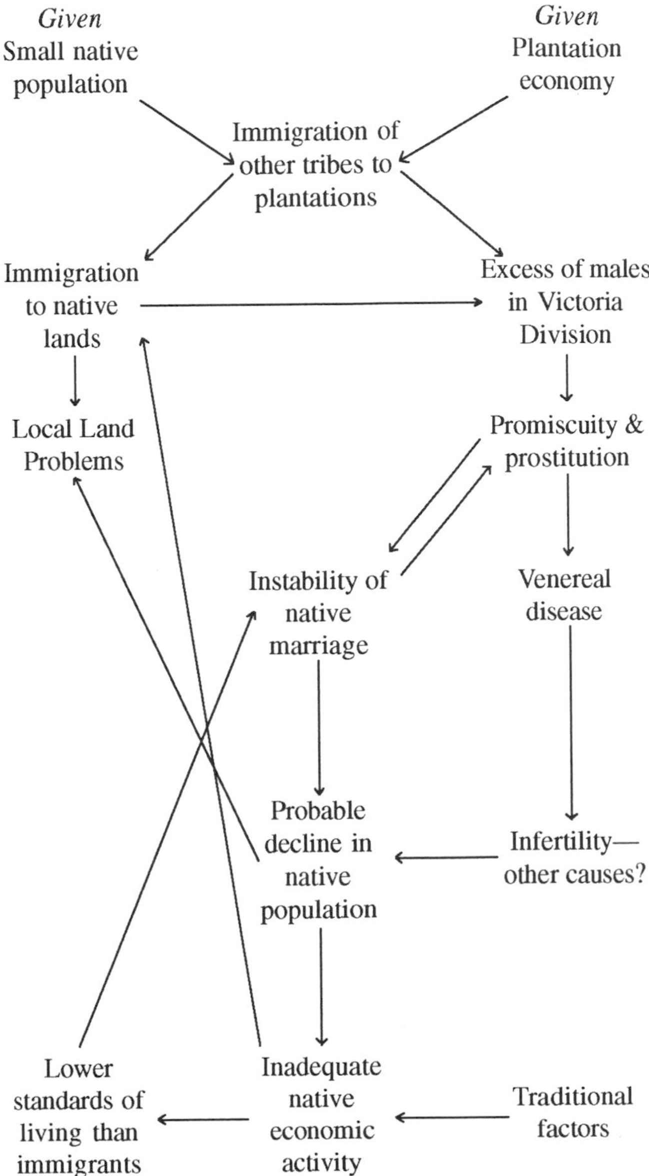

Positive measures to control true prostitution have been advocated but the wider question of promiscuity will remain while the excess of males in the population of the Division continues. The greater part of this excess is due to the structure of the immigrant population. Only small changes in this structure are likely to occur while immigrants are not settled permanently, although permanent settlement is not likely to be popular because, among other things, of probable adverse effects on the home areas from which immigrants come. Further encouragement by the plantation organizations to enable married workers to bring their wives with them, although useful, will only touch the fringe of the problem.

The further stimulation of native agriculture including subsistence crops might discourage some of the unnecessary immigration into the native areas themselves. The chief immediate value of these measures would be, however, to increase the supply of foodstuffs available in the Division. An improvement in native standards of living may help to stabilise indigenous village life including marriage and play a part in increasing the fertility of the indigenous population. Traditional factors have been mentioned as contributing in the past to the small scope of indigenous economic activity although they tend to be exaggerated, and have been largely overcome in recent years.

It is not impossible that the indigenous population may begin to expand in some areas in the next generation, provided, however, that village conditions do not worsen again, as by a collapse in the banana market. Meanwhile immigration onto native land remains a problem. It is therefore important that this should not be allowed to continue without control, and that there should be clear definition of landlords' and tenants' rights, and a precise and consistent application of legislation and customary law concerning alienation. Certain areas might eventually be designated as suitable for immigrant settlement and others as unsuitable. Where local land shortages have arisen, the indigenous peoples would be well advised to accept the offer to excise plantation land, provided that agricultural enterprise is managed cooperatively.

The proposals summarised here and embodied in earlier chapters are intended to sketch out a policy for the indigenous peoples, despite adverse factors which are out of the range of administrative control. There can be no lasting success if measures are confined to one or two problems; one essential basis for their execution is the compilation of adequate population records.

Conclusion

The relationship of the highly organized plantation system to the village communities of the Southern Cameroons has for more than 60 or 70 years been an unequal one. The plantations, as the sole economic outlet of the area for so long, have caused movements of population affecting in some degree or other communities several hundred miles apart. They have moulded the history of the Southern Cameroons. Now the relationship is slowly changing. Development in the hinterland Divisions is likely to weaken somewhat their all-dominating attraction. In the plantation area native banana production is reducing the contrast between peasant and labourer. The growth of the cooperatives there into an independent financial and commercial system, the supply of technical advice by the plantation organizations, the gradual levelling up of living standards on and off the plantations, and the introduction of an elective local government system covering both plantations and native areas, is leading to a better balance between them. At a time when the Southern Cameroons is undergoing rapid constitutional changes, an awareness of the complex social, demographic, economic and labour administration aspects of what is still its principal industry is more than ever necessary. Some of these have been discussed here.

Notes

1. [The original text was accompanied by important statistical appendices which have been omitted here. Frequent reference was made to Appendix K and its detailed notes. The text here has been edited down and the order of paragraphs changed to avoid repetition and to fit the text more coherently into the sequence of this book. Ed.]
2. Land Tenure and Land Administration in Nigeria and the Cameroons, by C. K. Meek, was published in 1957, after most of this text was written, but before its final revision for publication. Meek's section on the Cameroons is based on official reports available in 1950, and embodies together with their many virtues some misconceptions current at that time.
3. On the transfer of this area of the Cameroons to British rule, Rio del Rey District was made part of Kumba Division and the Victoria District retained as Victoria Division. In 1924 Victoria Division was reduced in area by the transfer of most of the Bamboko territory to Kumba, only the coastal strip, largely taken up by plantation land, being retained. In 1930 Victoria Division was enlarged to its present boundaries to include the Bakolle coast and the Fish Towns.
4. Bimbia, as has been stated, is the name by which Isubu territory has generally been known to Europeans for 150 years. The site of the plantation was at Man o'War Bay (Kriegsschiff-Hafen).
5. The Bibundi plantation later came to occupy the whole of the Bamboko coast. The original plantation is distinguished by those sections still named Thormählenfeld, Jantzenhof and Dollmannshöhe.
6. (1) Die wohlerworbenen Rechte Dritter sollen gewahrt bleiben; (2) der Grund und Boden der Städte und Ortschaften und der Bewohner soll das Eigenthum derselben verbleiben. (Grundstücks-Angelegenheiten: IV B 71, Nro. 4 d. N.R., 15 August 1885).
7. It is, however, doubtful whether this minimum was ever employed in the earlier coastal enclaves.
8. By this time a number of native land owners had had freeholds registered in the Government *Grundbuch*. These are shown in Maps 1 and 2.
9. The notes to Table 2 in Appendix K, p. 413 [of the original publication, q.v. ed.], on population contain complete lists of the villages comprising each Village Group and local council area, together with an outline of the system.
10. Based on the 1953 Census. The difficulties involved in the separation of the Bakweri proper from other tribes also enumerated as Bakweri are mentioned elsewhere The total may be reduced by 133 if the 'Bakweri' recorded on plantations in the Bamboko area are actually Bamboko (cf. Ardener, (1956), p. 14). Some certainly are. In addition, 372 'Bakweri', who also included some Bamboko, were enumerated in the larger centres in Kumba and Mamfe Divisions outside the true Bamboko native authority area in Kumba Division.

11. Some of the 'Bakweri' population of Victoria should be regarded as Isubu, however. [For an interesting history of Bimbia see Elango 1985 and 1989.]
12. Although the Bota Head Office area was built in German times on land of the Bakweri village of Kie and not actually on Wovea land.
13. The population of Mondole was apparently not given in the Census. It probably numbers about 60.
14. Ardener, 1956.
15. Robert R. Kuczynski, 1939. *The Cameroons and Togoland. A Demographic Study* London: O.U.P., p. 59, footnote.
16. H. H. Rudin, 1938. *Germans in the Cameroons, 1884–1914.* London p. 325.
17. The published Census bulletin could not be used because the tribal figures are not shown by villages, as is necessary for any analysis of trends in the indigenous population. There are also some defects in grouping which local knowledge is able to correct.
18. The Census enumerators from a misconception did not put French Cameroons tribes into the category 'Non-Nigerians' which here as a result only number 258.
19. Many Nigerian immigrants on the Bakolle and Rio del Rey coast refused to be counted, and there is no doubt that the actual proportion is even higher.
20. That is members of indigenous tribes living in areas other than their own. In most cases this is not known.
21. For the purposes of this table, with immigrants have been combined the few members of Victoria Division tribes living in tribal areas other than their own (in Mongo 175, in Balong 171 and in Bakolle 7). For their *proportions* see Table 1.
22. That is, those recorded as Bakweri, including Bamboko, Isubu and Wovea. There is no way of tracing members of other tribes in the Division, but they are unlikely to affect the proportion by as much as 1 per cent.
23. Possibly underestimates.
24. Such workers tend to be long-established with consequently higher ratios of dependents.
25. See Ardener, Ardener and Warmington, 1960, p. 196.
26. *Victoria Division Annual Report,* March 1933.
27. The boundaries for native, plantation, mission and other lands remain broadly unchanged, although the nomenclature of the estates has changed somewhat since 1933. Since 1953 the Bwinga plantation has leased part of the native freehold on its southwestern boundary, and additions were planned in 1960 to Batoki and Bakingili reserves.
28. *Petitions from the Bakweri Land Committee. Summary of the Findings and Recommendations of the Investigating Officer and the Preliminary Observations of the Nigerian Government* (Lagos, 1949).
29. Laws of Nigeria, 1948, Cap. 105.
30. Meek, 1957. pp. 370–8, examines some of these.
31. Technically a small patrilineage within which descent from the common

ancestor is directly traceable genealogically, without putative links. Its depth is limited by the memories of the oldest members. Further details of indigenous land tenure and inheritance will be found in Ardener, 1956, pp. 74–76.

32. The pledging (*tunge*) for a sum of money of land, which was redeemable at any time, was the closest indigenous practice to sale, but even this was not as common as among some Nigerian peoples, and is probably not ancient.
33. Warmington notes that plantation labourers in his sample who lived on native land in their own houses seemed to pay no rents (Ardener, Ardener and Warmington, 1960).
34. Rather confusingly *colocasia* is known outside the Division as 'mammy coco'.
35. The tone of reports on the Bakweri land problem has tended to be unnecessarily contemptuous of indigenous agriculture.
36. For a detailed description see S. G. Ardener, 1958. 'Banana Cooperatives in Victoria Division', Conference Proceedings, N.I.S.E.R.
37. Separate finance and materials supply societies were to be the next step.
38. The general advantages of cooperatives are as follows: A direct approach to the primary producers is possible. Because of the lien on produce, they are the best agency for the extension of credit in kind or in cash. Proper control on quality is possible. There is maximum return to the producer. Organized processing and marketing eliminates much waste of labour. Because of democratic control there is a greater realisation among members of the problems and difficulties facing marketing organisations.
39. The lack of any authoritative information on crop yields is a serious obstacle to any detailed scheme for increasing food production.
40. Group count.
41. Males 21,602, females 14,793; percentages are 59·4 per cent. (males) and 40·6 per cent. (females); the ratio is 146 males per 100 females.
42. Largely domestic servants and their families (see above). These were obtained by subtracting the Schedule 1 figures from the total of Schedules 1 and 2 in the published Census bulletin for Cameroons Province.
43. 'Anlage 2 zum Halbjahresbericht betreffend Landkommission vom 25 Juni 1903, *File IC 15 Sp., Vol. 2*, 1903, Buea.
44. Most of the immigrant population in the Bonjongo Village Group (Table 1) is located in Wonyalikombo ('Mile 4') and Wotutu Stranger Village which are excluded here.
45. This analysis by Miss Ruth Dedman and Mr. N. H. Carrier was included as an appendix to an unpublished report circulated in 1956.
46. A. Number of women in sample, 50 and over: 309.
    B. Number of female live births to A: 658.
    C. Number of surviving daughters to A: 302.

Approximate G.R.R. $= \frac{B}{A} = 2{\cdot}13$.

Approximate N.R.R. $= \frac{A}{C} = 0{\cdot}98$.

(This is the upper limit of the N.R.R. as not all daughters would reach reproductive age.)

47. 'A Demographic Field Study in Ashanti', part 2 of *Culture and Human Fertility,* edited by Frank Lorimer (UNESCO, 1954).
48. Lorimer, 1954, p. 75-78.
49. The low reproduction rates from the 1954 data seem to be due to the omission of the oldest age-groups from the women interviewed. The G.R.R. of 1·72 would exactly equal that for women 40-44 years old in our sample. The N.R.R. was further lowered by an exaggerated female mortality rate which was not confirmed by our survey.
50. See above.
51. Another feature of the figures for indigenous villages with few or no immigrants is for apparent excesses of males to appear in the 7-14 years age-group often balanced by excesses of females in the adult age-group. This effect is chiefly explained by the interpretation of the age 14 years by enumerators and informants in terms of physical maturity.
52. Comparable figures are 53 per cent and 18 per cent. (A. I. Richards and P. Reining, Part 4 of Lorimer, (1954), p. 386, 395).
53. Records made available by Miss Audrey Bulpitt, formerly sister in charge of rural clinics.
54. M. H. Hughes, 1954. 'Some Observations on the Pathology of Onchocerciasis', *W. Afr. Med 7.,* 3, 157. O. Ikeiiani, 1954. 'Studies on Onchocerciasis (iv). Successful treatment with Hetrazan of frequent abortion in two cases of Onchocerciasis', W. *Afr. Med. 7.,* 3, 169.
55. cf. Lorimer, 1954, p. 133 ff.
56. Ardener, 1956, pp. 83, 967.
57. For example the Banyang of Mamfe Division.
58. Remembering that some Bakweri workers living at home were enumerated in the native areas in the Census.

Chief Gervasius Endeley

Dr E. M. L. Endeley

Chief Manga Williams and Edwin Ardener

4

Bakweri Fertility and Marriage*

Members of the Nigerian Institute of Social and Economic Research and its predecessor (the West African Institute of Social and Economic Research), have undertaken various studies in the Southern Cameroons, beginning in 1953 when the present Region still formed two provinces of the Eastern Region of Nigeria. On the coast of the territory is an area in which plantations have been established since 1885. Various aspects of this plantation economy and its effect on the life of the territory were the subject of a team study by anthropologists and economists of the Institute, to be published in *Plantation and Village in the Cameroons* [for an extract see the previous section]. In this paper I shall examine one aspect of this study which I have recently been investigating in further detail.

The indigenous people of Victoria Division number only 18,000. They are grouped into seven Bantu-speaking tribes: the Bakweri (more accurately Vakpe), Balong, Bamboko, Bakolle, Isubu, Mongo and Wovea, of which the most populous is the Bakweri, with whom this paper is principally concerned. The Bakweri number about 16,000 and the bulk of their villages lie at an altitude of between two and three thousand feet above sea level. The reserved lands of the Bakweri lie adjacent to and in some cases surrounded by, the plantation estates, most of which have been vested since 1947, in the Cameroons Development Corporation, a body constituted by ordinance whose net profits go to the Southern Cameroons Government.

When the plantations were originally established by the Germans it was soon found that the local tribes could not supply enough labour for their cultivation. Labour was therefore recruited from other parts of the German Protectorate which included what are now the French and British Administered Trust Territories. This labour was mainly housed on the estates themselves in camps and labour lines, but further immigrants soon began to find their way into the areas reserved for the indigenous

* *Conference Paper, Ibadan, 1958.*

people. Some of these immigrants were plantation workers and their families who preferred the native areas, but many were traders and farmers and their families, who were attracted by the economic opportunities which arose from the presence of the plantation labour force. In many of the smaller native reserves the indigenous people were soon swamped by the influx of immigrants.

Today immigrants outnumber natives by more than three to one in the Division as a whole, and by two to one in the native areas alone; in some pockets in the native areas the ratio is as high as ten to one. In addition, the population of the Division contained twice as many males as females. Probably a third of the immigrants are unmarried. The situation is only a little better in the native areas. For two generations reports have become commonplace that the marriages between the Bakweri and other indigenous tribes were unstable, that the women ran away to live with immigrants, becoming concubines or prostitutes and that the indigenous population was declining. This then is briefly the background to a marriage stability survey which I have been undertaking among the Bakweri, to provide more detailed information on this problem than was previously available. In giving this preliminary description of the quantitative-study which formed one part of the investigations it must be emphasised that this is only a resume of some of the matters of most general interest to a conference of mixed disciplines. The needs of specialists, which will be served by the full report of this study [Ardener, 1964], have therefore been given less stress.

It was decided to interview about 1,000 women who should form the total female population of marriageable age of a sample of Bakweri villages. These were to be selected in the area of greatest concentration of the population of the tribe and to include Bakweri women living in at least one immigrant settlement. A number of villages were selected which illustrated most rural conditions among the Bakweri roughly in proportion to population. The first village contained a negligible number of immigrants, and was itself several miles from the nearest urban centre. The second village also contained very few immigrants and was not on a main road, but it was only a mile or two from the outskirts of the Southern Cameroons capital, Buea, and in frequent contact with the immigrant population there. The third village chosen for the survey was in a rural area in the heart of Bakweri country but it contained a small immigrant quarter which was also included in the survey. Fourthly, the Bakweri village of Buea attached to a quasi-urban centre and, fifthly, the large sub-settlement of Buea Stranger Quarter were selected.[1] Immigrants were not themselves to be studied but, because of the numbers of Bakweri women in the immigrant quarters, their presence had to be taken into account in selecting the sample, which did in fact form a very fair cross-section of village conditions, only excluding the most completely immigrant-dominated areas, in which Bakweri tribal life had largely ceased to exist. The number of women thus included in the survey who had had conjugal experience was eventually 1062.

For the survey to be successful complete coverage of the selected population was essential. Six weeks were allocated to it and during that time every woman living in the villages selected was to be interviewed in her own house. A further two weeks were eventually to be necessary for the following up of individuals whose papers were incomplete or for other reasons. The date of the beginning of the survey was the base-line to which all data were referred. It may be said at this point that in surveys on these fairly delicate topics the value of large numbers of generally inexperienced interviewers is questionable, and in this case, their use, (although it would have cut down the time devoted to the interviewing), was judged more likely to introduce possibilities of error than the use of a few interviewers over a longer time. I was fortunate in having the assistance of my wife and Mr Mbol'a Mwambo, a Bakweri clerk then in retirement. Both my wife and I were well known in the villages selected, while our assistant was born in one of them and had connexions in all the others. Mr. Mwambo is a quiet-spoken middle-aged man, with a tactful manner, qualities which were invaluable in a survey of this type.

Before the survey itself the legal and customary aspects of marriage problems had frequently been discussed with these villagers and discussions on matters relevant to the statistical survey were intensified before it began. The three of us went to each of the selected villages, which we divided into interviewing areas, and visited each house in turn. In the case of my wife and I, interpreters (where possible women) were usually within call, but our knowledge of the vernacular was sufficient for us to conduct all but the more complicated interviews ourselves. Mr. Mwambo, of course, spoke his mother tongue, being a Bakweri. This linguistic aspect was a great help in establishing confidence. The good-will towards the survey was increased by the fact that the Bakweri people have believed for some time that their tribe was in decline and they held a genuine interest in the subject studied. Not only did many women stay at home in order that they could be interviewed, but often a stream of helpers followed us to help point out houses and to give the names of absent women. If a woman was absent her name was recorded and a message left for her saying when we should call again. This was made easier by the fact that all houses had recently been numbered and could easily be identified on another visit. Some women were absent for the whole of the period of the survey on visits to other areas, and these were necessarily excluded. A few left the villages and others came back after the beginning of the survey; such elements of time-selectivity on the form of the sample may, in practice, be discounted, being largely mutually compensating, and are in any event negligible compared with the tremendous gains in accuracy and coverage resulting from the length of time given to the survey. Apart from the permanent absentees mentioned, all Bakweri women who had had conjugal experience in the villages studied including the aged, the infirm, even occasionally the insane, were interviewed.

On entering a house, the woman was reminded of the purpose of the interview, but as a result of the preliminary work most were prepared to take our presence on trust especially after the first few women had been interviewed. Very little time was in fact taken with preliminary explanations. Acquaintance with us and our work since 1953 was also a help here. A form had been prepared for each woman interviewed, and the first data recorded were her code numbers, her names, her village, and her house number. These were primarily for identification, in case any information given by her was later found to be inconsistent. The woman was then asked her religion and educational standard, if any, and her age was assessed. The rest of the data was set out by each conjugal union she had contracted. Each union was numbered and the type of union recorded, according to set criteria, as either customary, customary and inherited, customary and church, customary and civil (these four types were legitimate unions ultimately validated by the passage of bride-wealth). In concubinary unions no bride-wealth passed, 'Casual' unions referred to periods in which transient unions with numbers of men had occurred—that is periods of prostitution. A woman would admit to being 'outside' or 'travelling', common euphemisms in the area. Each such period was treated, (for the purpose of recording) as one union as, for example, when children resulted from them. This category was a convenient recording device but it clearly has special features which distinguish it from conjugal unions with one man, and it was separately treated in analysis. The age of the woman at contraction, and the date of contraction were arrived at by methods mentioned later, and the present state of the union was recorded as 'extant', 'widowed', 'divorced', or 'separated', as appropriate. The category 'separated' referred mainly, but not entirely, to illegitimate unions that had broken up, the criterion of divorce being the repayment of bride-wealth which, in such cases, had never been paid. The duration of the union was then ascertained and details obtained concerning the maximum number of other wives in polygamous unions and the informant's rank among them (first, second, third and so on), and concerning the partner (his religion, education and occupation). Lack of details about partners was of course normal in dealing with periods of casual unions. If a union had ended in separation or divorce the woman was then asked the reason for this. Finally, the numbers of children, living and dead, born to the union were recorded together with details concerning miscarriages, stillbirths and various other matters. Having completed the details of the first union, the whole process was repeated for any subsequent unions which the woman had contracted. Notes on other topics of interest, such as any infirmities of herself or her partner and so on, were also added.

Experience soon showed the best way of phrasing questions, both in English and Bakweri, and many interviews were conducted with considerable speed, although the most complicated marital histories could take an hour. It was usually necessary to spend the greatest proportion of the interview time on determining the age of the woman and on other durational aspects of the unions. This had to be done with care. First of all the woman's own opinion of her age was obtained, although she could rarely even hazard a guess, and a rough assessment was made by the interviewer, checked sometimes by other means. We had lists of prominent events in the area going back rather patchily to 1894, the year of the German invasions, and sometimes a women or one of her relatives could fix her age by reference to one of these. In addition, the duration of her total married life could be computed from the length of each separate union and the times between them. The durations themselves could be calculated by various ways, from data such as the number of farms made, and the births of children and their ages at the end of a union (gleaned sometimes from indications of their height). The age at the first union was guessed from the number of years it occurred after full breast development (taken as 14). The proven ages of some individuals gave checks on those of others. From all these and other methods a fairly sound estimate of the age of the informant usually emerged. Estimates to the nearest year were attempted wherever possible; afterwards in the tabulation of the results, most ages and durations were grouped in five-year intervals, in order to average out discrepancies while those ages in which discrepancies were likely to be greatest (the over-fifties) were grouped together as one category.

Experienced workers all agree that the establishment of this kind of data is the most difficult part of investigations of this type in African conditions. Very special efforts were therefore made to ensure the greatest possible accuracy within realistic and clearly known limits. In the case of the ages of living children, and the ages at death of dead children, these limits had to be more widely drawn, and children were assigned to three relatively easily determined age-groups: under two years old, two to fourteen years, and over fifteeen years. This could be done for dead children by collating reliable information on the ages of living children and the order of birth, and again by the use of dated events. The recording of children's data had to be tactfully done. Living children offered no special problem, but the discussion of dead children had to be taken slowly and with sympathy. Stillbirths and miscarriages were distinguished, although here semantic difficulties intervened and there seems in fact, as is not unusual in this type of survey, to have been some confusion between the two.

The only data which were difficult to elicit for any reason other than the perennial one of ensuring precision, were those concerning the so-called 'casual unions' or periods of prostitution. This was due usually to feelings of shame, or in the case of women still in prostitution, to groundless fears that legal measures might be taken against them. However, this reluctance was by no means as great as might have been expected. Some of the interviews actually took place in the *kpacha* or corn-beer houses which are the meeting-places for prostitutes. In those surroundings they were generally quite frank. In the case of married women or widows, unexplained blanks in their marital histories would generally lead to an admission of having been 'out' during that time. Husbands were often ready to give such information or pressed their wives to do so. It would perhaps be expecting too much for this survey to have recorded all periods of prostitution of the sample but the figures speak for themselves in that 8% of all reported conjugal 'unions' were shown to have been periods of prostitution. The survey itself was conducted in physical difficulties of mud, rain and mists and finished in an epidemic of Asian 'flu. This gave us all considerable sympathy with our women informants, who would in these conditions often be returning from the bush to leaking 'carraboard' houses with large baskets of firewood on their backs. The attraction of life in the *kpacha* house to the weaker spirits was only too obvious.

It is perhaps unnecessary to go into great detail here on the treatment of the results. The material was dealt with, after coding by us, by Hollerith punch-card machines. The final punching of the cards and the preparation of tabulations of the crude figures to our specifications were kindly undertaken by the London School of Economics Hollerith Unit for a very reasonable fee.

Some Results

A special study is being prepared embodying the results of the survey, but just a few of the salient features may be picked out. It will be realised that most of the essential commentary and very many qualifications are omitted. First of all: the question of Bakweri fertility. By the use of a well-tried method of approximation it was estimated that at the time when the women over 50 years of age in the sample had been bearing children (on average about thirty years before) their Gross Reproduction Rate was about 2·13, and the Net Reproduction Rate was approximately unity, meaning, of course, that the population was neither decreasing nor increasing. As this estimate is based on the figures for the daughters of women who had themselves survived to be interviewed in 1957, the group may *ipso facto* be biased towards longevity. The true Net Reproduction Rate of the female population as a whole may have been, therefore, below that necessary for replacements even thirty years ago. After that date fertility appears, however, to have dropped steadily below replacement for the next decade or two, possibly until very recently. By the use of an ingenious method (for which I am indebted to the Secretary of the Population Investigation Committee in London), an estimation of current fertility in the two and a half years before the survey can be made. This gives a Gross Reproduction Rate of 2·04, and (with an estimated survival rate of 583 per thousand up to the mid-point of the reproductive period) a Net Reproduction Rate of 1·18 or just over replacement level.[2]

I may quote my conclusion from a summary in the Institute's forthcoming team volume:

> Bakweri fertility has not therefore remained steady in the last two or three decades and seems to have fallen below and climbed back to replacement level in this period. It is quite possible that fluctuations of this sort also occurred in earlier decades, and that Bakweri fertility in this century has been generally low. It may be noted that, even at the highest levels computed from our data, fertility is low by some West African standards. The Gross Reproduction Rate of the Ashanti of Ghana is calculated by Forte (in Lorimer, 1954) to be about 3·0 (that of the Bakweri being about 2·0) and the Net Reproduction Rate about 2·0 (that of the Bakweri being about 1·0) Again, maternity ratios of 6·23 live births per woman living through the child bearing period are reported for the Ashanti, and ratios of about 6·0 for the Tallensi of Ghana and the Yao of Nyasaland. The comparable Bakweri figure is 4·5.

> The slump in Bakweri fertility in the last decade also shows itself in the figures for sterility in different age groups. While an average of 5%–8% of married women in Great Britain are usually considered to be 'involuntarily childless'. 8·7% of Bakweri women over 50 years of age were never pregnant rising to 15·7% of those in the 35–39 years age group. It is most improbable that, in the remaining part of the reproductive period, this age group could reduce its sterility rate to that of the oldest generation. It remains to be seen whether the possibility of a slight recent rise in fertility will be confirmed. The improvement in living standards, due to the introduction of cooperative banana farming, is the topic of another paper at this conference (Ardener, S.G., 1958) and this may provide more favourable conditions for fertility in time.
>
> The main conclusion of the marriage stability part of the survey is quite clear. Marriages are indeed unstable: 63% of all legitimate unions *completed* by the sample, and 40% of those *ever contracted* had ended by divorce. There was also a divorce frequency in the sample of 683 per thousand women. This does not take into account separations, which had not resulted in repayment of bridewealth. In addition, one in every six women was in an illegitimate union—about equally divided between concubinage and prostitution. It was notable that the peaks of the incidence of concubinage, prostitution, divorce and childlessness tended broadly to coincide among women aged 30–34 years, that is among women who reached puberty in the years about 1939. 26% of this group were in illegitimate unions and 11% in prostitution alone. This concentration of factors does strengthen the frequent suggestion that low fertility has been closely associated with promiscuity and instability of marriages, perhaps through the medium of venereal disease [E.W. Ardener, 1964].

The main conclusions having been stated some general characteristics of the sample population may be summarised.

1. Structure

The population showed a declining number of women in each age group from 30 years onwards, which is to be expected, as a result of mortality. From the age of thirty down to fifteen there is another progressive decline. This would partly be a reflection of the fact that these age groups were all born after 1927, the time of the apparently equally progressive decline in Bakweri fertility already mentioned, although the degree to which this is reinforced by the probably higher proportion of the younger age groups at school or employed in Victoria, on the plantations, or elsewhere, cannot be accurately determined.

2. Education

87% of the sample were illiterate, or had had brief periods of vernacular or German education. 5% were educated up to standard II, and 8% beyond this. Naturally, the younger generations were better educated: 30% of the15–19 age group were educated past Standard II, as opposed to about 4% of the generation around the age of 40.

3. Religion

89% of the sample were Christians, chiefly of the Basel (that is, Presbyterian), Baptist and Catholic Missions, the only three fully organised churches in the Southern Cameroons. The older generations were more Christian in general than the younger, 92% in the 40–44 years age group, 80% in the 15–19 years age group. The decline was most marked among the Basel mission adherents, and less so among the Baptists; the Catholic membership had remained relatively stable. It should be recalled that Christianity is fairly easily accommodated with indigenous magico-medical beliefs, and has been established in the Bakweri area since before the time of almost all the women interviewed.

4. Data concerning unions

The average number of unions of the women of the sample (defined, it will be recalled, as separate periods of conjugal experience, including periods of prostitution) was about two, but 28% had had three or more, including two women who had had nine. The average duration of the *extant* customary unions in the sample was 13 years; of customary inherited unions 15 years; of church unions 20 years; and of concubinary unions 6 years. Civil unions were too few for the data to be significant. Extant periods of prostitution exceeded the extant customary unions in average duration (14 years). The fact that all these figures refer to extant conjugal experience biases them towards duration, and these would not necessarily be the average durations of all reported unions. The relative durations are however interesting and largely speak for themselves.

5. Divorces in relation to other variables

Taking all customary and concubinary unions, and excluding periods of prostitution, reported by the sample: 36% of them were still extant, 20% ended by death of the male partner, 35% divorced (this refers to legitimate unions only) and 8·13% otherwise separated. These four conditions were tabulated against other variables. In this short paper there is only space briefly to run through their relationship to divorced legitimate unions alone.

Divorces by type of union

41% of all reported customary unions had ended in divorce. Only 24% of the customary inherited unions (these represented women still bound by tribal tradition), and only 10% of Church marriages, however, had so ended. It may be noted that 60% of all concubinary unions had ended in separation.

Divorces by religion of woman

The lowest divorce frequency occurred among Roman Catholic women (28%) followed in ascending order by Pagans (33%), Basel (37%) and Baptists (39%).

Divorces by religion of partner

Unions with Catholic men had also least divorces (25%), and Baptists again had somewhat more than Basel adherents. On the other hand, unions with pagan men were the most unstable (45% divorced). This figure would be influenced by short-lived unions between polygamous men (already quite old), and young girls; there were numerous examples of this in the early marital histories of our sample.

Divorces by similarity of religion

This point is also to some extent related to the last. The divorce frequency of marriages in which the partners' religions were different was 40%, and in which they were the same only 30%.

Divorces by education of women

The pattern here was: the more education over standard three, the less divorce of legitimate unions, but it may be remarked, other figures also suggest an increase of the chance of entering an illegitimate union with increase in education of the woman.

Divorces by education of partner

Here too, the same effect was seen in a more extreme form. 80% of marriages to illiterate partners were divorced, and only 32% of those to men educated merely to Standard II. The effect of age on these figures must of course be noted. The illiterate are on average older and their marriages have been at risk of dissolution longer.

Divorces by occupation of partner

The trends here are difficult to disentangle. Unions with village heads and elders had the lowest divorce frequencies (27%). Traditional values would probably be stronger in such households. Teachers also have low divorce frequencies, of the same order. This is probably related to factors both of education and religion, since most teachers were attached to missions. Clerks, who were of roughly the same education, had higher divorce frequencies. On the whole, unions with unskilled and semi-skilled men were more often divorced than those with the more skilled. On average, men who were employed in the villages in such work as carpentry and tailoring, as well as the farmers who made up the bulk of the group, were divorced somewhat less often than men employed outside the villages.

Divorce by number of unions

41% of the women's first unions were divorced, declining to 22% of their fifth unions. This decline is partly due to the fact that each later union of the sample stands a greater chance of being very recently contracted and therefore not yet divorced. On the whole, the pattern of divorce seems to start early in the marital career and to continue with remarkable persistence, often until well past the menopause.

Divorce by childlessness

Childless marriages showed a higher percentage of divorces (46%) than the average (36%).

Divorce by polygyny

Monogynous marriages had fewer divorces (33%) than polygynous (41%).

To sum up briefly, the factors associated with lowest divorce frequencies are: church marriage, monogamy in general, the same religion as the husband, Roman Catholicism, education of either partner, fertility of the union, and perhaps the employment of the husband in a milieu subject to traditional or strong mission influence. It should, by the way, be emphasised that, except for church marriage, none of the factors mentioned has the effect of bringing the frequency of divorced unions much below a quarter of all the sample of unions the figures refer to, and some reduce it only to about one third. These frequencies are still very high.

The women's own reasons for their divorces were of some interest, and may be briefly recapitulated, without much time for commentary. The most frequent explanation (given by 39%) was virtually a cliché, heard in every discussion of the subject, and a commonplace in the customary courts. This was 'lack of maintenance' to use the popular translation. The Bakweri word *liwongo* would really be better rendered as 'care', and clearly contained more tender elements than the word maintenance would suggest. On the other hand, as women tended to phrase it in terms of clothes and possessions, it is not inappropriate. The next group of about 25% blamed physical ill-treatment, temperamental differences, objection to polygyny or trouble with co-wives, the husband's adultery, his old age, his having a disease, various sexual matters and so on. About 17% blamed ill-health or bad reproductive history (5%). A specific complaint of 1% was the husbands failure to provide the pregnancy medicines to which every Bakweri woman had a right by custom. A further 6% blamed friction with in-laws on one side or the other. Another 2% had been accused of being witches, poisoners or adulterers, which caused them to leave their husbands. A further 2% had been driven out. In one such case I was shown a detailed reference written by the husband when dismissing the wife. From this one was to gather that a tolerable standard of cooking and cleaning had been outweighed by character defects.

There were many other individual reasons given for divorce, but the general pattern will have emerged. The two-fifths of unions that broke up because of 'lack of maintenance' are probably indirectly the most important indicators of the underlying cause of the instability of marriage. At various times, women were asked; what they would expect of proper maintenance; to which the common reply was 'clothes, fish and medicines'. We were present on various occasions at customary courts when young women filed divorce petitions. One such girl had run away from her second marriage as also from her first, because, she said, of 'lack of maintenance'. She was asked to give her idea of good maintenance for a year and gave a list which is worth noting for its own interest.

		£	sh	d
10	frocks[3] @ 8/-	4	0	0
5	headties @ 2/6		12	6
3	'simi' (petticoats)@ 4/-		12	0
4	pairs ear-rings @ 2/-		8	0
2/3	pairs of shoes @ 10/- to £1 (say)	1	10	0
2	cloths for warmth @ 10/-	1	0	0
	medicines (approx. minimum)	3	0	0
	fish @ 10/- per week	26	0	0
	per year	37	14	6
	per month	3	2	10

Modest enough demands perhaps by many standards, but beyond the pockets of her first husband (a PWD watchnight, earning then about £3 5 0 per month), and her second (a native doctor, whose monthly takings might average £1 17 6 in cash and £2 10 0 in fowls). Bakweri women nevertheless see such standards about them all the time among their own sisters and cousins who are 'out' or 'travelling' and this is no doubt a potent cause of dissatisfaction with life on the income of one man only. In this light, complaints concerning Bakweri as husbands largely lose their relevance. Women are in demand in the Division and they can command their own price.

To conclude this paper, it is worth examining (again this must be unfortunately brief), the attempts that have been made in the past to do something about the situation. These reveal the difficulty of treating the social symptoms of a problem in which the basic demographic aspects are inadequately realised. Broadly speaking, the population situation in the Division can be summed up as: three times as many immigrants as natives; twice as many males as females. The first attempts to ameliorate the problem of the area treated it as a Land Problem. The alienation of too much land to the German plantations was believed to be the evil from which all other problems stemmed. Although this was not quite an accurate diagnosis in the early days of the German Protectorate, the land aspect was certainly uppermost; the first plantation concessions were often full of Bakweri villages. Immigration into the main Bakweri areas also does not seem to have been important as late as 1903, and was probably confined to the enclaves around Victoria town and the west coast of the Division, but by 1914 the process appears to have been well under way. By the early 'twenties the situation, much as we know it today, was already troubling the first British administrators. The story of this decade is of the Administrations' pressure for the excision of more land from the plantations for the native areas; although this was not finally completed until the beginning of the thirties. The interpretation of the main social problems as caused by the alienation of land was a natural one at a time which was still within little more than a decade of the foundation of the very last of the estates land, and dominated policy thinking. Even then, however, it was realised by competent observers that increasing the size of the reserves was not a solution to the many other problems that had arisen, and it was correctly predicted that the disorganisation of the indigenous political system was such that the Bakweri would be unable to prevent the occupation of the best lands by immigrants (indeed they were accused by many, not without some slight justification, of actually encouraging this). In fact, the Bakweri problem is not in any true sense a problem of land shortages although this interpretation still appears in some quarters from time to time.

A second attempt to deal with the situation occurred in the thirties when the problems of the instability of marriage and the increase of prostitution were considered by administrators and local Native Authority leadership to be due to over-high bride-wealth levels (then about £40). This was thought to discourage young Bakweri from marrying and to encourage promiscuity and adultery. Parents and guardians were spoken of in reports as 'grasping', and in the middle 'thirties native authority rules were passed in the area limiting bride-wealth recoveries at divorce of £20 in Victoria and £25 in the Buea area. It is apparent now, of course, that this rule was made on the assumption that the problem of promiscuity resulted from some defect within Bakweri society, and ignored the fact that most promiscuity occurred where there were most immigrants, and that these were only rarely interested in marriage. The chief effect of the rule appears to have been to make even easier the repayment of bride-wealth by an absconding wife or her paramours and thus to reduce the vestigial stabilising influence of bride-wealth itself. As a postscript to this, at the time of my earliest investigations into this topic in 1953, a constant complaint of Native Authorities was that the Government had forbidden bride-wealths above the levels quoted and the native authority rule mentioned which enshrined the limitation has passed out of local memory.

So much for the treatment of the problem as a quasi-legal one of bride-wealth levels. With the forties we find the dominant trend of policy thinking summed up in the phrase 'Bakweri Apathy', that is: the problem was seen as one of what is known as welfare. The Bakweri were widely regarded as almost willing their troubles. Reports called for a 'social regeneration' and indeed the team that founded the well-known Man o' War Bay training centre was originally sent to 'rehabilitate' the Bakweri. There is no space to describe the reasons why this attempt failed, but, like all attempts to mend social problems by exhortation, it did fail. Finally and currently, in the 'fifties economic measures have the field and as will be seen in the paper by S.G. Ardener (1958), these have been more successful than any of the others in that the initiative came from some of the Bakweri themselves, thus disposing of the main arguments that gave colour to the term 'Bakweri Apathy'. This development is the successful and startling expansion of the banana cooperative movement. The economic arguments would be that anything which narrows the gulf between the income of native and immigrant, that makes village life more attractive, and that increases indigenous self-respect, should act to lessen the tendency of women to leave Bakweri husbands. However, it seems unlikely that, whatever the many and valuable benefits the banana cooperatives have brought, they will solve, in this simple way, the problem of the instability of marriage. Cooperatives are now beginning to enrich immigrants as well as natives, and are attracting fresh immigrants to the native areas. The basic demographic pattern remains at the moment almost certainly unchanged—without a more equal balance of the sexes the dice are still loaded, as they were, against early stabilising of marriage and against reduction in the high rate of prostitution; even with a more equal balance, there would be no certainty that the social trends, which now have their own momentum, would be immediately reversed.

Notes

1. It should perhaps be noted that Buea (population 3000–4000) is largely a government office and residential area, outside the fence of the Bakweri settlement, within which village life continues. Neither represent typical urban conditions as they are known in West Africa today,but are highly characteristic of the Victoria Division.
2. Even these figures may, however, be too high after adjustment to allow for the difficulty of separating girls in the lowest age group with no conjugal experience (16–19 years) from girls under 16 years.

5

Witchcraft, Economics and the Continuity of Belief

This study[1] is about the interrelations of the witchcraft beliefs of a certain African people and the various social and economic pressures that they were subject to over a period of fifty years or more. The story will show that the content of witchcraft beliefs may be subject to fashions: the beliefs change, as the world to which they refer changes. Among this people the particular and unusual form of the beliefs was associated with economic stagnation, and many of their neighbours blamed the stagnation on the failure of the people to move in some sense into the modern world. Yet, when the opportunity for economic expansion arrived, there was a skilful, if unconscious, adjustment of their beliefs which made it possible for the people to take advantage of the expansion, without shaking the basis of the beliefs themselves. In telling this story, and it is a very interesting one in itself, we shall come upon some sidelights on the nature of witchcraft beliefs, and also perhaps draw some lessons on how far one can blame a people's economic failure upon its cherished beliefs. Such lessons may even have relevance for populations of much greater size. The question of continuity in the structure of belief will also be raised.

The Bakweri[2] of West Cameroon are Bantu-speaking—the Bantu languages reach with them almost their farthest northern and western extension. Their population is not much greater than 16,000. Before the German conquest of 1894 they were living in scattered settlements round the southern slopes of Mount Cameroon. There are very few mountains in West Africa, and none is as high as this (more than 13,000 feet). It is also unusual in that it stands right on the coast, descending through a maze of foothills to the sea. At four degrees north of the equator it is not quite high enough for permanent snow. Instead, winds loaded with moisture from 4,000 miles of Atlantic travel precipitate copious rains, and swathe the slopes in mist and drizzle for many months of the year.

---

* *From M. Douglas (ed.), 1970.*

Inside the clouded summit is an active volcano from which new craters burst out every few decades. The rain and the volcanic soil have made the mountain area one of the most fertile in Africa, and forest covers the mountain up to 6,000 feet. The Bakweri lived (and live) in thickest concentration in a belt of villages between 1,500 and 3,000 feet above sea level, but they occupied the whole base of the mountain below this very thinly, as far as the sea. With the advent of German rule the fertility of the soils was quickly recognized, and the area was developed as plantations—initially for tobacco and cocoa, and then (with the failure of these) for various other crops of which bananas, rubber, oil-palm products, and tea remain important to the present day.

The acquisition of plantation land began through negotiation with village heads and the like, but after 1894, with the conquest of the mountain villages by the *laissez-faire* governor, von Puttkamer, alienation increased rapidly. In the 1900s, the process came under some official restraints, and reservations were established for the Bakweri on a fixed number of hectares of land per hut. Before the establishment of the plantations Bakweri settlements had been dispersed through the mountain forest in clusters of bark-walled huts occupied by close patrilineal kinsmen and their families. These clusters were grouped territorially into what may be called 'villages', but on the lower slopes of the mountain the Bakweri desire for elbow-room resulted in some of these villages occupying large territories. One, for example, occupied fifty square miles—the same size as Berlin, as one German noted—but with a population of only a few hundreds. On the upper slopes in the more densely inhabited belt the settlements were more compact and had less room for manoeuvre. The village was the normal political unit, under the control of the village head and lineage elders some times aided, or even superseded, by regulatory associations containing most of the male membership of the village.

The Bakweri cultivated a number of tubers, together with the coarse variety of banana which in West Africa is generally known as the plantain. In addition, the villagers in the upper belt of settlement were able to climb to the grassy higher slopes of Mount Cameroon, to hunt antelope and small game. The forest itself supported elephant, which were trapped in pits. While most agriculture was women's work, the originally staple plantain crop was a male concern. By 1890, the Bakweri economy had already changed considerably from what it must have been some forty years before. For one thing, the plantain as a source of food had been completely overshadowed by a new food crop, the *xanthosoma* cocoyam, an American plant which had been introduced at the coast in the period after 1845 by a small missionary settlement from the neighbouring island of Fernando Po.[3] The *xanthosoma* flourished in Bakweri country like Jack's beanstalk. The rich soils and the absence of any drought made it throw up huge stems, and leaves under which a tall man could shelter. The 'mother' corm in the soil was not dug up annually as it is in drier conditions. It continued to throw out knob-like cormels from itself for a period of years, and these were cut off regularly while the main plant still grew. This women's crop solved the problem of food supply, and diminished the incentive of Bakweri men to farm. Large quantities of small livestock flourished on the rich vegetation. Pigs grew fat on the cocoyam waste.

Between 1850 and 1890 the Bakweri became rich in other ways. By trading foodstuffs to the coast, and blocking the way of expeditions into the interior, they had acquired considerable trade goods and an armament of flint-lock guns. The largest village, Buea (later less than 1,000 in population),[4] had begun to instigate small raids which the German government began to advertise as a threat to the coastal establishments. By 1891 the Bakweri were at a peak: in that year Buea defeated a German expedition. The misty, forested mountain was a barrier which reduced the Germans to small importance in Bakweri eyes. The German colonial government was starved of funds at this time.[5]

All this was shattered at a blow in December 1894.[6] A well-mounted expedition found the Bakweri now unprepared; the commander, von Stetten, looked round in disbelief for the source of the threat. He saw a timid people living in small huts in the forest surrounded by fences to keep the flourishing livestock away from the even more flourishing cocoyams. In the next decade the Bakweri were systematically tidied up. Scattered huts were grouped in lines and lands alienated for plantations. Von Puttkamer enthused over the neat settlement he had made out of a village called Soppo: all that is now required, he said with full Prussian sentiment, is the village postman going from door to door.[7]

The plantations found it difficult to find adequate local labour. The Bakweri were neither numerous enough nor used to the work. So began an influx of labourers from outside, who came, over the decades, to outnumber the Bakweri by three or more to one. The predominance of males among the migrants began a drift of Bakweri women into concubinage and prostitution, which became a byword. The Germans were succeeded in 1914 by the British, who did not dismantle the plantation industry. They did pursue for several decades a 'pro-Bakweri' policy—reserves were enlarged and after the Second World War a land policy was suggested whereby plantation lands might be excised for Bakweri use.

By then, however, the Bakweri had acquired an unprogressive reputation. The term then in public use was 'apathetic'. Far from requiring more land (it was said) they wasted what they had; they let it out to strangers at a profit, or (worse) they were even too apathetic to make a profit. They did not respond to government exhortations. They were said by one observer to be 'unindustrious but grasping'. The women ran away from the men because they had to do all the work. The Bakweri men were too apathetic to control the women. They were about to die out. They lived with pigs, in huts that were falling down. This view of the Bakweri was heartily endorsed by the large numbers of industrious migrants working in the plantation industry—which after 1949 was nationalized and feeding its profits to the government. The territory itself became in 1954 partly autonomous, with an elected legislature. There was to be no putting back the clock, and the present Federated State of West Cameroon needs every franc it can get from its only major industry. But in the later 'fifties the Bakweri suddenly stopped being apathetic, and made fortunes in peasant banana-growing (Ardener *et al.,* 1960, pp. 329–332 [and see above]).

So what happened? It is in this context that one must turn to the witchcraft beliefs of the Bakweri. First of all, in the whole Cameroon forest zone in which the Bakweri live, there is an ancient and general belief in witchcraft. This kind is known under the name *liemba,* and the term itself goes back to a common Bantu word-form (it may therefore date from the Bantu dispersion). The belief in *liemba* was deeply seated just before the German conquest, we know because the first German expedition, which the Bakweri defeated in 1891, was believed by them to have been sent because they had just hanged two women for *liemba.* The names of these two women were given to me over sixty years later. Of course, coastal Christians, both black and white, were known to object to witch-hangings. It was common knowledge among the Bakweri that the missionary settlement of Victoria at the coast had gained its convert population from escaped witches and other malefactors from their own villages. *Liemba is* a 'classical' form of witchcraft. It is generally regarded as inborn, although it can sometimes be passed on to a person who is without it. Witches may be of either sex and are said to leave their bodies at night and 'eat' people so that they become ill and die. What is eaten is the *elinge:* the word means 'reflection' and 'shadow'. Many sicknesses would be attributed to witchcraft; but the essential diagnosis was always made by a diviner. In the milder cases a treatment was prescribed that would defeat the witch. In serious cases the suspected witch would be named and made to drink sasswood medicine. If the suspect vomited it he was innocent; if not he was guilty and was hanged. Every village had a witch-hanging tree (Ardener, 1956, p. 105).[8]

The Bakweri were not greater believers in *liemba* than were their neighbours; indeed, they lacked some of the elaborations of many of the forest peoples, in which there was a post-mortem examination in order to determine, from the position of blood clots, the actual kind of witchcraft from which a person died. However, the Bakweri belief partook somewhat of their misty mountainous environment. With plenty of room to move in, they came to believe that they were moving into scattered hamlets to avoid witches. It was well known that you should never live too near your patrilineal relatives for they suffered from that chief Bakweri vice: *inona*. This word may be translated 'envy', but the flavour is of the most ignorant, ill-wishing envy. Where *inona* was, there too was *liemba*. As among the Tiv, there were grounds for the belief that close patrilineal relatives would be the most envious, for relations with these would be influenced by the rules of inheritance by which a man's brothers and half-brothers had a substantial claim over his property at his death, prior to his own sons.

The Bakweri were very conscious of *inona*. The accumulation of property—chiefly in goats, pigs, and dwarf cattle—was the chief means of establishing status in this jealously egalitarian society. Yet it was collected mainly to be destroyed. At a potlatch ceremony known as *ngbaya*, performed only by the very rich, hecatombs of goats, fowls, and cows of a tsetse-free dwarf breed would be killed and distributed among those attending. To receive a great share at *ngbaya* was a mark of status, and also a severe blow, for the recipients would be expected to ruin themselves even more splendidly. As a fascinating by-product, it was only at an *ngbaya* ceremony that boys with certain mysterious headaches could be cured. The cured boys often went on to be medicine men. The extraordinary psychic energies bound up in the acquisition of property, and the twin emotion of *inona*, give Bakweri beliefs an interesting flavour of their own. The envy of relatives was further stimulated and assuaged by making any riches in livestock that survived a man's death the subject of another *ngbaya*-like ceremony, known as *eyu*. Here again the goats stood trembling, tethered in rows, their heads to be cut off one by one. The last prize sacrifice (if possible, a slave) was the subject of a special dance called *motio*, and the head was to be felled at a blow (Ardener, 1966, pp. 76–77, 89–90).

It seems, then, that the Bakweri attitudes to property, to envy, and to *liemba* witchcraft were closely bound up in a highly emotional knot. One should imagine an essentially proud, but rather inward-looking people, on average rather slight in build, shivering in a damp and foggy climate and dwelling in bark-walled huts; but having also enjoyed, for many decades, an environment where livestock and the cocoyam thrived, where extra food could be obtained from hunting on the isolated mountain top, and where trade goods arrived from the coast—a strange mixture of deprivation and riches. The conquest and the establishment of the plantations must have come as a great shock. The first carpet-bagger Bakweri interpreters and other servants of the Germans moved in, and many quaint iron houses were built in the villages by the new rich. Most of the Bakweri in the villages presented a dull, lifeless impression to the German administrators, the women now clad in colonial cotton frocks, the men timid and withdrawn. We now embark upon that period of Bakweri apathy to which reference was to be made so often for fifty years of this century.

I first went to Bakweri country in 1953 and by then they had for decades worried themselves with the problem of how to control the entry of their women into prostitution and concubinage with the large migrant population. They were convinced that they were dying out. Villages were dwindling. The spread of venereal disease from the plantation centres to the villages must have been responsible for the undoubted degree of reproductive disturbance among them, possibly exacerbated by environmental factors (Ardener, 1962). Anyone entering a Bakweri village in those years could not but be impressed by the lack of those hordes of children which are so typical of West Africa, and by the empty tin houses of the early Bakweri carpet-baggers. Empty, that is, except for the zombies.

For in the intervening years the Bakweri had come to believe in a new kind of witchcraft compared with which the old *liemba* was regarded as almost a harmless trifle. This new kind was called *nyongo*. It was believed to have been brought in from outside by 'wicked people' at about the time of the First World War. It took a peculiar form. A person with *nyongo* was always prosperous, for he was a member of a witch association that had the power of causing its closest relatives, even its children, to appear to die. But in truth they were taken away to work for their witch-masters on another mountain sixty or seventy miles to the north: Mount Kupe in the territory of the Bakossi people. On Mount Kupe, the *nyongo* people were believed to have a town and all modern conveniences, including, as will be seen, motor lorries. *Nyongo* people could best be recognized by their tin houses which they had been able to build with the zombie labour force of their dead relatives. How this belief grew up, and by what processes the association of dying children and the ownership of tin houses became so firmly fixed, cannot easily be traced. But by 1953 the belief had taken such a hold that no one would build a modern house for fear of being accused of possessing *nyongo*. Dying people who were being taken in *nyongo* were expected to be able to see the witch and to name him. I knew an old tailor, trained in German times, who lived in a plantation camp while his tin house in his home village was shunned, and people were dying with his name on their lips. A *nyongo* witch himself was not safe, it was believed, for one day his fellow *nyongo* people would come to him and take him too, and his house would stand empty. In this atmosphere, any conspicuous material success became suspect. Men with no deaths in their families, who built their houses visibly with their own hands, could hope to still the worst accusations, but most people were slow to exhibit the fruits of success for fear of suffering (or being accused of) *nyongo*.

The ancillary ornaments to the belief in *nyongo* were rich and circumstantial. When a person was taken in *nyongo* he was not really dead; the *nyongo* witch, acting as one of an association, would insert a dead rat under the body so that the corpse would appear to smell badly and would be quickly buried. Then he would invisibly abstract the body from the grave. Wherever the *nyongo* witches and their victims were, they manifested themselves as *vekongi*: zombie spirits. They occupied the tin houses, causing lights to be seen and noises to be heard. There would be unexplained knocks on doors in the night. A *nyongo* witch when dead was known to leave his grave himself as *ekongi*. To obviate this, known *nyongo* witches were buried face downward so that they would move deeper into the earth. Sometimes the head was severed.

In 1953 the belief in *nyongo* was deep-seated in all classes of the population, and there is no doubt that all 'economic' initiative was much affected by the climate of that belief. The non-Bakweri origin of some of its content can be confirmed. The name (= *nyungu*) is a foreign word, meaning 'rainbow' in the language of the neighbouring Duala people, among whom persons of unusual prosperity are supposed to have captured the magical python which manifests itself in the rainbow. Yet the Bakweri did not take over this belief in the rainbow source of the *nyongo* power. Again, the localization of the zombie town in another tribe, on a mountain they may not have heard of before the colonial period, tends to confirm the Bakweri belief that *nyongo* was a new witchcraft. It is, however, interesting that although the belief in zombies is found in East and Central Africa, it is not commonly found in West Africa. Its occurrence in the West Indies has been supposed by some to be a spontaneous growth. It is of some linguistic interest that the Bakweri word for the act of giving a relative to *nyongo* is *sómbà,* 'to pledge' or 'pawn', and in the tense used takes the form *sómbî.* For example, *à mò sómbî ô nòyngò:* 'he has pledged him in *nyongo'.* Possibly we should look somewhere in our area for the African transmission point of the Caribbean belief. Even if the circumstantial *realien* of the *nyongo* witchcraft were new to the Bakweri, an underlying belief in the possibility of witchcraft 'pawns' or 'pledges' may have long existed—an idea that could have become flesh on either side of the Atlantic. Once more, in any event, the property-gathering connotations of the 'pledge' may be noted.[9]

The whole tale in its extraordinary detail must be viewed as an exaggeration of those trends already marked in Bakweri belief: the powerful ambivalence towards riches and property; the sudden breach of the isolation of the society, accompanied, as is all too commonly the case with the victims of decline in power or status, by a sense of collective guilt; the low fertility, and the fear of dying out. Perhaps all this turned against those who were thought to have benefited by the events which had caused so much damage. Envy, disaster, property, and witchcraft were once more in close association. So much for Bakweri apathy. To anyone who knew them well, the quiet exterior seemed to cover a dangerously explosive mixture.

In 1954 things began to happen. After many years of rejecting all avenues of economic profit, the Bakweri had begun to take up commercial banana-farming. Things began very slowly at first, the stimulus coming from a group of educated Bakweri and from government officials. The idea was that individuals should not corner any economic markets, but that the villages themselves should work as cooperative units. There would be an office and organization: the old and the young would all gain. The commercial banana was a crop not dissimilar to the traditional plantain. The first steps were shaky and not free from *inona.* What clinched the operation was the immediate and disproportionate monetary return at the end of the first full year (1953). It had coincided with the great banana boom of the 'fifties. An *embarras de richesses* poured in: sums of the order of £100 per farmer entered Bakweri villages, with their tumbling huts and empty tin houses.[10] By common tacit consent the making of small improvements, such as cementing a floor, began to be taken as not necessarily of *nyongo* origin. Then, in 1955 and 1956, a masked figure called *Obasi Njom* began to glide about the villages. Bakweri villagers had used over £2,000 of the first banana revenue to purchase the secrets of a witch-finding association from the remote Banyang tribe. With the new advanced ritual technology they began to clear the *nyongo* witchcraft from the villages. The extraordinary logic of this behaviour makes one almost feel that it could have been done only by conscious reasoning. Jarvie (1963) would doubtless contend that this was so. For, with the *nyongo* threat removed, obviously the next revenue could be spent on self-advancement and, yes, even on tin houses. Yet the change came like this:

On 9 January 1955, in the village of Lisoka, a young man named Emange Isongo was found dead at the foot of a palm tree which he had climbed to tap palm wine. His climbing rope, it was said, was unbroken. The village was shocked. Soon after, the story spread that Emange's father was one of the *nyongo* people, and that it had been his turn to supply a victim. Emange, it seemed, had fought the *nyongo* people at the foot of the tree, but his own father had clubbed him to death. It was Emange's sisters and a surviving brother who came back from a diviner with this story. Somehow, this particular event greatly upset the youth of the village, and they held meetings, at which the proverb was often quoted, *mèfondo mekpâ mɛ̀ɛ̀sɔ mìikìsɛ̀nɛ̀* 'When the hair falls from the top of the head the temples take over'. This means that it was natural for the old to die before the young: whereas the reverse had been happening. Prominent in the succeeding period was a middle-aged traditional doctor named Njombe, who dealt with dangerous *nyongo* cases. As he put it to me in his own words in the local Cameroon creole:

> So Emange died. So everyone vex and the young men say they want to run out for town as he be young man too. So we begin to give advice to all young men: they can't run outside, so they begin cool their temper. From January, going February, March, April, dreams for sleep. People begin cry, time no dey, and man die on waking.

In June new events began to happen. On a Sunday, 3 June 1955, a youth named Njie Evele was attacked in broad daylight by *vekongi* zombie spirits who were hiding in the village Presbyterian chapel. Njombe, the *nyongo* doctor, was called in (as Njie put it) to 'doct him'. Njie was in a delirious state. What did he see? asked the doctor. He saw thirty-six *vekongi,* he said. Who led them? Njie called out 'Efukani!' Njombe put it rather charmingly: 'When he called Efukani, we say who is Efukani as we no get any Efukani.' Njie said this was the secret name of a man called Mbaki. Now Mbaki was a man with a large inguinal hernia which made it difficult for him to get about. But, Njie said, he had actually been driving the *nyongo* lorry, which was to take him away. Mbaki and three others who were also named were dragged to Njie's bedside, where they were ordered to let Njie go. The accused old men meekly did as they were ordered by the doctor Njombe. Njie made an excellent recovery.

The next day another young man, Manga ma Vekonje, suffered a similar experience. He gladly dictated to me his account. He had had a primary school education.

> I was working under Ekona Costains. Then it was payday of 4th of Juni [sic] of 1955. When I received my pay, when coming back to Lisoka I saw some little men of three feet high, black with white shirts and white trousers. They were plenty and I couldn't count them. They said we should go to Mpundu and sing *elonge* [a kind of part-song].

But Manga managed to get back to his mother's hut. She gave him a dish of mashed cassava meal. The *vekongi* were still outside, climbing about in a small mango tree in front of his mother's door. (It is an interesting sidelight that probably under the influence of the local schoolteacher he called these *vekongi* 'eskimos'.) Manga was eating, but the little men ran in and ate up his cassava meal, and took him off to Mpundu and made him dance. They ran away at the approach of Njombe the *nyongo* doctor. Manga woke up on his bed, naming a suitable Lisoka adult who had been with the 'eskimos', and who duly confessed, after being found hiding under the bed in his own hut. Manga recovered with no ill effect except that the *vekongi* had escaped with his money and a long bar of washing soap.

On the following day, 5 June, there was a big meeting in Lisoka to protest against the conditions in the town. Njombe was prominent at the debate. The need for a really good medicine was stressed. 'So dey make a price 1/-, 1/- general, man, woman, big man, small boy, 1/-. We was collect on that day £17 14s. 0d.' Two days later, the decision was made that only among the Banyang people, 150 miles away, did an appropriate medicine exist. After a further whip round, three delegates left for Banyang country with £30 . On the 16th they returned with the news that the Banyang men would come, but that their price was £100. The town meeting nevertheless agreed: part of the banana fund was subscribed. And so, on 10 August, the Banyang people came with their medicine and their masked dancer: *Obasi Njom*. The marvels of the succeeding days passed expectation. Witches were flushed out in large numbers. The father of the dead Emange of the palm tree was pointed out by the medicine. He confessed that he had killed his son, but swore repentance. He was made to dance a rhythm at the request of the Banyang visitors, which they identified as a *nyongo* dance, which he clearly knew quite well. Other revelations followed. A by-product was the exposure of an ordinary *(liemba)* witch: a woman, Namondo, who was accused of having sexual intercourse with other women in witch form. Before the Banyang people left they trained thirty doctors capable of performing *Obasi Njom*. They also left a powerful fetish in the bush to protect the village.

They left on 7 September. It was like a great load off the village mind. By 1956 the news had spread from village to village. Emissaries flowed to Banyang country from a long roll call of Bakweri settlements. Approximately £2,000 of the new banana money, as I have said, went to Banyang doctors. The newly constituted *Obasi Njom* lodges continued their anti-*nyongo* work for a year or more. Through 1956 and 1957 they came into conflict with the Churches and the law. In Wova, eight people were fined £5 apiece for digging up the floor of a wooden chapel, when the *Obasi Njom* masked figure indicated that the evil witchcraft medicine would be found there. As indeed it was: like all the others it was a latex rubber ball of nail-pairings and witchcraft symbols. Meanwhile, the villages resounded with the hammering as the new houses went up. On a visit at this time I could hardly hear what Njombe the *nyongo* doctor was saying, for the noise of the tin going on his enormous new house. We must leave this happy scene and reluctantly not pursue more of the details of the exorcising of *nyongo* from Bakweri land. Suffice it to say that from now on the new banana income was spent on village 'betterment'; the zombies retired and, as Njombe said, 'From there we no get trouble. They no die the same die. Plenty women conceived.' *Nyongo* was gone; there was *Obasi Njom* instead.[11]

Discussion

The general points I want to make are as follows. We clearly have three main elements in this situation: the questions of (1) a change in morale among the Bakweri; (2) a change in economic circumstances; and (3) a change in the supernatural situation. Of these only one, the economic change, was documentable or measurable by any 'objective' criteria. The economic change moved, indeed, from strength to strength, and began to show a downturn only about 1960 when, as we shall see, because of the weakening of the banana market, combined with certain political and economic factors that affected Cameroon particularly, the peasant cooperative movement in bananas began to lose money. The other two changes, the change in morale and the change in the supernatural situation, were, in rather different ways, what development economists would regard firmly as 'subjective'. Any Bakweri would, of course, have judged the change in the supernatural situation to be more important than either of the others. The change in the economic situation merely provided the means to rectify the supernatural situation. The change in morale followed this. The logic is perfect.

There are of course other logics. Here was a people who associated economic ambition with powerful forces of destruction which were supposed to be destroying the youth and fertility of the people. Suddenly, the attempt at communal betterment through cooperative exporting succeeds richly. Was not the previous body of hypotheses disproved? Such might be the neo-Popperian view. As Professor Evans-Pritchard has taught us to see, witchcraft beliefs express numerous situations of conflict and tension. While these conditions exist, and especially while individuals are thought to be able to project their wishes on reality and thus to change it, witchcraft beliefs are largely immune to disproof. The Bakweri hypotheses were not disproved. When the people were shaken by the shocks of fifty years, the pre-existing witchcraft beliefs took on a darker and more morbid form. When the 'objective' circumstances changed, they did not abandon the beliefs: they acted, as we have seen, according to the logic of those beliefs; they exorcized the zombies but the zombies were, to them, no less real: they were now powerless.[12]

When one reflects on this material certain coincidences seem to be worth exploring. The experience of the Bakweri in 1954 of the influx of cash from commercial banana-farming must have been of the same kind as the earlier experience in the second half of the nineteenth century. Then, too, there was a striking rise in material wellbeing with the new *xanthosoma* cocoyam, and the flow of trade goods into the otherwise isolated economy. We can thus recognize the following phases of economics and belief.

Phase	*Date*	*Economy*	*Belief*
I	Pre-1850	Pre-*xanthosoma*; isolated	?
II	1850-1894	*xanthosoma*; trade goods	No *nyongo*
III	1894-1954	Marginal to plantations	*Nyongo*
IV	1954-1961	Banana boom	*Nyongo* controlled

Some indication of a possible pattern has emerged since the decline of the banana boom. After 1961 the massive profits of cooperative banana production were reduced. The Bakweri who, during part of Phase IV, had even supplied a Premier to West Cameroon, suffered political setbacks in addition. They had generally been lukewarm to the unification of the two Cameroons. By 1963 the peasant economy was set back to a lower level than that of the end of the 'fifties, but not back to the level of Phase III. In that year a rumour spread from Bakweri villages on the mountain that the elders had ordered that no money should be picked up from the ground, since it was being scattered as a lure to entice men to the waterside. There, 'Frenchmen' would use them to work as zombies on a new deep-sea harbour, or use them to appease the water-spirits. For a number of months it was commonplace to see coins and even low-value notes lying about the streets of the capital. In June of that year the Chief of Buea pointed out to me with a significant gesture a disturbingly shiny 50 franc piece, lying in the garden of the British Consulate, during a gathering of notables for the celebration of the Queen's birthday. These interesting events merit more than this brief mention. It is enough here, however, to note the revival of the zombie theme with totally new *realien.*[13] We may then set up tentatively:

Phase V 1961+ Economic setback *Nyongo*-like resurgence

The old *nyongo* spirits still remained exorcised: Bakweri were firm on this. Since 1963 no more striking events have occurred. It now seems to me, however, that Bakweri statements about the novelty of the zombie witch beliefs are to be taken to refer to the incidental, 'syncretistic', dress in which they appeared. Taken together with the linguistic evidence, which suggests a longer history for the *somba* witch-pledge than the Bakweri are aware of, it seems likely that the 'template' for new versions of this belief is permanently in existence. Replication occurs, perhaps, when general prosperity *(inona* low) is replaced by times in which individuals of property begin to stand out (and to attract *inona*). Perhaps this speculative graph[14] may contain some truth:

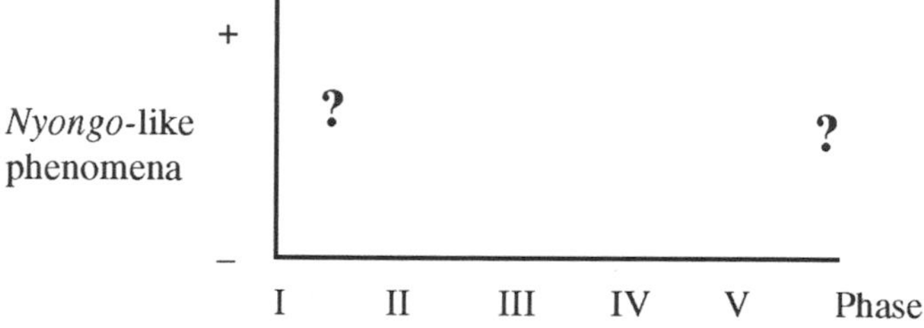

Perhaps the ambiguity of Phase V derives in part from the decline of the potlatch controls which may have helped to stabilize the property-versus-*inona* conflict during the great Phase II period of prosperity. The first (and still I think the only) *eyû* mortuary potlatches for a generation were performed in 1955 and 1960 during Phase IV, but no attempt has been made to revive *ngbaya.* There has been some discussion among psychologically minded economists as to whether some societies have innovating ideologies and others not. Such a distinction becomes unreal when one sees that the 'non-innovating' Bakweri have at least twice been supremely 'innovative': when they accepted the *xanthosoma* and when they accepted cooperatives.[15]

I have used the idea of the 'template' to express the persistence of certain themes in belief, from which 'replication' occurs only when other elements in the social and physical environment combine to permit this. The *realien,* the circumstantial details of 'content' through which the replicated element is expressed, may be different on every occasion—assembled, it may be, by that unconscious process of *bricolage* to which Lévi-Strauss (1962) has drawn our attention, and by that resolution of opposites upon which he (1964, 1966) as well as Needham (e.g. 1967) and others have worked to such effect.[16] When the Bakweri beliefs were 'live' during the critical months of 1955 the creation of new *realien* could be observed. For example, the novel and rather peculiar form of the zombies as lively little men of multi-coloured appearance is in striking agreement with a syndrome known as 'Lilliputian hallucinations' (a term invented by Leroy in 1909). It is found in Europe in combination with many states ranging from schizophrenia to relatively mild conditions-including measles.[17] In this connection it is interesting to note that the doctor Njombe had told me independently that the zombie spirits were twelve feet high. When Manga, an eye-witness, reported them as small, Njombe accepted this as evidence that they could change size. Manga, at least, I take to be a susceptible individual whose Lilliputian hallucinations were, in the prevailing excitement, assimilated to the general terms of Bakweri belief. Field (1960) shows how Lilliputianism is commonly reported by patients in terms of cultural beliefs, such as, for example, that in fairies.

Many will be struck by a fellowship in literary atmosphere of the Bakweri beliefs with those of the more remote parts of central Europe. The emergence of *nyongo* witches from their graves, and their general preying on the young, recall the whole complex of vampire beliefs. And the heroic position of *nyongo*-fighting doctors like Njombe, who braved the thick of the fray, rescuing victims at great spiritual risk to themselves

—enabled perhaps to see the invisible conflict by tying a seed of Aframomum, the so-called 'Grain of Paradise', to the brow—all this has the sound of Tolkien's *Lord of the Rings*. Such men knew themselves to be fated to succumb at death to the evil. *Nyongo* doctors too were specially treated at burial, for there was the danger that they themselves would rise from their graves. Njombe died a few years ago, in his own view, and in that of the people, fatally weakened. He had only one eye, a disability which was taken as a wound. Witchcraft beliefs are all too often ignoble and sordid. On the contrary, the mundane troubles of the small and insignificant Bakweri people gained a certain grandeur from their projection into the spiritual conflict.

Notes

1. An earlier version of this paper was given at Dr Mary Douglas's Seminar in London on 26 October 1967. An earlier version still was given for the, Oxford University Delegacy of Extra-mural Studies on 27 January 1965.
2. The following can be amplified from Ardener (1956, 1961, 1962) and Ardener, Ardener and Warmington (1960). The Bakweri call themselves *Vakpe* and (with the removal of the Bantu prefix) they are also referred to in the literature as *Kpe*.
3. Baptist missionaries landed at Fernando Po in 1841 and founded settlements at Bimbia (1844), Douala (1845), and Victoria (1858), finally evacuating Fernando Po itself. They often proudly claimed to have introduced the new crops. Saker *(Missionary Herald,* 1871, pp. 56–57) recalled that harvests on the coast had formerly provided only for three months' consumption. The *xanthosoma* bears in Bakweri and Duala the same name as the island of Fernando Po (Bk. *Likao,* Du. *Dikabo);* the Duala plural form *makabo* was later borrowed by inland peoples together with the crop.
4. Bakweri population of Buea (1953): 914. Preuss (*DKB,* II, 1891, p. 517) assessed the population in 1891 at 1,500 of whom 600 were men capable of bearing arms, 400 being provided with guns. Later, 600 guns were said to have taken part in the battle of Buea.
5. See *DKB,* III, 1892, pp. 14–18; Ardener, 1956, pp. 24–25. Von Gravenreuth, von Schuckmann, von Stetten, Dr Richter, and the gardener Pfeil, 150 African mercenaries, 10 Kru policemen, and a Maxim gun were halted at a barricaded ravine. Gravenreuth was shot dead, the Maxim gun jammed, and the expedition returned to the coast bearing its buried leader's head and heart.
6. *DKB,* VI, 1895, pp. 134, 321, 382–383. Dominik (1901, pp. 105–106) describes the unearthing of the rest of Gravenreuth's bones, finding them still clad, he says (as if echoing some grotesque advertisement), '*in den wohlerhaltenen gelben, festen, nägelbeschlagenen Schnürschuhen*'! The

remarkable obsequies of von Gravenreuth illustrate the peculiar muffling effect of belief on behaviour between foreign peoples. With Gravenreuth dead, the German belief system sought as if by antennae for the belief system of the Bakweri. The latter, as 'savages', were expected to prize a victim's head and heart: the Germans spared their leader's body the ignominy of losing those parts to the Bakweri by removing them themselves. Any explanation of the German behaviour must be found, then, in German belief, not in the belief of the Bakweri, for whom the events, had they been aware of them (and possibly they were), would merely have suggested (on the contrary) that it was the Germans who prized the heads and hearts of the dead. By such a dialectic, no doubt, colonizers and the colonized may come in time to produce a body of shared beliefs which differ sharply from either of the parent systems. For the possibility that the Germans shot Gravenreuth by accident, see now Ardener [above].

7. Most of this report appears in *DKB*, X, 1899, p. 513.
8. The sasswood mixture was not thought of as in itself killing the witch.
9. For some of the closely comparable elements to be found in the beliefs of peoples neighbouring the Bakweri, see, for example: Talbot (1912), Ittmann (1953). The Haitian vocabulary of West African origin (Huxley, 1966, pp. 237 241) seems to contain some other coastal Cameroon elements. We may compare Bakweri *lova,* 'god', 'sky', Haitian *loa,* 'gods', 'spirits'; more securely: Bk. *nganga,* 'doctor', Ha. *gangan,* 'magician'; Bk. *gbanga,* Duala *bwanga,* 'medicine', Ha. *wanga,* 'a magical charm used for selfish ends'; Bk. *mwana,* Du. *muna,* 'child', Ha. *ti moun,* 'a child'; Bk. *ngole,* Du. *ngokolo,* 'millipede', Ha. *gangolo,* 'centipede'; Bk. *maese,* Du. *mawasa,* Ha. *marassa,* 'twins'.
10. For the detailed history of the Bakweri Cooperative Union of Farmers, see Ardener, S. G. 1958 and Ardener *et al.* 1960, pp. 329–332 [and above]. The roots of the Union lay in a meeting of 5 August 1951. In 1952 it had an initial membership of only 73, yet in that year it shipped 8,000 stems of bananas valued at £2,500. There was a dramatic increase in membership. In 1953, the first full year of operations, it shipped 34,000 stems valued at £13,410. In 1958 the cooperators shipped 1,350,000 stems valued at nearly £1 million. In that year the villagers on the mountain received a net income of £300,000, about £150 per member. The 182 members at Lisoka (a village which looms large in this account) received £39,000 gross: an average of £216 gross each, about £75 net (Ardener *et al.*, 1960, p. 330 and Table 81 [and above]).
11. For *Obasi Njom* among the Banyang themselves (Basinjom), see now Ruel, 1969, pp. 210–213.
12. It is noteworthy that the cooperative nature of the venture enabled individual ambition to be achieved through collective endeavour. The higher and the more general the level of prosperity, the less likely may be the stimulation of *inona.* Whether all societies that lay great stress upon economic 'justice'

tend to react in a Bakweri way (that is, with the sensitivity to individual success increasing when the economy is stagnant, thus increasing the tendency to stagnation) is a good economic question.

13. Or a new arrangement of *realien*. The water-spirits are part of a different section of Bakweri belief: in *liengu (pl. maengu),* appropriate to the deep-sea wharf environment (Ardener, 1956, pp. 93–94, 98–100). A surprising linkage of all the themes occurs, however, in the account of Bakweri folklore given to the administrator B. G. Stone, whose MS report (1929) leans heavily on the work of the late Mr Steane, a Bakweri teacher of Victoria. He says (paragraph 110) that there is a powerful spirit 'at the bottom of the lake near the summit of Mount Kupe in Kumba Division. In the latter lake there is a great spirit market and spirits from all over the world are thought to meet there and barter their goods. *The new Nigerian coinage and paper money* were said first to have been introduced in this spirit market, and to have been distributed thence to the people' (my italics). Mount Kupe is, of course, the *nyongo* mountain.
14. Phases III–V are documented. Phase II (no *nyongo)* rests on the statement of the Bakweri, the relatively modern *realien* of the *nyongo* belief, and the saliency of the old *liemba* at the time of the colonial occupation. Phase I is merely a symmetrical speculation, aided by my guess that *sómbà* (*sómbî*) = Caribbean *zombi.* The transmission would have to occur before the almost total cessation of the slave-trade from this area after 1840 (the peak was from c. 1785 to 1830). The pre-*xanthosoma* economy is assumed not to be expanding, and to be based on the former plantain staple cultivated by men. There are some ritual hints of a yam staple before the plantain, based on the *D. dumetorum* species (Ardener, 1956, p.46). A shadowy economic 'Phase minus I' is perhaps remotely conceivable.
15. The Bakweri 'innovations' were group borrowings which differed from 'non-innovative' borrowings mainly in their unforeseen effects. Yet the second innovation is ideologically connected with the first: it restored the place of the banana (man's crop) which the *xanthosoma* (woman's crop) had overwhelmed. Whatever the reinforcing effect of the 'jackpot' consequence, the earliest steps towards acceptance of export banana-farming were aided by its being a 'man's' crop.
16. Lévi-Strauss, particularly in his latest studies (1964, 1966), analyses brilliantly the constant rearrangements of themes and motifs, and transformations in myth. He uses the term *bricolage* (1962) to indicate the impression of new structures being 'bodged up' out of pieces of other structures. In his terminology: every so often, by a process of *bricolage,* a new Bakweri myth is created out of old and new elements embodying a statement involving economics with zombie-like phenomena. Something is repeated and revived over time through these successive replications. Whatever 'it' is, it is to be considered at a different level of analysis from that used in even the sophisticated analysis of content. I call it the

'template'. Its simple meaning of a 'form' or 'shape' used for copying is self-evident. I have in mind, however, the word's use in molecular biology, in the description of the process whereby the genetic material (DNA) continuously replicates itself from the chemical materials that are presented to it. The analogy I wish to bring out is that the molecules that replicate do so because their structures are logically limited in such a way that the chemical reactions they can take part in always compel the same end: the repetition of the original structures. They are like puzzles whose lengthy solution is finally in the form of the same puzzle. I suggest, merely on the loosest analogy, that in systems of belief over time certain configurations continually recur. Across time, 'synchronically', they may from time to time be absent. The metaphor of the 'template' is a way of visualizing that diachronic continuity perceived in the phrase: *plus ça change, plus c'est la même chose. So* we see the ideological template of the father-despot replicated in Russian history through totally different (even 'reversed') *realien* in Tsarist and Stalinist times. In French ideology two templates in particular replicate with monotonous regularity: one summarized by *'l'etat c'est moi'* and one by 'the barricades'.

17. '[T]he patient sees very small, perfectly formed figures, usually active and mobile, gaily coloured, and pleasant to look upon.' In a case of scarlet fever, a child reported them as tiny 'clowning' who seemed to be moving across and under his bed. They reappeared at fifteen-minute intervals (Leroy, 1922; Savitsky and Tarachow, 1941).

6

The Bakweri Elephant Dance*

The Bakweri are a small tribe of some 16,000 people who live on the slopes of the Cameroon Mountain. They are quiet and reserved and are not widely known outside the Southern Cameroons—despite the fact that both the Premier of the Southern Cameroons, Dr. E. M. L. Endeley, and the capital, Buea, are Bakweri. Not many non-Bakweri have the opportunity of witnessing their ceremonies, and it is rarely indeed that the participants will allow photographs to be taken. As members of the Elephant Society Mr. Mbwaye and I were in a privileged position.

This is the season when the annual dances of the society *(Njoku Malé)* are held. Members, in the higher grades at least, claim the power to own elephant 'doubles' into which they can change at will. There are four grades in *Malé* known as *Lovè, Venjuka, Tamba* and *Vekpa* which have an ascending scale of entrance fees, and which are open to men only. Mr. Mbwaye, the Southern Cameroons Information Service photographer, is a member of *Tamba.* A member with an elephant double is thought to be able to trample on the farms of his enemies in elephant form, and to transport himself (and any friends he may link arms with) at tremendous speeds from place to place. Such a member must however take the risk that if his elephant double is killed by a hunter he too will suddenly die.

The society came from Womboko on the other side of the Cameroon Mountain. It was there that the belief in the power to change into an elephant *(njoku)* seems to have been grafted on to the widespread *Malé* society, which, without this belief, is found all over the inland Kumba Division. A number of Bakweri villages have the society. The most well-known is Wokpaongo near Buea, but less accessible villages such as Mafanja, Wova and Gbasa can sometimes show more of the traditional features of the society.

The evening before the annual dance of a society a bonfire is lit *(ewond' a Malé),* and that night members are believed to enter their elephant bodies and trample through the bush. Next morning, as I saw

---

* *First published in* Nigeria *No. 60 (1959)*

The 'elephants'. Sugar canes represent trees.

The climax of the elephant dance.

one year at Mafanja, the damage is visible on neighbouring farms, although it must be said that the 'elephants' seemed to have scrupulously avoided plots in use. On the next day—usually nowadays a Sunday—the public is allowed to witness a dim reflection of these activities in the annual dance. First there is a general dance of the members of the society dressed in head- and waist-cloths, with their bodies smeared with red mud and decked with vegetation of various kinds. This dance is known as *Veambe* and the participants, some of whom are quite young children, wind in and out of the village to the rhythm of the drums. This is said to represent the movement of the elephant herd through the forest, but some of the members almost seem to be dressed to resemble the forest itself. Most of the old meaning of this dance is lost and young members view it as an opportunity for bizarre fancy dress.

Then comes the spectacular part of the ceremony—the entry of the elephants themselves *(njoku),* not, alas, the real elephant doubles, but representations suitable for public view. The *njoku* are dressed from the waist down in large spreading skirts of palm frond, while the rest of the bodies and the heads and arms of the dancers are completely enclosed in loose head-dresses of sacking with a shaggy covering of raffia. From these extend 'tusks' of iron-wood, held from inside by the dancer. The whole head-dress is extensible to twice the height by raising the tusks at arm's length above the head. As the *njoku* dance they stamp their feet, and '*lisonjo*' nut-shells round their ankles make a rhythmic rattling. Senior members of the society pretend to hunt the elephants, and the elephants in their turn charge at the hunters and strike their tusks furiously into the ground.

After a time the elephant dancers rest and the popular 'clown' of the society comes on. This is *Moseke,* a dancer covered in a net costume from head to foot, with yellow garden eggs for eyes. There is a special *Moseke* drum theme with a catchy rhythm, and the spectators join in with clapping. His appearance is eagerly awaited and he has to be a good dancer or suffer the criticism of the crowd. At the end of his performance, after some humorous by-play, *Moseke* is presented with a fowl by one of the senior members. This year I noticed that at Wokpaongo he only received an empty dish, the members having failed to make the necessary subscription in time. On the other hand his dancing in general opinion did not reach the standard of great *Mosekes* of other years.

Another figure of the *Malé* celebrations is *Ekpang' a Teta,* the 'policeman' of the occasion. He has a wooden mask painted black and white and carries a knife and 'medicine', and strides about the dance ground, his ankle-shells rattling, threatening the crowd in a gutteral

Ekpang' a Teta carrying a knife attends the elephant dance to keep the crowd in order. He is borrowed from the Nganya Society.

language of his own. *Ekpang' a Teta* is traditionally lent for the occasion by the Nganya society (a more exclusive group that sings satirical songs at night).

Eventually, after further dancing by the 'elephants', the celebrations come to a close and the members repair to their own feast, and the real business of the society.

Dance of the Veamba. Members dance round drummers

Moseke, the 'clown' of the elephant dance.
He resembles the Nigerian Ekpe dancer.

7

The Boundaries of Kamerun and Cameroon*

I. A Note on the Boundaries of Kamerun

That which was to be bounded in the Bight of Biafra under the name of Cameroon may be conveniently dated from 1827. Fernando Po came to be the key to the consolidation of the tendencies which resulted in the creation of Cameroon. In 1827, a settlement was established there by Captain Owen, which was developed under Colonel Nicholls, a Marine Officer. It was planned for good reasons that the anti-slave trade Mixed Commission should be moved there from Sierra Leone. The move failed and the settlement of Clarence (Santa Isobel) was finally abandoned in 1835, leaving behind a mixed body of Sierra Leone settlers and the installations. Among those who came in Colonel Nicholl's time, in 1829, was John Becroft, sometimes spelt as Beecroft, a merchant seaman from Birkenhead who had acted as Superintendent under him. He stayed on as agent for Dillon Tennent, the timber exporting West Africa Company, a firm which took over the installations which sold the buildings, in their turn, to the London Baptist Mission in 1842.

In 1849 Becroft became British Consul, based on Fernando Po, for the Bights of Benin and Biafra. As is well known, this man more than any other was responsible for the successful establishment of Britain's 'informal empire' on that stretch of coast which subsequently became Nigeria, and particularly on that area of rivers east of the centre of the Niger Delta. Until 1884 that informal empire stretched to the Cameroons River.

---

* *This previously unpublished Note was probably given in 1968 as an oral presentation in Oxford at the African Affairs seminar convened by Prof. K. Kirkwood and Dr Anthony Kirk-Greene. It is followed by Part II 'The Nature of the Reunification of Cameroon' published originally in Hazlewood (1967) which takes the political history up to 1966.*

Boundary - 1

John Becroft

Becroft it was who appropriately enough laid down on the map one of the few inland points which would be used as a boundary when the Cameroons segment was divided off from Nigeria. In September 1842 he sailed in the *Ethiope* up the Cross River from Old Calabar turning back at some 'rapids'. This point on the Cross River is not really very important practically. To this day craft go every rainy season some 40 miles further upstream to Mamfe. But the point marked 'rapids' became the furthest extension of the boundary of Cameroon in 1885, as we shall see.

Becroft thus was a 'boundary maker' by his very activities. In broader perspective it may be said that the informal consular empire was inevitably the prime source of the information available for its own subsequent subdivision.

Missions

The second Fernando Po factor was the mission one. The Baptists had gone to the island to join the Niger Expedition there in 1841. By accident or design the expedition did not call there, however, and the missionaries set to work with the local population. This was really two populations: settlers and natives. The natives (the Bubi) were less amenable and harder to get at than the settlers. The settlers were a body of West African artisans and recaptives from the time of Captain Owen and Colonel Nicholls. They were mainly of Sierra Leone provenance, and often of ultimate origin elsewhere on the West Coast. They were already Christians and pidgin-speaking. The reclaiming of the island by Spain, variously implemented in the 'forties and 'fifties, and the pious imperialism of the Baptists led to a spilling of Fernando Po influences onto the opposing coast as early as 1844 in Bimbia and inland. In 1858 the loyal Baptist colony of Victoria was interposed between the people of Old Calabar/Rio del Rey, and the Cameroons River Duala people. The Cameroons River, because of Baptist influence and the proximity of Victoria, was a piece of the informal mangrove empire which had a particular style and flavour. The Fernando Po orientation of the Christianised population was a further subtle factor which has survived somewhat even until today. Old Calabar was visited by the Baptists from Fernando Po in the 1840's, but the ambitious Hope Waddell who arrived at the same time on behalf of the Methodists quickly claimed Old Calabar. He too had reached Fernando Po on the same wave as it were.

This split of the Fernando Po zone in mission terms was not without its minor significance later. Without Hope Waddell the Baptists would have no doubt claimed Old Calabar, and Hope Waddell, were it not for the Baptists, would have looked towards the Cameroons River. Either missionary organization came to carry sufficient prestige that if all the Bight coast had fallen under one or the other, it is likely that the junction of the Cameroons culturally to (the commercially supremely British) Old Calabar would have avoided the existence of this extra 'dotted line': a line which enabled the German Protectorate later to be torn off.

The 'mission factor' should not be underestimated. The 'informal empire', at its margin, fell between a Hope Waddell (Methodist) and an Alfred Saker (Baptist) zone. The idiosyncrasies of Alfred Saker, who rose to absolute power in the 1850's, made his zone inward-looking; we see him printing away at Duala bibles till he appears to us knee deep in the undistributed sheets. His failure to open up his hinterland turned his more adventurous missionaries of the 1870's to the south. The best was Grenfell who left Cameroon with his Victorian wife for the Congo where the Baptists became a great humanitarian influence, and where Grenfell's greatest contributions were made. In the eyes of the Foreign Office, though not in the eyes of the most iconoclastic Consuls, the small theocratic republic of Victoria, with the lively, multiple Duala state on the Cameroons River, seemed deceptively solidly placed. 'Settlement' was going on so well. Not like the turbulent Delta. As it happened the hopes of progress based on the retirement of Saker in 1876 were shattered by the death of his successor— and of a whole row of young men and women. The Baptists were reduced to a skeleton staff at the crisis of the 1880s.

Trade

The 'trade factor' was important. Behind the Cameroons Estuary the continuous belt of dense hinterland populations behind the West African coast begins to fade out. The last Oil River was not as rich especially in palm oil as some of the others and the entry of Woermann's German company into Duala in 1868 excited little comment. Thormählen, the Woermann agent, later split off with another employer and established a second firm Jantzen and Thormählen. The hulk-dwellers in the estuary (agents of six British firms in 1884) little realised that the newcomers would be instrumental in establishing German rule in the Cameroons Estuary.

The Annexation

The annexation of Cameroon has been discussed in many standard works; these would include Rudin (1938), Jaeck (1960), Gifford and Louis (1967), and Ardener, S. G., (1968). For the local side, in particular, S.G. Ardener throws a stream of light, documented in material from the Baptist records and German sources. We know that Bismarck in 1884 'changed his mind' in favour of a German bid for colonies. We know that the British were pre-occupied with the French threat, and feared the tariffs the French had imposed at Malimba. We know that steps were under way to annex the 'informal empire' to avert this, when the German Nachtigal suddenly arrived in the Cameroons River, just ahead of Hewett the British Consul. We know that Bismarck had selected areas on Woermann's advice over which British claims had not yet been made, but in which German interests could act.

In the end, it must be stressed, any of the Nachtigalian annexations depended on the ability of the local German interests to make treaties for Nachtigal to ratify. It is even now not fully realised just how touch-and-go it was that Nachtigal was given anything to ratify. Only two out of the four Duala chiefs could be induced to sign anything at all, while their howling Duala subjects cried 'we want English!'.

The merchant interest in Hamburg was dominant at the home end. Woermann and Thormählen in Germany virtually dictated Nachtigal's instructions to Bismarck. It only remained for their local agent to acquire the treaties. All this vast imperialistic weight and the succeeding consequences fell on one 25-year-old local Woermann agent, Eduard Schmidt, a jolly, popular, ex-salesman of confectionary. One has the impression, as he struggles for a treaty, of a total sacrifice of personality and of a reputation for integrity; and yet still he nearly fails. Kings Akwa and Bell were closetted with the Woermann men as the stakes were raised. King Bell offered one of them an island (not his own) to keep them off the horrible monetary offers. The Cameroons notables demanded confirmation of their middleman rights. This was conceded in writing by the German Consul (another Woermann agent) against specific Woermann policy. A treaty signed by Bell and Akwa only, which did not mention this all-important clause, was thrust as it were into Nachtigal's hands. No copies were left behind. Flags were hoisted on 14 July 1884. The Duala exploded in December and were put down brutally. But by then diplomacy had done its work in Europe and the impossible had been achieved. The 'informal empire' had lost its most secure possession.

Schmidt was brushed aside by Woermann like a fly. A Red Eagle 4th class was all Schmidt got. He went to live in Lagos where he suffered guilt for his part in the annexations. By 1911 Woermann was a millionaire, ship-owner, merchant and armaments manufacturer.

Schmidt's success created the circumstances for the Diplomatic foothold. How did it happen? The death of the Baptist element? Sheer luck? Why were the British so slow? Actually they were not slow: they left Cameroon last because it was safe. Why? Because of the Baptist element. Paradoxically, in the 1880s it was an area of constant pleas for British rule.

Boundary - 2

Although Duala was thus claimed by Nachtigal, Victoria had been annexed by Consul Hewett safely enough, thus realising, briefly, an old dream of the anglicised inhabitants. It seemed unthinkable that this territory, at least, should be added to Germany. Indeed for a time the treaty-making activities in the hinterland of agents of the British Government, official and unofficial, produced clashes with Germans on the same mission. The popular journalistic picture of the 'scramble' in the metropolitan countries at the time derived precisely from the events on the Cameroon mountain.

All this was taken very seriously in Germany where colonial mania was far in advance of the situation in Britain. By an exchange of notes of 29 April and 7 May 1885 the British drew the division between the new German sphere and their own near Calabar: 'along the Rio del Rey to its source and thence to the Rapids on the Cross River'. These were Becroft's rapids of old. They were later difficult to find; and there was no river Rio del Rey but this was settled in the 1890s. The colony of Victoria was excluded from the German sphere: however, a secret exchange of notes provided that if the Germans could make an agreement with the Baptists for their interest the British would not stand in the way. This was not achieved for two years.

*****

Meanwhile, the question of the position north of the rapids arose. From now on the extension of the boundaries of Cameroon ceased to express pre-existing socio-political realities, but expressed the *idea* of what an African colony should be. That idea certainly took into account certain views with a local basis—those of merchants and the like. The German idea *in Berlin* was, however, in part affected by what the two 'senior older colonial powers' (a respectful own term of the Germans of the time) thought or seemed to think an African colony's boundaries should be. The British who invented railways were obsessed by rivers in Africa, as inlets of trade, and their attempts to seize rights on them approached the disengenuous (the 1884 Congo Treaty with Portugal, after all, had horrified Europe). The Niger-Benue had virtually been secured for her by the Berlin Conference of 1884/85. *Rivers=trade* was one image offered to Germany by Britain. On the other side, France saw Africa, as ever, with a grander vision of the same theme. To her Africa was a country whose units were the river basins—'les grand bassins fluviales, les grands zones climatiques'. For her a colony would link as many basins as possible. The implied utilitarian view of rivers was no doubt British-derived too, but multiple Basin-pocketing gave French boundary-making a feverish purposiveness. As is ever the case, the Germans were awed by the examples of both brilliant neighbours. Faced with a fairly blank map, occupying a gap between the Niger and Congo basins, there was no choice on either model but to aim that the boundaries should reach a major affluent of each system, if not the main rivers themselves. In fact the Germans had little choice. For Britain, the Germans were thought to be better than the French as potential neighbours, and the Germans were dragged along at times in the British wake, to their advantage, only to have bits punched out of them by the French. Throughout the new boundary-making period the Germans had at farthest penetrated less than 300 miles from their coast.

For a few months in 1885, the Germans hoped that the inland western boundary of Cameroon would be the longitude of the Cross River rapids. Bismarck was soon conceding British claims as far up the Benue as Ibi. The West Africa Company soon reached Yola. Only then did the Foreign Office offer a boundary extension. A line was drawn from the rapids to a point East of Yola on the Benue. So far so good. The Germans were not then fully aware of all the implications of Yola's primacy in Adamawa. The agreement was made in an exchange of notes 27 July/ 2 August 1886.

Meanwhile, weary negotiations of the Germans with the London Baptists for the sale of Victoria dragged on. On the spot the elderly Jamaican missionary Fuller was not able to resist the overwhelming gentlemanly prestige of the German officers and their encroachments, exercised with brutal charm. He was essentially inexperienced, bewildered and left unsupported locally by a wave of missionary deaths, and was unaware that his home mission was sick of Government pressures to sell and was turning to the Congo. His own church in Duala had been recently reduced to matchwood by German guns. Other men, other times might have mobilized European, or American public opinion as lesser men had for lesser causes. A victim of excessive respect for white men, he was blamed by the Victoria Creoles for the sale of their settlement to the German-backed Basel Mission. The young white missionaries were naive or struck down with disease. Negotiations between Baptists and the Basels were completed in Europe over all their heads and in an exchange of Notes of 27/31 January 1887 the British Government ceded Victoria to Germany handing over in March. Fuller was glad to retire to Stoke Newington, where he died in 1908.

The social and political realities of the coast show conclusively that the Baptist organization was the entity which was invaded and transformed by the German power. The very buildings of the German government at Duala were those of the Baptists.

The important population base then was the Duala people. In this respect the subsequent social and political history reflects the division between Victoria—the quietistic Baptist republic—and Duala—the more rebellious Baptist congeries of kingdoms. The last Duala revolt against the Germans was expressed in the execution of their 'King' Rudolph Manga Bell just after the outbreak of the War of 1914. The Victorians never revolted, but they quietly made it seem impossible to British advisers in 1919 that this part of West Africa, at least, could return to Germany.

*****

Ironically, as the German colonial frontiers were expanded in Cameroon in the 1880s and 1890s on geopolitical grounds, so too did the Creole coast expand. Willy-nilly coastal pidgin English travelled with the Germans into a vast area. The necessary division of the country between the British and French in 1916/22 resulted in an apparent breach between the two parts of Old Baptist Cameroon. In the end, however, it was this unity which as much as any other single factor stirred the sentiments which led by a devious route to the 'reunification' of Cameroon.

None of this was to be realised by the German boundary makers. The native populations were never regarded by them as having any historical effectiveness. The 'ideal colony' continued to be created after the absorption of Victoria.

The French

The southern boundary of the German interest was fixed with relative ease in December 1885 (ratified 1886). The French whose approach to Cameroon had first alarmed the British, offered the Germans the Campo River as a boundary, continued by a straight line to 15° East.

For a time (between 1886 and 1893) it looked as if the final boundary might have to be a line joining Yola to the southern 15°E point. The Germans were bad at exploration in Cameroon. The lack of money in the early days (due to the parsimony of the Reichstag) was, of course, a significant factor. Caprivi's apathy was conveyed to Governor Zimmerer. Strange expedients were resorted to: for example the employment of Dahomeans by Gravenreuth.

The Chad was now the international aim. The 'race' was once more the product of a mixture of French grandeur and British empiricism. The romance of the Chad derived from its, roughly, central position in French basin-hopping. It was a convenient linking point for its expeditions from the Niger and the Congo and on the way to the Nile.

For the British it was a useful boundary for its North Nigerian interests. While the Germans humiliatingly failed to get a Chad expedition into the interior they were suddenly offered a Yola-Chad boundary by the British who preferred a German to a French neighbour there. This was ratified on 14 November 1893. The Germans were by now fully aware of the important position of Yola in Fulani Adamawa but they were firmly excluded. In the apology for the Treaty the German Government stressed how impossible a Chad boundary would have been without British help, since no German expedition had reached the region.

The final settlement of the Eastern boundary with France was less satisfactory. Hardly any German claims reached anywhere near the 15° longitude. The French had well-attested claims everywhere. The resulting negotiation is mapped in the peculiar Eastern boundary. The French wanted as much of the Chad shore as possible and access to what was thought to be a river system navigable to the Niger-Benue (the 'river basin aim'). Both points were inside the 15° line. The Germans wanted to touch the Congo affluents somewhere to appease colonial interests (outside the 15° line). These concessions, with minor adjustments, were balanced in the boundary of 11 March 1894.

Summary

We have here, therefore, a strange set of boundaries influenced at the coast by contradictory local realities,

a. linked with the 'Nigerian' coast by language and political experience of 50 years,
b. separated from it by a peculiar mission history expressed in political institutions for nearly the same period,
c. internally subdivided into a colonial segment (Victoria) and a free segment (Duala).

As time went on boundaries moved back and forth. In 1884 (b) had been expressed. In 1916-22, factors (a) and (c) were expressed. In 1961 reunificationist Southern Cameroons thought they were expressing (a) as well as (b). Only (b) came to be expressed in the new boundaries.

After 1894 the German ideal colony remained dormant at Berlin. Then, in 1911, it was given prongs to the Congo and Ubangi as a compensation for the German recognition of France in Morocco. It was extended round Rio Muni over which Germany claimed right of reversion. In the thought of Kiderlen-Wachter before 1914 the prongs pointed across the Congo to Angola, Mozambique and East Africa. The Mittelafrika dream, which in various forms had had on and off British support from 1898, lingered on into the appeasement period of the `30s. Spain, Portugal, Belgium and all native populations were ignored.

At the Anglo-French division of Cameroon in 1922 the boundaries of the mandate were neither the pre-1911 ones nor the post-1911 ones. The 1911 gains by Germany were taken back by France. She kept, however, one small gain of that year in the so-called duck-bill. That is now part of Chad.

Conclusion

My theme so far has been:

1. that boundaries on the ground are boundaries round ideas. The ideas are generated from many socio-political realities. You tear along the dotted lines. Stable is the zone where the dotted lines are few.
2. In Africa the diplomatic boundaries after 1884 represented certain geo-political ideas. Africa was unique in that a whole new set was internationally recognised at once. In some sense the Berlin Conference, Brussels

Conference, Algeciras Conference and League of Nations and Trusteeship systems expressed the same continuous internationalism in Africa. I have already documented in Hazlewood (1967) how this affected the re-unification movement in the Cameroon Trust Territories. The independent states, in my view, still view their boundaries as in this domain. They are possibly right to do so because

3. the socio-political realities and the geo-political were in tension in 1884. They remain so today but they are only partially known to the politicians themselves.

II. The Nature of the Reunification of Cameroon 1960-1966

The Federal Republic of Cameroon and its predecessors have been known by various names in the past, but there are now two official forms: 'Cameroun' and 'Cameroon', used in French and English respectively.[1] The republic is officially bilingual, while the official language of the West Cameroon State is English.[2] By the constitution of 1961, the Federal Republic consists of two States: East Cameroon and West Cameroon, constituted respectively from the territories of the Republic of Cameroun (independent in 1960) and of the Southern Cameroons, formerly under British trusteeship.

The two federated States are geographically and demographically unequal. The area of West Cameroon (approximately 42,000 sq. km.) is only a tenth of that of East Cameroon (432,000 sq. km) By the 1961 constitution, the populations of the two states were defined as: 'East Cameroon 3,200,000, West Cameroon 800,000', with the provision that the figures may be amended by a federal law in the light of significant variation established by census'.[3] These were to some extent conventional figures: each being an exact-multiple of 80,000, the prescribed size of a federal parliamentary constituency; they were however acceptable approximations. The latest figure (1964) for West Cameroon is 1,030,720. A reliable recent figure for East Cameroon is lacking, but the estimate for 1965 was 4,070,000, and the approximate relationship of four to one is thus probably maintained. The capital of West Cameroon is Buea (pop. 1964: 9,171). The capital of East Cameroon and of the Federal Republic are both at Yaounde (pop. 1965: 100,000).[4]

There is economic inequality also: the per capita GDP of West Cameroon is of the order of 20,000 francs CFA ($78 or £30) contrasted with 30,000 francs CFA for East Cameroon. The West Cameroon figure does not compare badly, however, with Nigeria (21,000 francs CFA), Chad (13,000 francs CFA) and the Central African Republic (12,000 francs CFA).

1. Introduction

Reunification: Formal Political Aspects

The German protectorate (*Schutzgebiet*) of Kamerun was set up in its primitive form by proclamation on 14 July 1884, passed through two main stages of redefinition, in 1894 and 1911, and existed until it was invaded in 1914 by British and French forces. A *de facto* partition followed in 1916.[6]

The Anglo-French occupation was perpetuated by a division of Kamerun into two mandated territories by the Council of the League of Nations on 20 July 1922.[7] Much subsequent political discussion, at the international and local levels, in the succeeding decades was to turn upon this partition of a unitary colonial territory, but the boundaries of the mandate were formally defined, after 1922, in a way that did not precisely match those of the German protectorate at any period. They were neither the boundaries of 1894 nor those of 1911, but a superimposition of the two, which had the effect of excluding all parts of Kamerun that had been occupied by France at either of those dates.[8] Since the partition which was enshrined in the mandate system was the one which engaged attention for forty years, it is important to note that the other partitions (which abolished the 1911 accessions of territory without restoring the boundaries of 1894) did not do so. The political movement for the reconstruction of Kamerun was, from the outset, held within new boundaries, which were stated after 1922 by the mandate and (later) trusteeship system. This system must thus be accorded one place in the set of forces which created the Federal Republic.[9]

The incorporation of the portions of the subdivided mandate into neighbouring political systems was of different kinds. The eastern and larger part was incorporated into the French African colonial structure, but as a separate administrative unit. Its later decolonisation as a whole, without further subdivision, was not to be seriously questioned.[10] The western part, itself geographically discontinuous, was treated for administrative purposes as part of Nigeria. This procedure was taken so far that the north-south subdivision, which was of long standing in Nigeria, was extended to the new territory. This resulted in the emergence within the British sphere of a 'Northern' and a 'Southern' Cameroons. Only the latter remained a separate administrative unit within its segment of Nigeria. In the north the mandated territory never had a separate administrative existence but became subdivided, in its turn, among several Northern Nigerian provinces. In the south the mandated territory existed as one province for more than twenty-five years. Its further temporary subdivision into two provinces in 1949 occurred on the eve of the modem political period, and was abolished by the new constitutional position of 1954.

At the United Nations plebiscite of 1961 the largely 'assimilated' North chose to maintain the two partitions that separated it from both the East and the South. In the southern part, the balance of opinion between perpetuation of partition and union with the French Trust Territory was evenly held for a time. In 1961 the balance swung heavily in favour of the latter.

The Federal Republic of 1 October 1961 therefore came into existence within even narrower boundaries than those of 1922. Neither East Cameroon nor West Cameroon has the boundaries it would have had if a simple reconstruction of German Kamerun had been achieved. It was not achieved, evidently, because of certain more powerful political forces deriving from the nature of British and French colonialism, and of Nigerian and French African decolonisation. For this reason, these forces must also form part of the set which created the present Federal Republic. Any picture of the Federal Republic as simply reconstituting a previous political entity is therefore bound to be inadequate. Since 1961 the political force represented by the mandate/trusteeship system may be said to have dissipated, except in so far as the international basis of the present boundaries derives from the last acts of the trusteeship system. The forces deriving from the other two points of the triangle have not, however, dissipated. To this extent therefore they remain expressed in the boundary between the two component states of the Federal Republic.

This discussion bears upon the nature of the frontiers of the ex-colonial countries: their supposed 'artificiality', combined with their proved durability. The diplomatic recognition and negotiation of colonial boundaries took place according to the operation of certain axioms and rules, in a special 'political space'.[11] By the axioms of this space, the boundaries of Kamerun were far from artificial. They were defined clearly in relation to other boundaries of the same type. The mandate and trusteeship agreements had legal reality only in so far as they referred to units in this space. So did international recognition of the status of independence. 'That which was to be re-unified' was such a unit. There was, for the purposes of formal political argument, no necessity that it should be a unit of any other kind (such as a 'tribal' or 'cultural' one). Many of the arguments leading up to reunification were, in fact, formal in nature. The boundaries of that which was finally 're-unified' were not willed by those who wished for reunification. It is important then to recognize at the outset the autonomy acquired by the system to which political boundaries belong.

In their institutional and political aspects the two parts of the reconstituted Cameroon still bear witness to the partition. The great difference in the sizes and populations of the two units means that the eastern segment has been required to make fewer adjustments than has the western segment. Those it has had to make have been initially those of outlook due to the presence of the new Western State, and to the contrast implied by the existence of the latter's own peculiar institutions. Institutionally, the creation of the Federal Republic required little of East Cameroon beyond the interposition of a further stage between the Eastern legislative and ministerial institutions and the Presidency. The East State and the federal institutions were essentially one in origin as well as in function. For West Cameroon they represented a level superimposed upon the pre-existing legislative and government organs which was different in kind as well as in hierarchical degree. The *de facto* relationship of the states to the federal government has differed from the *de jure* relationship. The pattern has been less:

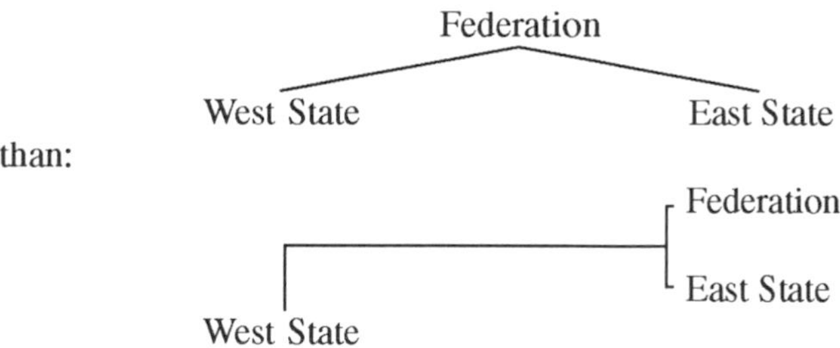

Because of the low degree of differentiation between the Federal and East State organs, the relationship of West Cameroon to them, in the first five years, at times partook of something of the relations of Northern Ireland to the United Kingdom government (which is also the government of Great Britain), at others, of the relationship between the Channel Islands and the British Crown. What its final form will be is not yet clear.

Given the imbalance between the two states, and other factors deriving from the isolation of West Cameroon, any study of the reunification must lay great stress upon the West Cameroon side of the situation. The story of the first five years is, broadly, one of various attempts to link West Cameroon in some effective way to its partner, and of the gradual discovery of new ways of doing this by the East. The vision from Yaounde of the West as an essentially marginal area, a remote 'Shangri La', reflects some of the lack of immediacy attaching there to the notion of the reunification. A study of East Cameroon could, for most of our period, ignore the West or relegate it to a footnote, without serious distortion. As far as the broader international and economic relations of the Federal Republic are concerned, they are those largely of a successor state of French Africa. Its undoubted peculiarities do not derive from the reunification but from the particular history of East Cameroon during the divided trusteeship. Any slight stylistic differences which may be gradually appearing in the 'Francophonity' of the Republic are also much more clearly perceived by approaching them from a consideration of West Cameroon. In West Cameroon, in contrast, the reunification is the dominant fact of life.[12]

West Cameroon: Topographical

The economic development of West Cameroon while it was under British administration was always circumscribed by poor communications. The country divides into a high northern 'rural' grassland plateau, and a commercially more developed seaboard, both with considerable population densities, joined (or separated) by a long forest belt, broken and hilly, and in part mountainous, of relatively thinner population. At the seaboard, access to waterways and to the sea provided reasonable communications, although the terrain itself was rocky. The great difficulty was always to establish adequate access to the northern highlands, and to exploit the thinly populated forest link. The problems presented by this fundamental pattern shaped the whole mandate and trusteeship period.

At the coast Victoria Division, dominated by the volcanic Cameroon Mountain (13,350 ft.), is an area of high rainfall and extremely fertile soils. It is separated from the neighbouring coastal areas of Nigeria (at Calabar), and of East Cameroon (at Douala), by the estuarine systems of the Rio del Rey and Wouri and their mangrove swamps. The mountain slopes were, after 1885, the site of a large plantation industry established by the Germans. The estates were maintained in operation throughout the mandate period, after 1924 mainly under their original German owners. In 1940 they fell under government custodianship. In 1949 the estates were sequestered and leased to a public body, the Cameroons Development Corporation, whose profits (under the terms of its charter) subsequently went to the Trust Territory. The CDC estates passed through various vicissitudes, but they still remain the chief industrial complex of the present West Cameroon. The ports are Victoria/Bota, and Tiko.[13]

From this area a main road runs north, through Kumba, where it is joined by a route from East Cameroon. It then continues north over a hilly watershed and drops through broken country to Mamfe, on the Cross River. Throughout the mandate period the most efficient means of communication with eastern Nigeria was by this river during the rains, to Calabar. Later, the only road communications with Nigeria have also been through Mamfe Division. Its northern part has a population density of only six persons per sq. km., the lowest in the State. From Mamfe, the main route runs north-eastwards climbing an escarpment from the forest to a plateau with a base height of about 3,000 feet. The whole of this area (the 'Grasslands'), with a savannah vegetation and a cooler climate, formed Bamenda Division until its partition in 1949. A ring-road circles the plateau, joining Bamenda with Wum and Nkambe, the headquarters of the divisions of the same name. Bamenda Division (population 1964: 338,580) was, before its further partition in 1966, the most populous of the three, as well as the most developed economically, Wum Division (105,710) and Nkambe (101,880) being less so. From Bamenda a road runs to the east.

Concomitants of Isolation

It is important to stress that throughout the period from 1922 to the early 1940s and even into the 1950s the isolation of the present West Cameroon ('Cameroons Province') was almost complete: one dry-season route to the west, two dry-season routes to the east. There was never at any time a road to the Northern Cameroons. The main mercantile and industrial area, Victoria Division, was also internally isolated, relying on one poor route to the north, while having only sea communication with equivalent coastal centres at Calabar and Douala. The provincial headquarters at Buea was itself in Victoria Division; it was isolated from Victoria by its position, reached by circuitous roads, 3,000 feet up the Cameroon mountain. In Kumba Division, the Rumpy mountains were isolated from the headquarters. In Mamfe Division the area north of the Cross River (the 'Overside') was isolated from the rest of the Division.

In Bamenda Division, as still now in Wum and Nkambe Divisions, there were whole belts of inaccessible country. At this period almost all the important centres lay not so much on roads as at the ends of roads, each in its own cul-de-sac. This isolation has remained central to the social, political, and economic development of the country ever since.

It was in the time of the mandate that a peculiarly (British) 'Cameroonian' way of life grew up in the province, although the time has often been regarded as one of stagnation. The isolation of the present West Cameroon in those days was not uncommon for extensive regions of West Africa. Its chief peculiarity lay in its possession of a full-scale plantation industry at its coast in speedy contact with world markets. The first crops had been tobacco (an early failure), cocoa, and rubber. The economic depression of the 1930s had been weathered by the widespread introduction of bananas, formerly a crop grown by only a single German company.[14] Throughout the inter-war period the bulk of the produce went to Germany. The Cameroons Province was thus not only detached from Nigeria geographically but it led a unique and partially independent economic life. From Nigeria came administration, and the introduction of local governrnent.[15]

The term 'isolation' has been used here to emphasize difficulty or slowness of land communication, not absence of communication. The difficulty was for many years almost insuperable for modern forms of transport. Nevertheless, throughout the mandated period, labour arrived at the coastal plantations, most of it on foot, and either from within the borders of the Cameroons Province or from the plateau area of the French mandate next to Bamenda Division. From these movements derived: (1) (in great part) the spread of pidgin English ('Creole') into all parts of the province; (2) a basis of unity greater than the tribe resulting from a common working history, in which spells of migration to the plantations had become a uniform experience for the adult males (and some females) of most ethnic groups; (3) the assimilation of migrants from the French mandate to the provincial career pattern. These three factors were of later political significance, but require before their consideration some discussion of terminology.

Ethnic' Context: Theoretical Remarks

There were no great partitioned peoples on the intra-Cameroon boundary. On the contrary, it could be argued that the only extensive group of recognised ethnographic status which was cut by any boundary was the Ejagham (Ekoi) of the Upper Cross River, through whose territory ran the old Nigeria-Kamerun frontier from its very earliest days. This survived as the western boundary of the mandate and trusteeship, of Cameroons Province, and of the Southern Cameroons. It is still the western frontier of West Cameroon, and thus of the Federal Republic. Yet despite this division to the west, the notion of 'our brothers to the East' was the one which acquired political force.[16] In Europe and America, Africans have been commonly assumed to be moved mainly by 'tribal' sentiment. The degree to which adherents of reunification felt that it was necessary to stress ethnicity if their case was to receive world support is illustrated by the circumstance that the assumption by many observers that the Bamileke (a large congeries of peoples in East Cameroon) were also the dominant people of Bamenda, was often left uncorrected. The sentiments which reunification expressed were genuine and compelling but they were not 'tribal', unless that term be accorded a subordinate reference especially designed for the Cameroon situation.

Political scientists and political commentators ultimately derive the idea of 'tribes' and 'tribalism' from the older social anthropology, but in West Africa, at least, all too often the social anthropologist was the unwitting follower of the administrator. Meillassoux speaks of the Gouro of the Ivory Coast as in origin an administrative unit resting on 'des réalités furtives'. The 'tribal consciousness' of the Gouro, he went so far as to add, developed later in the towns, where individuals from the Gouro area found it necessary to adopt a 'tribal' organization because the dominant *Rassemblement Démocratique Africain* (*R.D.A.*) movement was organized on a 'tribal' basis. 'La conscience d'être Gouro semble être née parallèlement a celle d'être Ivoirien, dans le cadre de l'expérience coloniale'.[17]

We can now more clearly see the logic of such apparent paradoxes. For, having pointed out this Gouro example, it is no longer possible to add, as would once have appeared natural: 'but, of course, this is not to argue that tribes do not exist' (that is: *somewhere,* or *elsewhere,* 'the Gouro being a case of peculiar type'). The 'peculiar' cases throw light upon the use of 'tribe' as a prior category in all cases, for we have in fact, no single set of criteria for the definition of the term. Linguistic criteria commonly purport to provide one, but in African circumstances the accepted 'linguistic' divisions are also frequently fed back from the 'tribal' divisions. A convenient device is to take populations to which certain names are applied and to assume that other criteria of community will be revealed by further study. Some conventionally accepted 'tribes' do name themselves, and those which do so commonly name their neighbours, whose only 'unity' may originally have consisted in their being the recipients of such a name (one unknown, possibly, to themselves). The period of colonial rule tended to favour the classifications used by the self-distinguishing 'tribes' and, indeed, to reward and reinforce the acceptance of 'tribal' categories. The modern use and widespread development of these categories therefore derives from both African and foreign sources. The intervention of colonial policies shaped the process whereby Africans became aware of each other: the 'tribe', as the Nigerian situation most clearly exemplifies, is now a socio-political category of daunting complexity.[18]

The prior question of the 'furtive realities' behind the accepted ethnic structure is nowhere less solved than for West Cameroon and the neighbouring part of East Cameroon.[19] The primary division is linguistic. In Victoria and Kumba Divisions all the peoples (with the exception of the Korup and Efik of the western borders of Kumba Division) speak Bantu languages of the North-Western Group. In Mamfe, Bamenda, Nkambe, and Wum Divisions, many languages are spoken of which the majority are to be classified as 'Bantoid' of two or three main branches. This linguistic boundary is a creation of genetic comparative linguistics, and its precise geographical position is fixed by the axioms upon which comparative Bantu studies are founded. I have chosen the position which requires least modification of those axioms, that is: broadly the position of Professor Guthrie. The laxer position of Professor Greenberg would draw that boundary much farther to the north.[20] It depends, therefore, to a real extent upon scholarly arguments. The philological frontier crosses the interstate line from west to east, but it can hardly be said (given the technical bases of its determination) to be a prominent feature on the ground. The Bantoid languages of Cross River type are cut from north to south by the Nigerian boundary. Superimposed upon the main linguistic division is a further one of economy and environment: it distinguishes the three Grassland Divisions from the rest. This boundary thus distinguishes the Mamfe Bantoid speakers from their close Bamenda congeners. The plateau/forest distinction extends eastward, and thus the speakers of plateau Bantoid languages in Bamenda are environmentally similarly placed to the Bamum Kingdom and the Bamileke congeries of East Cameroon.[21]

Within the forest divisions distinctions may be made between peoples looking towards the Cross River for their social and economic contacts (Mamfe and part of Kumba Divisions), and those looking towards the coast (the rest of Kumba Division and all of Victoria Division). Within the latter we may set up a further distinction between those focused upon the Rio del Rey system and those upon the Wouri system and Douala.

The last evidently had East Cameroon connexions, but the other forest sub-divisions had their connexions in the present Nigeria.

We may lay upon the map more and more overlapping sets according to different criteria. Linguistic comparison can distinguish clusters of languages, in both the Bantu and Bantoid areas.[22] Sociological and cultural criteria enable further ones to be made. The plateau environment is associated with a particular cultural style variously expressed in Bamenda, Bamileke, and Bamum (Foumban: one of its most fruitful areas of development). Among its striking features are the institution of kingship and common elements of art and decorations. Other cultural sets cover the Cross River basin jointly with much of Bamenda plateau, thus distinguishing the people of the latter from those to the east. And so on.

The final units to be distinguished are the present named sets, the 'tribes'. These units, as generally listed, are not all of the same taxonomic order. Some could be termed 'artificial', if we believed in the existence of 'real' tribes. The most effective set of criteria, which give modern validity to the tribal list, are those deriving from the Native Court areas established, according to certain classifying assumptions, by the administration in the mandate period.[24] These are defined by their organs (courts, treasuries, and the like). By this final classification there are over 80 'tribal' units in West Cameroon. It is impossible to come to a 'real' figure. By the criteria (especially linguistic) used of the forest, the Grasslands 'tribes' are often bundles of tribes. If the handful of state-like chiefdoms of the Grasslands are taken as the measure, many other tribes are meaningless groupings of independent villages.

One or two general remarks can, however, be made. Linguistically the fragmentation is very much greater in the Bantoid-speaking area than in the Bantu-speaking zone, but nowhere are we dealing with large areas of mutual intelligibility. The largest socio-linguistic group in 1953 numbered under 60,000 people (Nso' in Bamenda Division). A modal figure for West Cameroon should be close to 10,000. As has already been hinted, only specialists can distinguish Bantoid from Bantu languages. Of the tribal units normally defined by all these criteria, those which were clearly split by the Anglo-French boundary belonged to the forest or the forest/plateau edge—generally small groups of minor political importance later.[25] On the plateau the boundary usually divided groups which were already politically independent and linguistically divergent. In particular the vast 'Bamileke' area of East Cameroon with its peculiar social, linguistic, and demographic characteristics was trimmed only at the edges.[2]

The 'Ethnicity' of West Cameroon

There were no 'Ewe' therefore and certainly no 'Somali'. For the 'ethnic' basis of the reunification (the quotation marks must be carefully preserved) we must look back to a previous section. My argument has been that the area, far from being one in which broad common tribalities occur, is a test-case for any scientific analysis of the various significances attached to the term 'tribe'. The fallacy in our thinking is to conceive of an ethnic pattern as having been laid down once and for all, at (say) 1884 or in the 1930s (with 'indirect rule'). The process of differentiation has continued up to the present. If the canoe trade with Calabar could stamp a common ethnicity upon the Balundu, and the primitive salt industry of the Cross River do the like for the Banyang-Ejagham border; if the Duala people, as we know it, is the creation of the slave-trading society of the eighteenth and nineteenth centuries: then we must not assume that this process of continuous creation has ceased.

West Cameroon was, we saw, isolated by its geography from developments in Nigeria between the wars. Although there were social and linguistic links across the western border, the Nigerian population was itself here thinly distributed, creating a kind of intervening marchland which tended to add to the isolation on this side. On the eastern side, however, certain other boundaries continued into East Cameroon: (1) that of the 'catchment' area from which labour migrated to the plantations of West Cameroon; (2) the area of the 'Old Cameroons' at the coast; and (3) the area of spoken pidgin English.

The plantation catchment area, as we have seen, extended over the eastern border to include the Bamileke Plateau, and shared to some degree a common life-style, deriving from the exigencies of labour migration. By the 'Old Cameroons' may be understood the coastal stretch between Douala and Victoria. It formed a common area of modernization from 1827, at first linked with the official, subsequently mercantile, settlement at Fernando Po. It then became subject to the Baptist Mission influence (either from Fernando Po or at the coast) from 1841 to 1887, and finally formed the main administrative and commercial core of the German Protectorate. The Old Cameroons was linked largely by water-transport, and some interchange of population through education and administration was maintained until, and even after, the mandate settlement of 1922. Although this old unit was divided, and the parts became more and more isolated from each other in the next thirty years, the influence of living individuals in maintaining a sense of contact remained important at the coast. Both these areas were overlapped by the distribution of pidgin English (Creole), a development originally from the Old Cameroons.[27]

It was, I suggest, these new and important socio-linguistic sets which came to be felt as an 'ethnicity', in a context in which internal and external political pressures favoured the expression of all wider communities of this type in 'ethnic' terms.[28] Whether this feeling was equally shared by both sides of the border is another matter. It rested ultimately upon the movement of individuals. The migration of Bamileke to West Cameroon, for example, was a tiny part of the whole movement of this very mobile people. Some members of the 'ethnicity' (for example Ewondo [Yaounde] migrants settled in West Cameroon) never returned to their home areas. Their children, nevertheless (often unilingual in pidgin), were embodiments of 'unification'.[29] West Cameroonians were generally unaware of the rapid changes among their Eastern neighbours who were after 1945 drawn into vortices of much greater power and importance.

The use of the term 'ethnicity' has been forced upon this discussion by the language which is generally offered for the examination of these matters. It has been made clear that this language is already inadequate. It is to be hoped that no one will be tempted to interpret these remarks in the form: 'there "really" was an "unrecognized" ethnic group which was re-unified or which sought to be re-unified'.

'Tribes' are not permanent crystalline structures, belonging to one 'stage' of historical and social development. Certain of the criteria by which sets of people differentiate themselves from other sets have received the label 'tribal'; but the process of self-classification never ceases. The term 'ethnicity' has been introduced to illustrate only the Cameroon situation. 'Ethnicities' no more 'exist', with fixed criteria of definition, than do 'tribes'. They should certainly not be seized upon as some fixed stage on the path from tribe to nation. The discussion may merely help us to see how an ambiguity could arise in the Cameroon situation as to the nature of the reunification. The question will be raised in the next section of the source of that mass support which experience showed could always be evoked by skilled leaders in West Cameroon politics. The source lay, I suggest, in this 'ethnicity'. It would be possible to refer to it as a kind of West Cameroon 'nationalism' by which the borders of West Cameroon were idealised to include somewhat more territory than its legal ones. The terms 'nationalism' and 'tribalism' refer to overlapping sets of phenomena, and their ambiguities can only be resolved by avoiding any tendency to nominalism in their study.

A final remark should be made. After 1945 the influx of Ibo migrants from Nigeria to the plantation areas of West Cameroon grew very rapidly, and Cameroon separatism was marked by hostility to the Ibo, who in their turn came for many to symbolize the Nigerian connection. The relationship of Ibo migrants to receiving communities is a study of its own: hostility to this people was not confined to West Cameroon. It is sufficient here to note that the Ibo did not enter into the West Cameroon 'ethnicity'. In part they excluded themselves by their roles (as traders especially), as well as by aspects of their behaviour, which perhaps would have become less noticeable in time.[30] Since they came in large numbers only after the war, they had no opportunity to become assimilated, had they wished to be. By the 1950s the movement for political devolution was under way, and the very Nigerian-ness of the Ibo acted as a catalyst to the political expression of the West Cameroon 'ethnicity'. It is possible that the Ibo would always have symbolized the alien-ness of the Eastern Nigerian regional government to which until 1954 the territory was attached. As it was, the 'Nigeria' and the 'French Cameroons' of West Cameroon politics were very much reflections of the different esteem in which migrants from the two areas were held.[31]

2. The Political Movement

The Devolution Period: The Southern Cameroons

The transformation of the mandate into a Trust Territory of the United Nations (1946) was accompanied by (and to some extent caused) a quickening of the rate of economic and political change. Already, during the war the need for new sources of tropical products had directed attention to the Cameroons. A development plan had been drawn up by the Provincial Resident, as early as 1943. The vesting of the ex-German plantations in the Nigerian government for the benefit of the Trust Territory, the creation of new administrative entities, and the establishment of the Commissionership of the Cameroons all occurred in 1949. This coincided with several new waves of thinking, both among administrators and the growing political group among Cameroonians. The isolation of the Plateau from the provincial capital and the poor communications generally were now felt to be a scandal, and the northern roads were much improved. The growth of the independence movement in Nigeria had, at the same time, drawn Cameroonian expatriate organizations in Lagos into the National Council of Nigeria and the Cameroons (NCNC). A tour of the Cameroons Province by local politicians in 1946 as part of the campaign against the 'four obnoxious ordinances' was one of the first public manifestations of the new political period.[32]

It has been said earlier that the reunification of the Trust Territories of the Cameroons was a result of forces deriving both from the mandate/trusteeship system, and from the decolonisation of French and British Africa. The beginnings of the independence movement in the southern British Cameroons are inseparable from those of the Nigerian independence movement. This early stage was associated with P. M. Kale and others in the founding of the Cameroons Youth League (CYL) on 27 March 1940. It was Dr Endeley who most clearly grasped that the existence of the trusteeship provided an alternative mode of political action to that offered by Nigerian politics.[33] That two real alternatives existed may readily be seen. Had Nigerian politics been of no account at the critical period the United Nations might have become the only channel of appeal to sympathetic political circles outside the colonial territory. As it was, the NCNC agitation provided such an approach to circles of this type in England. In practice, the momentum of devolution came always from the vast energy of the Nigerian political movement. It soon became clear, however, that the use of the alternative political opportunities could differentiate the Southern Cameroons more and more within the Nigerian movement. It was as if, while the Nigerian machine was working for separation from the United Kingdom, the British Cameroonians had a simple device which could draw off some of the power generated and gear it to separate their own territory from Nigeria. The history of the political movement shows that each operation of it was irreversible.

The groupings which came into existence during the late 1940s need not detain us, except to note the participation of the French Cameroons Welfare Union, created by settled Easterners, and the early contacts with the nationalist leaders of the *Union des Populations du Cameroun* (UPC) Basically the personal divisions between the two future Premiers of the British Southern Cameroons, Dr Endeley and Mr J. N. Foncha, derived from that period, when they for a time belonged to different branches of the political movement. In 1951 the Macpherson constitution in Nigeria led to the representation of the Kamerun United National Congress (KUNC) and the Cameroons National Federation (CNF) in the Nigerian assemblies, in alliance with the NCNC. During the Eastern Region constitutional crises of 1953, Dr. Endeley, as leader of the 'Cameroons bloc', took the opportunity to press for the creation of a separate legislature for the southern British Cameroons. A group who wished to retain the NCNC connection with the Eastern Region formed the Kamerun People's Party (KPP) under P. M. Kale and N. N. Mbile. The remnant of the KUNC and the CNF united to form the Kamerun National Congress (KNC). At the 1953 Nigerian constitutional talks in London, Endeley received provisional acceptance of his demands, provided he won an election on the issue. This he achieved with ease and in 1954 the 'quasi-federal territory' of the Southern Cameroons was constituted. Dr Endeley became Leader of Government Business, after capturing nearly all the seats in the new House of Assembly.

Dr. Endeley's evident satisfaction with the Southern Cameroons' new position in the Nigerian Federation led, soon after, to the defection of John Ngu Foncha, who founded in 1955 the Kamerun National Democratic Party (KNDP), with the policy of complete secession from Nigeria and ultimate reunification of the two Cameroons. He was joined by Augustine Jua, then a 'Native Authority' member.[34] In that year the abortive revolt of the UPC in the French Trust Territory led members of the party to seek asylum within the Southern Cameroons, where they settled in Kumba. They fought an election without success, before being deported. The strong ideological background of the UPC gave some stimulus to the KNDP leadership, but the success of Foncha's party in increasing its membership in the House in the 1957 elections was based upon a non-radical programme (with the exception of the central theme of secession).

At the Nigerian constitutional conference of the same year, . Endeley achieved a further step in the advance to full regional status within the Federation. His virtually complete abandonment of reunification occasioned the crossing of an experienced member of the government, S. T. Muna, to Foncha's KNDP. The KNC, its majority threatened, sought the support of the KPP to form a governing 'Alliance'. On 15 May 1958 Endeley became Premier and ministerial government was introduced, but at elections in January 1959 the KNDP won control of the House of Assembly, and Foncha assumed the premiership. With Nigerian independence due the following year, much discussion took place at the United Nations and in the Southern Cameroons as to the timing of and questions to be asked at a plebiscite in which the territory would finally decide its future.[35]

By late September 1959 it was clear that the KNDP leadership were not inclined to early reunification after secession from Nigeria: some period of continued trusteeship was envisaged. Despite popular support for this conclusion, the two leaders eventually agreed at the United Nations to secession from Nigeria when it became independent on I October 1960, with continued trusteeship only until the implementation of the decision of a plebiscite on the future of the Southern Cameroons, to be held before March 1961.[36] It was held on 11 February of that year, and was fought by the KNDP government under the Premier, Mr Foncha, and by the KNC/KPP Alliance, now renamed the Cameroons National Peoples Convention (CPNC), under the Leader of the Opposition, Dr Endeley.[37]

Contradictions in the Reunification Movement

Two terms were used to express this situation as it developed: 'the Kamerun Idea' and the 'quasi-Left'. The former was intended to label that theme which singled out this special area from the mainstream of Nigerian political history'. It was partly symbolised by the common use of the German spelling *Kamerun,* which 'also carried with it the ideal of reunification of the two Cameroons'.[38] Its political appeal was not connected with any exact apprehension of the nature either of the undivided protectorate or of the future reunified state. As we saw at the beginning of this chapter, part of the effectiveness of the reunification argument derived from those simple formal properties which made it suitable for international political discussion. Its ready and permanent appeal to West Cameroonians of every level of education was less explicable. The term 'quasi-Left' was intended to elucidate this problem.

In Nigeria it was true that the most politically active groups aimed at the attainment of power through the direct control of the 'masses'. The ideology of the process was definable as 'Left' in tendency by foreign commentators, because: (1) the European Left was in general in agreement with the aims of such movements, (2) the leaders had often been influenced by writings of the European Left, (3) the alliance of 'the masses' with the intelligentsia against a dominant 'imperial' authority was thought to be a movement properly defined as 'Left'. It is true that many movements definable as 'Left' by these criteria were also 'Left' by other foreign criteria. The preoccupation of European and American observers with their own political categories led the general similarities to be stressed in such cases. But, while the movement for Nigerian independence answered for a time all three criteria of Leftness, the reunification movement in West Cameroon was only weakly definable by them as Left. In many respects there was little overlap with other criteria for Leftness. Thus the appeal to reunification by J. N. Foncha captured a mass following but was accompanied by moderate, even 'traditionalist' and 'pro-British', policies. In contrast, the losing pro-Nigerian party of Endeley at the peak of its achievement (at about 1958) had developed a strongly 'anti-traditionalist' and 'anti-imperialist' approach.[39] Within West Cameroon, the movement for reunification was a step to the 'Right' in many ideological senses, despite its ability to attract mass support.

Confusion was brought into the situation by the special development of the idea of reunification in the neighbouring French Trust Territory. There it had always been firmly attached to a 'Left' which was ideologically impeccably based upon world models. The UPC from 1951 pursued under Reuben Um Nyobe, and later Félix Moumié, a strongly Marxist line. After the rising in May 1955, and up to and after the independence of the eastern territory in 1960, the UPC movement carried on a running 'revolutionary' war whose repercussions have still not ended.[40] The reunification aim was a part of an ideological framework of a Marxist type. The mass support of the West Cameroon political movement, combined with its reunificationist purpose, thus gave it a Leftish gloss by association, and in the later years before 1961 it was supported by students and others who were repelled by the excesses of the UPC Left in the neighbouring territory. Once this happened a point of no return was reached. Each successive shift from the orbit of the Nigerian independence movement sent West Cameroon politicians at an accelerating pace into the orbit of reunification. The intermediate aim of 'secession' (with reunification in an unspecified future) was passed over in 1959;[41] there was no resting place to be found there, because of the 'quasi-Left' position of Foncha's party. From now on, any halt on the stages to reunification was greeted by impatience and disbelief on the part of the true 'Left': students, and intellectuals at home, abroad, or in the United Nations.[42] Foncha, probably remembering the fates of P. Kale and Endeley, never risked losing control of the mass movement to anyone offering a purer version of the Kamerun Idea. 'With each incipient split in his own party he hopped nimbly to the leftward.'[42]

The 'Kamerun Idea' was a compound of the 'ethnicity' described above and the political arguments for reunification. This accounts for its otherwise surprising self-contradictions. The Kamerun Idea had its own mythological consistency: West Cameroonians saw reunification as merely a grand affirmation of what West Cameroon already was. Only the isolation of the territory's politics could have enabled this idea to remain unmodified so long by experience of the actual development of events in the French Trust Territory. In East Cameroon the combination was quite other. The political argument for reunification was a consistent subordinate aim of that Marxist ideology which informed the independence movement from the beginning, and which made the running for the non-Marxist politicians who actually achieved power. In so far as the term 'Left' achieves its clearest definition only when used as a label for the Marxist political theory, this was a movement of the true Left. The West Cameroon movement would in its terms have been best called a bourgeois nationalist movement (merely 'secessionist' from Nigeria).

Lest these distinctions seem remote from local support it is worth citing a young West Cameroonian, who remarks:

> It is significant to note that there existed a slight and subtle difference between the movements for unification in the two Cameroons. In the British sector it was conceived not as a means to an end, that is: a weapon to achieve independence and sever relations with the colonial powers. It was an ideal and end in itself. On the other hand in the French sector it was in the short run a means to an end: it was like a weapon to rally the masses against colonialism, to get independence and to dictate terms on which French or British presence was to continue.

He adds that the question of recreating Cameroon 'involved the whole of the Cameroonian Personality'.[44] Njeuma's 'Cameroonian Personality' grows from anglophonic roots. But the East Cameroon movement was not without its own higher mysticism, derived in this case from more universalistic origins. It is well illustrated by the statement of Reuben Um Nyobe, cited by Willard Johnson: 'Chrétiennement parlant, tout le monde reconnaîtra que Dieu a créé un seul Cameroun; c'est là le point de départ'.[45] This kind of language provided a meeting point for the movements in the two Cameroons after reunification as much as before.

The Approach to Independence

The French Trust Territory moved to internal autonomy (1 January 1959), and to independence (1 January 1960). The UPC rebellion had by then lost its leaders, but the Cameroun Republic came into existence under President Ahidjo in a very perilous position.[46] Nigerian troops had been moved into the Southern Cameroons to guard against any spread of terrorism from the border. When Nigeria became independent herself on 1 October 1960 and withdrew her forces, British troops were brought, for the first time, into the territory. The Cameroons Trust Territory as a whole became also for the first time, a nominally separate unit under British administration. The previous federal services in the Southern

Cameroons were run by the Nigerian government on an 'agency', or contractual, basis.

At the plebiscite of 11 February 1961 Foncha received massive support:

	S. Cameroons	N. Cameroons
For the Cameroun Republic	235,571	97,659
For Nigeria	97,741	146,296

The Northern Cameroons passed to the Federation of Nigeria where it became Sardauna Province.[47]

Before the plebiscite, the British Administering Authority published a pamphlet which was widely distributed in the Southern Cameroons and contained the proposals of the two main parties regarding the future constitutional and administrative arrangements for joining the Cameroun Republic and Nigeria respectively. Both parties favoured federations. The pro-Nigerian CPNC had the advantage of an already operating federal system and their proposals were comparatively detailed. The KNDP, in favour of unification with Cameroun, on the other hand, drew up its proposals after meetings in 1960 with a partner which had no experience of federation, and with a very different political and administrative history. The Administering Authority had 'on several occasions enjoined upon those concerned the need for clarification of these terms'. The result from the pro-Cameroun side was two communiques (one of which included a 'Joint Declaration') totalling about 1,000 words, from the Prime Minister of the Southern Cameroons and the President of the Cameroun Republic, outlining certain constitutional possibilities.[48]

Soon after the plebiscite a conference of Southern Cameroons party representatives and chiefs was held at Bamenda (26-28 June 1961) to discuss the government proposals for the constitution of the reunified Cameroons. The course of the discussions is of some interest. It was decided not to press for 'concurrent' subjects in the new federal constitution, but to make a clear distinction between the rights of the States and of the Federation. This was done apparently to secure the greatest degree of autonomy for the States. There was some basis for this in the terminology of the Joint Declaration ('In non-federal matters the Authorities of each of the Federated States will have exclusive competence'). The Bamenda proposals for exclusive State rights were, however, later extensively whittled down. The absence of a concurrent field meant that wherever the Federation could prove a constitutional primacy the State government had no defined powers at all. The optimism (even the innocence) of the Bamenda proposals again reflect the isolation of Southern Cameroons politics. Separate State and Federal citizenship was to exist. There were to be Governors of the two States, and a quota of ministerial portfolios at the federal level for each State. Later there were even proposals that the federal capital should be established not at Yaounde, the capital of the Cameroun Republic, but at Douala. Nevertheless the *Two Alternatives* had foreshadowed certain of the Bamenda proposals, for example the establishment of a bicameral legislature at the centre.

In July an all-party delegation from the Southern Cameroons went to Foumban and met Presidential Ahidjo and his representatives. There they received the proposals of the Cameroun Republic. These passed over in silence most of the Bamenda proposals. The Southern Cameroons delegates found it necessary to devote their energy to salvaging a few only of their central points: the most notable of which was the preservation of the Southern Cameroons House of Chiefs (this promise had been made by Foncha before the plebiscite). The rest went—including certain items such as control of the police, and of education above the primary level, to which the Southern Cameroons had attached high priority. The federal capital was to be at Yaounde. 'The bicameral system in a federation is, without doubt, classic', said President Ahidjo, but 'it is necessary to lighten as much as possible our Parliamentary apparatus in relation to the resources at our disposal.'[50]

A tripartite conference of representatives of the British, the Cameroun, and the Southern Cameroons governments met at Yaounde in August.[51] The territory was faced with the departure of British troops on 1 October. Expatriate civil servants were already offered posts with the preservation of full pension rights (especially those to the valuable lump-sum compensation) in Nigeria. No comparable alternative terms were ever offered to those who wished to stay. The doubts over security had by now permeated all sections of the population.[52] At the conference the question of the phasing of replacement of British by Republic forces was solved. The final shape of the constitution was fixed. The atmosphere of haste and doubt of the months between February and October 1961 is superficially surprising, in view of the fact that reunification had been a recognised political aim for over a decade. Given the nature of the West Cameroon political movement this should, however, be comprehensible. During the same months red pillar-boxes (mail-receptacles) marked with the royal monogram E II R were delivered and set up in Buea, and duly announced to the press, as the first pillar-boxes in the Southern Cameroons.[53]

Since few observers have reported of that period in West Cameroon, some points may be noted. The worries over internal security were exaggerated by the heavy mantle of official silence preventing its discussion in West Cameroon. The British administration chose, perhaps correctly, to interpret security as a political matter having undoubted relevance to the plebiscite, and therefore not a matter for discussion by them, lest charges of interference be made. The representatives of the Cameroun Republic unwittingly compounded this situation. They came prepared to deal with hidden terrorists in the West who would burst out upon independence. Because of UPC operations near its borders, West Cameroon appeared to them to be the mountainous home of radicalism. On 8 August twelve labourers were shot in a plantation camp in West Cameroon.[54] Despite denials that security forces were involved, other fears were added to the fear of terrorists. It was quite clear, however, that there was then no real internal danger. The population, the security forces on both sides, the politicians, and the administration were the victims of the policy of silence. An 'invasion' by terrorists was impossible (they would have had to use the roads, without any transport). It remained to be seen whether there were any secret encampments near the capital: despite wild rumours, there were not.[55]

The evacuation of some dependents of foreign citizens took place (this was a year after the Congo crisis), a precaution which could not fail to exaggerate the pre-independence fears. The removal of British experts at this time appeared to many as a betrayal. There is no doubt that the career factors were overriding: many British advisers would have stayed if some clear guarantee could have been given concerning their position after independence. The suggestion of a United Kingdom Aid Mission foundered on this problem. The career choices of the highest officials had already been made, and there was no leadership for the middle and lower ranks. Certain officials were in addition asked not to stay. The uncertainties concerning security added further confusion, but by October many officials left with great reluctance. It is significant that most of those who did stay were, either through juniority or otherwise, relatively less affected by the Nigerian guarantees. Recently recruited 'contract' officers for example, who might have been expected to be influenced to leave by the prevailing uncertainty, remained—as did virtually all British plantation staff. In particular, the loss of British education officers was a blow.

It is unfortunate that the end of trusteeship should have been clouded in this way, for there is no doubt that West Cameroonians felt at a relative disadvantage after reunification compared with their well-advised

Eastern neighbours. But in retrospect it does not appear that much was lost. The crucial Permanent Secretaryship to the Ministry of Finance was occupied, by special arrangement, by a British Adviser for a considerable time. Sir Sydney Phillipson was also retained for six months. The Attorney-Generalship passed to a British West Indian of high calibre, who had served in the pre-existing legal department, and who occupied the post until September 1966. British Advisers remained with the Ministries of Education and Local Government. Not all these departments, however, found their negotiating position necessarily any stronger than those deprived of British advice. A highly-respected British official stayed on secondment to the Foreign Office as British Consul (1961-5) in Buea.

The Constitution

The federal constitution was signed by President Ahidjo on 1 September 1961, to come into force on 1 October 1961. A number of subjects were, by Article 5, to come under federal jurisdiction immediately upon independence. Of particular importance was 'internal and external security'. By Article 6 another list of subjects was to be temporarily placed under the jurisdiction of the respective States, but these were to become federal subjects as conditions permitted. This list was very comprehensive indeed. Most of these transitional powers were taken over to some extent or other by the federal government by 1967.

The subjects which were to fall permanently within the jurisdiction of the State government were less clear. None were specifically listed in the Law to Establish a Constitution for the Federated State of West Cameroon, which received the President's assent on 26 October 1961. The powers of the federated States were described in the federal constitution in this way: 'Any subject not listed in Articles 5 and 6, and whose regulation is not specifically entrusted by this Constitution to a federal law shall be of the exclusive jurisdiction of the Federated States, which within those limits, may adopt their own Constitutions' (Art. 38 (1)). The customary courts of West Cameroon (excluded from federal jurisdiction by name) and primary education (by inference not included under 'secondary and technical education') have some constitutional warrant for being taken as state subjects. It was further assumed by convention in the early years that there were also left to the West Cameroon State legislature: Local Government, Social Welfare, Archives and Antiquities, Agriculture, Forestry, Co-operatives, Internal Trade, State Public Works, and some other minor functions, but no list can be made which has any constitutional validity. In 1965, in fact, aspects of these subjects were also taken over. The West Cameroon State constitution does provide for the governing of the Police and Civil Service by independent Commissions, but even these powers of the State constitution might be excluded by Article 38 (1) of the federal constitution, should they be interpreted as being covered by Articles 5 and 6. The federal constitution also contains a safeguard (An. 18) by which the President or a State Prime Minister may demand the confirmation of federal legislation by a majority of the (federal) deputies of each State. This potentially powerful provision[56] turned out not to be directly relevant to the constitutional relations between the West and the Federation in the first five years, which were mainly mediated by the decree powers of the President.

One effect of the new constitution upon West Cameroon was apparent immediately. The principles of revenue allocation (by which the Nigerian regions had been financed) were not included in the new constitutional arrangements. It was the application of the rules of reallocation of federal revenues (from customs, and the like) that had enabled the Southern Cameroons to increase its services so rapidly in the last few years of its association with Nigeria. During the period of separation in 1960-1 the Southern Cameroons continued to rely upon customs and similar revenues collected within its territory. These fell disastrously after independence, and an annual federal subvention became necessary to balance the budget. The West Cameroon authorities regarded this as a temporary expedient to be replaced by a negotiated permanent system of revenue allocation.

The principle was not lost sight of by the West Cameroon State government, and it was a prominent concern of the present Prime Minister of the State, who was for so long the Minister of Finance. Nevertheless it seems unlikely that West Cameroon will ever be permitted any greater financial autonomy.

In devising a federal constitution that would incorporate West Cameroon, President Ahidjo and his advisers had to avoid creating one which would dangerously differentiate a new autonomous East Cameroon from federal control. It will be recalled that the structure of the Eastern State was created by an act of internal redefinition of the former Republic of Cameroun. Observers viewing the Federal Republic from within the West State usually fail to grasp that the constitution had to be worded in such a way that the federal organs could retain full control over the East State, while avowing a degree of *de facto* autonomy to the West. The possibility of the use of a state constitution by political groups in the East to detach the Presidency from the popular base was by no means a fantasy. President Ahidjo was a politician from the north of the State. Several regions in the southern part of the East State had been at one time or other in partial or full rebellion (Sanaga-Maritime, Bamileke, and Moungo), and only in 1964–5 did they really begin to return to normal. Curfews were still in operation through this period.[57] It has never been suggested what courses would have been open to the President if the autonomy West Cameroon sought at Foumban had been constitutionally accorded to the East. The Nigerian example did not encourage imitation, although no one foresaw the disaster that was to overtake that system in 1966.

President Ahidjo's own proposals provided for a constitution more centralized in some respects than that of the pre-existing Cameroun Republic, and enabled his control over the new East State to be increased:

> Under the Republic, President Ahidjo had been Head of State only, assisted by a Prime Minister who shared his powers with his Council of Ministers, but, under the Federation, the new President . . . was both Head of State and Head of Government. No longer would the Council of Ministers have a constitutional basis, or have to be consulted on the items that previously required its accord.[58]

The President acquired control over courts, the magistracy, and the civil service, and the right to exercise emergency powers without the existing controls of the legislature and the Council of Ministers. Nevertheless, the potential of the new East State appointments, which included a Prime Minister, cannot be entirely ignored.

What should surprise and interest is that West Cameroon achieved those *de facto* powers that it did under the circumstances. President Ahidjo's evident success at Foumban does not, I think, merit a recent judgment that Foncha's only 'victories' were 'hollow'. It would be a mistake to think that the Eastern negotiators experienced no anxieties themselves. The south of the British Trust Territory was in their view all too similar 'ethnically' and politically to the rebellious south of their own country, but its strong institutions inspired respect as well as disquiet. The Eastern representatives would have been guilty of neglect of their duty if they had not felt it necessary to negotiate as many overriding powers in the constitution as possible. That Foumban was marked by few concessions from the Eastern side should not obscure the fact that the West State, despite its undoubtedly inferior negotiating position, achieved (indeed was accorded) a degree of autonomy which survived at least for five years, and outlived the Nigerian regions in whose company it had begun its existence.

3. Economic Consequences of Reunification

The effects of reunification were felt by West Cameroon most consistently in the economic sphere. When only the West State was called upon to make institutional adjustments it was clearly not in the interest of the Federal Republic as a whole that it should be a serious liability. There is no doubt, however, that the West Cameroon economic position in the 1950s was much sounder than it subsequently became, and even at that time warnings of its delicate basis had been given.

In the years 1959–61, two reports of economic relevance to the West State were commissioned by the old Southern Cameroons government, and one by the Cameroun Republic. The Phillipson report was compiled between July and October 1959 to determine the fiscal viability of the Southern Cameroons if it *seceded* from the Federation of Nigeria. At that stage (it will be recalled) government opinion had crystallised momentarily in favour of a fairly long period of secession from Nigeria under British trusteeship. Sydney Phillipson specifically did not consider the consequences of an early unification with the French Trust Territory (then some months before independence), nor the possibility of separate independence. He concluded that the revenues of a seceded Southern Cameroons 'might just suffice to enable it to maintain and even modestly to expand its recurrent services, but it would be a precarious hand-to-mouth existence'.[60] Moreover, capital expenditure of £1 million a year was needed for the development of the infrastructure, especially communications. The report did not favour a customs barrier between a seceded Southern Cameroons and Nigeria, but considered a customs union between the two countries combined with a revised system of revenue allocation, as the 'least unsatisfactory' solution. The report was superseded by events, even during its preparation. The contingency it envisaged was rejected at the United Nations. It may be noted that Phillipson accepted the Agricultural Department's view that the output of export crops might be doubled in twelve years. This belief reflected the optimism of the period of the export boom of the 1950s. Since, as we shall see, this prediction (after half the period has elapsed) has not begun to be realized, it is not surprising that the modest limits of viability foreseen by the report were not maintained.

The Berrill report,[61] presented in August 1960, only seven months before the plebiscite, was a more general survey of the economy of the

Southern Cameroons. Berrill noted that in the previous five or six years (which coincided with the period of regional autonomy) there had been a great rise in expenditure on public works and roads, and the government's recurrent and capital outlays had doubled. By early 1961 recurrent expenditure alone would be £2½ million. The great expansion in government recurrent expenditure, he stressed, had been 'made possible rather by revised revenue allocations between the regions and the Federation [of Nigeria] than by the natural buoyancy in Government income'. It was estimated that the revenue in 1965 would be about £3¼ million. This would scarcely meet probable recurrent expenditure; it would not support any capital investment programme at all. However, the Cameroons Development Corporation had received £1 million of a £3 million loan expected from the Commonwealth Development Corporation and this was giving grounds for optimism.

Berrill's report shows the efforts made by the Southern Cameroons government to cope with the problem of communications and, once more, the precarious balance upon which the rapid recent progress had been made. The remarks on revenue allocation underline the significance of the loss of that prop at reunification. The estimated revenue for 1964-5 turned out to be 2,000 million francs CFA (£3 million) and the estimated deficit 240 million francs CFA (£360,000).

The Berrill report largely ignored the problem of the political future of the Southern Cameroons. A third report, commissioned by the Cameroun Republic in the pre-plebiscite period, examined the economic aspects of any possible reunification of the Southern Cameroons with the Republic. This report, by K. Andersen, a Norwegian, was prepared in the period from early December 1960 to the middle of February 1961, and deals with problems of finance, trade, and administration.[63] Andersen considered the possibility of (a) keeping a sterling currency in use in West Cameroon and a franc currency in East Cameroon; (b) allowing two currencies to circulate at once in both areas;[64] and (c) changing from the pound to the franc in West Cameroon. He favoured the third possibility for the following main reasons: that a change from the Nigerian pound to another currency would probably be insisted on by Nigeria;[65] that entry to the franc zone would make West Cameroon eligible for the relatively generous French aid and also to aid from Common Market sources; and in general that access to the markets of the EEC would be beneficial.

Andersen also recommended a harmonisation of import policy, and hoped that it would be possible for Commonwealth preference for bananas to be phased off gradually over a number of years. He suggested that, temporarily, the federal budget should be financed by contributions to be determined with due regard to the economic conditions prevailing in the two territories. The problem of raising additional revenue to cover the rise in total public expenditure was to be the responsibility of the States or regions, until appropriate revenue sources could be federalized. For administration, Andersen hoped that technical aid would be available to tide West Cameroon over the transitional period. He ended by underlining the need for the Federation to plan carefully in order to encourage foreign capital investment. Incidentally, it is interesting that, in the February before reunification, Andersen had been given no clear indication of the constitutional nature of the reunified Cameroon for which he was to plan.

Currency and Banking

Andersen's currency recommendation was adopted. Following independence, and after several months of preliminary propaganda, the CFA franc became legal tender on 2 April 1962. Nigerian notes, and all bank and book balances, were converted at the rate of 692 CFA francs to the £ sterling (coin to be changed at 35 CFA francs to the shilling). Exchange counters were opened in all the main centres, usually at the branches of banks, and mobile exchange offices circulated in all areas. A period of two months—later extended to three—was given for the change-over. On the same date, certain exchange-control measures were brought into effect in West Cameroon. With the introduction of the CFA franc, West Cameroon left the sterling zone for the franc zone, and ceased to be a Scheduled Territory. The official exchange rate of the CFA franc to the £ sterling later dropped a little from that at independence; in December 1964 it fell to 681 francs to the pound, but began climbing almost immediately.

In general, the physical conversion went smoothly, although there were inevitably some local misunderstandings.

> The Government issued a propaganda poster, in which was printed in large letters, '692 FRANCS=£1'. In each bottom corner of the sign was a hand, one with four pound notes, the other with four thousand franc bills. Seeing such a graphic suggestion of equality many people refused to accept the established rate, demanding 1,000 francs instead of 692. To prevent further misunderstanding, the Government blocked out the offending bands.[66]

In contrast there were also stories circulating of innocent villagers who exchanged their pound notes to more knowing neighbours for 100 franc notes. There was a reluctance in some remote places to accept the new money, especially where trade moved to and from Nigeria, and Nigerian currency was hoarded and used for some time, although for official purposes, such as tax, Nigerian currency was invalid. In addition, a widespread disdain arose for the low-value 1- and 2-franc aluminium pieces, known from their appearance as 'white francs', and eighteen months after their introduction, at the government party conference in August 1963, it was even suggested that traders should be forced to accept them. West Cameroon had, however, seen currency changes before, and the idea was not novel. The Mark was remembered by many, and the Mark itself had been commonly known as the 'shilling' in the German period: a memory of the pre-Mark currency dominant in the Old Cameroons before 1884. In the minds of some the successive changes were linked with the long-term inflation throughout the colonial period. The 'rounding-up' of prices which occurs with such changes was even expected and foreseen by some West Cameroonians.

The banking structure was for a time only slightly modified. Barclays Bank, DCO, had long been established in West Cameroon, and in 1958 a branch of the Bank of West Africa had been opened in Victoria. These banks remained in operation after independence. It was not until 1965 that a branch of the Banque Camerounaise de Développement was established in West Cameroon.[68] The population at large was more affected by the closing down of all Nigerian Post Office Savings Banks. Investors were asked to withdraw their deposits, and it was not until 1 July 1963 that post offices in West Cameroon began again to operate Savings Accounts.

A new bank with West Cameroon government support (the Cameroon Bank Ltd) opened in Kumba, branches being set up soon afterwards in the main urban centres. West Cameroonians served on the Board of Directors, and the staff was expanded to include foreign and Cameroonian personnel. State government accounts were lodged with it, and a considerable saving business was done. Disastrous mismanagement, including an over-liberal loans policy, led the Bank into difficulties and, in 1966, civil service salaries could not be paid. Financial help had to be sought from the federal government. The Board of Directors was replaced by a committee, mainly of senior West Cameroon civil servants, under the chairmanship of the Financial Secretary.

Commonwealth Preference and Bananas

At the peak of their importance, in 1958, bananas contributed about one-half the total value of exports from the Southern Cameroons. In the United Kingdom they enjoyed a 15 per cent preference over non-Commonwealth imports, amounting to £7 10*s* a ton. Preference on the other main exports (cocoa, rubber, timber, coffee, palm oil, and palm kernels) either did not exist or was of smaller importance. Nearly all the bananas exported at this time, as well as the bulk of other exports, went to UK markets.

Andersen argued that the immediate discontinuance of the preference 'would have serious effects on banana exports, the incomes of producers and traders, on the Government's financial position and, indeed, on the whole economy of the territory'.[69] The possibility of recouping from trade with the EEC was not very great. There was little hope of increasing exports to France, while in Italy there was a state import monopoly which discriminated in favour of Somalia. Andersen recommended that an agreement be sought with the United Kingdom to remove the preference only gradually over a number of years. He viewed the difficulty over bananas as an urgent but essentially short-term problem, which a gradual switching of production to other crops and long-term expansion of EEC markets would ease.

Andersen's recommendation was accepted, and under the United Kingdom Finance Act, 1961, it was arranged for the Southern Cameroons to remain within the Commonwealth preference area until 1 October 1962. This period was extended to 30 September 1963, before which time the position was to be reviewed again. In 1962 West Cameroon bananas accounted for one-fifth of the total banana consumption of the United Kingdom.[70]

On 6 May 1963 President Ahidjo arrived in London on an official visit, during which the continuation of Commonwealth Preference for West Cameroon was discussed. But objections had been raised by West Indian banana-growers, and legislation for the removal of the preference was passed on 22 July 1963.[71] It is probable that the introduction into West Cameroon (even in modified form) of the import-licensing and exchange-control policies of East Cameroon, which would be likely to divert West Cameroon purchases away from the United Kingdom, also influenced the British government's decision. The abolition of the preference after only two years was a disappointment in Yaounde and in Buea.

The latest figure for banana exports available to Andersen was that for 1958, the peak year of banana income. But by 1960 (the last complete year under United Kingdom trusteeship) the income from banana exports had already fallen off, because of low prices (the tonnage exported was almost the same as in 1958), and they now formed only 31 per cent of total export earnings. Thus the banana industry was already playing a diminished part on the eve of independence. The profitability of bananas was already declining because of disease, rising labour costs, and lower world prices. After independence, and after entry into the franc zone, the value of banana exports did indeed fall further. In 1964 (when they provided 21 per cent of total export earnings) they amounted to only 39 per cent of the figure for 1958. But if banana exports declined, so did the value of other exports from West Cameroon. The year 1960 had seen their peak, of which their value in 1962 was only two-thirds, although in 1964 it climbed to 82 per cent. West Cameroon exports in total were also highest in 1960. In 1964 they fell to 72 per cent of this value, or only about the same as in 1957. The effects of the cancellation of Commonwealth Preference, as such, were highlighted then by a general export decline from the boom days up to 1960. It was a misfortune for West Cameroon that her trading difficulties should have coincided with her embarkation on a new political venture.

Economic Interregnum 1961—5

For the first four or five years of the reunification the major economic achievement for West Cameroon was limited to the change in her currency.[72] It was an irony that the State existed in an unbalanced version of that autarky which had been specifically excluded from consideration as early as the Phillipson report. On 1 October 1961 a customs barrier was established with Nigeria, and that between the East and West States was maintained. The latter decision could be defended: the difference in cost of living between the two newly united States (generally higher in the East, or in that part of the East closest to West Cameroon) made it seem rash to abolish the customs barrier without careful consideration of the consequences. Perhaps this *cordon douanier* would have been to the advantage of West Cameroon if (1) the flow of imports from Nigeria had been maintained at its pre-unification level, (2) the East-West customs barrier had not exempted locally-produced goods, other than major export products (such as bananas, coffee, rubber, and cocoa). The first repercussion was a sudden drop in revenue from taxes on beer and cigarettes from Nigeria with the influx of these items from East Cameroon. In the first year, the federal government agreed to make a subvention to offset this loss. By 1964–5 the subvention accounted for two-thirds of the estimated West Cameroon revenue of £3 million. The necessity to apply annually for federal help over the years made the economic arguments for the federalization of many State services irresistible.

The contrary flow of cheap foodstuffs to the East was widely held to have produced a steep rise in the cost of plantains, cocoyams, and other staples in the West. Furthermore, the local retail trade, like the traffic with Nigeria, depended upon Nigerians, especially Ibo, who could hardly view reunification as a good trading prospect. The West Cameroon Minister of Internal Trade stated later[73] that at independence many retailers left and prices rose. In addition the entry of West Cameroon into the franc zone involved strict exchange regulations. In June 1962 offices of the Federal Exchange Control and of the Department of Foreign Trade were established at Victoria. Although traders might apply for currency for the importation of goods from Nigeria, the effect was to reduce their flow considerably. A further factor in the slowing of internal trade between 1961 and 1963 lay in the frequent road-blocks of the Federal Gendarmerie, which increased the difficulties of local entrepreneurs, in an area already notorious for poor communications. Mamfe, the former entrepôt for Nigeria, ceased its growth, and the half-finished houses of traders, begun in the pre-independence period, gave part of it the appearance of a ghost-town.

The exchange-control system, even though not applied with the same rigour as in East Cameroon, introduced difficulties into overseas trade. Trade with the sterling area was limited to a part of the needs of importers, who had difficulty in obtaining suitable non-sterling supplies. As Andersen had noted, the import policies of the two Cameroons had been different as a result of their connexions with sterling and the franc. In the Southern Cameroons most goods could be imported from anywhere without restriction, except that imports from the Eastern bloc were subject to licensing. In the Republic there had been no restrictions on imports from France—which was the source of between one-half and two-thirds of the Republic's imports—or other franc zone countries, whereas imports from all other sources were subject to licensing (although the restrictions with EEC countries were being relaxed). Andersen had argued that since the liberal import policy of the Southern Cameroons would have to be continued if Britain were to be persuaded to maintain the Commonwealth preference for Southern Cameroons' bananas, the harmonisation of the foreign-trade policies of the two parts of the Federal Republic would have to be gradual. He recognized that this gradual harmonization would require the continuance of customs between West and East Cameroon, in order to prevent the free importation through West Cameroon of non-franc goods intended for the East.

Commenting on the situation in 1964 the West Cameroon budget memorandum said:

> Exchange Control and Import Licensing are still the vexing question they have been since their introduction in West Cameroon. However, though not much success has been achieved in convincing the Authorities concerned to modify them or to fit them to the particular circumstances of West Cameroon, their effect on the trade of the country appears to be less pernicious and less deleterious now than was once the case, this being so partly because the staff operating them are becoming more experienced and therefore more deft, and partly because the initial irritation they caused to businessmen when they were newly introduced has lost much of its sting as people are learning to accommodate, or maybe, to resign themselves, to the new situation.[74]

For two or three years the total effect of all the new measures was to increase the tendencies to stagnation in the West Cameroon economy, and to encourage a rapid rise in the cost of living. In 1963 it was reported that a rise of 25 per cent was estimated over 1960-1 prices.[75] Nevertheless, prices were still markedly higher in East Cameroon. It is clear that the West Cameroon government, despite institutional appearances, lacked any control over the economy. The population blamed the situation upon the franc; the government was convinced that only the East-West customs barrier held back complete chaos. The function of this barrier was, as we have seen, ambiguous, and several visiting economic observers recommended its abolition. While it existed the whole question of the different wage structures, within and between occupations, obtaining between the two states was postponed. The fact that the West Cameroon structures underlay its state institutions, for example the civil service, made the postponement a partially political matter. From the Federal/East side the possibility of the need for financial subsidies to tide over the West and even of unanalysed repercussions upon local interests, added to the arguments for caution.

Private investment showed a marked decline during the years immediately following reunification,[76] from 215 million francs CFA in 1958 to 113 million in 1962. The 'parting gift' of the United Kingdom to West Cameroon (£575,000) was almost all absorbed by 1962 in meeting a deficit on the Development Fund, due to outstanding capital works.[77] During the years 1962-4 many attempts were made by the West Cameroon government to improve the economic situation. The West Cameroon Development Agency engaged in several joint projects: for example in December 1963 a trading corporation (UCTC) was established with the co-operation of the Swiss Union Trading Company. At the same time the Cameroon Commercial Corporation was established as a retail distributor for both rural and urban areas in an attempt to counteract the shrinkage of retail trade since independence. Indian firms began to play an important role for almost the first time at West Cameroon. Attempts were made to establish new industries but on a small scale and with limited success.[78] The details of the finance of some of these operations contained obscurities and there was some critical press comment. Praiseworthy attempts although they were to bring new enterprises into West Cameroon, perhaps the impossible had been expected. This was a high-risk area; the need to secure adequate profit margins was not clearly grasped. The most successful government intervention was the introduction of a West Cameroon State Lottery, which was set up with technical assistance from Israel.

Plantation and peasant agriculture remained, despite all difficulties, the only mainstay of the economy. The Cameroon Development Corporation (CDC— CamDev) had, on reunification, lost eligibility for £2 million of the £3 million originally promised for future capital development when its management was taken over in 1960 by the British Colonial (subsequently Commonwealth) Development Corporation (CDC—ComDev).[79] The cutback in banana production, begun after the boom of the 1950s, continued. Many estates were completely replanted with other crops, and the labour force continued to decline from its peak of 25,000 in 1953-5 to 13,000 in 1963. The co-operative ventures which had increased peasant export production spectacularly in the 1950s[80] ran into difficulties. The vast banana co-operative movement, which was associated with the Leader of the Opposition, Dr Endeley, passed through a gloomy period in which its management fell under political scrutiny. Nevertheless, in 1964 peasants still exported 50,000 metric tons of bananas against CamDev's 17,000. They also exported 4,600 tons of cocoa against CamDev's 154 tons, and 16,000 tons of palm-oil and kernels against the Corporation's 6,000 tons. Peasant coffee exports were in addition over 6,000 tons.[81]

The memorandum accompanying the State budget for 1964-5 exclaimed:

> The West Cameroon Budget . . . has been drawn up in circumstances not dissimilar to those which surrounded the Pharisee, Nichodemus, who, perplexingly overwhelmed by his realisation of the greatness of the miracles of the Great Master, decided to pay the latter a nocturnal visit in order to enquire of Him about the way to eternal bliss. We too, engrossed in the overwhelming magnitude of the great task with which reunification has confronted us, may consider visiting some sage in order to enquire how we can, in the light of the problems involved, successfully accomplish this complex experiment of reunification.[82]

Observers who arrived during this economic period were inclined to imagine that it was due to the condition in which the country had been left after thirty years of British rule. It is worth remembering (without glossing over the fact that the Trust Territory was never given development priority within Nigeria) that even the conditions of 1959 had not been restored. Without minimising the important building and other developments of the post-independence period, and recognizing the inadequate investment in roads at all times, communications were better maintained in (say) 1960 than at any time in the following five years. The strain upon government recurrent expenditure was in no small measure responsible for the almost derelict appearance of the country. Such as it was, the economy of the old Southern Cameroons had still been running and the optimism reflected in parts of the Phillipson and Berrill reports was that of the political and administrative leadership of the time. One effect of reunification was the complete eclipse of all previous work upon the economic problems of West Cameroon. It was assumed that no information of any kind was available, and the state was approached like some nineteenth-century slab of darkest Africa. One amateur prospector even appeared. The duplication and reduplication of effort was ultimately valuable, but it can be said that not until 1964 did as much basic information about West Cameroon emerge as had been known in the British period. In this the British suffered the oblivion which for so long, in their own day, had covered the work of the Germans.

The New Period

If the first five years be regarded as economically an interregnum, the new period may be said to begin with the coming to fruition of various movements begun after 1963. Symptomatic of these were: the creation of a Statistics Department (1963), the undertaking of a demographic survey (1964), the activities of the United States Aid mission mainly after 1963, and the report of the Stanford research team (1964-5). An important change at the federal level was the entry of Cameroon into the *Union Douanière et Economique de l'Afrique Centrale* (UDEAC) by a treaty of 8 December 1965.

Among the most important signs of the new period were the beginnings of a serious attack upon the physical isolation of West Cameroon, which had had so dominating an influence on its affairs. In the first years after reunification little progress in land communications had been made, unless the change-over from driving on the left to driving on the right be so considered (it turned out to be a formality attended with no dislocation).[83] The virtual cessation of the traffic with Nigeria had not been balanced by a significant improvement of road communications with the East, while the internal roads began to deteriorate because of the government's financial difficulties. An improvement of the link between the capital and the coast (begun before reunification and completed by 1963) was the exception to this. To some extent Buea ceased to be a mountain suburb. New town roads were built in 1964 and 1965. The developments largely destroyed that picturesque quality which its centre had possessed in the previous fifty years of its existence, and marked its movement into a new urban phase.

Otherwise the interregnum had been marked by the growth of air services. An airstrip at Bali, near Bamenda, brought the plateau within an hour of the coast. Flights to Douala and Yaounde were scheduled after independence, and regular flights were instituted to Bali and Mamfe. In 1964 the first aeroplane landed precariously at Akwaya in the remote Mamfe 'Overside'. Cameroon Air Transport was a firm which grew out of the charter opportunities of the plebiscite period. The increased traffic arising from the needs of AID and the Peace Corps and, for inter-state services, of political leaders and technicians was an important reason for its expansion. To anyone who knew the country in the previous decades the development of air services was perhaps the most striking feature of the interregnal quinquennium. It was possibly symbolic that in 1966 Cameroon Air Transport encountered grave financial difficulties. An essentially small-scale organisation, managed by a British pilot, it had possibly reached the point at which the informal methods of its heyday were no longer appropriate.

On land the first important development was the surveying in 1963 of a link between the northern railway in East Cameroon and the West Cameroon entrepôt of Kumba. Since long before independence it had been the dream of some West Cameroon politicians, including S. T. Muna, to connect West Cameroon to Douala by rail. The project was no doubt furthered by the fact that Muna became Federal Minister of Communications. It was, however, part of a large expansion programme of the federal railways system which was to join Chad and Cameroon.[84] Also in 1963 a survey of the Kumba-Mamfe road (the central north-south route) was begun by AID engineers, and in May 1965 the United States gave the Federal Republic aid to the value of $5 million, including a loan of $3·2 million at a low rate of interest for the reconstruction of the roads (confirmed by an agreement between the United States and Cameroon in April 1966). To this valuable accession was added, in June 1965, 725 million francs CFA from the Common Market *Fonds Européen de Développement* (FED) for improving the metalled part of the road south of Kumba (which had since 1961 become almost impassable) and making a new road connexion with the East Cameroon network. FED experts arrived in West Cameroon in March 1966 to examine the scheme.

The new period was thus marked by real progress in the most ancient of West Cameroon's problems. The most striking decision, however, and one which may be said really to inaugurate the period (and indeed to mark a break with the whole of the previous economic history of Cameroon) was that to unite the coastal modernised belt of West Cameroon with Douala, in the East, the main port of the Federation (population 130,000). The intervening joint estuarine system of the Mungo and Wouri rivers barred access by land except by the circuitous route north to Kumba, from there to the East Cameroon northern road, and then south to Douala (over 150 miles). The port facilities of West Cameroon were at Victoria and Tiko. The former was a roadstead, and the latter had a wharf which could hold one ship. An expert of the World Bank had noted that the capacity of Douala was limited by its own estuarine position, and by the need to dredge the channel for tankers. He recommended that Victoria be enlarged and linked with Douala by road via Tiko. At the time, this proposal appeared almost outrageous in its implications, but a study made by the Société Générale d'Exploitations Industrielles (SOGEI) showed that Ambas bay with a combined Victoria/Bota port could be made into a deep-water harbour 'serving the Cameroon and probably the land-locked republics to the North and West'. It would accommodate 'many of the vessels composing the world tanker fleet'.' The recommendation was repeated in the report of the Stanford research team, which proposed that about 3,500 million francs CFA should be spent upon the deep-water port, which was expected to come into use in 1970, before Douala port reached its natural limits in 1972. It was recommended that it should specialize in handling petroleum products, for which an oil refinery should be built near

Victoria. Tiko would specialize as a banana port.[87]

On 10 October 1965 President Ahidjo inaugurated work on the new road which ran from the national route north of Douala to the West Cameroon road-head at Tiko. It was to cost 800 million francs CFA, towards which French financial aid was provided. Work, which began at both ends, was expected to be completed in 1967, reducing the distance from Tiko to Douala to approximately 56 kilometres. Soon afterwards, on 6 December 1965, the first train reached Ediki in West Cameroon on 'Mr Muna's' railway line. This part of the line was financed by France. The second phase, to take the line north to Kumba, was to be financed by FED.

During this time the fiscal isolation of West Cameroon was also at last abandoned. The UDEAC Treaty, which came into effect on 1 January 1966, required that the West Cameroon tariff system should be completely and finally harmonized with that of East Cameroon, and the internal barrier abolished. A transitional period was granted until 1 July 1966. One account of the consequences states that:

> the most serious repercussions of this new system will be on the cost of living in West Cameroon. So far the new duties are just beginning to be felt in West Cameroon, though they did not apply to goods shipped in 1965 for delivery in 1966. But what they are likely to mean can be seen from a few examples. Under the old tariff both rice and flour, two fairly staple commodities, were imported into West Cameroon free of duty. Under the new rate, rice from non-Common Market or non-OCAM states will pay 20 per cent common external tariff, while flour will pay 30 per cent; both commodities will pay 10 per cent import duty, 14 per cent supplementary tax and 4 per cent 'transaction' tax. Rice and flour from Common Market or OCAM countries will pay the last three duties only.[88]

In addition, all imports into West Cameroon *except* those from the franc zone became subject, as in East Cameroon, to full import licensing and exchange-control regulations. The nettle was at last grasped. As some compensation for the adverse effects of the tariff harmonisation, West Cameroon was to receive a further subsidy from the federal government to increase government salaries. In addition a subsidy would be paid to the state of 15 million francs CFA to 'help distribute foodstuffs in the West'. Subsidies were also to be paid to help food production and the improvement of feeder roads from farms to markets.

Finally, the bases for a new development plan became available after the growth of new statistical services. The old Southern Cameroons Five-

Year Development Plan 1961–6 which appeared before reunification was never implemented. In 1964 the federal government commissioned an economic survey. It was contracted by AID to the American commercial Stanford Research Institute, whose report appeared in June 1965. The report, while noting that West Cameroon exports had not yet been restored to the levels before independence, that foreign investment had declined, and that prices and wages might rise on the harmonization of customs procedures, recognized the economic importance of the new road programme and of recent arrangements for the banana industry.[89] The report outlined a ten-year development programme of 48,800 million CFA francs ($194·8 million, or £75 million), with an annual investment rising from the 1962-3 figure of just over 2,000 million francs CFA to about 7,000 million by 1975. This programme, it estimated, would result in an average annual increase in per capita GDP of 5·2 per cent, which is comparatively rapid by standards prevailing in most developing countries.[90] The recurrent budget was expected to be increased from the 1963/64 figure of 2,200 francs CFA to at least 4,500 in 1975, partly because of the harmonization of the fiscal regimes of the two States.

Economic Factors: Conclusion

The first five years of reunification required economic adjustment from West Cameroon. In retrospect, the chief symptoms of decline in what is called here the interregnum period were apparently a direct consequence of the stopping of the momentum of development by the political change itself. If the movements of after 1963 had been welded to the situation of (say) 1960, it is possible that the poor situation of West Cameroon might have been avoided. This would be, however, only an argument for earlier reunification and that was, for political reasons, not feasible. The financial dependence of the State upon the Federation, which had begun with the subventions to offset the loss of customs receipts, was increased in 1966 by the collapse of the Cameroon Bank, and crowned by the repercussions of UDEAC. The illusion of economic independence was over. The new period seems certain to be of much deeper significance. The growth of Victoria as a deep-sea port will require the first significant adjustments on the part of the East Cameroon economy. More important, the isolation of West Cameroon looks as if it will be decisively breached.

4. *Social and Political Adjustments*

Administrative

Administratively, the first years were marked by a process of adaptation between the powers of the West Cameroon Prime Minister, J. N. Foncha (who was, until 1965, also Vice-President of the Republic), and of the Federal Inspector of Administration, an official appointed to West Cameroon by the President. Under the Federal Inspector the District Officers, by now all West Cameroonians, were also appointed as Prefects (*Préfets*). They had thus a dual role. For State purposes, including local government, they came, as District Officers, under the West Cameroon Prime Minister and the West Cameroon Ministry of Local Government. For federal purposes, including security and the co-ordination of federal services in the Divisions (as Prefectures) they fell under the Federal Inspector. As more and more departments became federalized after 1963, his position became inevitably more important.[91]

The situation can be viewed from two points of view: (1) from that of the growth of the administrative structure, and (2) from that of the relations between West Cameroon and the Federation. The conclusions from these two points of view are not identical. It is commonplace to render a chain of command in the form of a quasi-genealogical chart. It is thereby easily assumed that all power relations expressed in the form of such a chart are those of a chain of command. This is a fallacy: relations of competition and power may be similarly mapped out, in which the power at each level in the structure may not be *delegated* to lower levels, but may be (on the contrary) a kind of residuum (continually being redefined) deriving from unresolved conflicts at the lower levels. Although this distinction is known to all students of affairs, the formulation in advance of 'chains of command' tends to direct the attention merely to the former aspect of administrative structures. It is also true that this is the one most often expressed in the French mode of administration, upon which the federal levels in Cameroon were based. The British mode, because of its stress on 'development from below',[92] was always to some extent a mixed system. The attachment of local-government organs to the British administrative hierarchy did not, as a result, constitute a chain of command. Similarly the attachment of the whole West Cameroon system to the federal hierarchy did not constitute a chain of command. Since it may be argued that the 'French' system is in itself only an idealized construct (a 'model'), and that the chain of command is everywhere a compromise, it may be adequate to say that discontinuities occur in the administrative relationship between the Federation and West Cameroon which that 'model' does not reveal.

The administrative structure, as it had become by September 1964, is well depicted in the chart in the Stanford report.[93] On 7 May 1965 it was further modified after the separation of the Vice-Presidency from the Prime Ministership of West Cameroon[94] and (soon afterwards) by the transfer of several more of the functions of the State ministries to the federal level. The position of the Federal Inspector is clearly of great academic interest. To revert to the terminology used earlier, the Federal Inspector operates in a different logical space from that in which the West Cameroon system operates. By the axioms of this space, he is part of a chain stretching from the President to the subdivisions. The elements in this space are, however, already organised into sets which form parts of the West Cameroon political space. This applies even to some federal departments which from the chart appear, in their administrative aspects, to belong to the Inspector's space. Thus the chief Law Officer, paid from federal funds, was the Attorney-General, an official of ministerial status, with a seat in the West Cameroon Executive Council.

The period 1961-5 was thus not marked by the administrative 'absorption' which was stressed by many observers. The Inspectorate appeared to interpret itself initially as virtually of equivalent status to the Prime Ministership, although possibly of a lower one than the Vice-Presidency. Since both these offices were held by Mr Foncha at the time, a certain ambivalence appeared in the relationship. The West Cameroon interpretation was certainly that the official had a lower status than the Executive Council. At the funeral of the Speaker in August 1966, the Inspector was given precedence after State Parliamentary Secretaries, but before the Attorney-General, Chief Justice, and members of the legislative assemblies. In part the uncertain position of the Inspectorate derived from the *de facto* allocation of 'local government' to West Cameroon. Under the British system, as is well known, much of the local administration devolved upon the Native Authorities and, in some areas, their elected successors: the local government councils. They had their own organs: treasuries, courts, works, and the like. The administrative officers were, in the last years of British rule, in the process of 'withering away'. In their role as Advisers to the local government councillors they were essentially agents of the Ministry of Local Government. Their responsibilities for security and as members of a career service came under the Deputy Commissioner. In a sense the Federal Inspector inherited directly only some of the powers of the British Deputy Commissioner, which by the logic of British colonial policy had at independence been largely devolved out of existence.

On the other side the local government organs, based firmly upon ethno-administrative tribalities created in the 1930s, acquired a constitutional strengthening at independence by the recognition of the West Cameroon House of Chiefs and of the non-federal nature of the customary courts. The members of both were selected from defined members of these local units, by criteria firmly under the control of the Ministry of Local Government and the Prime Minister. It is probable that the drafters of the constitution did not expect the boundary between local government (visualised provisionally as a state subject) and administration (a federal subject) to be drawn in this way.

The Inspectorate thus initially lacked the *de facto* control that it appeared to have on paper. Nevertheless, tours of the Divisions by the Inspector, in their aspect as Prefectures, and the practice of personally installing incoming District Officers, in their aspect as Prefects, were not without their function in building up the role of the new official. Any careful analysis of the reunification period up to 1966 would require a more detailed consideration of the Inspectorate than would be appropriate to attempt here. In retrospect it can be seen that, with the relaxation of fears about internal security, the office entered into a less self-conscious relationship with the state government. In many respects this period matches that which I have called the economic interregnum. In 1966 the number of federal services in West Cameroon was such that West Cameroonians themselves were representing the federal government at ministerial level. 'Federalization' was also to some extent 'Westernisation', and the 'foreignness' of the federal services symbolised by the French-speaking Federal Inspector was becoming rapidly dissipated. Nevertheless, a structural tension remained inherent in the relationship of this official to the Prime Minister and Executive Council of West Cameroon.

The present discussion is closely linked to that concerning the constitution, of which the administrative structure is merely one of the manifestations. Constitutional rules, administrative chains, and the like lend themselves to analyses the elegance of which may illuminate experience but should not be confused with it. The federal constitution, as we have seen, ultimately guarantees almost no specific autonomous fields to the States. Yet the operation of the constitutional powers of the federal government in West Cameroon in fact produces authority and structural relationships which cannot be described in terms of the constitutional statements. The political spaces of West Cameroon and the Federation are still in part autonomous.[95]

Legal

The harmonisation of the legal systems of East and West Cameroon has for similar reasons been slow. Such progress as has been achieved relates to the most formal parts of the law, where differences were of least moment. For several years up to 1966, British- and French-trained jurists (and subsequently a commission including lay politicians) met to produce a harmonized criminal code, the 'general part' of which came into force on 1 October 1966, and the 'special part' in the following year.[96] In Part 1, the introduction of suspended sentences, minimum sentences, the ideas of 'prescription' and 'rehabilitation', and a tripartite division of offences, derived from the Eastern system. From the West was taken the concept of 'conspiracy'. The death penalty was retained: to be administered by hanging as an alternative to shooting (in concession to the West), and in public unless otherwise decided (in consideration of the East). In Part 2, Eastern practice was followed in the determination of offences, including the establishment of the criminal offences of adultery by a woman (and by a man if in the matrimonial home), desertion of the matrimonial home, the neglect of duties by civil servants, and excessive demands for dowry (bride-wealth). Certain of these derive from French laws which had long been dormant in France.

No agreement concerning criminal procedure was reached, owing to the greatly different assumptions in the two metropolitan systems concerning the role of the judge in relation to the prosecution, whether he should have prior knowledge of the details of a case, and the placing of the onus of the proof of innocence or guilt. A set of draft principles was drawn up, but it was thought that the Eastern (French) trial procedure would become standard, with the possible introduction of the cross-examination of witnesses from the Western (English) procedure. It seemed likely that actual practice in the two states would continue unmodified for some time.

No attempt was made, or was thought feasible, to reconcile the two systems of civil law. The body of jurists on the commission for harmonization was dispersed. The policy would be the piecemeal application of Eastern practice in, for example, laws relating to commerce and insurance.

Education and Bilingualism

The constitutional responsibility of West Cameroon did not include Higher Education and Scientific Research (Art. 5), nor Secondary and Technical Education (Art. 6). The latter were finally taken over by the Federation in 1963. The federal post of Cultural Delegate in Charge of Education was combined for a time in the person of the West Cameroon Director of Education, and was then filled by another West Cameroonian. In West Cameroon, pupils were still prepared for the General Certificate of Education, and the pressure of expansion of education in the state only made it less and less feasible to depart from the main lines of the English-language education system which was in being. Despite the establishment of a bilingual grammar school at Man o'War bay near Victoria, the largest single influence was not French but American. There were in all years sizeable contingents of Peace Corps Volunteers, who were absorbed into the educational system. The Cameroon College of Arts, Science, and Technology at Bambui-Bambili received considerable American aid. The federalisation of education took fresh steps after 1965, and in 1966 it was announced that secondary schools in both East and West Cameroon would soon have a common syllabus and time-tables.[97]

Although much information is available concerning the expansion of educational opportunities within the State itself, the question of the harmonization of the educational systems turns fundamentally upon the future relationship of English and French in the Federal Republic. It is, in fact, the conception of bilingualism which is truly federal in Cameroon: the one theme which has had a significant influence upon the thought of both States. A bilingual journal *Abbia* (first issue February 1963), published at Yaounde with UNESCO support, became the vehicle of discussion on the subject. The unifying nature of the idea of bilingualism derived, in part, from the threat to national unity which the general rise in levels of education would otherwise present. Contacts between people from the two states tended to be expressed in terms of 'English' and 'French' stereotypes. This second-order cultural nationalism was certainly not restricted to French-speakers. The metropolitan stereotypes were applied freely by Cameroonians to each other.[98]

The cultural influence of the former colonial language in African states (which I call here 'metropolitanism') is no longer underestimated.[99] The influence may, however, be exerted even when the linguistic performance of individuals appears poor. Thus the mass of Creole-speakers in West Cameroon are less conscious of a break in continuity between their derivative of English and the educated standard than many visitors imagine. The educated language is perceived as a *Hochsprache*, certainly, but in its spoken form (of course the primary barrier is of literacy) it is not unintelligible. Many have a one-way knowledge (hearing, not speaking) of its most common forms and usages. In the towns mixtures of various kinds occur in speech at all educational kinds. Although the case for literary Creole is itself argued frequently, too much should not be made of the Creolization of West Cameroon English. It presents a pedagogic problem (as in the West Indies), but it is no less a vehicle for a popular 'metropolitanism' of the type under discussion than the standard language. For this reason Creole (despite the existence of bilinguals in both states who speak it as well as a vernacular) is unlikely to be an acceptable national tongue for the Republic in the near future.[100]

Bilingualism in English and French from primary level upwards was proposed by Dr Bernard Fonlon, as a mode of reducing the divisive effect of the two cultural influences. He accepted that no Cameroon language could command universal support. He argued persuasively that the failures of bilingualism in Canada and Belgium rested on bases non-existent in Cameroon: (1) both languages were of comparable status in Africa and of similar intellectual prestige; (2) neither was the property of a particular racial or national group; (3) neither was the language of a conquering element. Fonlon underestimates factors in the Cameroon situation which may approximate in sentiment to the second and third situations. It is, however, clearly in order to avoid the metropolitanisms which would emphasise such factors that he proposes his programme of individual bilingualism:

> The University recently started in Yaounde is supposed to be a bilingual university. But the nature of its bilingualism needs to be defined clearly and efforts made, right from the start, to put that definition into effect; else the French element will become so predominant as to make the Federal University of Cameroon, to all intents and purposes a French university.[101]

The movement for true bilingualism became part of the stirrings of the new intelligentsia in West Cameroon (see below), and derived some impetus from the apparently unequal status of English and French in many federal contexts (for example the official phrase: 'The French text is authentic').[102] The educational policy of West Cameroon was not to teach French at primary level. Nevertheless the bilingualism idea has captured some of that idealistic sentiment in both States that marked the pursuit of reunification. In a speech delivered in West Cameroon on 1 October 1964 (and published in English and French) President Ahidjo referred to 'the alienation of our civilisation resulting in the adoption by our elite of two fundamentally different languages and cultures' and added:

> When we consider the English language and culture and the French language and culture we must regard them not as the property of such and such a race but as an acquirement of the universal civilisation to which we belong. That is in fact why we have followed the path of bilingualism . . .

He spoke of an 'original civilisation' which should preserve the elements of both cultures 'together with what is proper to our own genius', and which could transform Cameroon 'into the catalyst of African unity'.[103]

The New Politics

The fears for security at independence proved illusory. Nevertheless, the years 1961-3 were marked by the activities of the Federal Gendarmerie whose encampments were established in or near the major centres. The occasional severities of the new forces of security[104] can be attributed to their limited education, and to their experiences in terrorist areas of the East. It had been feared that the West was a haven for bandits. The searching of lorries, the questioning of travellers, and the use of public violence, were a novelty to the West Cameroon population. Complaints finally appeared in the press alleging that even police and officials and their families were not immune from assaults. The situation quickly eased after 1963. It was during this period that East Cameroonian officials began to acquire a genuine respect for the high degree of law and order in the West, and in due course the public behaviour of the gendarmerie began to approximate to that of the unarmed West Cameroon police. To West Cameroonians must go the credit that their attitude to the gendarmerie was kept separate from their attitude to reunification. No political voices were raised in criticism by either the CPNC opposition, then in eclipse, or, publicly, by the KNDP government.

The electoral developments in West Cameroon will be only briefly mentioned. The KNDP government remained in power after reunification J. N. Foncha remaining Prime Minister, as well as becoming Vice-President of the Federal Republic. The Opposition CPNC continued in existent and Dr Endeley remained salaried Leader of the Opposition,

His party was much weakened at new elections in January 1962 to an enlarged House of Assembly. No further state elections have been held at the present time.[105]

The dominant political question throughout the period was the formation of a national party. In the early years after reunification President Ahidjo's governing party, *Union Camerounaise* (*UC*), completed the process (well described by LeVine)[106] by which it emerged as the only East Cameroon party. In West Cameroon, the Opposition CPNC had renounced its support for a pro-Nigerian policy after the plebiscite. Both it and the governing KNDP stated that they were prepared to join the national party, but it was the latter's consistent demand that the CPNC first dissolve itself, and its members join the KNDP. The long coexistence of two parties, one in government and one in opposition in West Cameroon, and of both with the *Parti unifié* of East Cameroon, was no doubt one of the more subtle influences upon the development of political experience in East Cameroon which resulted directly from reunification.[107]

In 1963, however, a movement of complex origin began in West Cameroon. It contained elements of a generational revolt, of a reaction of a new intelligentsia against the leadership, of the rights of the federated state against the Federation, and others also. At the KNDP National Convention of that year the choice of the acknowledged deputy and successor-apparent to Foncha became important, in view of the approach of the date after which the posts of Prime Minister and Vice-President would, under the constitution, be separated. At the same time the Secretary-Generalship of the party had become vacant. Both posts were contested: the greater by A. N. Jua (the West Cameroon Minister of Finance, and S. T. Muna (Federal Minister of Transport and Communications), and the lesser by E. Egbe (Federal Deputy Minister of Justice) and Nzo Ekhah-Nghaky (Federal Deputy Minister of Foreign Affairs). Muna was commonly regarded as a 'Federation' man, possibly because he was a man of great energy and determination who was genuinely bound up in his ministerial responsibilities, which he saw as the way of bringing to his State those great constructions and public works which he admired in the East. He was respected for his ability by the President. A. N. Jua was believed to be a West Cameroonian first and foremost. This was also probably an overstatement. He had never antagonised any section of the party, and he had a good, even flamboyant, record of political activity when KNDP had been in opposition.[108] He had retained a keen sense for movements in West Cameroon popular feeling, and he had played a large role in maintaining the impetus in favour of reunification in the pre-plebiscite period. He had done good service as Minister of Finance through the difficult economic period. Jua was the party's choice. For the Secretary-Generalship the selection was Nzo Ekhah-Nghaky, a member of the new intelligentsia.

During this time the articles by Dr Fonlon began to appear in *Abbia*. One of these, 'Shall we make or mar?', appeared in the issue of March 1964, and was serialised in the one-sheet *Cameroon Times* a few months later. It is hard to convey the effect of this article upon West Cameroonian opinion. It began, almost alone, a thaw in the congealed political attitudes which characterised the interregnum period. Further, there had been before 1963 federal pressure upon the *Cameroon Times*, hardly more than a broadsheet although it then was. The Nigerian *Daily Times* had been banned outright. That outspoken political discussion which was typical of the pre-independence period was completely absent in the new West Cameroon. The Fonlon articles reintroduced into discussion the aims of reunification, and demonstrated that it was not necessary to be *Upéciste* to express the deficiencies of the time. The article was essentially a development of his plea for a bilingual state, but it marshalled strong attacks upon the cultural metropolitanisms affected by the users of French and English, by attacking French and American policies and national attitudes.[109]

The force of Fonlon's article was the greater because he had not then entered politics, was a graduate in French—indeed regularly interpreted for President Ahidjo (who was said to think highly of him) and was a well-known supporter of the Federal Republic. Serialized articles by Fonlon appeared on two main political occasions: at the federal elections of 1964, and after the Presidential and Vice-Presidential elections of 1965.[110] These stressed *inter alia* the need to cease the divisions between government and opposition. While it is not to be imagined that Fonlon was responsible for any particular political event or decision, it is rarely given to a relatively young man to be heard and read with respect by his elders, as well as to become a hero to the young. Yet all this he achieved by a few articles written in an English of such fluency that many of his mass readership could wrest its finer shades only after frequent re-readings. In 1964 he was appointed Deputy Federal Minister of Foreign Affairs by President Ahidjo.[111]

The national Presidential and Vice-Presidential elections of 20 March 1965 resulted in the unopposed return of President Ahidjo and Vice-President Foncha. It was now required that on 7 May Dr Foncha[112] should occupy his post at Yaounde, and relinquish the Prime Ministership of West Cameroon. It was understood in West Cameroon, as we have seen, that A. N. Jua would succeed. It was, however, learned that Mr Muna had laid claim to the succession and might have powerful support. The ensuing period was one of considerable tension. President Ahidjo travelled to Buea to assess the situation for himself. His careful sounding of all shades of opinion resulted in his choice of Jua. Mr Jua's announcement of the news on 12 May was made before the West Cameroon House of Assembly, which was waiting in sombre mood. The ensuing jubilation left no doubt that the President's choice had wide support, and his own prestige in the state rose to unprecedented heights.

The *Cameroon Times* compared the new Prime Minister's later entry into Bamenda to that of Christ into Jerusalem. His public speeches promised a rapprochement with the opposition. At the same time Mr Muna, two West Cameroon ministers, and six other members of the House, who had heavily committed themselves to his cause, were expelled from the government party. They at once formed the Cameroon United Congress (CUC). The rapid sequence of events was completed by the formation of a 'national government' of the KNDP and the CPNC opposition, and the return of Dr Endeley to ministerial rank on 31 August 1965 with the title of Leader of the House. Mr Mbile, his most loyal supporter, received the Ministry of works.[113] The final healing of the old rift in the independence movement was well received in West Cameroon, and recalled that moment of jubilation on 30 September 1959 when Dr Endeley and Mr Foncha had temporarily united to present a joint plan to the United Nations (a policy with which Mr Jua had been associated). The resemblances were not entirely fortuitous. The new intelligentsia was fired again with that idealistic sentiment which it has been suggested was the source of the popular appeal of the 'Kamerun Idea', as now of the 'Bilingual Culture'. The separation of Mr Muna and his CUC was deplored by the Presidency. Mr Muna hinted that he had been 'encouraged' to take his stand for the succession. At the KNDP party conference Dr Foncha, Life President of the party, was reported to have been under some criticism.

The departure of Dr Foncha to Yaounde on 3 August 1965 marked in yet another way the end of that interregnum period to which reference has been frequently made. The following year a new political period began. On 14 June 1966 it was announced that the KNDP, the CPNC, and Mr Muna's CUC had agreed to merge with President Ahidjo's *Union Camerounaise* into the Cameroon National Union (CNU). On 1 September the three parties, having each held its final convention, had formally united. The activity in the press which had developed since 1963 began to come under restraining influences.[114] The *parti unique* was now a reality.

5. Conclusion

From outside, the reunification of the two Cameroons appeared to be a simple matter; it was widely assumed that there were bases for the reunification at least as strong as those which led to many historical examples of the achievement of unity. As we have seen, the term 'reunification' could have meant the reconstruction of the boundaries of Kamerun in 1894, or those of 1911. It came to be used of those defined by the mandates in 1922. The present Republic, in its turn, represents only a partial reunion of the two mandates. The idea of the reunification had formal, legal, aspects which made its discussion at the United Nations a relatively simple matter. It had ideological, even mythological, aspects, the bases of which were widely and inadequately assumed to be 'ethnic'. It was subsequently often forgotten that the actual choice which created the union (and in the absence of which the union would not have come into existence) was made by West Cameroon. The situation from which the choice was made was one of social and economic isolation, in which a community of sentiment and experience arose, to which was assimilated the idea of the reunified Cameroon. Chance events and outside pressures played their part, no doubt, in weakening the pro-Nigerian party and strengthening the reunificationist party at critical moments. But, in the main, the course of events has a compulsively *voulu* air. The West Cameroonians were never pro-Nigerian; they were at most pro-British.[115] The first five years of reunification demonstrated the continuity of many of these features. In many respects the isolation was maintained. Indeed, it may be said to have defeated the early attempts to attach the federal representatives to the West Cameroon government. The physical isolation of the representatives from Yaounde was increased by the sense of psychological distantiation. As an East Cameroonian official exclaimed: 'Nous sommes occidentalisés!'

Since 1 October 1961 it has been constantly predicted that the West State would be 'swamped or swallowed'. These judgements do not reflect a very high opinion of the Federal Republic. This is quite surprising. The Federation is in undoubted military control of the Western Federated State, and yet institutions of the latter have not been dissolved, nor has the constitution been suspended, as has occurred in Nigeria. A liberalism was even tolerated after 1963 that would have been regarded as impracticable in the East. There was no 'mass take-over' either by East Cameroonians or by French technicians, in part for good linguistic reasons. Such a term is more applicable, indeed, to the influx of American nationals, who might well have appeared to the French-speaking East as an accession to the 'Anglo-Saxon' influence. The development of a certain pessimism, even cynicism, in the face of African affairs is certainly in part a defensive reaction against the constant surprise-value of political events on the continent. This is surely due to the low predictive power of most of the 'models' used by foreign observers (if many of the formulations based upon unarticulated assumptions are worthy of the name). One of the reasons for this is the preoccupation with the formal properties of political institutions on the one hand, while associating with them, on the other, sentiments and interpretations deriving from other societies and periods, eked out with certain special 'African' categories, among which those clustering round the 'tribe' are noteworthy.[116]

For the reunified Cameroon, it is most valuable to direct one's attention away from political and constitutional matters to (for example) the momentum of education in West Cameroon, which makes the number of employable people educated in English an important vested interest. This expanding group will be a factor for the coming decade. There has never been, nor can there be, any question of legislating it out of existence. The collapse of the Nigerian Federation has made West Cameroonians very contented with their choice. To some extent West Cameroon will by the pressure of her own interests attach herself more firmly to the federal centre. Her enthusiasm for the ideal of cultural bilingualism is unlikely to diminish.[117] In 1966 there is no doubt that the economic weakness of West Cameroon, following on the collapse of the Cameroon Bank, combined with the dissolution of the old parties, led to a significant rise in the status of the federal authorities, who were now unchallenged in many fields. It is conceivable that the present federal constitution may be superseded, either with the participation of the West Cameroon authorities, or in response to wider movements involving the whole Republic. Possibly the creation of the six administrative regions, of which West Cameroon is taxonomically one, may foreshadow a future, more centralized, republic, in which the position of West Cameroon will be reduced in constitutional importance. But the basic realities will have to be accommodated in any succeeding structure.

The force of the various movements which led up to reunification did not play itself out until five years after the foundation of the Federal Republic. This has been demonstrated in all fields. The great changes implied by the reunification only began in 1966. The economic ones have the greatest potential importance, with the investment on East-West communications and the prospective development of Victoria/Bota, Tiko, and Douala as virtually a one port complex, distributed over thirty miles of coast and estuarine system. These changes must affect the Republic as a whole, and West Cameroon, quite fundamentally. It may be that in later years they will loom as the one solid argument for unification—and one which I, at least, do not ever remember having heard, except in the most general terms, in the time of the political movement.

Notes

1. The use of *Cameroun* in English is now inappropriate, and hybrid forms such as *West Cameroun* especially so. A rule of thumb for English-speaking usage is: Period of Mandate/Trusteeship: *The Cameroons* (divisions: British [Northern, Southern]/French); The independent French-speaking Republic of 1 Jan. 1960–1 Oct. 1961: *Cameroun Republic;* the independent reunified Federal Republic of 1 Oct. 1961: *Cameroon* (divisions: West/East). French-speaking usage has been consistent through all periods: *Cameroun*
2. For the federal law see Constitution of the Federal Republic (Engl. version). Art. 1; for the State law see 'A Law to Establish a Constitution for the Federated State of West Cameroon', Suppl. to *Extraordinary Gazette* (*Buea*), 8 Nov. 1961, Art. 55.
3. Federal Constitution, Art. 60.
4. East Cameroon population figures are from estimates of the Statistical Dept of Feb. 1965. For West Cameroon, all population figures unless otherwise stated are from *La population du Cameroun Occidental* (Yaounde, 1965); Engl. version: *The Population of West Cameroon* (1966), p. 11 (a sample demographic survey). The English version, despite stylistic deficiencies, can be generally relied upon. To the total figure for the State should be added an estimate of 18,000 for the transhumant Fulani population. At the Nigerian census of 1953, the present West Cameroon had a population of 753,000 (*Population Census of the Eastern Region of Nigeria,* 1953, Bulletins Nos. 2 and 5). Another figure for West Cameroon made public in 1965 was 1,058,000.
5. The protectorate acquired the coastline between Rio del Rey and Campo and limited inland boundaries by agreements with England and France in 1885. By agreement with Great Britain the western frontier was extended to Yola (1886) and the Chad (1893). The eastern boundary was agreed with France in 1894, thus fixing the frontiers for the main period of the protectorate. They were greatly expanded in 1911, when in return for recognition of rights of protection over Morocco, France ceded 275,000 sq. km. to Germany. The new protectorate now reached the Congo and Oubangui rivers and surrounded Rio Muni. France received a small portion of Kamerun territory near Lake Chad (Riebow, (ed.), 1893. *Die deutsehe Kolonial-Gesetzgebung* vol. I. Berlin; Ruppel, (ed.), 1912. *Die*

Landes-gesetzgebung fur das Schutzgebiet Kamerun, Berlin; H. R. Rudin, 1938. *Germans in the Cameroons 1884–1914,* London).

6. Between 1914 and 1916 the British had administered Douala. This was given up but they retained responsibility for 'The north-west half of the Dschang district (including Dschang)', i e. part of the Bamileke area of modern East Cameroon (*Nigeria Gazette*, 1916, pp. 212, 377).
7. The British now gave up Dschang to the French thus breaking the unity of the 'Grasslands' plateau. One reason given was the desire not to block the natural hinterland of the Northern Railway, which went to France.
8. The German gains of 1911 were reabsorbed by France's Equatorial colonies, but these (specifically Chad) retained her own gains of the same date.
9. In criticism of this view Dr Moumié (*West Africa,* 1958, p. 876) stated that UPC policy had never accepted the loss of the 1911 boundaries. Yet all reunificationists devoted themselves only to unifying the two mandates.
10. D. E. Gardinier, 1996, *Cameroon,* London, pp. 127–8 discusses the reasons for the separate administration of Cameroun by France.
11. The operation of rules based upon the axioms of the political space, as of any other space similarly defined, have a logical autonomy. No doubt in old-established states, the political space coincides approximately with certain other spaces. That this did not occur automatically with colonial units accounts for the intuitive impression of 'artificiality'. At the time of colonial expansion, however, this impression of 'artificiality' was not dominant: the boundaries of Cameroon were then based upon the 'realities' of German movement towards the Niger, the Chad, and the Congo, meeting the reaction of British and French interests (see Rudin).
12. For independent support for these remarks see *West Africa*, 1966, p. 371.
13. E. Ardener and others, *Plantation and Village in the Cameroons* (*1960*). The CDC has 220,000 acres, of which 57,000 are planted. It is still the largest employer (13,000 workers: *West Africa,* 1966, p. 563; 28 May 1966, p. 599).
14. A recent history of the Afrikanische Frucht-Compagnie is H. Domizlaff and others, 1961, *FL: Die Geschichte einer Reederei.* Hamburg.
15. E. M. Chilver, 'Native Administration in the West Central Cameroons, 1902–1954', in K. Robinson and F. Madden, (eds), 1963. *Essays in Imperial Government.* Oxford, pp. 89–139. A forthcoming paper by Gardinier outlines the administrative history of the period.
16. Even the movement for retaining the connexion with Nigeria rarely used any ethnic argument. The Ogoja Ejagham had their own separatist movement within Nigeria (as part of the COR state).
17. C. Meillassoux, 1964. *Anthropologie économique des Gouro du Côte d'Ivoire.* Paris, pp. 15–17.
18. For the growth of the modern urban and political aspects of the 'tribe', which has resulted in terms like 'supertribalism', see A.L. Epstein, 1958. *Politics in an UrbanAfrican Community.* Manchester; J. C. Mitchell, 1966.

'Theoretical Orientations in African Urban Studies', in *The Social Anthropology of Complex Societies.* London: ASA Monograph No 4; The many uses of the term 'tribe' now much reduce its explanatory value. Thus E. Gellner is enabled to apply the term to North Africa only by special *ad hoc* definitions ('segmentary', 'marginal'). See 'Tribalism and Social Change in North Africa', in W. H. Lewis, (ed.), 1965. *French-Speaking Africa: the Search for Identity.* New York.

19. Conventional tribal lists will be found in Ardener and others, 1960, pp. 353–67. The onomastic confusion resulting from the flexibility of tribal classification is illustrated by ibid, pp. 368–370, and pp. 23–27. The lists in UK Annual Reports before 1958 are for similar reasons to be used with caution. In 1958 the lists were corrected, but there are typographical errata which were themselves corrected in 1959. G.P. Murdock's classifications and nomenclature in *Africa: its Peoples and their Culture History* (New York 1959) are based on inadequate material and are unreliable. P.A. Talbot, 1926. *Southern Nigeria.* Oxford. Vol. iv, is to be used now with caution.
20. See M. Guthrie, 1948. *The Classification of the Bantu Languages*. London. and *the Bantu Languages of Eastern Equatorial Africa* (London, 1953); I. Richardson, 1955. *Africa,* pp. 161–9 and *Linguistic Survey of the Northern Bantu Borderland,* vols. i & ii (London, 1956–7); J. H. Greenberg, 1963. *The Languages of Africa.* Indiana; D. W. Crabb, 1965. *Ekoid Bantu Languages of Ogoja,* pt. 1. Cambridge; J. Ellis, 1966. *Towards a Comparative Linguistics.* The Hague. The last discusses the logical bases of 'genetic' comparison. Recent work by the Grassfields Bantu Working Group under the inital inspiration of Professors Voorhoeve and Hyman have refined the work on Grassdield languages.
21. Dugast, *Inventaire ethnique du Sud-Cameroun* (Paris 1949); C. Tardits, 1960. *Les Bamiléké de l'Ouest Cameroun.* Paris; J. Hurault, 1963. *La structure social des Bamiléké.* The Hague.
22. See works cited above. An early classification was G. Tessmann, 1932. 'Die Völker und Sprachen Kameruns', *Petermanns Mitteilungen*, 78/5–6, pp. 113–20; 7–8, pp. 184–90.
23. P. M. Kaberry, 1962. 'Retainers and Royal Households in the Cameroons Grassfields', *Cahiers d'ét. afr.,* pp. 282–98.
24. Chilver, in Robinson & Madden, pp. 113–18.
25. Mongo (E. 300; W. 600), Balong (E. 2,406; W. 2,000), Bakossi (E. 4,257=Muamenam +Manehas; W. 17,086), Elung (E. 2,665; W. 1,447), Mbo (E. 7,816; W. 5,041) were the most notable cases (E. W. Ardener, 1956. *Coastal Bantu of the Cameroons*, p. 15; Ardener and others, (1960), pp. 405–7, 409, n.2; Dugast).
26. The Bangwa (18,959) and some villages on the Bamenda/East border are classifiable as Bamileke. The 'Bamileke' (the 'tribal' name is foreign) of East Cameroon numbered about half a million people. V. T. LeVine, *The Cameroons from Mandate to Independence* (Berkley, Calif., 1964), in giving 51,800 Bamileke in West Cameroon, is misled by the category 'Bakossi-Bamileke' in the Nigerian census where it was used only in Bulletin no. 5 for Cameroons Province (Victoria, Kumba, and Mamfe Divisions). By a

convention this was to be read as 'Bakossi' in the Bakossi and Basossi areas, 'Mbo' in the Mbo areas (accounting for about 30,000), and as 'Bamileke' in the Bangwa area (in fact the latter were recorded among 'Other Cameroons Tribes'!). The remaining 20,000 under Bakossi-Bamileke consists of people of all these Western origins as well as probably some 'real' Bamileke, mostly in the towns. In Kumba Division in 1953 they were certainly in part migrant 'British' Bakossi and congeners, while Victoria Division showed only 1,489 in the category. LeVine, in combining Bakundu with Mbo, is further misled by Murdock's classification which rests on the conception of a 'Bakundu Group' deriving from a very early German ethnic classification (in e.g. Schnee, *Deutsches Kolonial-Lexikon,* 1920). Although the present writer, like others, provisionally accepted it a decade ago (Ardener, *Coastal Bantu*). it was in fact an arbitrary category.

27. For an idea of the geographical distribution of Creole in the Republic see J. A. Kisob, 1963. 'A Live Language: "pidgin English"', *Abbia,* Feb.
28. For a related usage, see Wallerstein, *Cah. d'ét afr.,* 1960, p. 133, where 'ethnicity' describes 'the feeling of loyalty to [the] new ethnic group of the towns'.
29. For the nature of the East Cameroon catchment area see Ardener and others, (1960), pp. 196–7. For labour-force relations see pp. 101–4. French Cameroons workers had eight per cent mixed marriages, the highest of all plantation workers due, it is likely, to their long settlement (ibid., p. 105). The relative 'naturalisation' of French Cameroon workers was clearly marked. M. Z. Njeuma, 1964. *The Origins of Pan-Cameroonism,* p. 14. Buea, traces the Ewondo element to refugees from the railway construction in the early French period. See also LeVine, *Cameroons,* pp. 196–7.
30. E. W. Ardener, 1954. 'Democracy in the Cameroons', *West Africa,* p. 203 (the political reaction), Ardener and others, 1960, pp. 105–6 (reaction to Ibo in the work-force). Njeuma, p. 16, while stressing the experiences of Cameroonian traders (surely rather few) who visited Aba and other Ibo centres, well expresses the West Cameroon view of the Ibo: 'Competition was generally unfavourable in such strange and highly competitive lands. The too trusting and unsuspicious ones fell prey to pick-pockets or were the victims of dishonest men at the houses of their hosts. Also the Ibos had a greater acumen for trade and took up business with all enthusiasm, having been long inured in almost intolerable hardship in their own country.'
31. It may, finally, be noted that the ethnicity did not derive from the 'Bantu' or 'Bantoid' nature of the languages of the area, since these languages stretch over many thousands of square miles of Africa from Northern Nigeria to Zululand.
32. For the political background: J. S. Coleman, 1958. *Nigeria.* Berkeley, Calif., pp. 284–93; LeVine, *Cameroons*; D. E. Gardinier, 1963. *Cameroon, United Nations Challenge to French Policy.* London, 1963; E. W. Ardener, 1962. 'The Political History of Cameroon', *World Today*; C. Welch, 1966. *Dream*

of Unity. New York, which became available too late to be cited in detail.

33. Dr E. M. L. Endeley, a member of a chiefly family at Buea (but not the son of Chief Endeley), had been associated with the CYL since the foundation, as were L. Namme, and N. N. Mbile. Mr Kale, who was eclipsed by him, re-emerged as a proponent of separate independence at the plebiscite but achieved no following. He was always popular, however, and soon after reunification became the Speaker of the West Cameroon House of Assembly. He died suddenly in August 1966. A brief account of the CYL occurs in his unpublished MS: 'Political Evolution in the Cameroons' (Buea).
34. Mr Jua in time became the most popular of all the KNDP leadership after Mr Foncha, and ten years later succeeded him as Prime Minister.
35. The all-party Mamfe Conference of 10–11 August 1959, under the chairmanship of Sir Sydney Phillipson, closed without any decision on the issue.
36. LeVine, *Cameroons*, pp. 207–11.
37. The question of the Northern Cameroons will not be gone into here. The UN fixed a plebiscite for the area for November 1959. The result was inconclusive and there too a plebiscite was held (to be separately counted) on 11 February.
38. E. W. Ardener, 1958. 'The Kamerun Idea', *West Africa*, pp. 533, 559, and in *World Today*, 1962. The first of these papers contains printers' errata later corrected (*West Africa*, 1958, p. 661). It also contains an uncorrected factual error (the date of the Baptist evacuation of Victoria was 1887). The correspondence following it between myself and Dr Moumié (*West Africa*, 1958, pp. 876, 972), discusses the 'Kamerun Idea' as a symbolic concept, not susceptible therefore to weakening by scientific criticism. The term itself has, of course, no special validity; Njeuma (p. 11) prefers the term 'Cameroon Aspiration'. The 'Kamerun' spelling appeared in the party names: KUNC (Kamerun United National Congress) which helped to found KNC, and in KPP, KNDP, and OK (One Kamerun: the successor after 1957 in West Cameroon of the banned UPC). The acceptance of the independence name of *Cameroon* has now made this factor in the reunification movement fade out of present significance.
39. In 1958, so violent were Dr Endeley's public attacks upon British administrative officers that they awakened the protests of the KNDP opposition. The suddenness of these attacks derived, some thought, from the appearance of encouragement of anti-Endeley sentiment given by the Resident Special Duties, Bamenda, of the day. For the strong sentiment in Bamenda which led to the establishment of the special duties post (in addition to the usual Divisional appointments) on the abolition of Bamenda Province in 1954, see Chilver, p. 138. The plateau chiefs at this time favoured Mr Foncha. The Resident, like many officers posted to the plateau, tended to share the Bamenda feeling of isolation from Buea. Later the Bamenda posting was abolished.

40. The UPC history is well covered by Gardinier and LeVine, *Cameroons*. The early contacts between the UPC and the West Cameroon movement, between 1948 and 1951, were briefly revived with the KNDP when Dr Moumié's group fled to Kumba in 1955.
41. In July of 1959 Sir Sydney Phillipson was asked to report on the fiscal consequences of the separation of the Southern Cameroons from the Federation of Nigeria with a further period of trusteeship, because 'this is the policy favoured by the political party returned to power at the General Election held early this year' (Sir S. Phillipson, 1959. *Financial, Economic and Administrative Consequences to the Southern Cameroons of Separation from the Federation of Nigeria.* Lagos, p. 2). By the time of his final report (in October) this policy had already been abandoned (LeVine, *Cameroons*, pp. 208–11).
42. The Kamerun Society (1956–61), a non-political debating group of young civil servants and plantation employees, became later the architects of reunification. The role of students: in 1956 the Ibadan Cameroons Students Union wrote to Dr Endeley urging secession from Nigeria. Its secretary J.N. Ekang was, a mere six years later, to become Deputy Federal Foreign Minister of the reunified Cameroon, under the name of Ekhah-Nghaky (Kale, MS, 1966). On the role of the UN: LeVine, *Cameroons*, pp. 209–21.
43. *World Today*, 1962, p. 346.
44. Njeuma, p. 26.
45. W. Johnson, 'The Cameroon Federation' in W. H. Lewis (ed.), *French-speaking Africa*, New York, 1965, p. 205.
46. M. Roberts, 'Political Prospects for the Cameroun', *World Today*, July 1960. By 1960 the UPC revolt was concentrated in the Bamileke Region and in the area of Manenguba. Both bordered on West Cameroon. A considerable influx of refugees and/or terrorists sought asylum in the Southern Cameroons. The doubt as to which they were was difficult to resolve. Le Vine, 'The Course of Political Violence', in W.H. Lewis, examines the UPC in a wider context.
47. The non-acquisition of Northern Cameroons was not allowed to pass unchallenged by the Republic, which took a case against the UK government to the International Court of Justice at The Hague, which ruled in favour of the UK plea that the case was out of order (see 'Law Report' in the *Guardian* and *The Times*, 3 Dec. 1963). President Ahidjo declared 1 June every year a national day of mourning (*Cameroon Times*, 3 Dec. 1963). In March of the following year A. Jua replied to complaints made in the Northern Nigeria House of Assembly, that hundreds of people were crossing from Sardauna Province into East Cameroon. It was said that they had been offered free land and other concessions (ibid., 14 March 1964).
48. *The Two Alternatives: Southern Cameroons Plebiscite, 1961* (Buea, 1961).
49. *Record of the all-party conference on the constitutional future of the Southern Cameroons held at the Community Hall, Bamenda, from 26th to 28th June, 1961* (Buea, 1961).

50. Foumban Conference, 17–21 July: Press Release, nos. 1438, 1467, 1468, of 17, 20, and 24 July 1961.
51. Press Release nos. 1473, 1477, 1486, 1488, and 1492, of 31 July 1961, 2, 4, 5, and 8 Aug. 1961.
52. Press Release no. 1428 of 1 July 1961: 'Southern Cameroons Constitutional Conference: KNDP and CPNC Memoranda on Security Matters'.
53. Press Release no. 1364 (29 May 1961).
54. Press Release nos. 1501, 1505, 1509, of 11, 15, and 18 Aug. 1961; Johnson, in W. H. Lewis, pp. 213–14. Press Release no. 1505 said: 'The representative of the Government of the Republic of Cameroun has undertaken to conduct a full investigation and to make the facts known. We both agree that whoever is guilty of this cruel murder will be severely punished.'
55. E. W. Ardener, *West Africa,* 1961, pp. 878–79, 1071.
56. As the Federal Assembly had 40 Eastern and 10 Western members, 'ultimately any 20 easterners or . . . any 5 westerners could block any legislation' (LeVine, 'The Cameroun Federal Republic', in G. Carter, ed., *Five African States* (London, 1964), p. 312).
57. They were finally lifted in Yaounde in mid–1966 (West *Africa,* 1966, p. 729).
58. Johnson, in W. H. Lewis, p. 209. Levine, in Carter, p. 310, shows that the Presidency was a completely new amalgam of Western constitutional models.
59. Johnson, in W. H. Lewis, p. 211.
60. Phillipson, p. 42. The report also concluded that 'As a completely independent state the Southern Cameroons at its present stage of development, would not be viable'.
61. K. Berrill, 1960. *The Economy of the Southern Cameroons under United Kingdom Trusteeship.* Buea.
62. The stress on road-building was confirmed in the Southern Cameroons Five-Year Development Plan, 1961–6, which also appeared on the eve of reunification, after separation from Nigeria, in which 69 per cent of the £8·8 million capital investment recommended over this period was to be spent on road construction and public works.
63. K. Andersen, 1961. 'Report on the Economic Aspects of a Possible Re-unification of the British Cameroons with the Republic of Cameroun.' Yaounde, mimeo.
64. There was a precedent for this in Morocco.
65. Until the end of June 1959 currency of the West African Currency Board was in circulation in the Southern Cameroons. From 1 July 1959 this was withdrawn in favour of the Nigerian currency issued by the new Central Bank of Nigeria. If a sterling currency was to be retained in West Cameroon after independence, one possibility would have been to reintroduce the West African Board currency.

66. C. E. Welch, 1963. 'Cameroun since reunification, (2)', *West Africa,* p. 1213).
67 Ibid., p. 973.
68. It may be noted that UK banks had been represented in the East before reunification, while in October 1961 the Bank of West Africa was a partner to an agreement to set up a banking company, the Banque Camerounaise de Développement, jointly with Crédit Lyonnais and the government of the Federal Republic.
69. Andersen, p 26.
70. H.C. Debates, 12 July 1962, cols. 1667–70.
71. See letter to *Financial Times,* 10 May 1963. The Minister of State at the Board of Trade put the position to the House of Commons: 'Jamaica and the Windward Islands, [are] both concerned to increase their export earnings and worried about the tendency, especially in the winter months, for the British market to be over-supplied with bananas. These countries have made it clear that they are strongly opposed to sharing their preferential advantages in our market with West Cameroon given that the territory is the only area of the world which enjoys preference both in Britain and in the EEC' (H.C. Deb., 22 July 1963, col. 1204). West Cameroon products did not then reach EEC countries in important quantities.
72. The metric system may be mentioned here. Its introduction in West Cameroon was announced by decree to take place on 1 April 1963. It was then postponed to 1 July, and finally to 1 January 1964. The collection of scales and measures took place between January and March. It was hoped to sell them to offset the cost to those who had to buy new ones. The planing of inch rulers (reported from one commercial organisation) symbolized the practical importance of this step.
73. *Cameroon Times,* 14 Dec. 1963.
74. *West Cameroon Estimates*, 1964–65, p. 126.
75. No true index of retail prices had been then calculated, but a statistical office was just beginning its operations.
76. It was unfortunate that a large timber company (Kamerun Ltd.) failed at this time, partly, at least, due to its operations elsewhere.
77. West Cameroon Budget Speech, 30 March 1962 (Press Release no. 1784).
78. Tiko Ironworks was opened in 1963, with an investment of 50 million francs' to make cooking pots and the like from scrap. This enterprise was short-lived. In August 1964 Indian finance was involved in the establishment of Britind Ltd (at Moliwe), an umbrella assembling factory which used imported frames and materials; it was also to make plastic shoes and sandals (*Overseas Review*, Sept. 1964, p. 62; Press Release nos. 3424, 3429). A bag factory followed in 1966.
79. Ardener and others, 1960.
80. S. G. Ardener, 1958. 'Banana Co-operatives in the Southern Cameroons', Nigerian Institute of Social and Economic Research, *Conference Proceedings.* Ibadan.

81. *West Africa,* 1966, p. 599.
82. West *Cameroon Estimates,* 1964–65, p. 125.
83. In July 1962 it was announced that the change-over would take place on 1 October, but this was postponed. Much public explanation went into the operation, which came into effect from midnight on 3 January 1963, with no difficulty (Press Release no. 2148, 4 Jan. 1963).
84. *Financial Times,* 7 May 1963 10 Nov. 1964, *West Africa,* 1962, p. 485.
85. Stanford Research Institute, 1965. *The Economic Potential of West Cameroon, i,* p. 42 (hereafter Stanford); *Overseas Review,* May 1965, p. 66.
86. Stanford, *i,* p. 30.
87. ibid. p. 73.
88. *West Africa,* 1966, p. 447.
89. An agreement was made in 1965 between the West Cameroon government and the marketing corporation Elders and Fyffes (United Fruit Company) guaranteeing a stabilized price and a guaranteed outlet for 45,000 tons of bananas, with an opportunity to sell a further 20,000 tons at a slightly lower price. Tonnages nearly equivalent to the total export volume of 1964 were thus assured (Stanford, *i.* 40). Markets in Italy had been developed largely since 1963.
90. West Cameroon has approximately 20 per cent of the total population of the Federation, yet her exports (for the year July 1963–June 1964) amounted to only approximately 14 per cent of total exports. She imported a slightly higher proportion of the total imports for that year (15 per cent). in 1962–63. West Cameroon had an unfavourable trade gap, while in 1963–64 there was a slight credit balance on exports over imports (p. 2 of Tables in *Quaterly Economic Bulletin,* Ministry of National Economy, second quarter, 1964).
91. The office was one of six regional Inspectorates (the other five being in East Cameroon) responsible to a federal minister (cf. Johnson, in W. H. Lewis, p. 212).
92. Welch, 1963. 'Cameroon since reunification (1)', *West Africa,* p. 1175.
93. Stanford, *i,* 12–14. The administrative areas were gradually changed by federal decree. Subdivisions, with concomitant modifications of Victoria and Mamfe Divisions, were a creation of the federal authorities after 1963. In 1966 the Divisions of West Cameroon were increased from six to nine. Bamenda was partitioned into Bamenda, Nso', and Gwofon, to the last of which were attached parts of Mamfe. Kumba was split into Kumba and Ndian. An inadequate diagram of the structure of the Federal Republic is to be found in V. P. Verin. 1963, *Prezidentskie Respubliki v Afrike.* Moscow. p. 278. The chart is reproduced with the permission of the Stanford Research Institute.
94. Press Release no. 3899 (22 Apr. 1965).
95. In the new period many of the earlier adjustments may be superseded. The question of the harmonization of the federal and state civil services

with their widely different salaries and emoluments was by 1966 becoming urgent. Despite the efforts of the West Cameroon government it seemed quite unlikely that there would be any revision of the federal civil service in the direction of the British-derived system.

96. *Penal Code*, Book I (Buea, 1966).
97. See also Welch, *West Africa,* 1963; Johnson, in W. H. Lewis, p. 217.
98. A West Cameroonian wrote that stereotypes of the French ('sophisticated, talkative, artistic, passionate, and witty') and the English ('sportsmanlike, reserved, trade-loving, conventional, intelligent . . . courteous, honest, extremely nationalistic and humourless') were applicable to Cameroonians of the two segments (M. Manga, 1964. 'Cameroon: A Marriage of Three Cultures', *Abbia,* p. 133).
99. J. Spencer, (ed.), 1963. *Language in Africa.*
100. J. Kisob, *Abbia,* 1963. G. Schneider, 1963. *First Steps in Wes-Kos.* Hartford, uses the too general term *Wes Kos* (West Coast) for what is essentially the Bamenda dialect of Cameroon Creole, which is itself simply known as *Ingris* or the like. Several writers (e.g. Stanford, *i*, 9) take a narrow view of creolization, when they complain of 'low penetration' of English in West Cameroon. Creolized and dialectical English is an almost universal second language, and for some a first language, in the State and a neighbouring part of East Cameroon.
101. B. Fonlon, 1963 'A Case for Early Bilingualism', *Abbia,* p. 88.
102. The name and style of the Federal Republic is in French only on postage stamps, although other inscriptions on them are bilingual.
103. A. Ahidjo, *Message to the Nation* (Buea), 1 Oct. 1964. The President supported the Fonlon policy of eventual bilingualism at primary level.
104. Johnson, in W. H. Lewis, pp. 214–15.
105. They should have been held in December 1966 but they were delayed for a year.
106. *La presse du Cameroun,* 30 June 1962, W. Cameroon Press Relase no. 1895 (4 July 1962); see also Johnson, in W. H. Lewis, p. 210.
107. The federal legislature had no political significance during this period. West Cameroonians participated in federal ministries: S. T. Muna (Minister of Transport, Mines, Posts and Telecommunications); E. T. Egbe (Deputy Minister of Justice), N. Ekhah-Nghaky (Deputy Minister of Foreign Affairs). See Federal Commissariat General Information Release, 20 Feb. 1962. By a decree of 1 July 1964, Dr B. Fonlon became Deputy Minister of Foreign Affairs and Ekhah-Nghaky became Minister of Public Health.
108. He had stimulated the women's *Anlu* movement (on which see R. E. Ritzenthaler, 1960. 'Anlu: A Women's uprising in the British Cameroons', *African Studies,* pp. 151–6)
109. '. . . for although the Anglo-Saxon uses and institutions that we have inherited are British, the British themselves, to their lasting credit, on our quitting the Commonwealth decided to pack out, and today, their more wealthy, more vigorous and more redoubtable cousins are swarming in, from across the Atlantic, to take their place' (*Abbia,* 1964, p. 26).

110. *Cameroon Times* serialized 'A case for early Bilingualism', 27 Feb.–10 Mar. 1964. From 17–27 April 1965 it serialized 'Under the Sign of the Rising Sun', from which the following is a quotation: 'For trained minds will hardly submit to a clumsy, bungling, muddle-headed leadership which, even with all the good will in the world, they cannot sincerely bring themselves to respect'.
111. The most highly educated West Cameroon public figure since Dr Endeley, Bernard Fonlon was born in the Nso' chiefdom of West Cameroon, and educated at Onitsha and Enugu. PhD National University of Ireland, Diploma of Education, Oxford; studied at the Sorbonne; Chargé de Mission at the Presidency, Yaounde 1962–4.
112. On 2 June 1964 the Vice-President was awarded an honorary LL.D of St John's University, New York, and use of the title 'Dr' became customary as a result (*Cameroon Times*. 4 June 1964; Press Release no. 3223, 4 June 1964).
113. Press Release nos. 4203 and 4244 (20 and 31 Aug. 1965).
114. In 1966 certain single-sheet newspapers (*Iroko* and *Cameroon Star*) acquired notoriety for their thinly disguised attacks upon prominent politicians, including the Vice President, and upon the CNU constitution. *Iroko* was banned.
115. E. W. Ardener, 1961. *West Africa*, pp. 878–9.
116. Political journalists have been most open to this criticism: for a recognition or this see R. Hinden, 1966. 'Africa without tears', *Encounter*, pp. 55–59.
117. The last pages of the MS of the elder statesman P. M. Kale, completed just before his death in August 1966, endorsed this policy.

[Note: In the original paper Edwin frequently used the style 'Mr' for J. N. Foncha and other politicians, which was the local practice of the time. Following the publishers house style this form of reference has usually been omitted here.]

Bibliography

Anderson, H. C., 1940. (ed. Goodliffe, F. A.). An Intelligence Report on the Isangele Community of the Kumba Division (1940) based on a Report by H. O. Anderson, A.D.O., 1933 (or 1934), *Buea MS.* Ae 35 (1080).

Annual Report on the Administration of the Cameroons. 1958. London: H.M.S.O.

Ardener, E. W., 1954. 'Democracy in the Cameroons', *West Africa.*

— 1956. *Coastal Bantu of the Cameroons,* London.

— 1958. 'The Kamerun Idea', *West Africa.*

— 1959. 'The Bakweri Elephant Dance', *Nigeria* (60).

— 1961. 'Social and Demographic problems of the Southern Cameroons Plantation Area', in Southall, A., (ed.), *Social Change in Modern Africa,* pp. 83–97. London: Oxford University Press.

— 1962. *Divorce and Fertility.* London: Oxford University Press for the Nigerian Institute for Social and Economic Research, Ibadan.

— 1962. 'The Political History of Cameroon', *World Today.*

— 1965. *Historical Notes on the Scheduled Monuments of West Cameroon,* Buea.

— 1968. 'Documentary and Linguistic Evidence for the Rise of the Trading Polities between Rio del Rey and Cameroon, 1500–1650', in Lewis, I., (ed.) *History and Social Anthropology.*

Ardener, E. W. and Ardener, S. G., 1958. 'Wovea Islanders', *Nigeria* (59) pp. 309–321. Lagos.

Ardener, E. W., Ardener, S. G. and Warmington, W. A., 1960. *Plantation and Village in the Cameroons,* Oxford University Press for the Nigerian Institute for Social and Economic Research, Ibadan.

Ardener, S. G., 1958. 'Banana Cooperatives in the Southern Cameroons', *Conference Proceedings,* Nigerian Institute of Social and Economic Research, Ibadan.

— 1968. *Eye-Witnesses to the Annexation of Cameroon, 1883-1887.*

Asmis, D. R., 1907. 'Der Handel der Duala'. *Mitt. aus den deutschen Schutzgebieten* 20 (2). pp. 85–90.

Bankes, T., Blake, E. W. and Cook, A., 1787. *A New Royal Authentic and Complete System of Universal Geography. . .,* London.

Barbot, John, 1732. 'An abstract of a voyage to New Calabar river, or Rio Real, in the year 1699. . .' in Churchill (q.v.) (Vol. V).

Barlow, Roger, *A Brief Summer of Geographie.* (See Taylor, E. G. R.).

Barros, Joam De, 1732. *Asia, reedição da edição princeps.* Coimbra.

Basel Mission, *Annual Report,* 1 July 1896.

Basto, Raphael Eduardo De Azevdo, (ed.). 1892. *Esmeraldo de Situ Orbis. Edição commemorativa da Descoberta da America por Christovão Columbo no seu Quarto Centenario,* Lisbon.

Berrill, K., 1960. *The Economy of the Southern Cameroons under United Kingdom Trusteeship.* Buea.

Blake, John W., 1937. *European Beginnings in West Africa, 1454–1578.*

Blok, D. P., (ed.). 1966. *Proceedings* of *the Eighth International Congress of Onomastic Sciences.* The Hague: Mouton.

Bouchard, Joseph, 1952. *La côte du Cameroun dans l'histoire et la cartographie: des origines à l'annexion allemande* (*1884*). Douala.

Brown, B., 1896. *The History and Description of Africa. . . by. . . Leo Africanus,* London (ed. of Pory, q.v.).

Brun, Samuel (ed. Naber, S. P.), 1913. 'Samuel Brun, des Wundartzet und Burgers zu Basel, Schiffarten . . .', Basel, 1624, in *Werken Uitgegeven door de Linschoten-Vereeniging,* Vol. VI.

Brutsch, J. R., 1950. 'Les relations de parenté chez les Duala', *Études camerounaises* 3 (31–32), Sept.-Dec.

— 1956. 'Anniversaires d'histoire Douala', *Études camerounaises* (51), March.

Bry, J. T. & J. I. De, 1628. *Descriptio Generalis totius Indiae Orientalis et Occidentalis.* Frankfurt.

Burton, R. F., 1863. *Abeokuta and the Cameroons Mountain.* Vol. II, London.

Chilver, E. M., 1962. 'Nineteenth Century Trade in the Bamenda Grassfields', *Afrika und Übersee* 45 (4), June, pp. 233–58. Hamburg.

— 1963. 'Native Administration in the West Central Cameroons, 1902–1954', in K. Robinson and F. Madden (eds), *Essays in Imperial Government,* Oxford.

— 1966. *Zintgraff's Explorations in Bamenda, Adamawa and the Benue Lands, 1889-1892.*

Churchill, Messers, 1732. *A Collection of Voyages and Travels, some now printed for the first time from Original Manuscripts. . .* London.

Coleman, J. S., 1958. *Nigeria.* Berkeley, Calif.

Comber, T. J., 1879. 'Explorations inland from Mount Cameroons, and Journey through Congo to Makuta', *Proceedings of Royal Geographical Society* 1879.

Cordeiro, Luciano, 1881. *Viagens explorações e conquistas dos portuguezes Collecção de documentos1574–1620.* Lisbon.

Crabb, D. W., 1965. *Ekoid Bantu Languages of Ogoja.* Pt. I. Cambridge.

Dapper, Dr O., 1668. *Naukeurige Beschrijvinge der Afrikanische Gewesten.* Amsterdam (2nd impression 1676).

Delp, *Dicionário Etimológico da Língua Portuguesa* (ed. Machado, José Pedro). 1st edition.

Deutsches Kolonialblatt (DKB). Berlin (series).

Dias, Augusto Epiphanio Da Silva, (ed.). 1905. *Esmeraldo de Situ Orbis. Edição critica annotada.* Lisbon.

Dinkelacker, E., 1914. *Wörterbuch der Duala-Sprache.* Hamburg.
Doke, C. M. & Cole, D. T., 1961. *Contributions to the History of Bantu Linguistics.* Johannesburg.
Dominik, F. W. H., 1891. *Sechs Kriegs und Friedensjahre in deutschen Tropen.*
Domizlaff H. et al., 1960. *FL: Die Geschichte einer Reederei.* Hamburg.
Dugast, I., 1949. *Inventaire ethnique du Sud-Cameroun.* Paris.
Ellis, J., 1966. *Towards a Comparative Linguistics.* The Hague.
Enciso, Martin Fernandez De., 1518. *Suma de geographia q trata de todas las partidas & provincas del mundo. . .* Saragossa.
Epstein, A. L., 1958. *Politics in an Urban African Community.* Manchester.
Evans-Pritchard, E. E., 1961. *Anthropology and History.* Manchester.
Fage, J. D., 1962. *An Introduction to the History of West Africa* (3rd edition). Cambridge.
— 1962. 'Some remarks on beads and trade in Lower Guinea in the Sixteenth and Seventeenth centuries', *Journal of African History* 3 (2) pp. 343–47.
Field, M. J., 1960. *Search for Security.* London: Faber.
Field, M., 1969. *The Prime Minister's Lodge.* Buea Archives office.
Figueiredo, Manoel De, 1614. *Hydrographia. . .* Lisbon.
Fonteneau, Jean (alias Alfonse De Saintongue), 1904. (ed. Musset, Georges) *La Cosmographie avec l'Éspère et Régime du Soleil et du Nord.* . Paris.
Forde, D., (ed.), 1956. *Efik Traders of Old Calabar.* London: Oxford University Press.
Forde, D. & Jones, G. I., 1950. *The lbo and Ibibio-speaking Peoples of South-eastern Nigeria.* London: International African Institute.
Fortes, M., 1954. 'A Demographic Field Study in the Ashanti', in Lorimer, F. (ed.), *Culture and Human Fertility II*, UNESCO.
Gardinier, D. E., 1963. *Cameroon, United Nations Challenge to French Policy.* London.
Goldie, Hugh, 1874. *Efik Grammar.* Glasgow.
Greenberg, J. H., 1963. *The Languages of Africa.* Indiana.
Grenfell, G., 1882. 'The Cameroon District, W. Africa', *Proceedings of the Royal Geographical Society* (10), Oct., pp. 586–95.
Guillaume, G., and Bedermann, S. H., 1967. *Subsistence Activity in Five Villages on and around Mount Cameroon in Victoria Division, West Cameroon.* Atlanta: Georgia State College.
Guthrie, M., 1948. *The Classification of the Bantu Languages.* London.
— 1953. *The Bantu Languages of Eastern Equatorial Africa.* London.
Hair, P. E. H., 1967. 'Ethnolinguistic continuity on the Guinea Coast', *J. African History* 8 (2): pp. 247–68.
Harleian Coll., 1745. *A Collection of Voyages and Travels. . .* Vol. II, pp. 511–517.
Hurault, J., 1963. *La structure social des Bamiléké.* The Hague.
Hutchinson, Thomas J., 1858. *Impressions of Western Africa. . .* London.
Huxley, F., 1966. *The Invisibles.* London: Hart-Davis.

Ittmann, Johannes., 1939. *Grammatik des Duala (Kamerun) unter Mitarbeit von Carl Meinhof.* Berlin and Hamburg.
— 1953. *Volkskundliche und religiöse Begriffe im nördlichen Waldland von Kamerun.* Berlin.
— 1956. 'Der Walfang an der Küste Kameruns', *Zeitschrift für Ethnologie* 81 (2).
— 1957. 'Der kultische Geheimbund "djengu" an der Kameruner Küste'. *Anthropos* 52 (1–2).
Jarvie, I. A., 1963. *The Revolution in Anthropology.* London: Routledge and Kegan Paul.
Johnston, Sir Harry H., 1908. *George Grenfell and the Congo.* London: Hutchinson.
— 1919, 1922. *A comparative study of Bantu and Semi-Bantu languages. 2 Vols.* London.
Johnson, W., 1965. 'The Cameroon Federation', in W. H. Lewis (ed,), *French-speaking Africa,* New York.
Jones, G. I., 1956. In D. Forde (ed.), *Efik Traders of Old Calabar.* London: Oxford University Press.
— 1963. *The Trading States of the Oil Rivers.* London.
— 1965. 'Time and oral tradition with special reference to Eastern Nigeria', *Journal of African History* 6 (2), pp. 153–160.
Kaberry, Phyllis M., 1962. 'Retainers and Royal Households in the Cameroons Grassfields', *Cahiers d'Etudes Africaines* 8 (10), pp. 282–298. Paris.
Kale P. M. 1939., *A Brief History of the Bakweri,* Lagos.
Kernkamp, G. W. 1908., 'Zweedsche Archivalia uitgegeven door G.W.K. 1. Brieven van Samuel Blommaert aan den Zweedschen Rijkskanselier Axel Oxenstierna, 1635–1641', *Bijdragen en Mededeelingen van het Historisch Genootschap (Gevestigd de Utrecht).* 29, pp. 3–196.
Kimble, George H. T., (ed. and translator). 1937. *Esmeraldo de Situ Orbis.* London.
Kingsley, M., 1964 (reprint). *West African Studies.*
Kisob, J. A., 1963. 'A Live Language: "Pidgin English"', *Abbia,* Feb.
Kuczynski, R. R., 1939. *The Cameroons and Togoland. A Demographic Study* London: O.U.P.
Labarthe, P., 1803. *Voyage à la côte de Guiné. . .* Paris.
Langhans, P., 1902. 'Vergessene Reisen in Kamerun, 1. Reisen des Missionars Alexander Ross von Alt-Kalabar nach Efut 1877 und 1879', *Petermanns Mitteilungen* 48 (IV), pp. 73–78.
Leers, Arnout, 1665. *Pertinente Beschryvinge van Africa. . . Getrocken en vergadert uyt de Reysboeken van Johannes Leo Africanus.* Rotterdam.
Leroy, R., 1922. 'Syndrome of Lilliputian Hallucinations', *Journal of Nervous and Mental Disease* (56), p. 325.
LeVine, V. T., 1964. *The Cameroons from Mandate to Independence.* Berkley, Calif.

— 1964. 'The Cameroun Federal Republic', in G. Carter, (ed.), *Five African States*. London.

— 1965. 'The Course of Political Violence', in W. H. Lewis (ed.), *French-speaking Africa,* New York.

Lévi-Strauss, C., 1962. *La Pensée sauvage*. Paris: Plon.

— 1964. *Mythologiques: Le cru et le cuit.* Paris: Plon.

— 1966. *Mythologiques: Du miel aux cendres.* Paris: Plon.

Lewis, W. H., (ed.), 1965. *French-Speaking Africa: the Search for Identity.* New York.

Linschoten, Jan Huygen Van, 1596. *Itinerario, Voyage ofte Shipvaert van Jan Huygen van Linschoten naer Dost ofte Portugaels Indien. . . t'Amstelredam. By Cornelius Claesz.* Amsterdam.

Lisboa, Joaode, 1514. *Ho Tratado de Angulha de marear. . .* Lisbon. In Rebello (1903).

Lobato, João, 1952. Relatório de João Lobato a D. João III (13.4.1529) Arquiva da Torre do Tombo, CC-1-42-90. *MMA* 1, pp. 505–518.

Mareez Pieter De, 1605. *Description et Récit Historique du Riche Royaume d'Or de Gunea* [sic], *autrement nommé la côte de l'or de Mina, gisant en certain endroit d'Afrique. . .* Amsterdam.

Massmann, P. J. C., 1910. *Realienbuch für deutsche Schulen in Kamerun; A: Geschichte.* Limburg a.d. Lahn.

Meek, C. K., 1957. *Land Tenure and Land Administration in Nigeria and the Cameroons.* London.

Meillassoux, C., 1964. *Anthropologie éonomique des Gouro du Côte d'Ivoire,* Paris.

Missionary Herald, Baptist Missionary Society. London (series).

Mitchell, J. C., 1964. 'Theoretical Orientations in African Urban Studies', in *The Social Anthropology of Complex Societies.* London: ASA Monograph No 4.

Monod, T. H., 1928. *L'industrie des pêches au Cameroun.* Paris.

MMA., 1952+. *Monumenta Missionaria Africana, Africa Ocidental,* Coligida e Anotada por Padre António Brásio C.S. Sp. Lisbon.

Mota, A. Teixeira & Carreira, Antonio, 1966. '*Milho Zaburro* and *Milho Maçaroca* in Guinea and in the islands of Cabo Verde', *Africa,* 36 (1), Jan., London.

Murdock, G. P., 1959. *Africa: its Peoples and their Culture History.* New York.

Mussett, George (see Fonteneau).

Mveng, Englebert, 1963. *Histoire du Cameroun.* Paris.

Myers, J. B., 1889. *Thomas J. Comber, Missionary Pioneer to the Congo.*

Naber, S. P. L'Honoré, 1913 (see Ruiters).

— 1913 (see Brun).

Needham, R., 1967. 'Right and Left in Nyoro Symbolic Classification', *Africa* 37 (4), pp. 425–452.

Njeuma, M. Z., 1964. *The Origins of Pan-Cameroonism.* Buea.

Ogilby, John, 1670. *Africa. . .* London.
Ortelius, Abraham, 1570. *Theatrum Orbis Terrarum.* Antwerp.
Pall Mall Gazette, 10 March, 1885.
Pereira, Duarte Pacheco (see Basto, Dias and Kimble).
Phillipson, Sir S., 1959. *Financial, Economic and Administrative Consequences to the Southern Cameroons of Separation from the Federation of Nigeria.* Lagos.
Pigafetta, Filippo, 1591. *Relatione del Reame di Congo et delle circonvicine contrade tratte dalli scitti & ragionamenti di Odoardo Lopez Portoghese.* Rome.
Pory, John, 1600. *A Geographical History of Africa. . .* London.
Poutrin, M., 1930. *Enquête coloniale dans l'Afrique français occidentale et equatoriale. . .*
Puttkamer, J. von., 1912. *Gouverneursjahre in Kamerun.* Berlin: Georg Stilke.
Ramos-Coelho, Jose, (ed.), 1892. *Alguns documentos do Archivo Nacional da Torre do Tombo ácerca das navegaçoes e conquistas portuguezas. . .* Lisbon.
Ravenstein, E. G., 1901. *The Strange Adventures of Andrew Battel of Leigh in Angola and the adjoining regions. . .* London.
Rebello, J. I., De Brito (ed.). 1903. *Livro de Marinharia.*
Richardson, I., 1955. *Africa.* pp. 161–9.
— 1956–7. *Linguistic Survey of the Northern Bantu Borderland,* Vols i & ii. London.
Roberts, M., 1960. 'Political Prospects for the Cameroun', *World Today,* July.
Rodrioges (Roiz), Duarte, 1954. Carta de Duarte Roiz a El-Rei (10-5-1529). Arq. da Torre do Tombo CC-I-42-116. *MMA* 4, pp. 144–146.
Rosa, Gasparda, 1955. 'Lembranças de Gaspar da Rosa', *MMA* 6, pp. 346–350.
Rudin, H. H., 1934. *Germans in the Cameroons, 1884–1914.* London.
Ruel, M. 1969., *Leopards and Leaders: Constitutional Politics among a Cross River People.* London: Tavistock Publications.
Ruiters, Dierick, (ed. Naber, S. P.), 1623. *Toortse der Zee-Vaert. . .* Flushing. 1623. In *Wertken Uitgegeven door de Linschoten-Vereeniging,* Vol. VI, 1913.
Ryder, A. F. C., 1965. *Materials for West African History in Portuguese Archives.* London.
Santarem, Viscomte De, 1899. *Atlas composé de cartes hydrographiques et historiques depuis le VIe Jusqu'au XVIIe siècle, pour la plupart inédites, et tirées de plusieurs bibliothèques de l'Europe. . .* Paris.
Savitsky, N. and Tarachow, S., 1941. 'Lilliputian Hallucinations during Convalescence of Scarlet Fever', *Journal of Nervous and Mental Disease.* (93), pp. 310–312.
Schwartz, B., 1886. *Kamerun: Reise in die Hinterlande der Kolonie.* Leipzig: Paul Frohberg.
Stone, B. G., 1929. Notes on the Buea District. (MS.) Victoria, Cameroon.
Talbot, P. A., 1912. *In the Shadow of the Bush.* London: Heinemann.
— 1926. *Southern Nigeria.* Oxford.

Tardits, C., 1960. *Les Bamiléké de l'Ouest Cameroun.* Paris.
Taylor, E. G. R., (ed.), 1932. *Barlow, Roger, A Brief Summe of Geographie,* London.
Tanreiro, F., 1961. *A Ilha de São Tomé.* Lisbon.
Tessman, Gunter, 1923. *Die Bubi auf Fernando Poo. . .*
— 1932. 'Die Völker und Sprachen Kameruns', *Petermanns Mitteilungen* 78 (5/6), pp. 113–120; (7/8), pp. 184–190.
Thomas, Northcote W., 1914. *Specimens of Languages from Southern Nigeria.* London.
Thomson, Q., 1882. 'A Native Court or Palaver at Victoria, West Africa', *Missionary Herald,* 1 December.
Vansina, Jan, 1965. *Oral Tradition.* London.
Victoria Division Annual Report, March 1933.
Waddell, Rev. Hope Masterson, 1863. *Twenty-nine Years in the West Indies and Central Africa.*
Welch, C., 1966. *Dream of Unity.* New York.
Zintgraff, E., 1895. *Nord-Kamerun.* Berlin: Gebrüder Poetel.

The largest of these islands is
the traditional home of the Wovea people

Appendix A

The Wovea Islanders of Ambas Bay*

It takes no little courage to pursue and kill whales from dug-out canoe and the Wovea of the Cameroons are one of the few tribes of the West Coast who can claim to have performed this feat. Although the Wovea admit that they have no longer the skill and confidence to hunt whales, their claim to have done so in the past is shown to be more than bravado not only by the documentation of others, but by the existence today of the gear for this activity. The whale harpoon, called by the Wovea *liongo,* has a single barb and is about eighteen inches long, while an impressive iron spike, called *esoni,* which is about nine feet long, was used to finish off the whale. These implements, although rusty from lack of use, are proudly displayed by the Wovea to their visitors.

The small Bantu-speaking Wovea tribe, numbering only about 550 altogether, has another unusual claim to interest, for the senior village is on a tiny island of rock just off the coast of the Ambas Bay. This island is the largest of a small group called the Pirate Islands, and is itself known by Europeans as Bota Island. On this tiny area of land, hardly more than half a square mile, live 200 people together with their livestock. When it is considered that the island is quite unable to support crops of any kind and that the only vegetation consists of bushes and small trees which cling to the rocky surface, one cannot but admire the determination of its inhabitants to remain in what appears such an inhospitable environment. The island even lacks springs or natural drinking water of any kind.

The Wovea, in their traditions of origin, tell how they came to settle on the island. They claim to be descended from a man of the *Bubi* tribe of Fernando Po who was shipwrecked on the Bamboko coast of the mainland, where he married a Bamboko woman named Ekoli and came down the coast and settled on Bota Island. There seems little doubt that the Wovea had ancestors among the Bubi as their name Wovea is itself

* *Article published in* Nigeria, *59, 1958.*

derived from their name for the Bubi, which is Wove or Bove. That the ancestors of the Wovea intermarried with local tribes is also evident from the fact that the Wovea language shows close affinities with those of the neighbouring tribes such as the Bamboko and Bakweri and little with the present speech of the Bubi. As the population expanded, the two larger islands in Ambas Bay which are not part of the Pirate group, Ambas (known to the Wovea as Ndame) and Mondoleh (Mondoli) Islands, were also settled. The date of these events is not known but the islands were certainly inhabited in the seventeenth century, being known as the three Amboises or Ambozes Islands. Dapper (about 1670) said the people made frequent visits to the mainland to obtain the necessities of life, and Barbot (about 1700) agreed that the islanders obtained a great amount of provisions from the mainland, but he maintained at the same time that the islands produced enough food for the inhabitants. Presumably, if this was true, crops must have been planted on the two larger islands, Ndame and Mondoli. In the nineteenth century the Wovea are clearly mentioned as 'Boobees''. After a serious quarrel with a neighbouring tribe on the mainland, the Isuwu of Bimbia, in about 1855, the Wovea were forced to abandon Ndame Island and founded the village of Molondi, known to Europeans as Bota Land. This village is now the largest of the Wovea villages, having a population of 300, and has given its name to the headquarters of the Cameroons Development Corporation. In 1907 the Germans transferred the inhabitants of Mondoli, the other large island in the Bay, to the mainland in order to use the island as a leprarium, and this settlement now numbers about sixty. The two large islands are now uninhabited.

Since there is neither soil nor water on the inhabited island, the Wovea people have adopted a specialised economy. They have become, as might be expected, and as has already been said, skilled fishermen, and virtually the whole population is concerned, one way or another, in the fishing industry. Even the children take tins and nets and catch tiny fish in the surf on their small beach. Women fish with·fish traps, called *ico,* and men used a variety of nets and harpoons, and formerly a fish-spear consisting of twelve iron spikes lashed round the end of a pole. Some fishing takes place at night when the men go out in their canoes and attract the fish with lights. Various kinds of nets are made on the island from imported string; and canoes, necessary for transporting persons and essential supplies to and from the island as well as for the fishing industry, are made of ironwood or iroko. The Efik fishermen and traders who pass frequently along the coast from the Calabar area, have introduced sails to the Wovea, and have given their word for sail to the

Young men making nets in 1958

Wovea language. Fish appear to be plentiful in the area, and the hunting of whale in the past is not likely to have been due to economic necessity. The season for hunting whale is said to have been in August, when they can still be seen in the waters between the Cameroons and Fernando Po.

After the fish have been caught the women of the island bring them to the mainland to barter them with women of the neighbouring tribe for coco-yams and other foodstuffs. Even in these days of a cash economy, this direct barter still takes place near the mainland village of Ngeme. The women thus control most of the marketing of the fish, bringing them to the shore in their own canoes for sale at Victoria as well as for barter at Ngeme. It has been said that the great demand for fish has, in fact, restricted their supply, for fishermen are able to satisfy their own needs with little work at fishing.

The Wovea people who are settled on the mainland have their own farms, and some of the islanders cultivate plots on the mainland at Isokolo near to the Bota settlement. In the mainland villages the agricultural economy is similar to that of the other tribes of the area, but on the island, since no crops can be grown, the keeping of pigs is one of the few other economic pursuits, and these very under-nourished beasts spend much time on the beach searching for the oil palm nuts which are frequently washed up from the sea.

Anyone visiting the island is paddled across in a dug-out canoe to the small beach and from here makes his way to the foot of a high stairway up the cliff to the island top. High irregular steps have been hewn in the solid rock-face and smoothed with cement. On arriving at the top, he will find the houses of 'split carraboard' and iron sheets with palm mat roofs, similar to those of the neighbouring mainland tribes, crowded together on the uneven surface of the island. He must jump down and climb up the pathway between the houses, the close proximity of which must give welcome protection when the sea breezes that continually cool the island change into violent storms. At such times the islanders regret their isolation and the need to go to the mainland for water and firewood regardless of the weather. The very closeness of the houses and the lack of any top-soil make it necessary for burials to take place inside the house, a custom formerly practised for choice by many of the mainland tribes, but practised of necessity by the islanders to-day.

Although the Wovea people are skilled fishermen, fishing is not the full-time occupation of all, and many of the men are employed in a variety of work on the mainland, especially in the Cameroons

Spear used to finish off whales

Whale (*njonje*) is hunted with this harpoon

Development Corporation, which has plantations on the neighbouring shore. However, one of the occupations most favoured by the Wovea men is the loading and unloading of cargo on the ships visiting Victoria and the manipulation of the winches. The loading of the produce exported by the plantations requires a large amount of labour and men of all tribes can be found in this work, but the loading and unloading of general cargo from the holds is mainly in the hands of the Wovea people. Following the practice of sailors throughout the West Coast, such workers are frequently referred to as 'Kru boys' since they perform tasks associated with men of the Kru peoples of Liberia. Although, therefore, the Wovea people no longer go out in their canoes to hunt the whale, they are still closely associated with the more skilled tasks connected with the sea by which they live.

Shirley and Edwin Ardener

Postscript:

Since this article was written some time ago, the Islanders have begun to press the Government to be allowed to migrate to the mainland and to settle permanently at Isokolo where they have already some farms. More land is to be made available to them. Why are they moving? Motives are various and mixed. Since their old chief retired in 1954 they have lacked steady leadership. Petty fears and jealousies have begun to split the old unity. These are partly symptoms of the fact that the island is so congested. There is barely room for a single new house and its healthy protein-fed population is still growing. Some say the fish have become less plentiful since the activity last year of Spanish and French trawlers in nearby waters. Some eyes are also cast on the success of Bakweri co-operative banana farmers on the coast. Not all the islanders say they intend to move at first, and some migration is probably the only way to relieve the congestion. But a certain loss of confidence in their way of life is visible. The fishing communities need an economic stimulus which the introduction of fishing co-operatives might go a long way to provide. The idea already has some local support. In the centenary year of the foundation of Victoria, and the year that the Southern Cameroons achieved Ministerial Government, it would be a pity for one of its most distinctive communities to fade quietly away.

Edwin Ardener.

[By 1996 the Wovea people were reported as all living on the mainland, but visting the island from time to time. For more illustrations see original publication. Ed.]

Appendix B

Preliminary Chronological Notes for the Cameroon Coast*

This chronology of the Coast of Cameroon amends and augments the picture deriving from Bouchaud, as well as throwing light on some topics going back to Avelot (in Poutrin). We give a skeletal chronology of the coast therefore. This is selective of items which have either been firmly dated since the standard literature, or which are frequently misdated. This chronology is followed by a skeletal chronology drawn from several papers in this volume. A few references only are cited here. [For further details see the first contribution above.]

Chronology of selected events at the Cameroon Coast

1474 Fernam do Po reaches the Island of Fernando Po, and, by presumption, the Coast of Cameroon. The prime source is Barros, 1552; the date 1474 was arrived at by Bouchaud from an examination of Barros (Bouchaud 1952: Ch. 3, 4).

1503–1505 Pacheco Pereira gathered material on this area most probably at the time of his second visit to India (1520–22 is another, less likely, possible period). Pacheco's account of trade in slaves, pepper and ivory, in exchange for manillas, with the people called *Caaboo* took place on the Cameroon Coast (Bouchaud, 1952, E. W. Ardener, 1968) and not, as Kimble believed (see above). on Fernando Po. Ardener suggests that the obscure topographical feature, *Bota,* was the Cameroon Mountain. Although the fishing grounds of the Cameroon estuary were know, trade did not take place at this point.

* *Edwin and Shirley Ardener. From Rapport de Synthèse - Colloques Internationaux du C.N.R.S. No. 551—Contribution de la Recherche ethanologique à l'histoire des civilisations du Cameroun.*

Lisboa's account, more or less contemporary with Pacheco's, confirms the existence of fishing grounds, specifying those at the entrance to Rio del Rey. The latter existed continuously to the present day.

1518 Andreas Pires, a Portuguese pilot, wrote a manual which was translated in the same year into Castillian by Martin Enciso. Several topographical features have been identified with existing places *(cabo de Fernando polo* with Cape Debundscha or Bimbia point; *golfo d'l galo* with Suellaba point). We learn of people who possess gold, palms (coconut) and palm wine, raffia cloth and iron, but the location of the population is not clear.

1529 (10th May) A Letter from Duarte Rodrigues to the King of Portugal refers to trade with the Ambos, identified with inhabitants of islands in the Bay of Victoria (known today as Ambas Bay), or of Bimbia Island nearby.

In this same year (13 April), it is recorded in a letter to the King that boats for rowing were required at Fernando Po, possibly for voyages to the mainland.

1600 (c.) The supposed founder of Douala, Ewale, and his father Mbedi, would belong to a milieu about this date (see below.). 'The Mbedine events' (Dugast, 1949: p. 10–21; Ardener, 1956: pp. 17–18, 20–21) can hardly have occurred later than some time in the sixteenth century. Traditionally movement took place from *Bitti* above the Cameroon Estuary in the Dibamba affluent (Moneba's Channel as it was later known). The Kole and Malimba and others attach their ancestors to this same movement. The movements were possibly in response to the trade mentioned by Pacheco.

1826 Britain signs anti-slave-trade Convention with Brazil.

(March–May) Capt. Owen, of British Navy survey vessel, surveys shore of Cameroon on way back from Congo.

(26 Dec.) Brazilian slave ship 'Invincible' captured in river Cameroons with 440 slaves on board. (B.P.P., 13 July, 1830).

1827 (22 Oct.) Capt. Owen establishes British post on Fernando Po. Lynslager, later Acting British Consul with jurisdiction in the Cameroon area, probably arrived on Fernando Po in this year.

1828 (5 Aug.) Brazilian slave ship 'Clementina' captured in Cameroons River (156 slaves). (B.P.P., 13 July, 1830).

(20 Aug.) Brazilian slave ship 'Voadore' captured in River Bimbri (Bimbia ?) but no slaves on board. (B.P.P., 13 July, 1830).

(30 Oct.) Brazilian slave ship 'Arcenia' captured in Cameroon River with 269 slaves. (B.P.P., 13 July, 1830).

(30 Oct.) Brazilian slave ship 'Estrella do Mar' captured in Cameroons River, but no slaves on board.

1829 (June) John Beecroft (or Becroft), later to become British Consul, brought to Fernando Po by Col. Nicholls, Superintendent of the British settlement on Fernando Po.

1831 (16 Dec.) Anti–slave–trade Treaty between Britain and France.

1832 British settlement on Fernando Po formally abandoned.

1834 (30 June) Spanish slave ship, 'Pepita', captured at River Cameroons (179 slaves). (B.P.P., 29 June, 1842).

1837 Possible first mention of 'the natives called *Esoubou*' (Isubu), as opposed to the more common use of the term Bimbe (or its variants) as a place name. (J. Purdy, 1837: 334–336 (footnote)).

King Billeh of Bimbia reputedly hands over sovereignty of his area to the British Crown, through the mediation of Col. Nicholls. (Allen, Vol. II, Ch. VII, cited also in Burton, pp. 49–50). This agreement was never ratified by the British Government.

1838 (1 August) Final abolition of Slavery in British

Territories.

1839 (April–Nov.) Capt. on British vessel in Cameroon River reports absence of slave ships (except for one small vessel manned by blacks). (Jamieson's 'letter' to Lord Russell, dated 8 August 1840).

1840's French open station at Malimba (Le Vine, 1964: 20).

1840 (18 March) King Bell and King Acqui (Akwa) make Agreement with Merchants trading in the Cameroon (witnessed by representatives of British Government) concerning regulation of trade. (S. G. Ardener, 1978, p. 70. This reprints Treaties as given in Hertslet. The 1968 publication is cited here since it is more easily obtainable than Hertslet).

(10 June) King Acqui (Akwa) and King Bell make Declaration that there should be no slave trade in Cameroon River, in return for a 'Dash' from the British Government. (S. G. Ardener, 1968. p. 71).

1841 Beecroft ascends Wuri River (John Whitford, 1877, p. 152).

(1 Jan.) First Baptist Missionaries arrive at Fernando Po (Clarke and Prince). Visit mainland of Cameroon soon after the Niger Expedition.

(7 May) King Bell makes Treaty with British Government concerning Cessation of Slave Trade. (S. G. Ardener, 1968, pp. 71–72).

1842 Capt. Allen surveys Victoria Bay.

(11 May) Agreement between Allen and Gandah, King Acqua (FO 84/1087).

(7 Sept.) Beecroft ascends Cross River. (T.J. Hutchinson, 1858, p. 114).

1843 Beecroft made Governor of Fernando Po and its dependant islands.
Land Agreement between King Akwa and Baptist

Missionaries. (BMS Archives). Merrick starts work in Bell Town.

1844 (16 Feb.) Slave Ship 'Carlitos' (no slaves on board) found at Bimbia Creek. (B.P.P., 29 June, 1842).

(17 February) King William and Chiefs of Bimbia (Prince George, Dick Merchant, John Bimbia, Old Amba) sign anti–slave treaty with British Government. Ratified in 1846. (S. G. Ardener, 1968, pp. 63–4).

(April) Merrick climbs Cameroon Mountain.

1845. (June 19) Saker begins work in Douala. Merrick moves to Bimbia.

1846 Merrick visits Esunggi and Dibanda.

(July) Death of King Akwa (T.J. Hutchinson; E. Saker: 75). War of succession lasted 5 months. Peace restored by British Naval vessel. Eldest son succeeds.

1847 (5 July) King John Batanga and King Batanga at Banaka make agreement with representatives of Great Britain for suppression of slave trade. This was reinforced by a further agreement on 18 July, 1860. (S. G. Ardener, 1968, pp. 83). Provision is made for France to become a party to this agreement.

1848 Clarke gives languages identified by E.W. Ardener as: Efik, Ekoi, Kenyang (Banyang), Barnum ?, Bamileke, Ndob, Lundu, Ngolo–Batanga, Ekumbe, Mbo, Balong, Bonken, Bakweri, Wovea, Isubu, Duala, Kole, Bubi, Benga, Lombi, Nkon, Basa, Bakoko, Banen, Bafia. Material collected mainly 1841–47. References to Bali fighting in Bamum area. (For Clarke's 'geography' of Cameroon see: E. W. Ardener, 1972, Commentary in edition of Clarke).

Saker takes over Baptist Mission at Fernando Po, and thus becomes head of mission in this area.

(31 March) King William and Chiefs of Bimbia (Prince William, Quan, Nacco, Dick, Young Ambie, Dick Mer–chant, John Bimbia) sign engagement abolishing custom of human sacrifice, with representatives of British

Government. (S. G. Ardener, 1968, pp. 64–5).

(31 March) King Pass, Prince Jumbo, Headman, Young Pass (King Pass's son), King Dyer and Duke, all of Malimba, make treaties with representatives of the British Government for the suppression of the slave trade. (S. G. Ardener, 1968, p. 83). Provision is made for France to become a party to this agreement.

(7 April) King Dick Moondah and Dongo of Boquah make agreement for the suppression of slave trade, similar to that made between British Government and King William of Bimbia in 1844. Provision is made for France to become a party to this agreement. (S. G. Ardener, 1968, p. 83).

1849 (30 June) Letter appoints Beecroft as British Consul. In 1853 his jurisdiction over the Lagos area is removed. Beecroft dies on 10 June 1854, aged 64. Is succeeded by Lynslager, as Acting Consul.

1849 Merrick dies.

1850 (17 December) King Bell, King Acqua (Akwa) and Chiefs of Cameroon (Tuccotoo, Ned Dido, Tim Acqua, Joss Bell, Sam Tory) make Treaty with representatives of British Government concerning regulation of trade. (S. G. Ardener, 1968, pp. 72–73).

(19 December) King William and Chiefs of Bimbia (Nacco, Young Ambey, Tom Bimbey, John Bimbey, Dick Merchant, Duke Merchant) enter into treaty concerning rules of trade with representatives of British Government. (S. G. Ardener, 1968, pp. 65–67).

1852 (8 March) Election of King Acqua under auspices of Beecroft. Petition with many signatures asking for Jim Acqua to be installed.

1853 Koelle's *Polyglotta* published. For Koelle's Linguistic Geography of Cameroon see also Commentary in E.W. Ardener's edition (1972) of Clarke (1848).

1855 (28 January) Ned Acqua murdered by supercargo Walker (FO/84/975/47–55).

(30 January) King Acqua (Akwa) and Chiefs of Acqua Town, Cameroons, make Declaration concerning safety of traders and resumption of trade, with representatives of British Government (S. G. Ardener, 1968, pp. 73–74).

(1 February) King Bell enters into Engagement to pay his trading debts, witnessed by representatives of British Government.

(2 February) King Bell and King Acqua (Akwa) and Chiefs (Dido Acqua, Jim Quan, Eyo, Preso Bell, Moss Coko, Taman, Ben Hickory Town, Sam Peter, Joss Bell, Jackoo, Green Ned Dido, Big Tom Dido) engage not to use firearms except in self defence. King Acqua (and Ned Dido, Big Tom Dido, Dido Acqua, Jim Quan and Eyo) agree to make payment to the people of Wuri for men killed. Engagement witnessed by representatives of British Government. (S. G. Ardener, 1968, pp. 74–75).

(7 February) The Chiefs of Boobee (= Wovea) Mahoua and Moutout, acknowledge their allegiance to King William and Chiefs of Bimbia (Dick Merchant, Dick Bimbia, Harry King William, Nacco), by an Engagement, witnessed by representatives of the British Government. (S. G. Ardener 1968, pp. 66–67).

1856 Rev. Anderson of Calabar corresponds with Hutchinson on subject of Tikar, Mbafu and Mbudikum (T. J. Hutchinson, 1861, p. 321).

(January) Hutchinson, who was appointed as British Consul in succession of Beecroft in 1855, arrives on first official visit to Cameroon River.

(January) War between Dido and Acqua; Dido town burnt down. Many deaths.

(14 January) Treaty with the Kings, Chiefs and Traders of Cameroons, concerning Bye–Laws for establishing an Equity Court to be established in the River Cameroons, on which the Kings and traders are to sit. Witnessed by

representatives of British Government. On 14 January Chiefs of Dido and Acqua Towns agree to accept ruling of Equity Court in matter concerning two freemen killed in the late war. (S. G. Ardener, 1968, pp. 75–78).

1858 Hutchinson publishes *Impressions of Ethiopia,* giving reference to Arumbi, Duwalla, D'ambedi, Collambedi, Mungo, Baboubi race, Isubutribu.

(9 June) First Settlers arrive from Fernando Po at Victoria.

(19 May) King Acqua (Akwa) and Chiefs (Prince Dido, John Anguah, Jim Quan and Eyo) agree to abolish 'Makoko' custom, on condition that slaves headed by Yellow Acqua, Senior, and Yellow Acqua, junior, shall abolish the 'Manganga' custom. Witnessed by representatives of the British Government, and by F. Pinnock, Bonny Acqua and Long Tom Acqua. (S. G. Ardener, 1968, p. 78).

1859 Alexander Innes 'annexes' Acqua Town (not ratified) for Great Britain. (S. G. Ardener, 1968, p. 56).

(July) Duala people are celebrating human sacrifices commemorating death of King Bell, who was succeeded by Bonny Bell.

(8 July) King Acqua and Chiefs of the Cameroons River (Bonny Bell, Josse, Preso Bell) agree to adhere to Treaty of 11 May 1842, and abandon human sacrifice, and further, to settle disputes between the Chiefs and people of one town or towns and another or other towns, through the arbitration of traders. (S. G. Ardener, 1968, pp. 78–79).

Capt. Close 'annexes' Douala for Britain (not ratified). (S. G. Ardener, 1968, p. 56).

1860 King Krabbe of Kribi tries to seize Kru agent of European merchants. Disturbances at Batanga. First visit of British naval ship with Consul since treaty of 1847. Krabbe angry because no factory established.

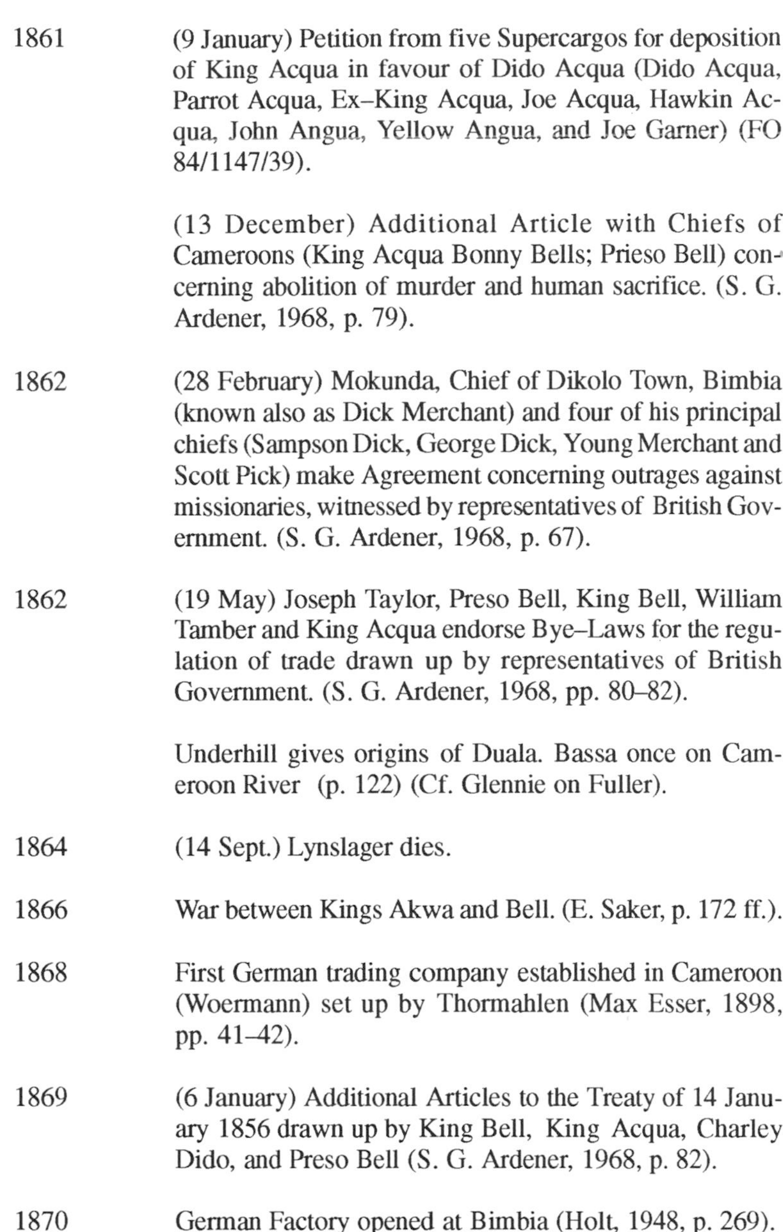

1861 (9 January) Petition from five Supercargos for deposition of King Acqua in favour of Dido Acqua (Dido Acqua, Parrot Acqua, Ex–King Acqua, Joe Acqua, Hawkin Acqua, John Angua, Yellow Angua, and Joe Garner) (FO 84/1147/39).

(13 December) Additional Article with Chiefs of Cameroons (King Acqua Bonny Bells; Prieso Bell) concerning abolition of murder and human sacrifice. (S. G. Ardener, 1968, p. 79).

1862 (28 February) Mokunda, Chief of Dikolo Town, Bimbia (known also as Dick Merchant) and four of his principal chiefs (Sampson Dick, George Dick, Young Merchant and Scott Pick) make Agreement concerning outrages against missionaries, witnessed by representatives of British Government. (S. G. Ardener, 1968, p. 67).

1862 (19 May) Joseph Taylor, Preso Bell, King Bell, William Tamber and King Acqua endorse Bye–Laws for the regulation of trade drawn up by representatives of British Government. (S. G. Ardener, 1968, pp. 80–82).

Underhill gives origins of Duala. Bassa once on Cameroon River (p. 122) (Cf. Glennie on Fuller).

1864 (14 Sept.) Lynslager dies.

1866 War between Kings Akwa and Bell. (E. Saker, p. 172 ff.).

1868 First German trading company established in Cameroon (Woermann) set up by Thormahlen (Max Esser, 1898, pp. 41–42).

1869 (6 January) Additional Articles to the Treaty of 14 January 1856 drawn up by King Bell, King Acqua, Charley Dido, and Preso Bell (S. G. Ardener, 1968, p. 82).

1870 German Factory opened at Bimbia (Holt, 1948, p. 269).

1871 Court of Equity re–established (King Bell, Prince Acqua, Black Acqua, Mokuri, Lock Priso in place of Priso Bell,

	Charley Dido. Witnesses, eight agents of whom one was German and missionary Quintin Thompson).
	Saker finishes translation of Bible into Duala. (Underhill, pp. 51–62).
1872	Chiefs of Bonjongo (Fondo Mbome, Motut Mo Ngumba, Diyunga, Esuka, Biwule, Eko Mbonze Bwele) sign land agreement, permitting establishment by Q.W. Thompson of Baptist Mission Station. (S. G. Ardener, 1968, p. 62).
	(March) Hopkins reports that the two Kings of Joss Town were King Joss and Coffee Joss.
	Quintin Thompson visits villages on Cameroon Mountain (Bosumbo, Boana, Mapanya, Banjango, Makunda, Botta—chiefs named).
	(November) War in Douala.
1875	School founded at Butu (Malimba) (Underhill, p. 165). George Grenfell explores estuarine area. (Hemmens, p. 49).
1876	Saker retires from Cameroon. He died in 1880.
	Smallpox epidemic up 'Lungarsi' River decimates villages. Butu (Malimba) abandoned. Kotto in ruins (Underhill, pp. 166–168).
	End of year, headman of Bonjongo just died (George Thompson, p. 185).
1877	Chief (Msassu?) and his brother Mungola of Mafanja mentioned.
	Yellow Joss or Priso of Cameroon claims Nicholl Island, in opposition to King William of Bimbia.
	Comber crosses the Cameroon Mountain from 'Bibundi to Rickards–See' (Barombi–Kotto Lake, Kumba) in Bambuko land.

1879 (January) C. H. Richardson and T. Johnson, and their wives, found mission station at Banga (Bakundu). (MH, 1879, pp. 252–253).
(7 August) King Acqua (Akwa) and others send letter to Queen Victoria.

1881 (6 November) Kings Bell and Akwa write to Gladstone.

1882 King of Bimbia killed by Woloa, Chief of Soppo (Bakweri). (E. W. Ardener, 1956, p. 92, S. G. Ardener, 1968, p. 58).

1882 Njanga Gladstone of Dibombari sells land to Fuller (BMS archives).

Bimbia petitions Britain for annexation (FO/84).

1883 King 'Pass–All' of Malimba makes Treaty with France (negotiated by Godin). (Stengers, in Betts, 1966, p. 45). See also letter from Kings Bell and Akwa to Gladstone (April, 1883). (S. G. Ardener, 1968, p. 19–20).

1884 (9 July) Edward Schmidt, Adolf Woermann and German Consul Emil Schultze arrive from Gaboon in Cameroon River.

(10 July) Chief of Dido Town and Voss sign Treaty.

(11 July) King and Chiefs of Bimbia sign treaty with Schmidt, Woermann and Schultze (text in S. G. Ardener, 1968, p. 58).

(12 July) Kings of Douala sign Treaty with German Traders.

(14 July) German Traders hand over the treaties to Nachtigal at a formal ceremony, when German flag is hoisted.

(19 July) Assumption of British Sovereignty over the Settlement at Amboises or Ambas Bay. (S. G. Ardener, 1968, p. 68).

(28 August) Preliminary Treaties made by Chiefs on Coast West of Victoria, with British Government (Batoki, *et al.*). Names of Chiefs given.

	(November) Bell family take refuge in Mungo Creek (S. Silvey – BMS archives).
	(20 December) Germans attack Hickory and Joss Towns.
1885	(7 May) Agreement between Britain and Germany as to western boundary of Cameroon, along the Rio del Rey to its supposed source and thence to Cross River Rapids, is confirmed. The British enclave at Victoria is still recognized.
1885	(24 December) Germans conclude agreement with French concerning western boundary (Ruppel Ed., 1912, pp. 10–11).
1887	(27 and 31 January) Victoria enclave officially transferred from England to Germany by an exchange of Notes.

General remarks

(a) *General: Duala.* Work on the chronology of the Duala has tended to confirm the general reliability of the genealogical record. It begins to seem probable that the present coastal populations were established already by 1500. However, the existing genealogies express the reaction to trading penetration. The 'Mbongo' ancestries are undifferentiated. The *Mbedine* ancestries in contrast, differentiate new 'big man' polities, circa 1600. Monneba (Mulobe) c. 1650, should probably be regarded as the true founder of Duala's fortunes, due to decline of Rio del Rey and the Ambos of the islands. (For some possible chronological implications of the Di- prefix see Ardener, Commentary to Clarke: 1972, pp. 38–39, s.c. Diwala). The many accounts of migrations seawards suggest that the *littoral* was not already inhabited, but it is improbable that even the Batanga had far to go to reach it.

(b) There is no reference to the Basa in the XVIIth Century sources [See contribution above]. *Monebasche* and the like all go back to maps based on the Leers source, and are Dutch forms referring to Monneba, e.g. *Monneba'sche Gat* (literally the 'Monneba'ish creek'). For the same reason these forms do not refer to the *Malimba.* There is, however, no reason to doubt that the Basa were on the Cameroon estuary in the XVIIth century and earlier (cf. Laburthe–Tolra).

(c) The Cameroon *Ambos* are now firmly fixed by a contemporary Portuguese letter (1529) to the *islands* in Victoria bay. They should be excluded from discussions of the mainland. [The Ambos question is treated above.]

(d) In tying the inland peoples to fixed coastal dates we should note that Coastal Bantu and neighbouring Efik and/or Kwa distributions much the same as now go back to c. 1650, definitely, and to first Portuguese contact, probably. This confirms the general conclusions of Hair about the Guinea coast as a whole period. We are dealing with slow drifts in small numbers towards the growing trading points and the paths leading to them. For West Cameroon some general patterns can be discerned, which have been presented orally. We should note, however, that the major ethnic groups south of the Cross River were fairly certainly in about their present sites before the XIXth century. A probably historical Buea chief can be attested as far back as 1800.

(e) A lesson of recent work is that oral traditions tend to fall into two strata or levels:

1. *A legendary or mythical stratum.* To this stratum belong the ultimate myths of origin and the most distant and general ancestral' names.
2. *A political stratum.* To this belong genealogies ultimately expressing the emergence of significant politico–economic groups. These genealogies seem to have rather outstanding chronological reliability.

Diagramatically this may be represented as:

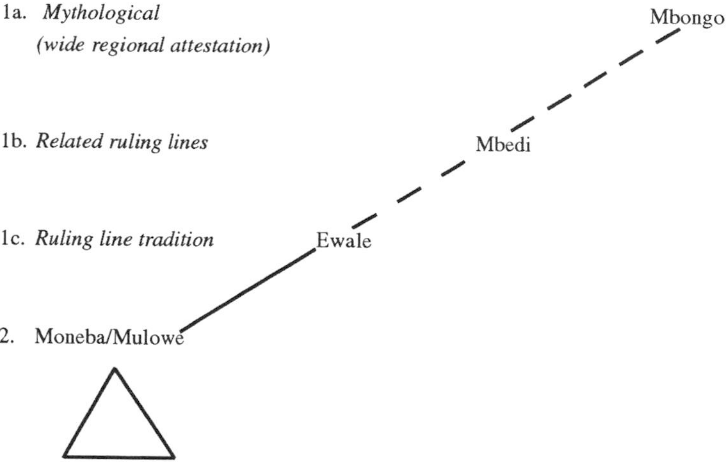

It is important to note that level (2) genealogies will be attached to level (1) material. If level (1) traditions have any chronological implications at all, they are totally discontinuous from those at level (2). With good material we can guess several intermediate linkages: as below for the Duala.

The political stratum (2) is a now fairly well authenticated genealogy from 1650. The next supposed ' ancestor ' (Ewale) is possibly not merely one generation up from before that. *Mbongo* (1a) certainly symbolizes a much more ancient period, or better still belongs in a timeless zone of regional mythology. For poorly documented peoples it is important not to exaggerate the scope of stratum (1) or stratum (2). Broadly all eponymous stories, in the absence of other evidence, should be ascribed to stratum (1). In assessing the possible scope of stratum (2), the 'reliable ' political level, it is important to assess what conditions would assist the transmission of material of this sort. It is very likely that European politico–economic contact is a powerful cause of such transmission — creating as it does new vested interests. These interests may however have grown up some time before direct contact with Europeans themselves.

Appendix C

A Bibliography of Edwin Ardener's Papers on Africa

1952 'A Socio-economic Survey of Mba-Ise' (Ibo, Eastern Nigeria), West African Institute of Social and Economic Research, typescript (bound).

1953 'The Origins of Modern Sociological Problems Connected with the Plantation System in the Victoria Division of the Cameroons', West African Institute of Social and Economic Research, conference proceedings, sociological section, March, pp. 89–105.

1953 'A Rural Oil-palm Industry: 1. Ownership and Processing', *West Africa,* 1909, 26 September, p. 900.

1953 'A Rural Oil-palm Industry: 2. Opposition to Oil Mills', *WestAfrica,* 1910, 3 October, pp. 921–3.

1954 'The Kinship Terminology of a Group of Southern Ibo', *Africa,* 24, April, pp. 85–99.

1954 'Some Ibo Attitudes to Skin Pigmentation', *Man,* 54 (101), May, pp. 71–3.

1954 'Democracy in the Cameroons', *West Africa,* 1932, 6 March, p. 203.

1956–9 Various sections in *Annual Reports on the Cameroons under United Kingdom Administration* (unattributed), HMSO, London.

1956 Coastal Bantu of the Cameroons *(The Kpe-Mboko, Duala-Limba and Tangayasa Groups of the British and French Trusteeship Territories of the Cameroons),* London, International African Institute (Ethnographic Survey of West Africa, 11).

1957 'Sociological investigations of the West African Institute of Social and Economic Research in the Southern Cameroons—Digest of Principal Findings', WAISER, duplicated.

1957 'Cameroons Swing to Tribalism', *West Africa,* 2090, 4 May, p. 411.

1957 'Numbers in Africa', *Man*, 226, November, p. 176.

1958 Various sections in *Victoria, Southern Cameroons, 1858–1958* (unattributed), Victoria Centenary Committee, Victoria, Southern Cameroons, London, Eyre and Spottiswood).

1958 'Marriage Stability in the Southern Cameroons', Nigerian Institute of Social and Economic Research, conference proceedings, mimeographed. Reprinted above as 'Bakweri Fertility and Marriage'.

1958 'The People', in *Introducing the Southern Cameroons* (unattributed), Federal Information Service, Lagos, pp. 17–21.

1958 'Wovea Islanders', in *Nigeria,* 59, pp. 309–21.
1958 'The "Kamerun" Idea', *West Africa,* 2147 p. 533 and 2148. p. 559.
1959 'Lineage and locality among the Mba-Ise Ibo', *Africa,* 29 (2), pp. 113–34.
1959 'Cameroons Election Aftermath', *West Africa,* 2185, February, p. 195.
1959 'The Bakweri Elephant Dance', *Nigeria,* 60, pp. 31–8.
1959 (with D. W. MacRow), 'Cameroon Mountain', *Nigeria,* 62, pp. 230–45.
1960 'The Linguistic Situation in the Southern Cameroons', Nigerian Institute of Social and Economic Research, mimeographed.
1960 'A Note on Intestate Succession', Nigerian Institute of Social and Economic Research, mimeographed.
1960 (with S. G. Ardener and W. A. Warmington), *Plantation and Village in the Cameroons,* Oxford, Oxford University Press.
1961 'Duala', in *Encyclopaedia Britannica.*
1961 'Kpe' (Bakweri), in *Encyclopaedia Britannica.*
1961 'Historical Research in the Southern Cameroons', third conference on African history and archaeology, School of Oriental and African Studies, mimeographed, July.
1961 'Crisis of Confidence in the Cameroons', West Africa, 2306, 12 August.
1961 'Cautious Optimism in West Cameroon', West Africa, 2313, 30 September, p. 1071.
1961 'Social and Demographic Problems of the Southern Cameroons Plantation Area', in Southall, A. (ed.) 1961, *Social Change in Modern Africa,* Oxford, Oxford University Press.
1962 'The Political History of Cameroon', The World Today, 18 (8), pp. 341–50.
1962 *Divorce and Fertility—An African Study*, Oxford, Oxford University Press.
1963 'Imperialism and the British Middle Class', *West Africa*, 2391, March, p. 357.
1965 Contributions to *La Population du Cameroun Occidental*, (unattributed), Société d'Etudes pour le Développement Economique et Social, Paris.
1965 *Historical Notes on the Scheduled Monuments of West Cameroon*, West Cameroon, Buea Archives Office.
1966 Contributions to the English version of *La Population du Cameroun Occidental*, (unattributed), Société d'Etudes pour le Développement Economique et Social, Paris.
1967 'The Nature of the Reunification of Cameroon', in Hazelwood, A. (ed.) *African Integration and Disintegration*, Oxford, Oxford University Press.
1967 'The Notion of the Elite', *African Affairs*, February.
1968 'Documentary and Linguistic Evidence for the Rise of the Trading Polities between Rio del Rey and Cameroon 1500–1650', in Lewis I. M. (ed.) 1968, *History and Social Anthropology* (ASA monographs 7), London, Tavistock.

1970 Review of *Custom and Politics in Urban Africa: A Study of Hausa Migrants in Yoruba Towns,* Cohen, Abner, *Oxford Magazine,* 7, Hilary, pp. 199–200.

1970 'Witchcraft, Economics, and the Continuity of Belief', in Douglas, M. (ed.) *Witchcraft Confessions and Accusations,* London, Tavistock, pp. 141–160.

1972 'Belief and the Problem of Women', in La Fontaine, J. (ed.) 1972, *The Interpretation of Ritual,* London, Tavistock; also in Ardener, S. G. (ed.) 1975, *Perceiving Women,* London, Dent.

1972 Introduction and commentary to reprint of *Specimens of Dialects: Short Vocabularies of Languages: And Notes of Countries and Customs in Africa,* Clarke, J. 1848 Farnham, Gregg International.

1975 The Problem of Women Revisited' in *Perceiving Women,* (S. G. Ardener, ed.) London, Dent; USA, Wiley, pp. 19–27 (also contains 'Belief and the Problem of Women', pp. 1–17, first published 1972, in La Fontaine, J. (ed.)

1982 with Ardener, S. G. 'Preliminary Chronological Notes for the South of Cameroon—Rapport de Synthèse', *Contribution de la Recherche Ethnologique à l'Histoire des Civilisations du Cameroun,* 2, pp. 563–77 ed. Claude Tardits, Centre National de la Recherche Scientifique, Paris, 1982.

1994 'The Personal Enemy in African Politics', *The Journal of the Anthropological Society of Oxford (JASO),* Oxford, Institute of Social and Cultural Anthropology with a comment by David Zeitlyn. (Originally written in 1960 and previously unpublished.)

Edwin Ardener

Appendix D

Selected Further Reading

As explained in the editor's introduction, it has not been possible to make complete reference to all the excellent work which relates to this area that has appeared since Edwin wrote the texts above. Edwin himself published other, including later, texts which are listed in his personal bibliography (Appendix C). For readers' convenience a few publications relating to the Cameroon Mountain area published *since 1970* by other authors are given here. Each will contain its own bibliography, and it is recommended that these be referred to.

Note that general texts on the political and economic development of Cameroon, of which there are many, have been omitted here. These studies and other titles on Cameroon, including the Mount Cameroon area, can be found in two bibliographies which are indispensable for Cameroon studies: the *Historical Dictionary of the Republic of Cameroon*, second edition 1990, eds. Mark W. Delancy and H. Mbella Mokeba, London, the Scarecrow press, and the annual *Africa Bibliography* issued for the International African Institute by Edinburgh University Press.

Bedermann, S. H. produced a report for the Cameroon Development Corporation in 1968, and a number of studies since then on the plantations in Victoria Division, including 'The Demise of the Banana Industry in West Africa', in *Journal of Geography*, Vol 70, No. 4. (1971).

Benjamin, Jacques., 1972. *Le Camerounais occidentaux: la minorité dans un état bicommunautaire*, Montreal, Les Presses de l'Université de Montreal.

Chiabi, E. M. L., 1982. 'Background to Nationalism in Anglophone-Cameroon: 1916-1954', Ph.D. Thesis, University of California.

— 1989. Administration britannique et nationalisme dans le 'Southern Cameroon' 1914–15', in Njeuma, (ed.).

Carter, E. J., 1992. *Limbe Botanic Garden and Rainforest Genetic Conservation Report; Socio-Economic and Institutional Study*, London, Overseas Development Adminstration.

Clarence-Smith, W. G., 1983. 'From Plantation to Peasant Production in German Cameroun', in Geschiere and Konings (eds.) (1983).

Clarke, J. 1972 [1848]. *Specimens of Dialects*,Annotated by Edwin Ardener, Farnborough, Gregg International.

Connell, B. and Maison, K.B. (in press). 'A Cameroun homeland for rthe Lower Cross people? , *Sprache und Geschichte in Afrika,* 15.

Connell, B. (in press) 'The role of language contact in the development of Usaghade. *Sprache und Geschichte in Afrika*, 16.

Courade, G. has written extensively on Cameroon, among his works are *The Urban Development of Buea. An Essay in Social Geography*, Yaounde, ORSTOM, 1972, and *Victoria, Bota: Urban Growth and Immigration*, Yaounde, ORSTOM-ONAREST, (1976), 'Marginalite voluntaire ou imposée? Le cas des Bakweri (Kpe) du Mont Cameroun', *Cahiers ORSTOM, ser. Sc.Hum.*, 18, 3, (1972).

Curly, R., 1983. 'Private Dreams and Public Knowledge in a Camerounian Independent Church', in M. C. Jedri and R. Shaw (eds.) *Dreaming, Religion and Society (entry 42).*

DeLancey, M. W. and DeLancey, V. have produced a number of publications on the area. Here we might mention DeLancey, Mark W. 'Health, and Disease on the Plantations in Cameroon, 1884–1939' in G.W. Hartwig and K. David Patterson (eds.), *Disease in African History*, Duke University Press, Durham, USA, (1978), and 'Plantation and Migration in the Mount Cameroon Region' in Mainz, Hase and Keohler (eds.), *Kamerun*, (1974), and DeLancey, V. 'Women in the Cameroon Development Corporation: How their Money Works', *Rural Africana* (n.s.) 2, (1978).

Derieule, B., 1983. 'Risques volcaniques au Mont Cameroun', *Revue du Géographie du Cameroun*, Vol.3, No. 1.

Doh, Jonas N., 1983. *Missionary Motivations and Methods. A Critical Examination of the Basel Mission in Cameroon, 1896–1914*, Basel, Universitat Basel.

Elango, Lovett Z., 1985. *The Cameroon Coast in Maritime History, c.1472 to the Present*, Douala, Editions CAPE.

— 1989. 'Trade and diplomacy on the Cameroon Coast in the Nineteenth Century, 1883–1879; the case of Bimbia', in Njeuma, (ed.).

Epale, S. J., 1974. 'The Impact of Early Christian Missionary Contact on Economic Growth in Cameroon, 1800–1884' in Haberland, E. et al, *Symposium Leo Frobenius Deutsche-Uniesco Kommission,* Munich, (1974).

— 1985. *Plantations and Development in Western Cameroon, 1885–1975: A Study in Agrarian Capitalism*, New York, Vantage Press.

Fanso, Verkijika G., 1989. 'Trade and Supremacy on the Cameroon Coast, 1879–1887', in Njeuma, (ed.).

Fongang, M., 1981–82. 'Case Study: The Cameroon Development Corporation and the Smallholders' Scheme', Buea: PAID/WA Student Report.

Gann, L.H. and Peter Duigan, 1977. *The Rulers of German Africa, 1884–1914*, Standford, California, Standford University Press.

Geschiere, P., 1993. 'Chiefs and Colonial Rule in Cameroon: Inventing Chieftaincy, French and British Style', *Africa* 63 (2).

Geschiere, P. and P. Konings, (eds.). 1983. *Les Itinéraire d'accumulation au Cameroun*, Paris: Karthala.

Hair, P.E.H. 1969. The earlist vocabularies of Cameroon Bantu. *African Studies*, 28, 1.

Hediger, R. 1987. *The Manenguba Languages (Bantu A.15, Mbo Custer) of Cameroon. London, SOAS.*

Heinzen, B.J., 1983, 'The United Fruit Company in the 1950s: Trusteeships of the Cameroons', *African Economic History*, Vol.12.

Kofele-Kale, Ndiva, (ed.). 1980. *An African Experiment in Nation-Building: The Bilingual Cameroon Republic since Reunification*. Oxford, Westview Press.

Konings, P. has produced a series of papers and books on the plantation economy of anglophone Cameroon, based on detailed fieldwork. All of them are relevant to an understanding of plantations today. A recent contribution is *Labour resistance in Cameroon: managerial strategies and labour resistence in the agro-industrial plantations of the CDC 1947–1987*, London: Curry (1993).

Kuperus, J. 1985. *The Londo World: its phonological and morphological structure.* Tervuren: Musée Royale de l'Afrique Centrale.

Maitland, T. D., 1932. 'The Grassland Vegetation of the Cameroons Mountain', *Kew Bulletin*.

Matute, D. L., 1988. *The Socio-Cultural Legacies of the Bakweri of Cameroon*. Yaounde, CEPER.

— 1990. *Facing Mount Fako, An Ethnographic Study of the Bakweri in Cameroon*, Milwauki, USA, Omni Press.

Mbake, S. N., 1975. 'Traditional Authority among the Bakweri', thesis for Postgraduate Diploma in History, University of Yaounde.

Michel, Marc, 1969. 'Les plantations allemandes du mont Cameroun (1885–1914), *Revue Française d'Histoire d'Outre-Mer*, 57, 207.

Molua, H. N., 1985. 'The Bakweri Land Problem 1884–1961: A Case Study', M.A. thesis, University of Ibadan.

Mosima, Fritz, M., 1985. 'Imperial Business in Cameroon under United Kingdom Administration', Yaounde, *Africa Zamani*, Nos 12/13.

Ngu, J., 1989. 'The Political Economy of Oil in Cameroon' in Geschiere and Konings, (eds.)

Ngongo, Louis,1982. *Histoires des forces religieuses au Cameroun: de la première guerre mondiale a l'indépendence (1916–1955)*, Paris, Editions Karthala.

Njeuma, M. (ed.), 1989. *Introduction to the History of Cameroon in the Nineteenth and Twentieth Centuries*, London, MacMillan.

— 1989. *Histoire du Cameroun, XIXe siècle-debut XXe siècle*, Paris: Harmattan.

Osuntokun, Jide, 1977. 'Great Britain and the Final Partition of the Cameroons, 1916–1922', Yaounde, *Africa Zamani*.

Takoukang, J., *Victoria, an African Township under British Administration, 1960–61*, Ph.D. thesis, University of Illinois at Chicago.

Zeitlyn, David and Ian Fowler, have edited three works recently, of which one is in this series: 'Perspectives on the State: From Political History to Ethnography in Cameroon', special edition of *Paideuma*, (1995), *African Crossroads; Intersections Between History andAnthropology in Cameroon*, Oxford, England, and New Jersey, USA, Berghahn Books (1996) and a special edition of *The Journal of the Anthropological Society of Oxford (JASO)*, Oxford, Institute of Social and Cultural Anthropology, (1996). All three publications are dedicated E. M. (Sally) Chilver, and provide a range of papers by Cameroonian and other scholars.

Index

Ian Fowler

Index of Names

Subject Index